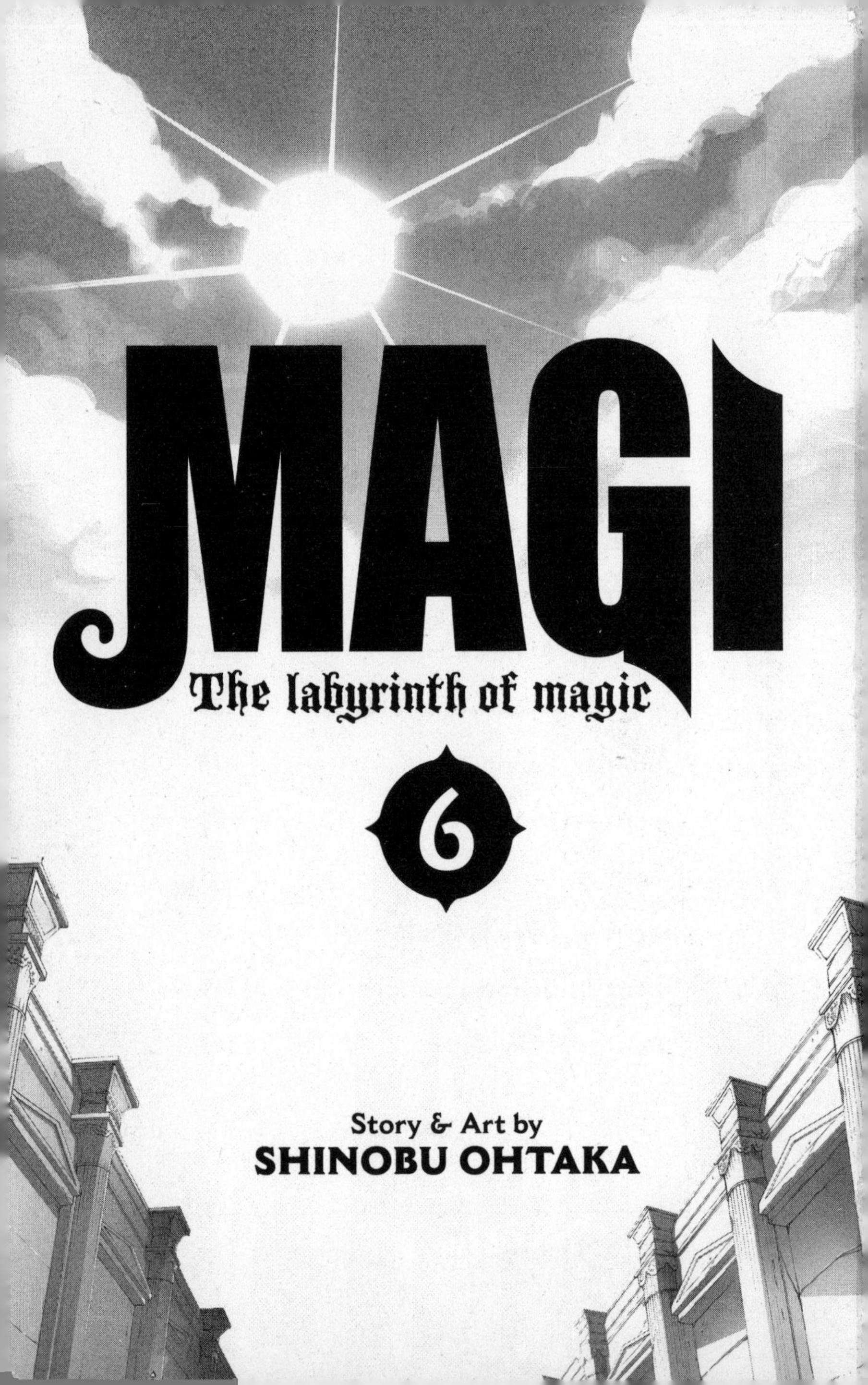

MAGI

The labyrinth of magic

6

Story & Art by
SHINOBU OHTAKA

MAGI
The labyrinth of magic
6

CONTENTS

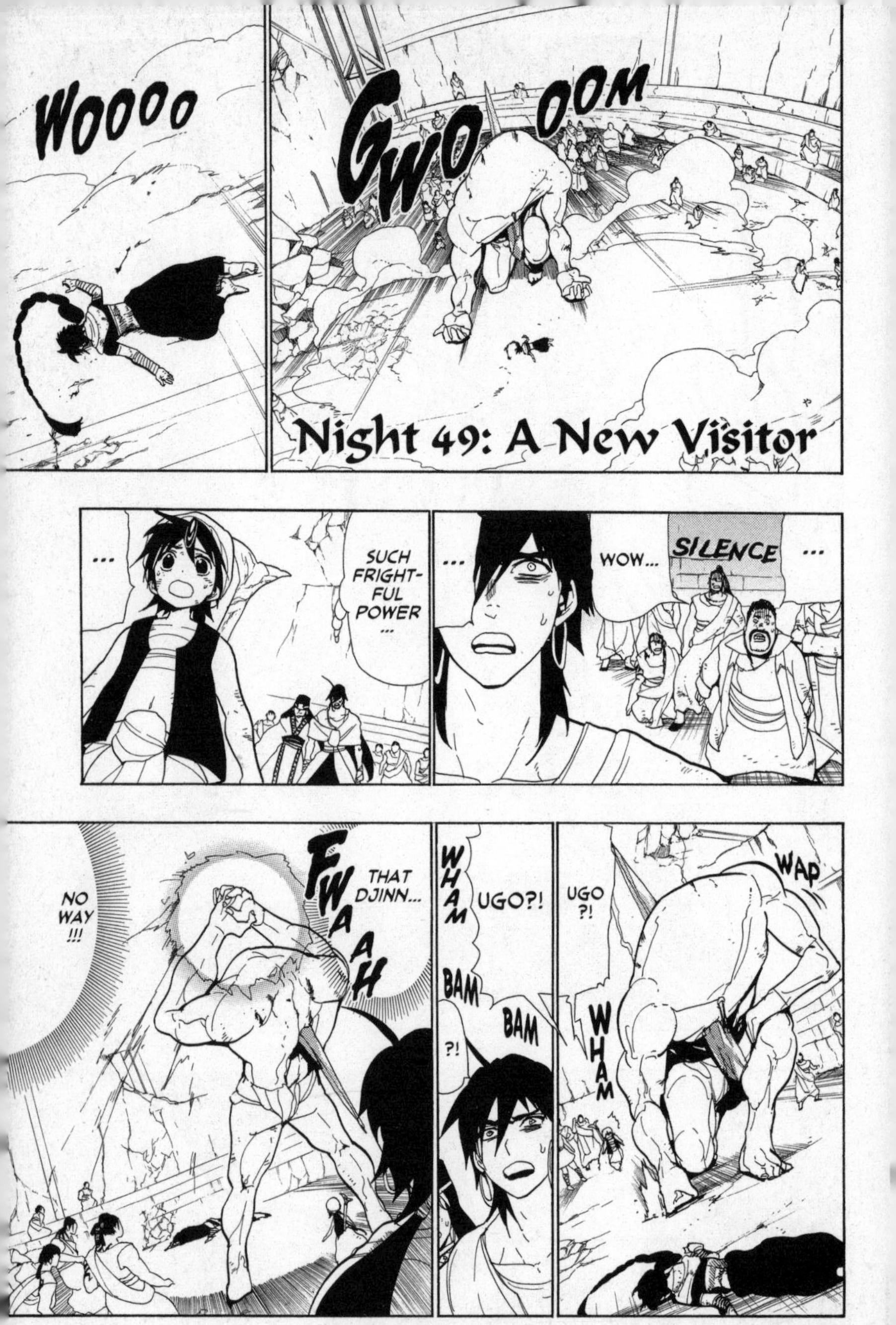
GWO OOM
Night 49: A New Visitor
WOOOO
...
SILENCE
WOW...
...
SUCH FRIGHTFUL POWER...
...
WAP
WHAM
UGO?!
UGO?!
WHAM
BAM
BAM
?!
FWAAAH
THAT DJINN...
NO WAY!!!

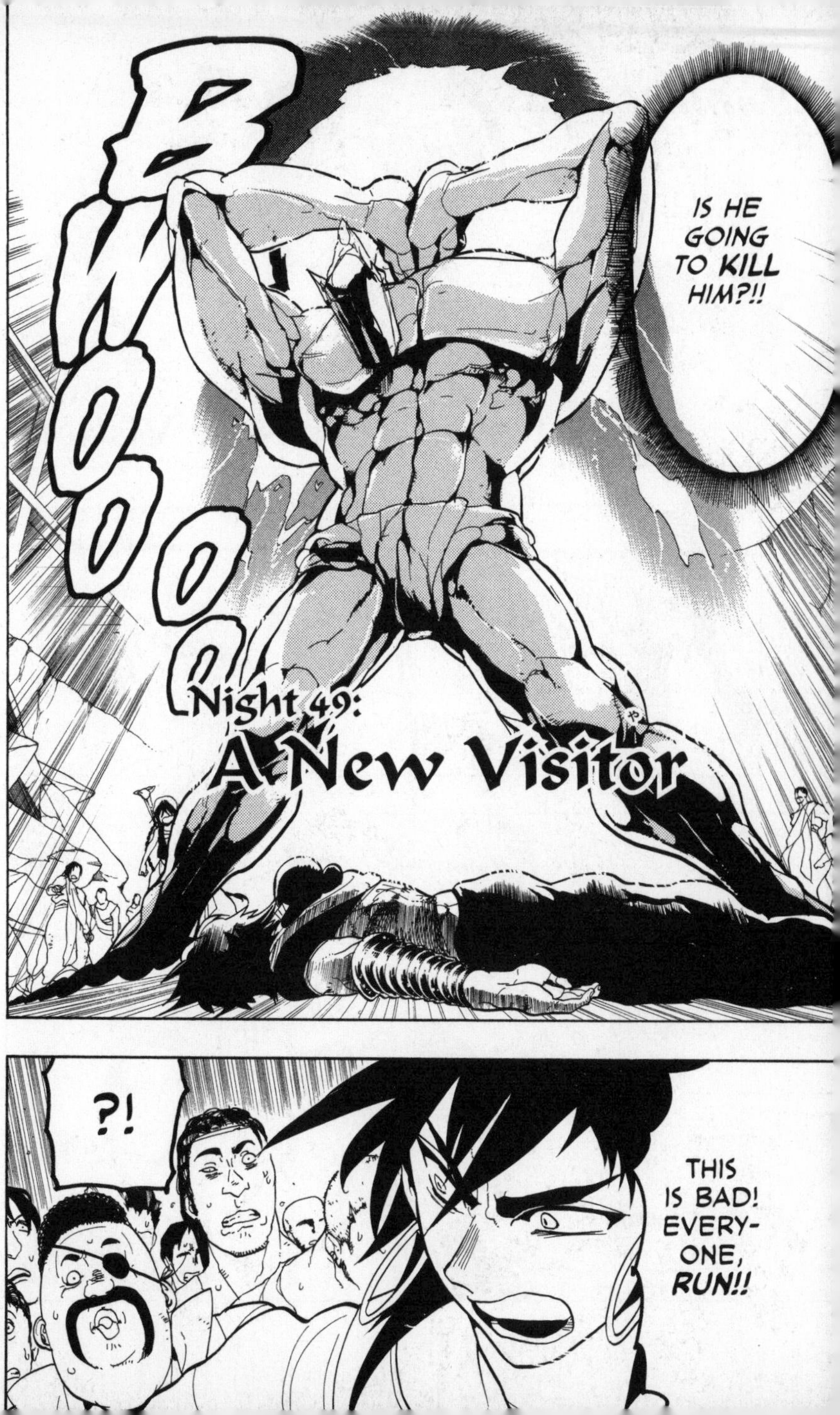
IS HE GOING TO KILL HIM?!!
BWOOOO
Night 49:
A New Visitor
THIS IS BAD! EVERY-ONE, RUN!!
?!

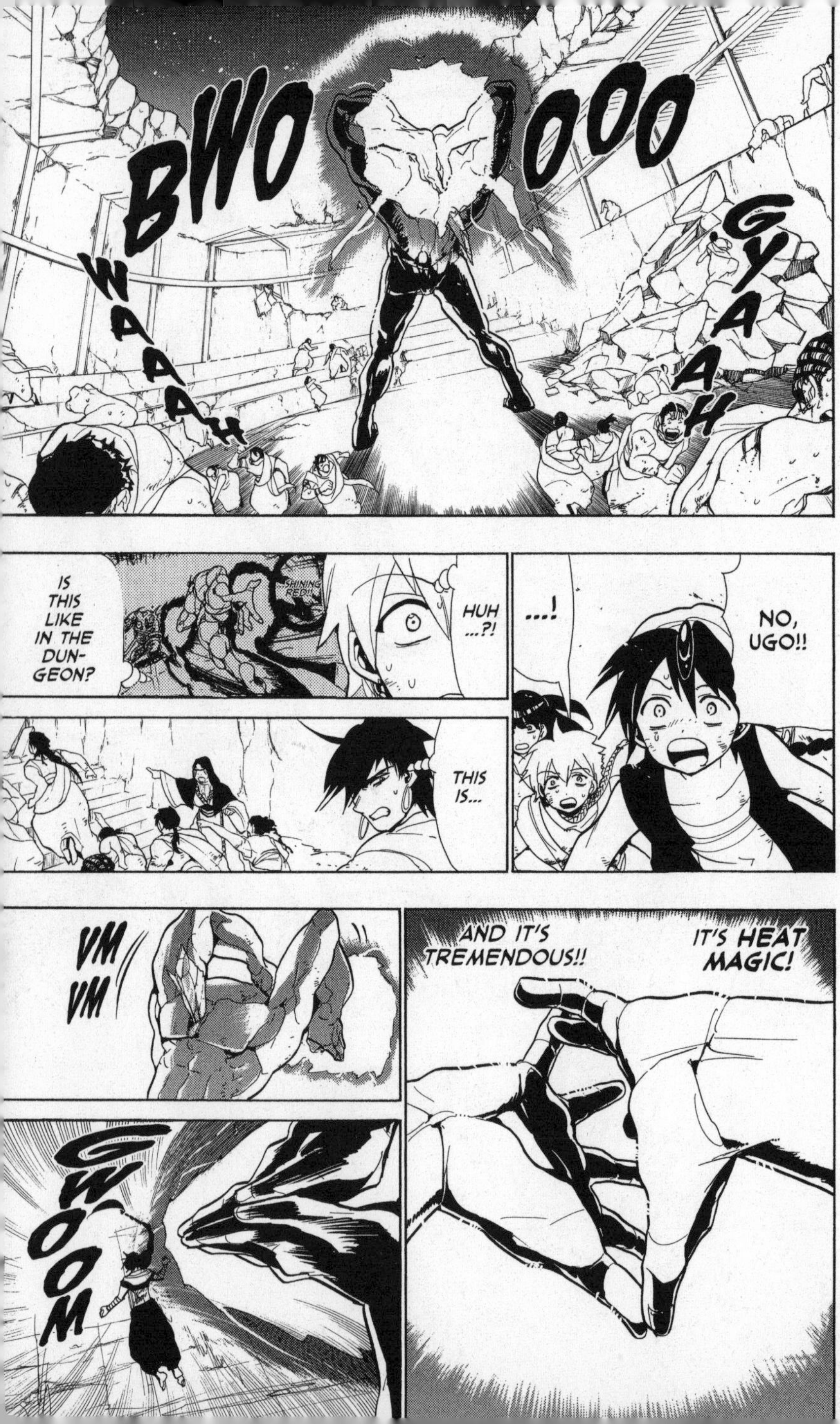
BWOOOOO
GYAAAH
WAAAAH
NO, UGO!!
...!
HUH ...?!
SHINING RED!!
IS THIS LIKE IN THE DUNGEON?
THIS IS...
IT'S HEAT MAGIC!
AND IT'S TREMENDOUS!!
VM VM
GWOOOM

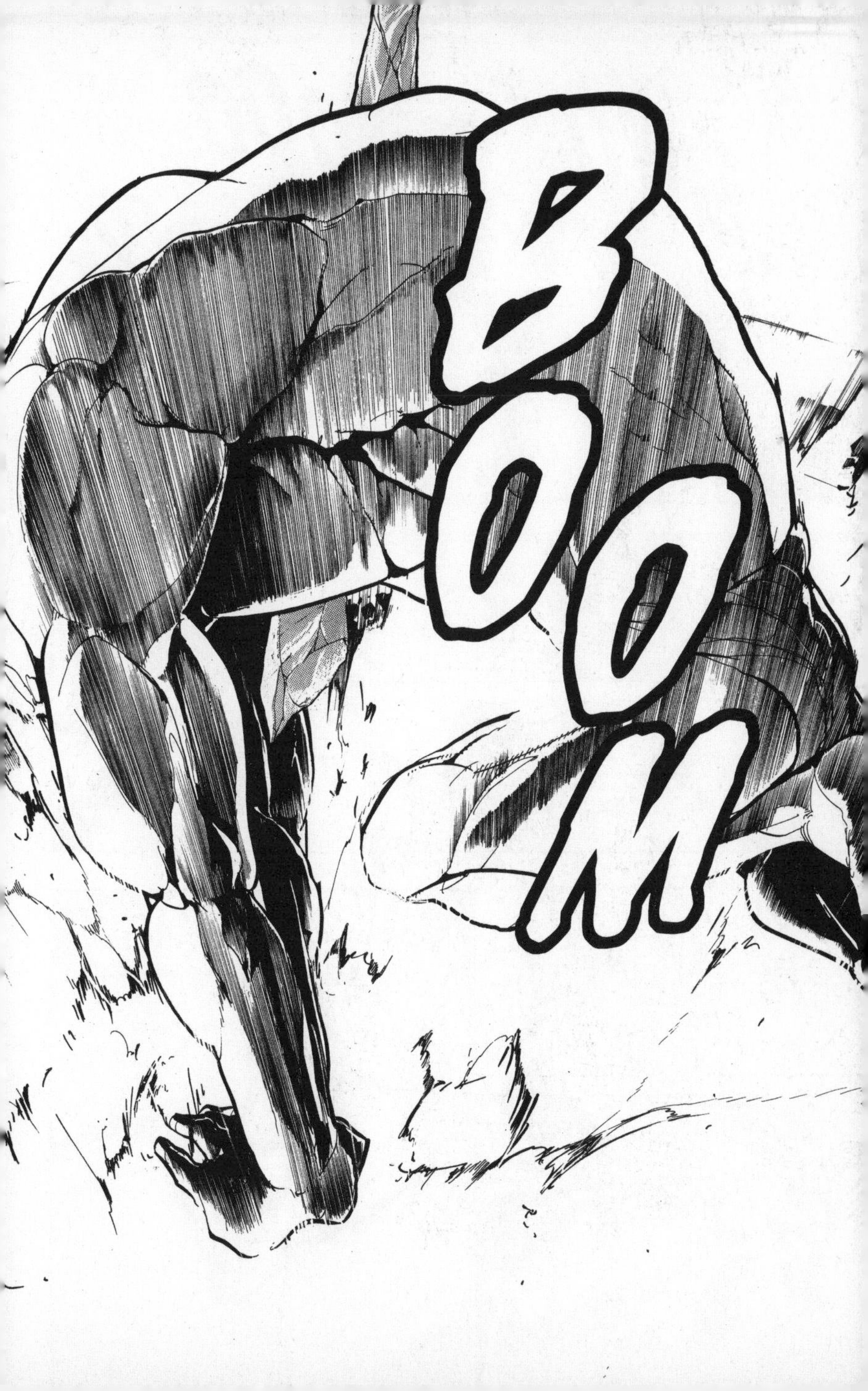
BOOM

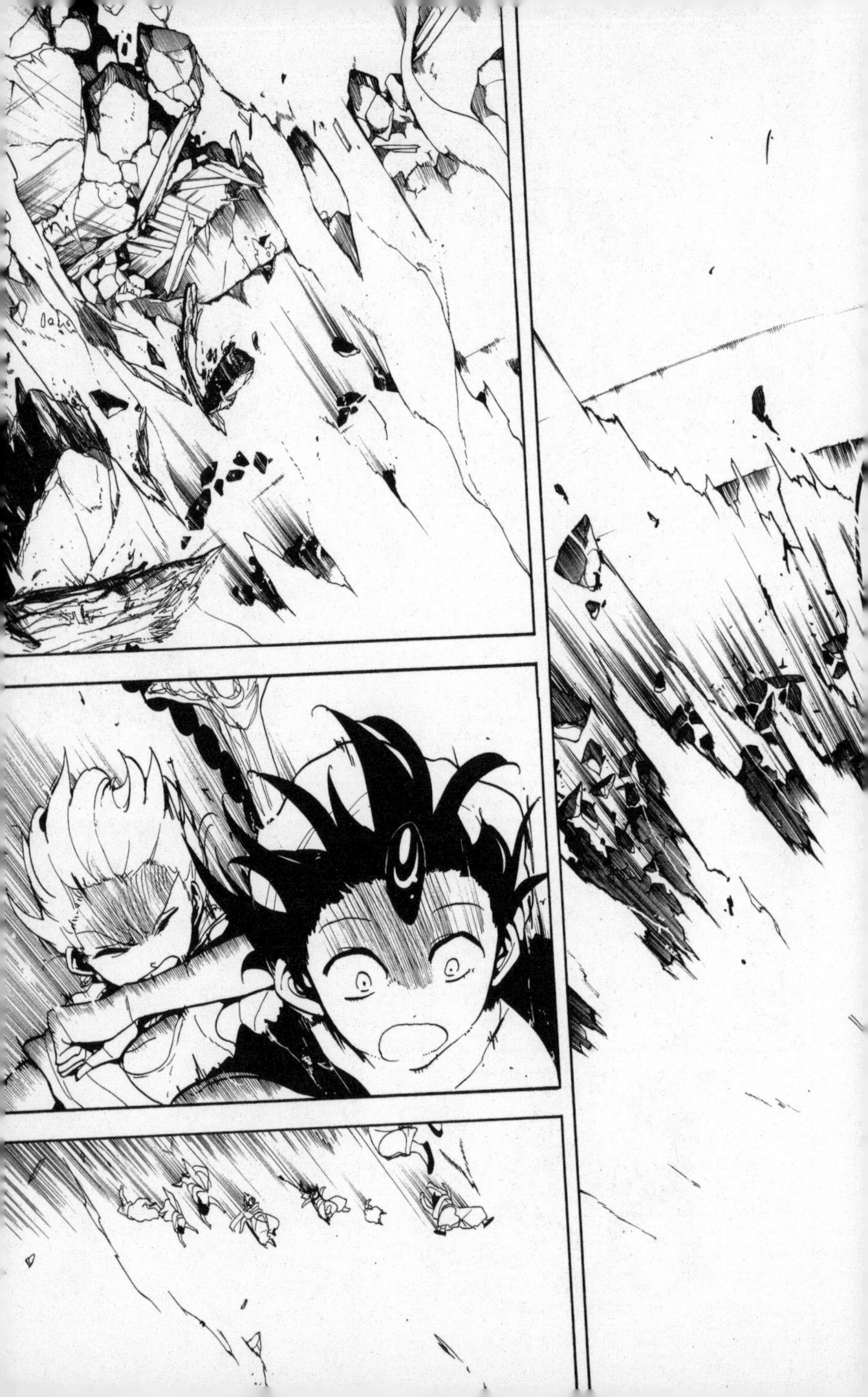

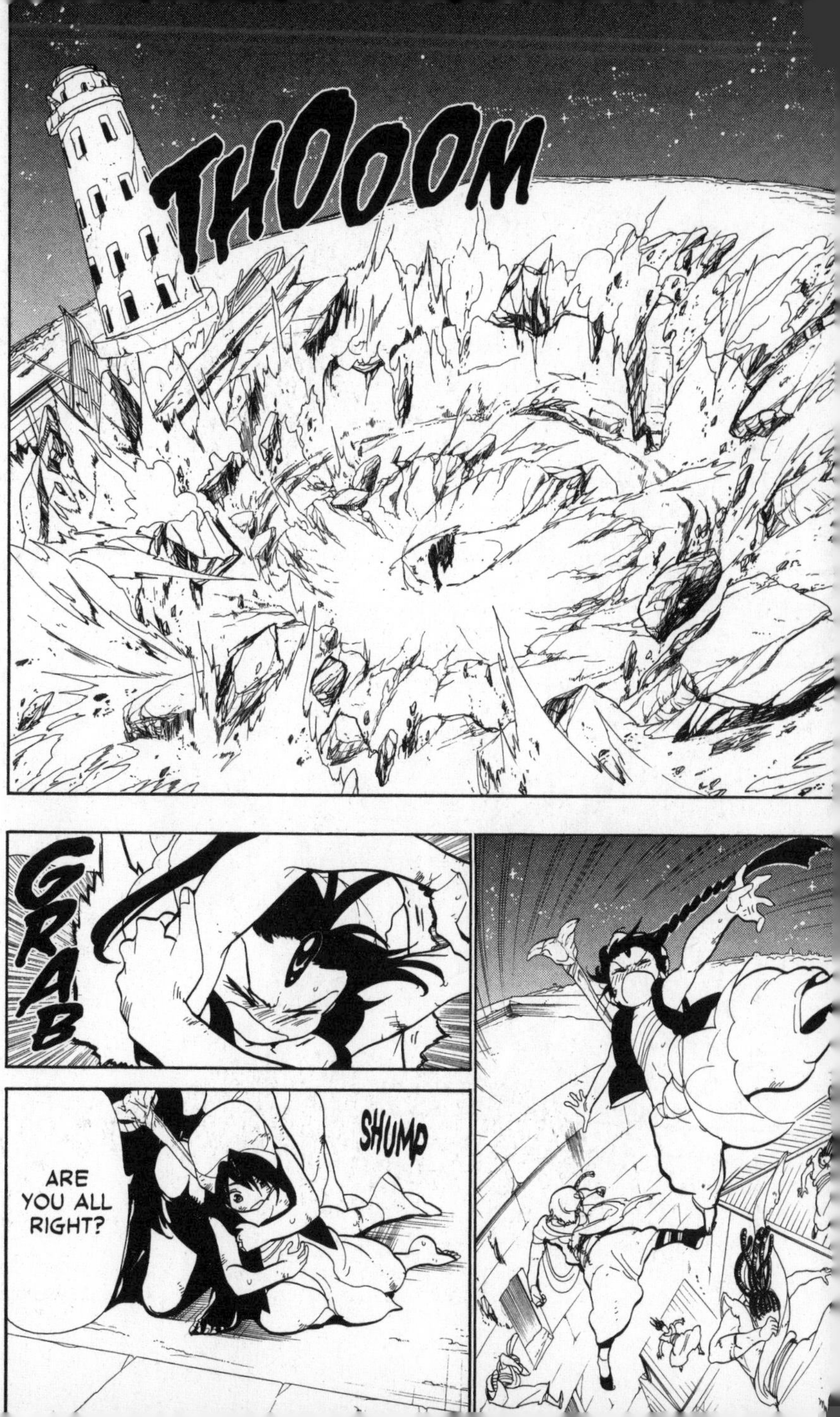
THOOOM
GRAB
SHUMP
ARE YOU ALL RIGHT?

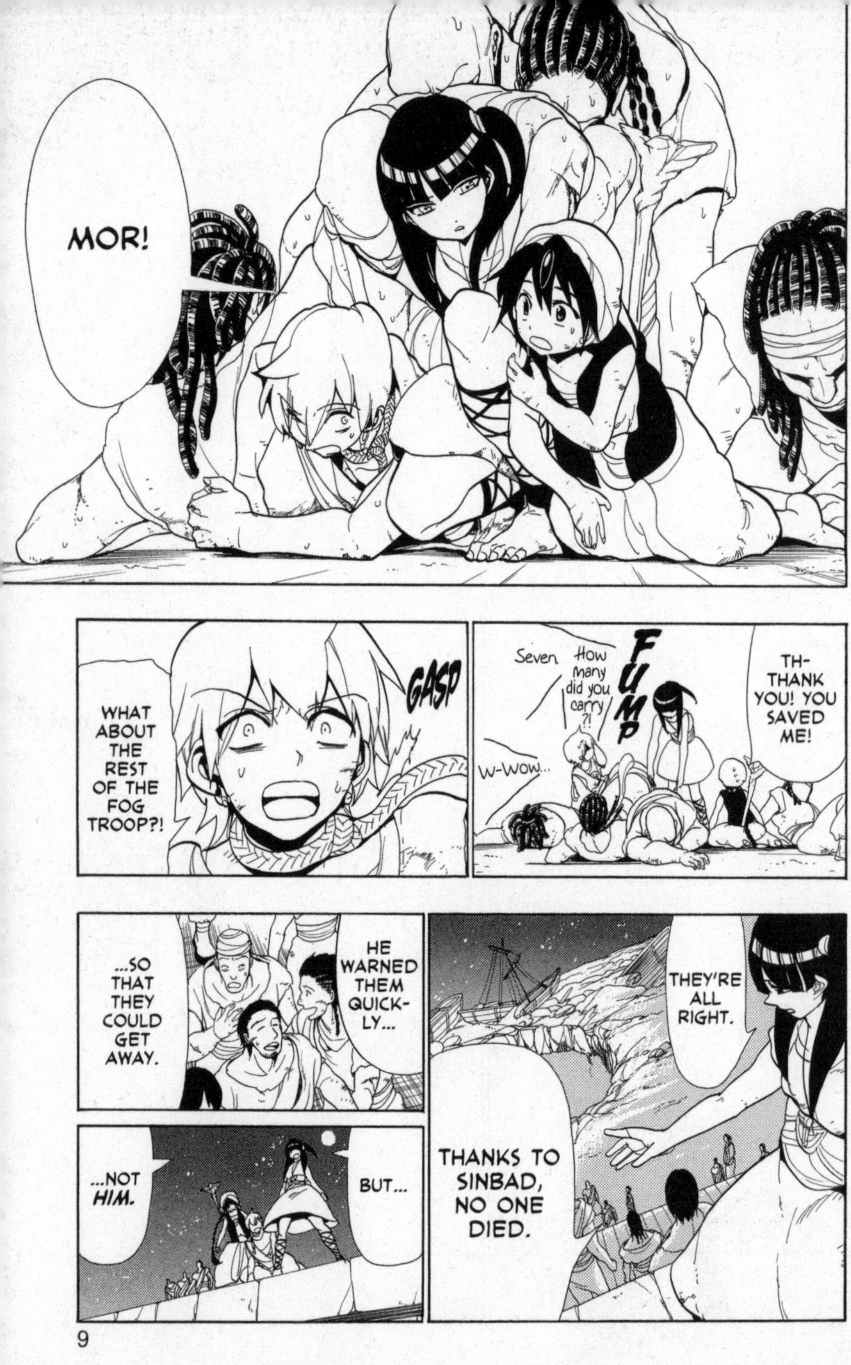
MOR!
TH-THANK YOU! YOU SAVED ME!
FUMP
How many did you carry?!
Seven.
W-WOW...
GASP
WHAT ABOUT THE REST OF THE FOG TROOP?!
THEY'RE ALL RIGHT.
THANKS TO SINBAD, NO ONE DIED.
HE WARNED THEM QUICKLY...
...SO THAT THEY COULD GET AWAY.
BUT...
...NOT *HIM.*

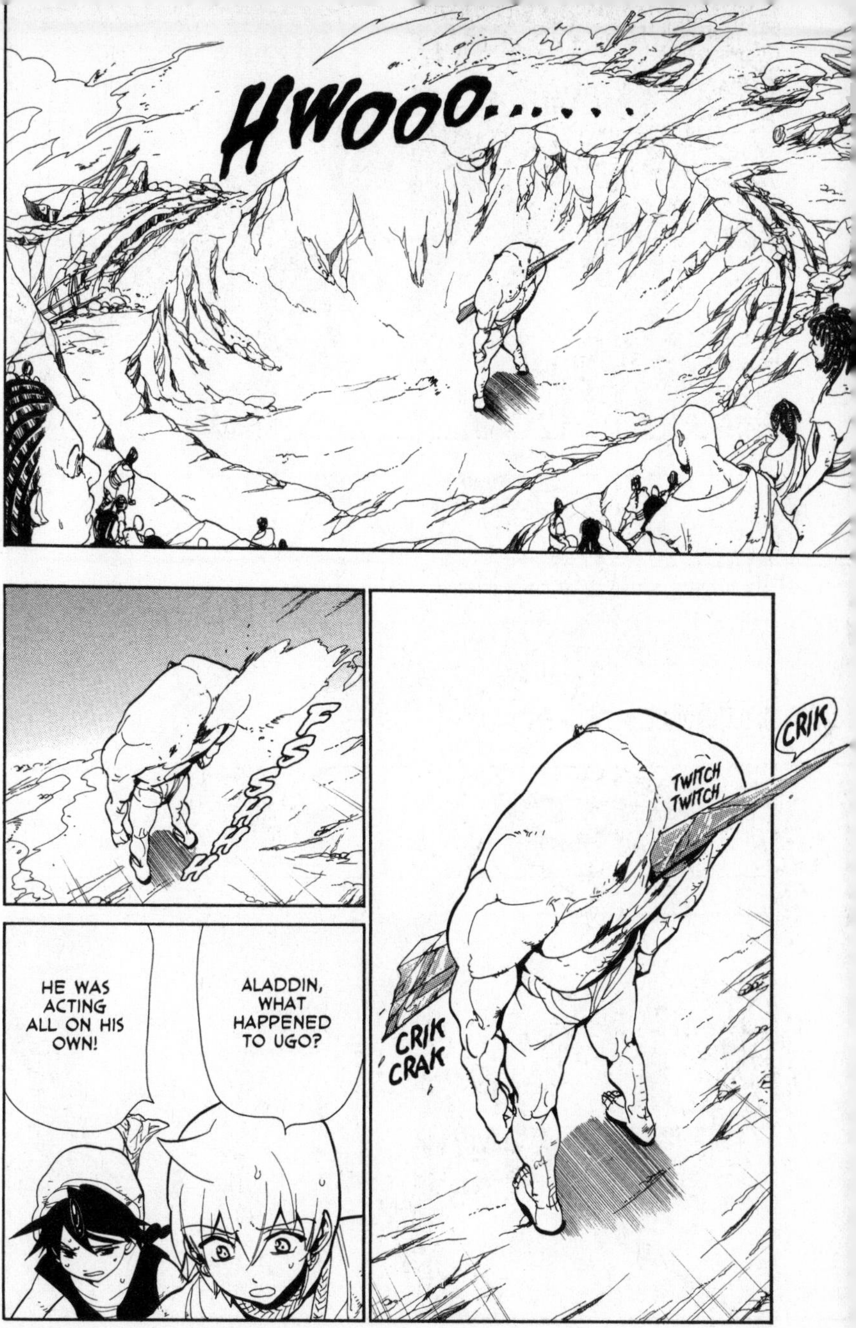
HWOOO.....
CRIK
TWITCH TWITCH
CRIK CRAK
FSSSHHH
ALADDIN, WHAT HAPPENED TO UGO?
HE WAS ACTING ALL ON HIS OWN!

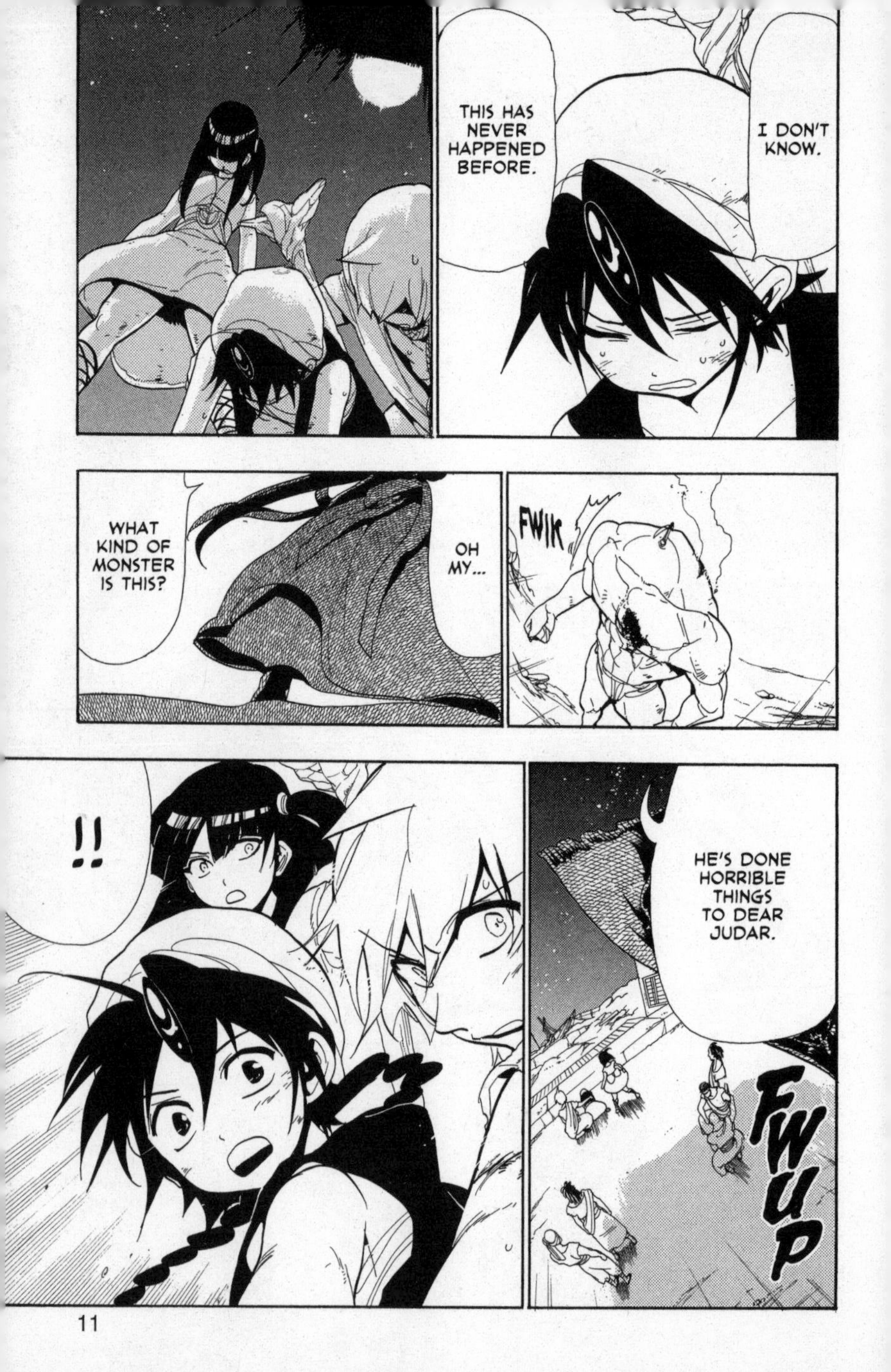
I DON'T KNOW.
THIS HAS NEVER HAPPENED BEFORE.
FWIK
OH MY...
WHAT KIND OF MONSTER IS THIS?
HE'S DONE HORRIBLE THINGS TO DEAR JUDAR.
FWUP
!!

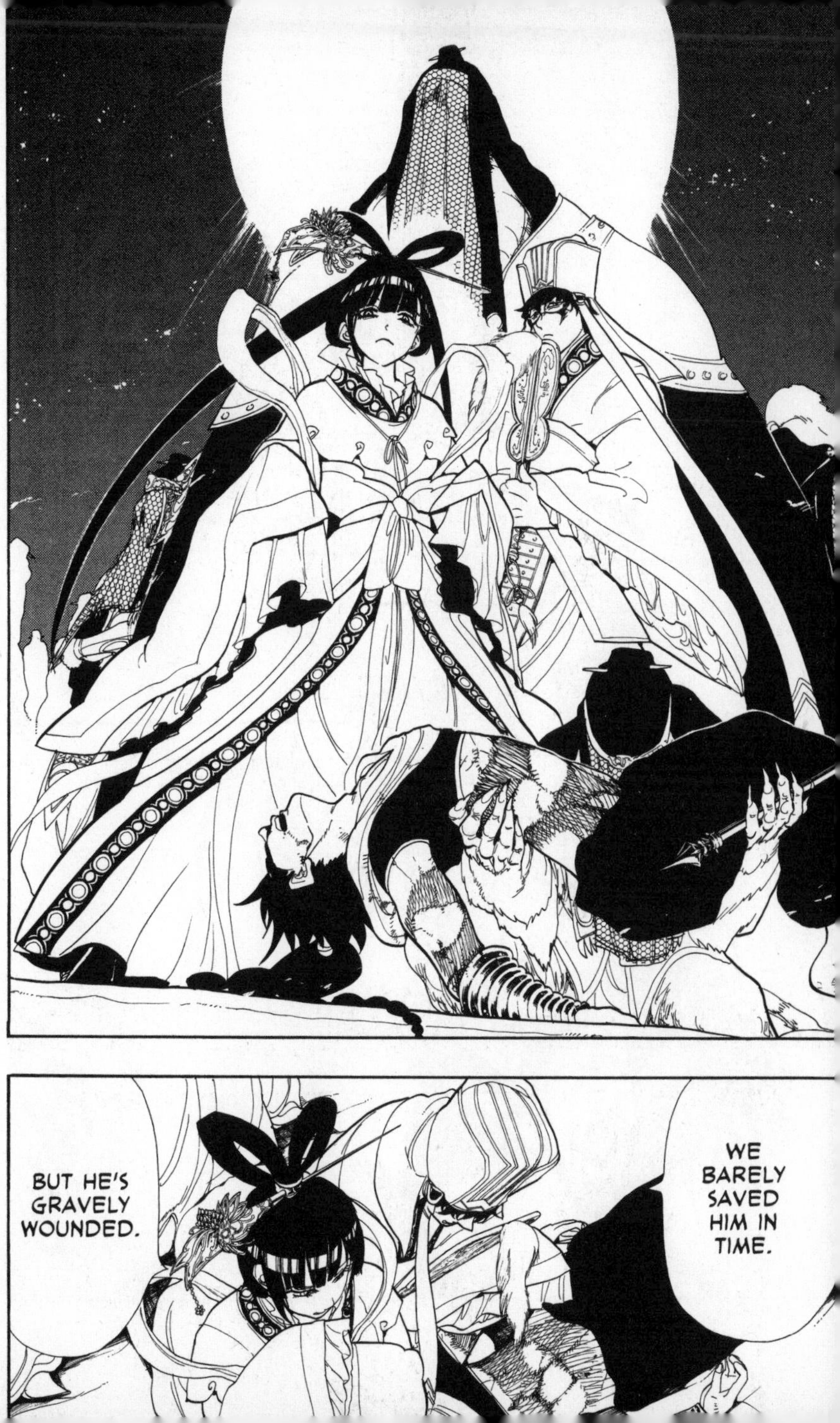
WE BARELY SAVED HIM IN TIME.
BUT HE'S GRAVELY WOUNDED.

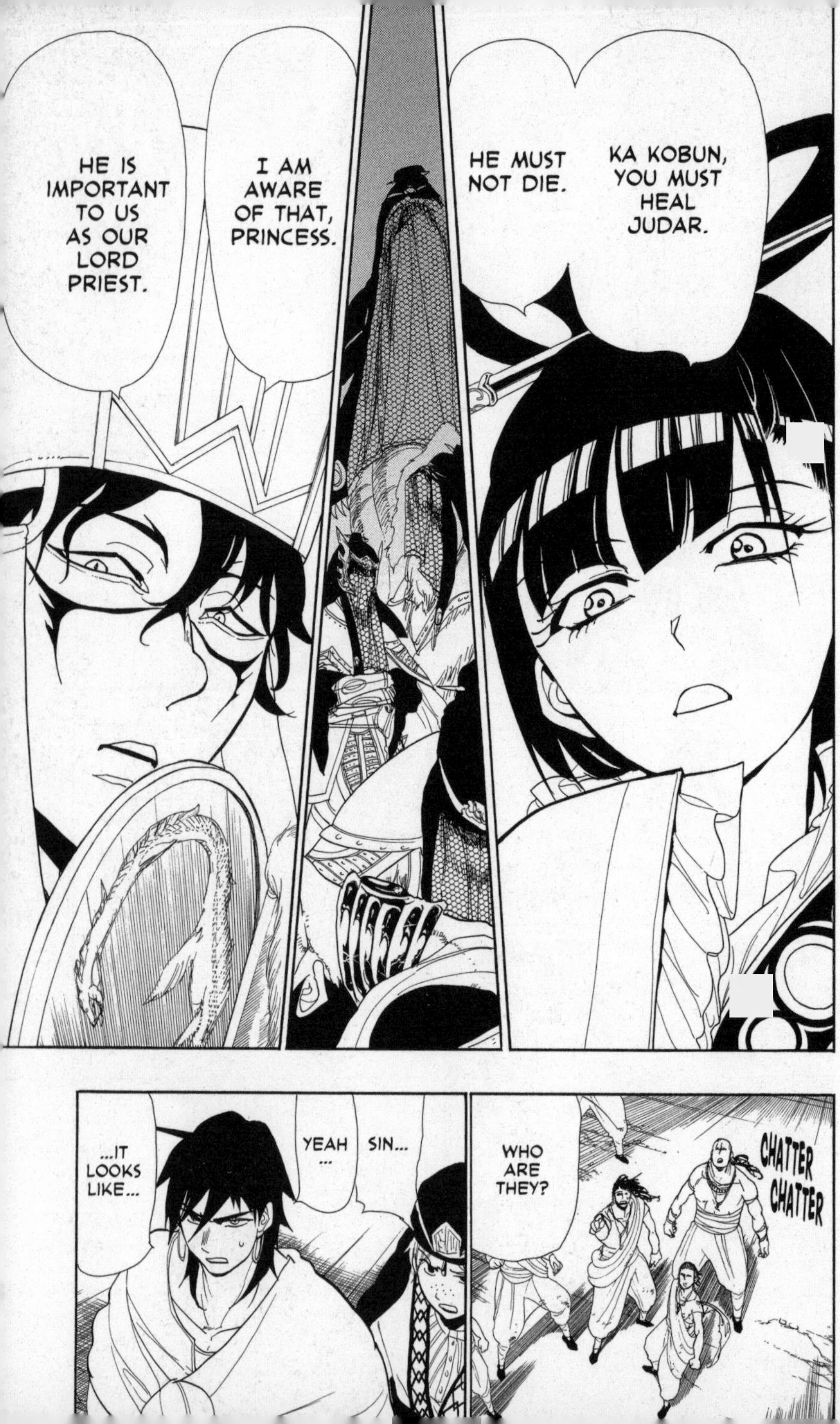
KA KOBUN, YOU MUST HEAL JUDAR.
HE MUST NOT DIE.
I AM AWARE OF THAT, PRINCESS.
HE IS IMPORTANT TO US AS OUR LORD PRIEST.
WHO ARE THEY?
CHATTER CHATTER
SIN...
YEAH...
...IT LOOKS LIKE...

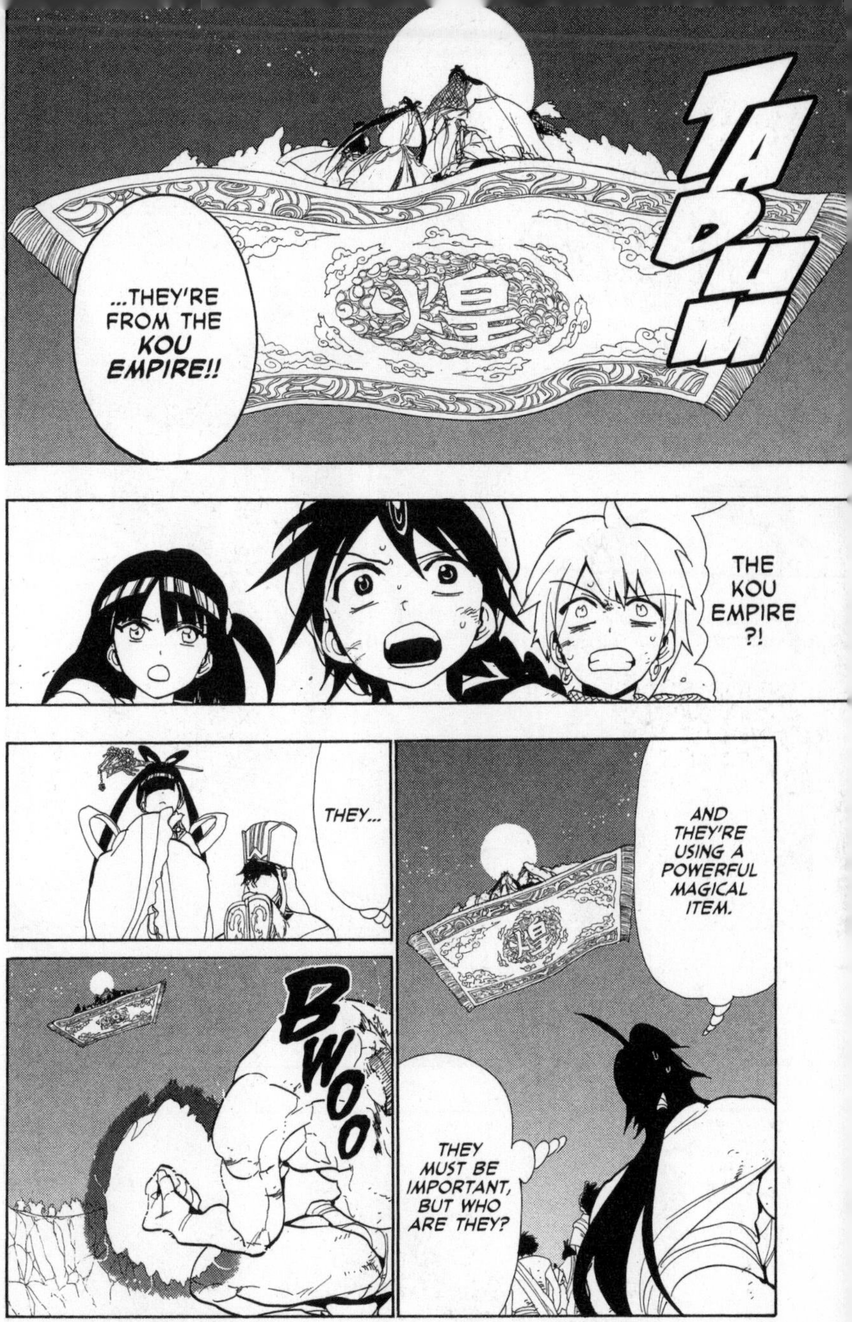
TADUM
...THEY'RE FROM THE KOU EMPIRE!!
THE KOU EMPIRE ?!
AND THEY'RE USING A POWERFUL MAGICAL ITEM.
THEY MUST BE IMPORTANT, BUT WHO ARE THEY?
THEY...
BWOO

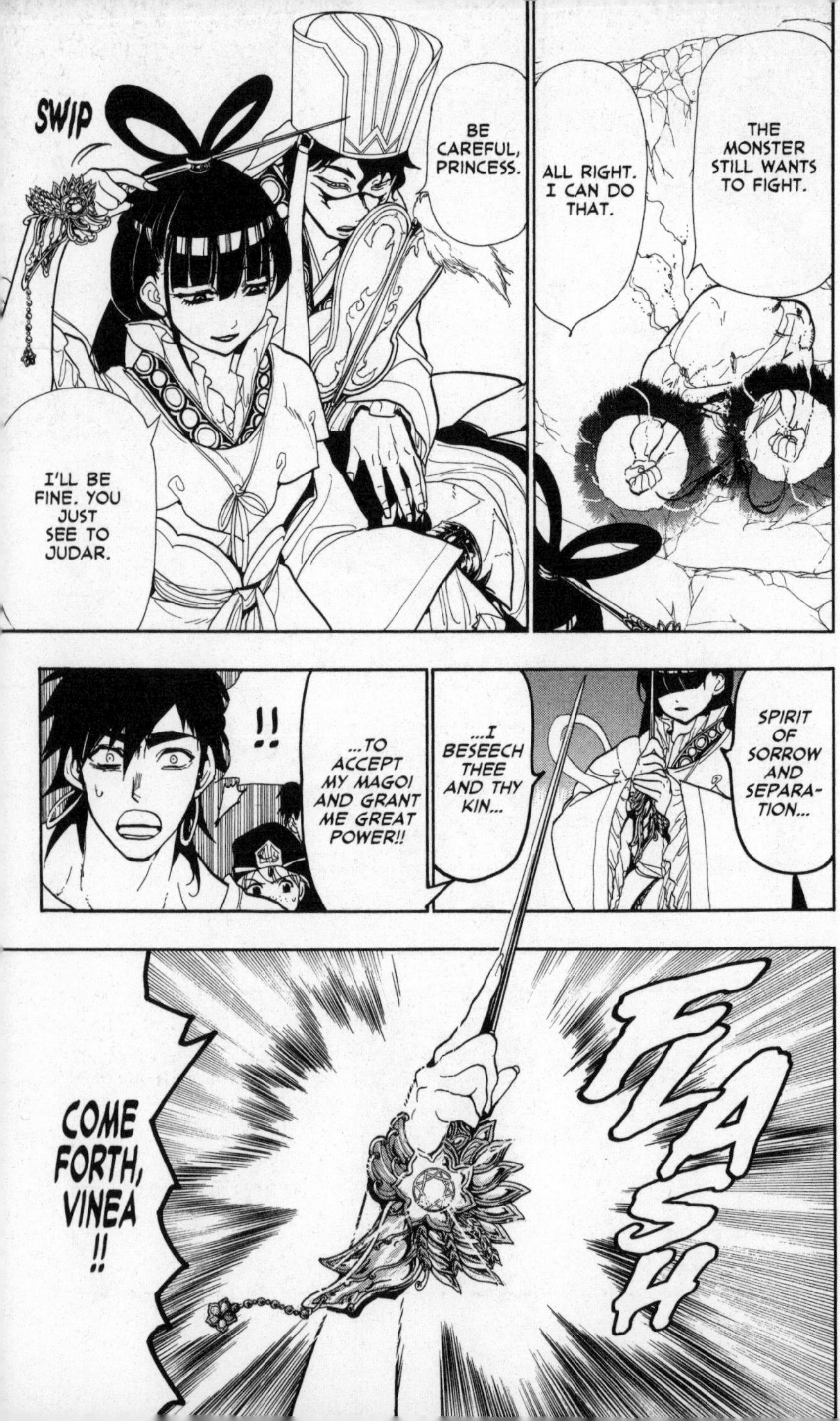
THE MONSTER STILL WANTS TO FIGHT.
ALL RIGHT. I CAN DO THAT.
BE CAREFUL, PRINCESS.
SWIP
I'LL BE FINE. YOU JUST SEE TO JUDAR.
SPIRIT OF SORROW AND SEPARATION...
...I BESEECH THEE AND THY KIN...
...TO ACCEPT MY MAGOI AND GRANT ME GREAT POWER!!
!!
FLASH
COME FORTH, VINEA!!

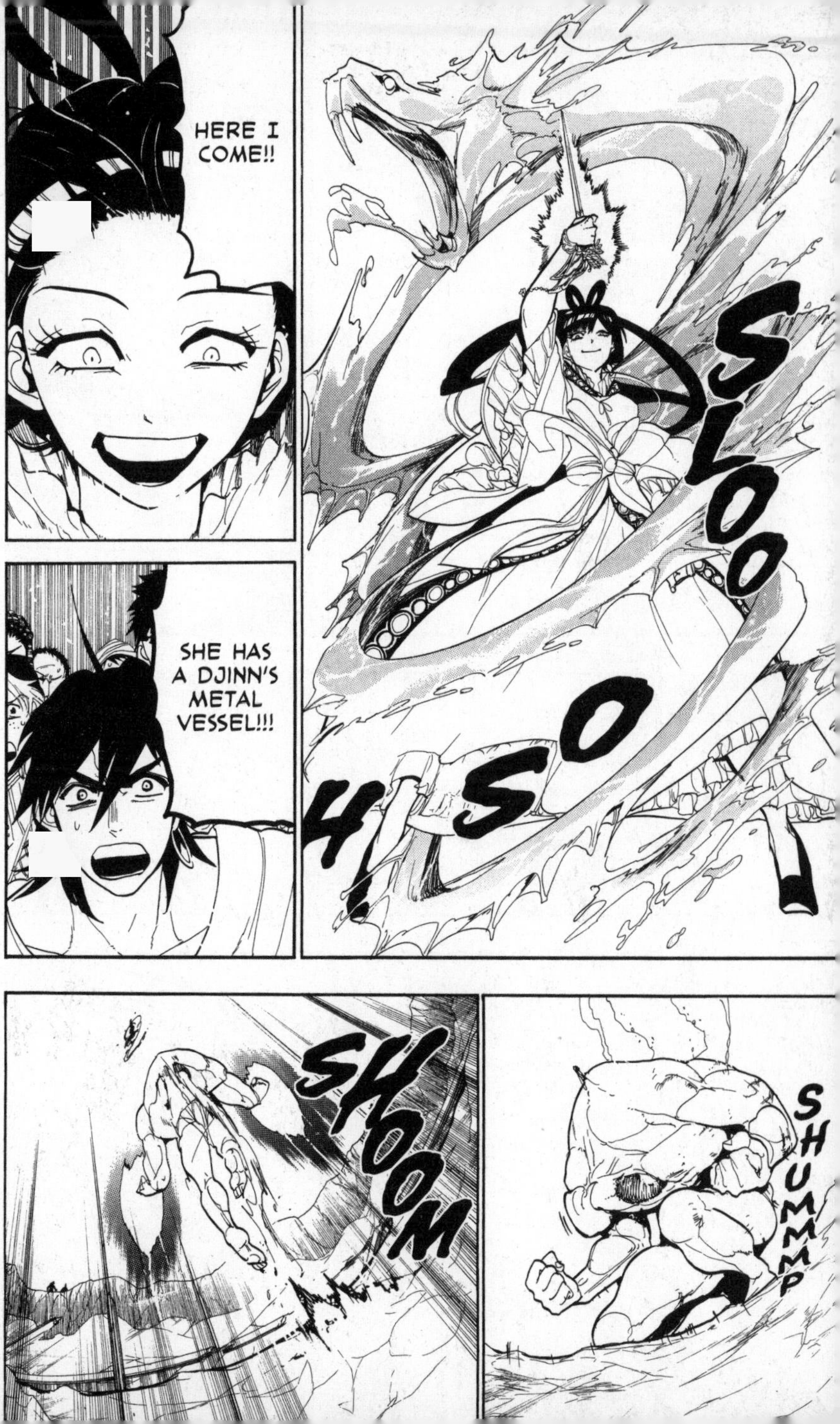
SLOOOSH
HERE I COME!!
SHE HAS A DJINN'S METAL VESSEL!!!
SHUMMP
SHOOM

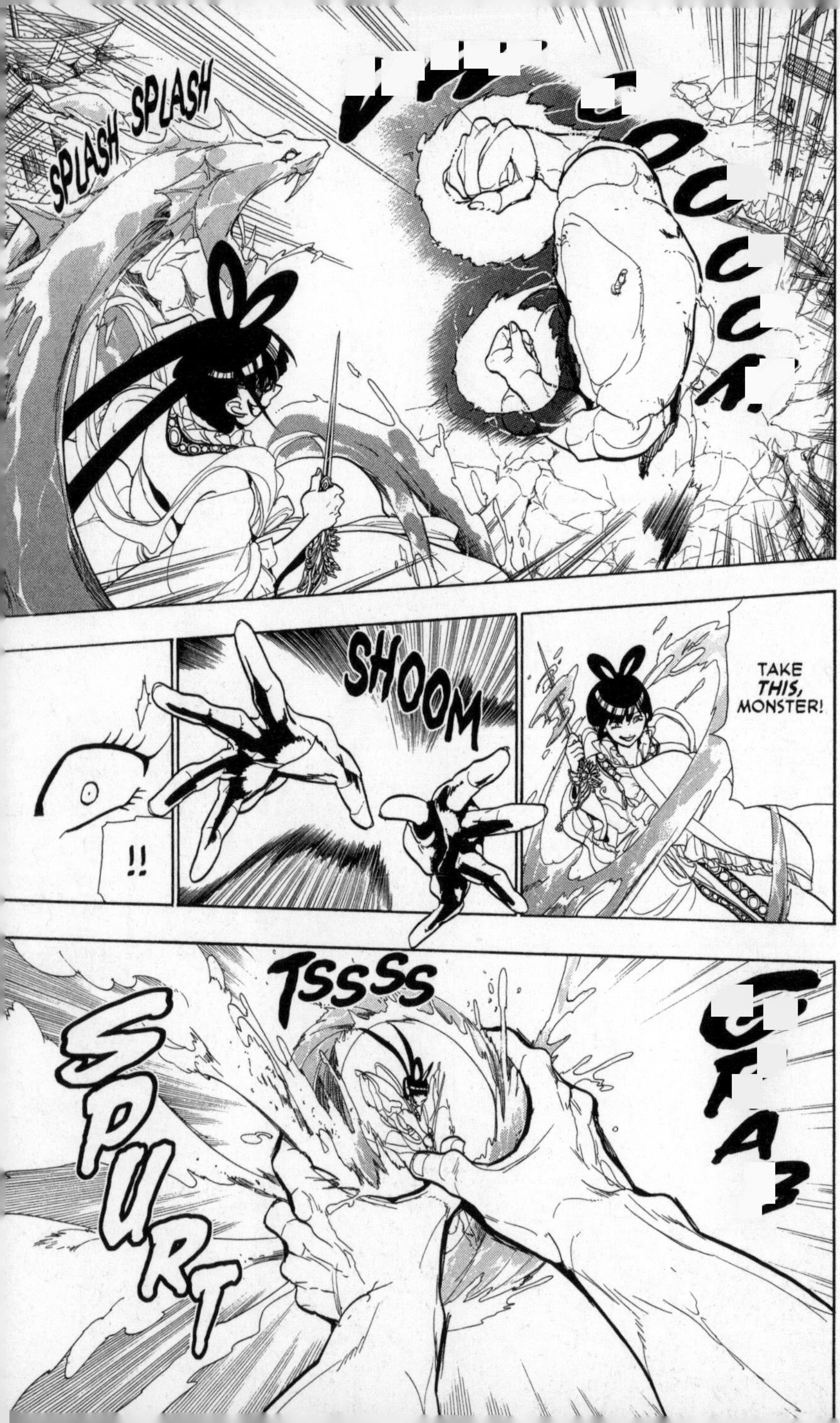
SPLASH SPLASH
TAKE THIS, MONSTER!
SHOOM
!!
TSSSS
SPURT

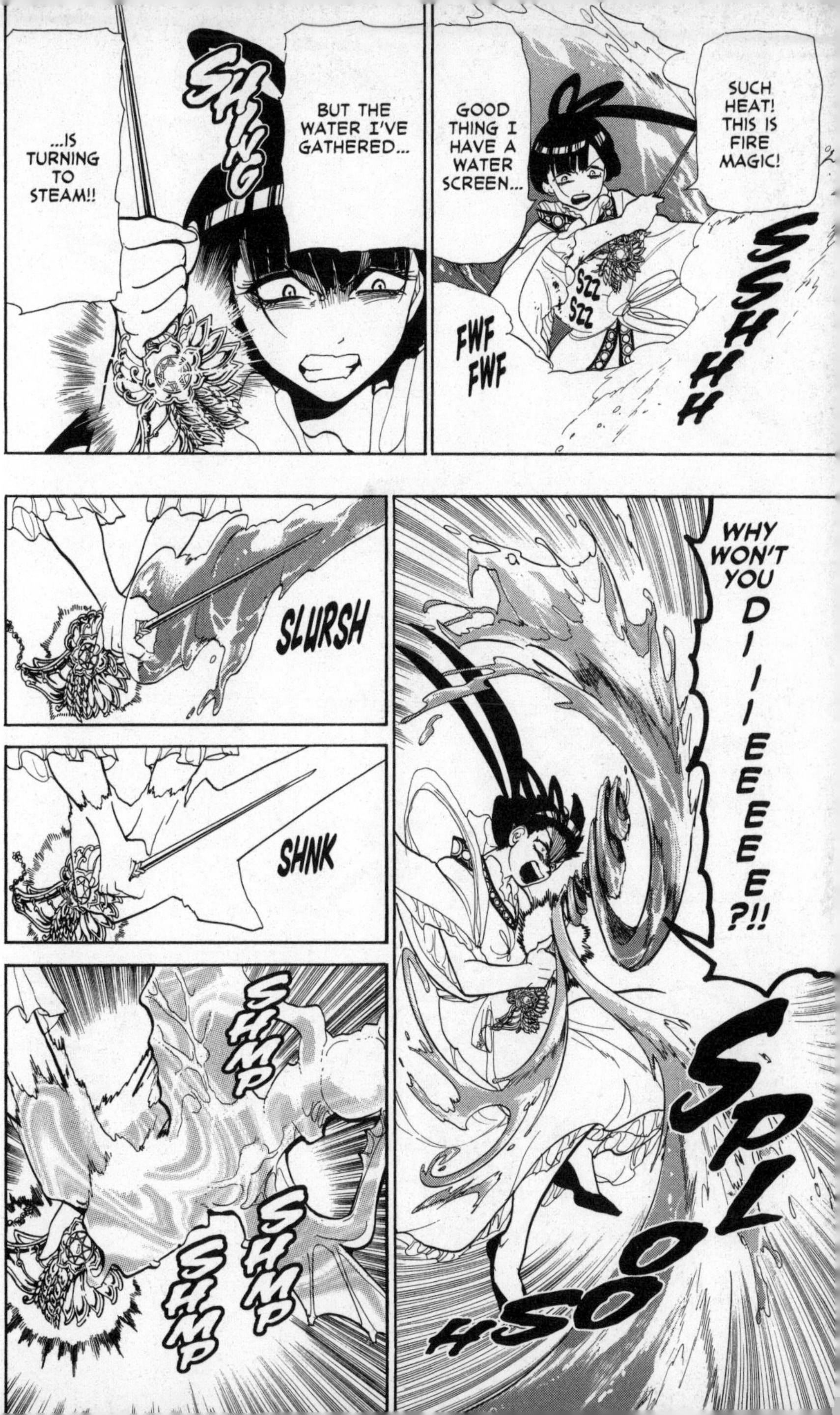
SUCH HEAT! THIS IS FIRE MAGIC!
GOOD THING I HAVE A WATER SCREEN...
SSHHHH
SZZ SZZ
FWF FWF
BUT THE WATER I'VE GATHERED...
...IS TURNING TO STEAM!!
SHING
WHY WON'T YOU DIIIIEEEEEE?!!
SPLOOOSH
SLURSH
SHNK
SHMP
SHMP
SHMP

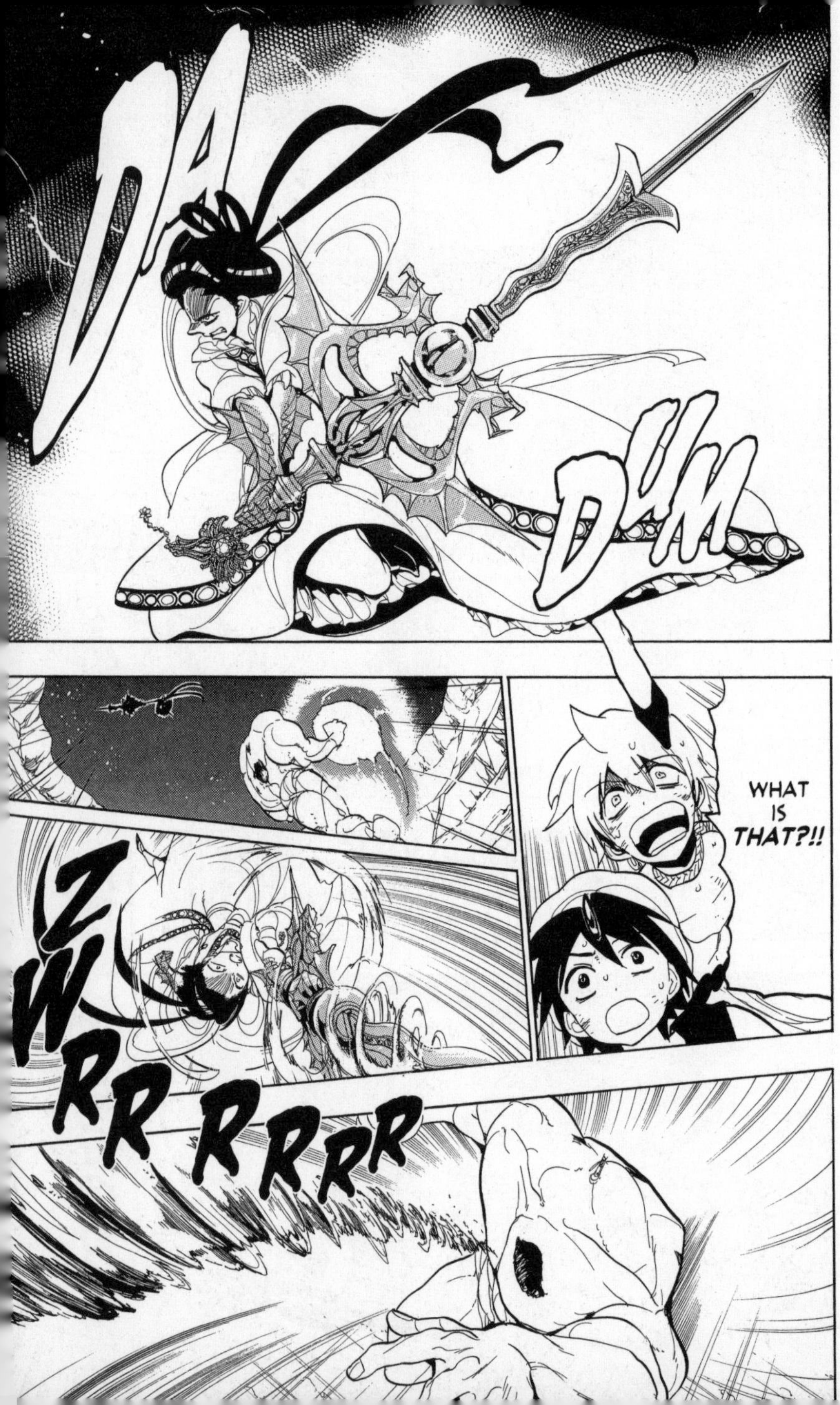
DA
DUM
WHAT IS THAT?!!
ZWRR RRRRR

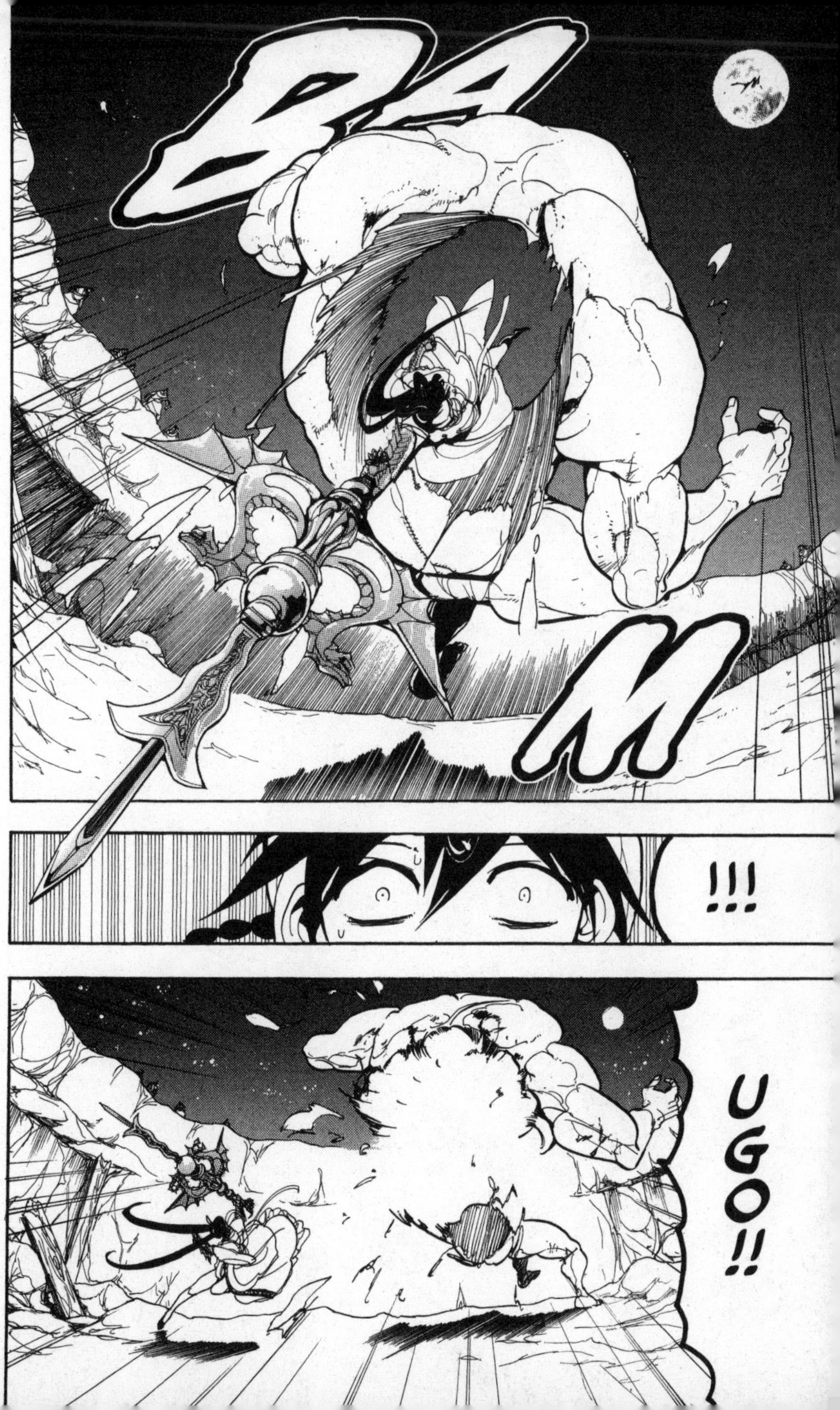
BAM
!!!
UGO!!

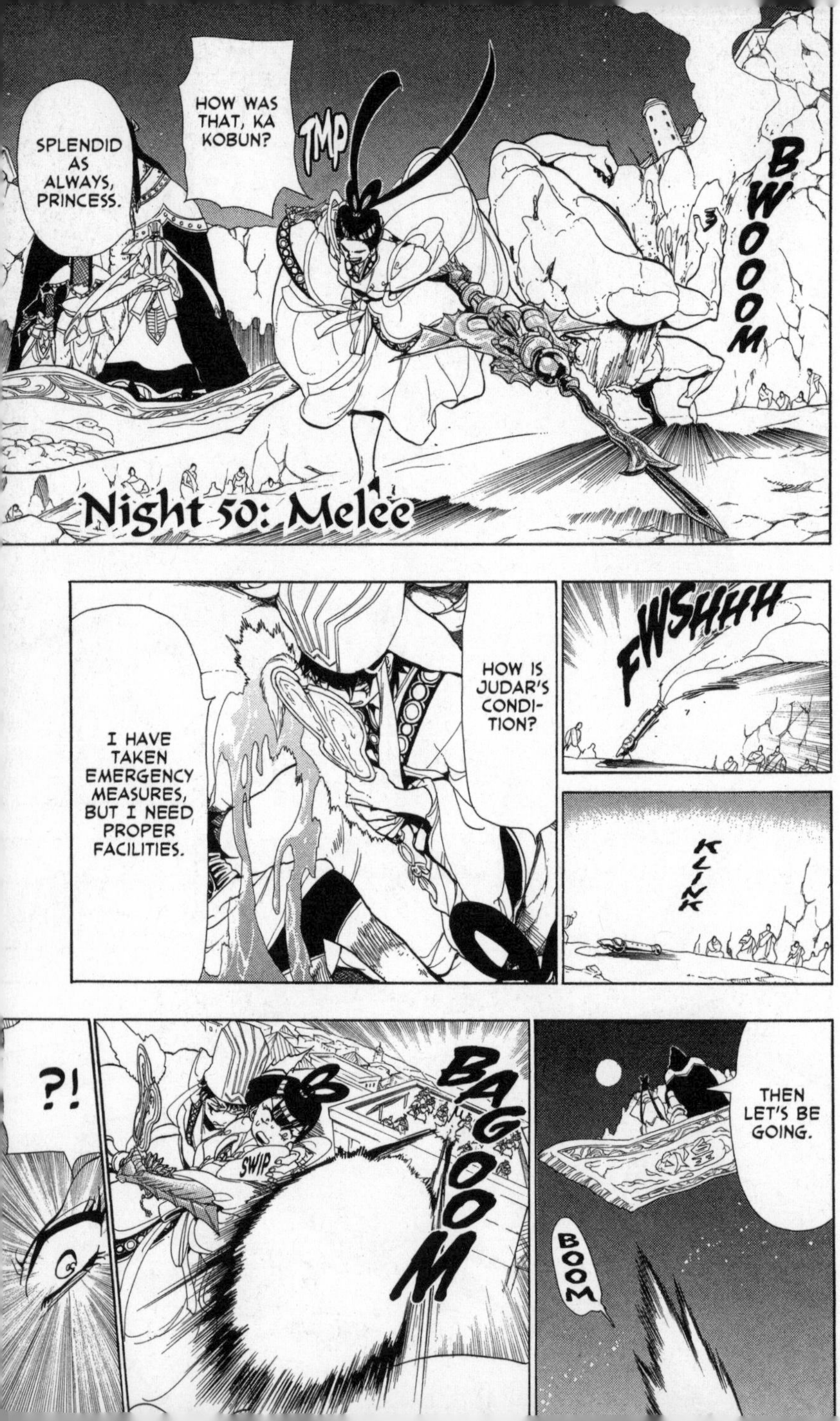
BWOOOM
TMP
HOW WAS THAT, KA KOBUN?
SPLENDID AS ALWAYS, PRINCESS.
Night 50: Melee
FWSHHH
KLINK
HOW IS JUDAR'S CONDITION?
I HAVE TAKEN EMERGENCY MEASURES, BUT I NEED PROPER FACILITIES.
THEN LET'S BE GOING.
BOOM
BAGOOOM
SWIP
?!

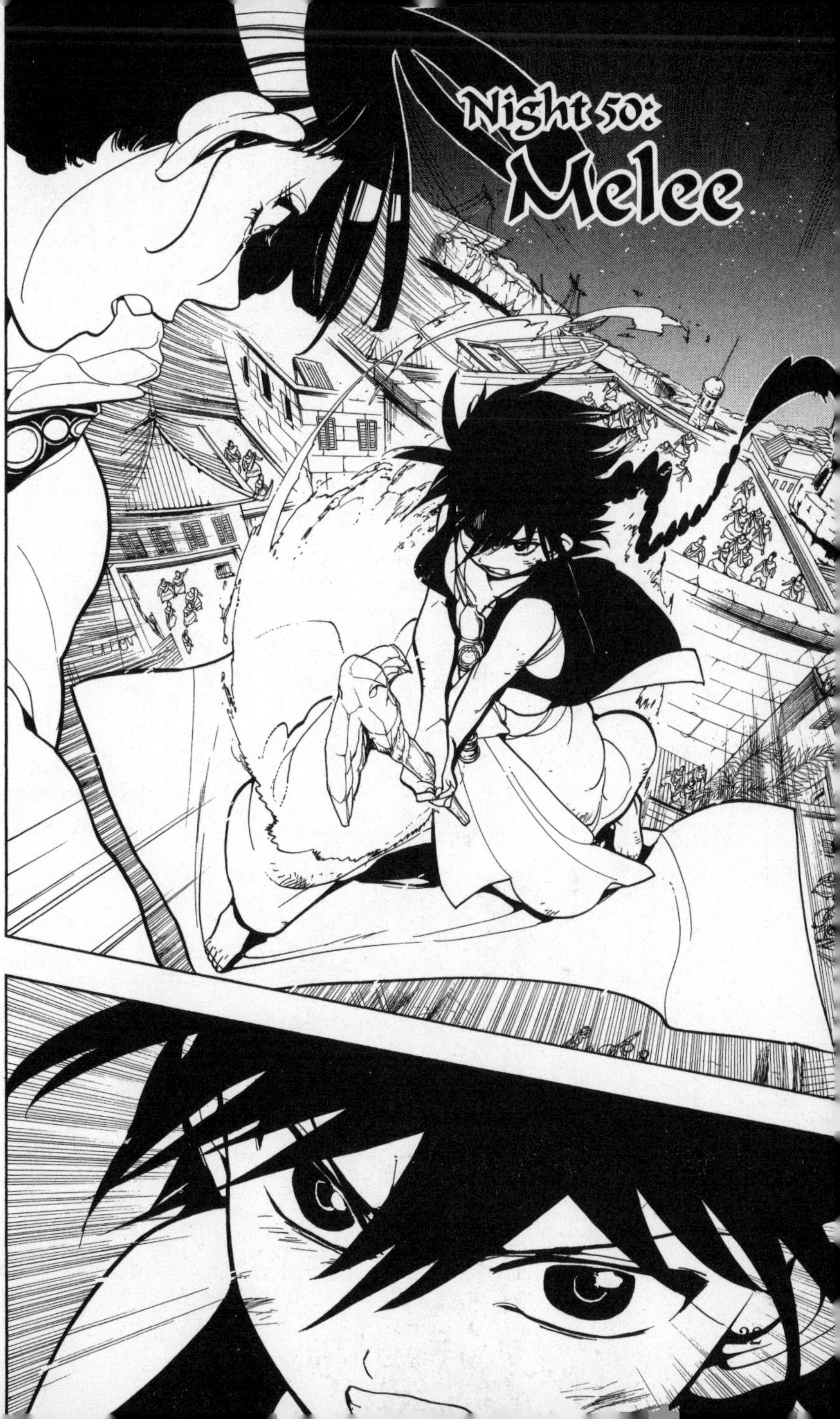
Night 50:
Melee

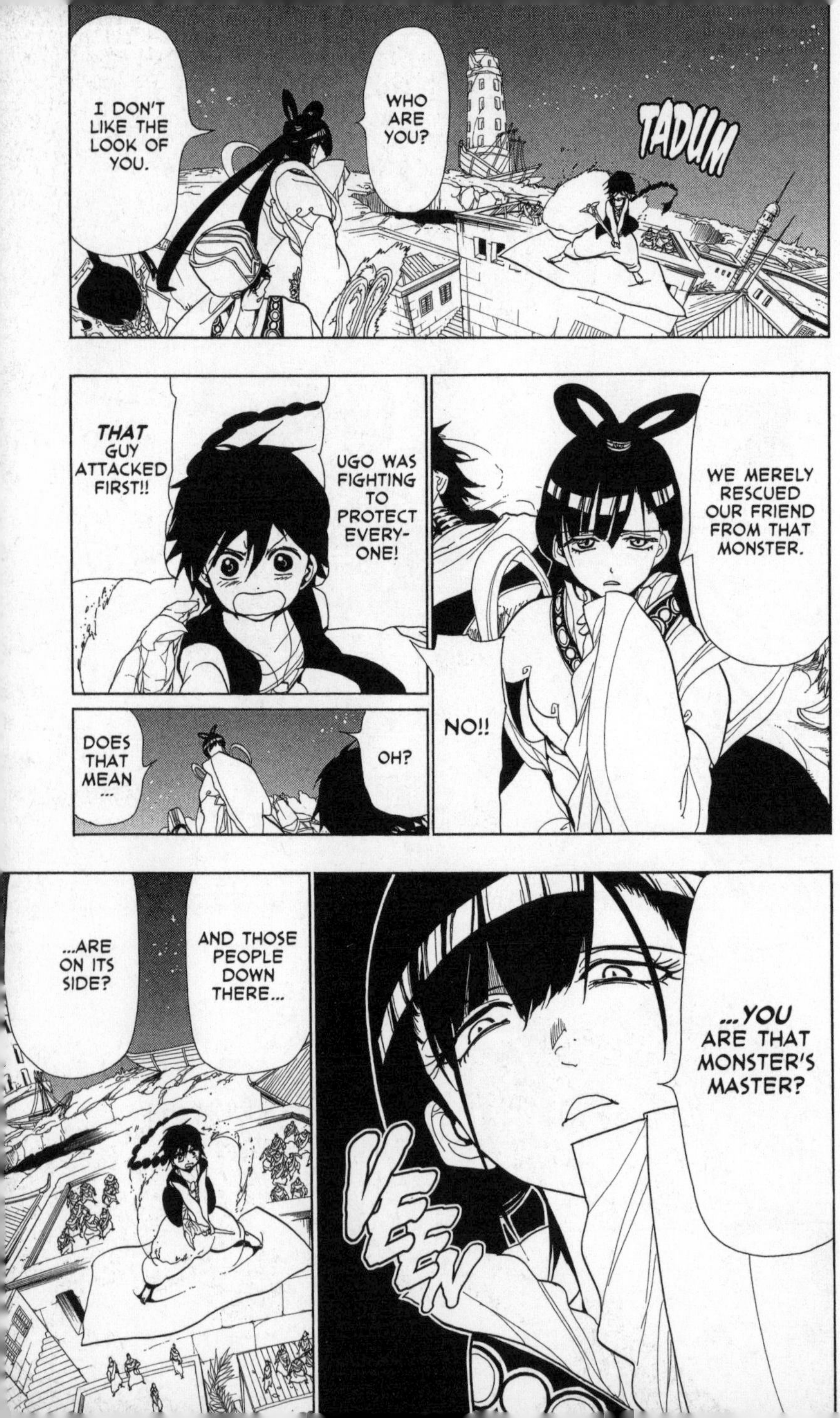
TADUM
WHO ARE YOU?
I DON'T LIKE THE LOOK OF YOU.
WE MERELY RESCUED OUR FRIEND FROM THAT MONSTER.
NO!!
UGO WAS FIGHTING TO PROTECT EVERY-ONE!
THAT GUY ATTACKED FIRST!!
OH?
DOES THAT MEAN ...
...YOU ARE THAT MONSTER'S MASTER?
VEEEN
AND THOSE PEOPLE DOWN THERE...
...ARE ON ITS SIDE?

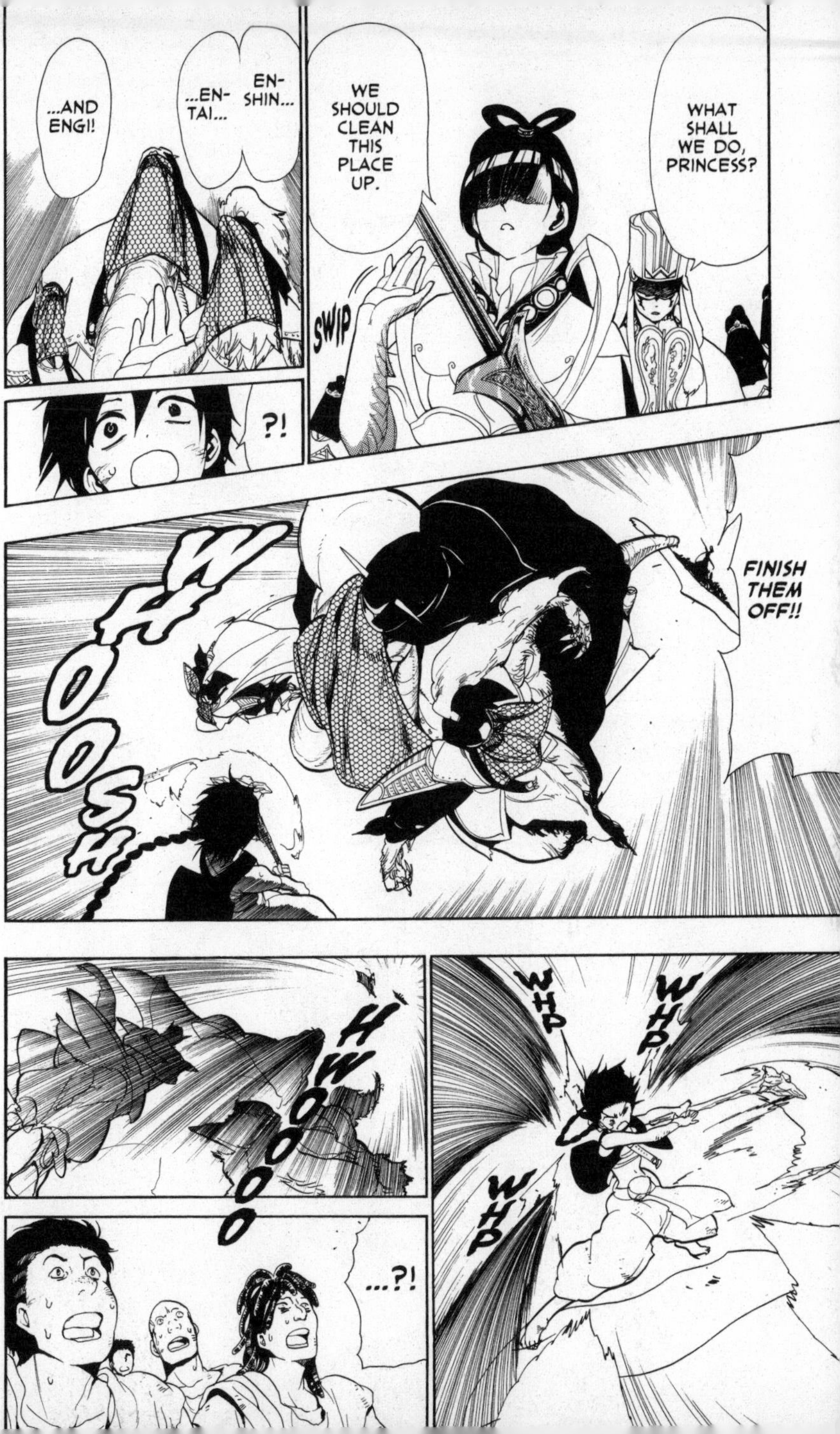
WHAT SHALL WE DO, PRINCESS?
WE SHOULD CLEAN THIS PLACE UP.
SWIP
EN-SHIN...
...EN-TAI...
...AND ENGI!
?!
FINISH THEM OFF!!
WHOOOSH
WHP
WHP
WHP
HWOOOOOO
...?!

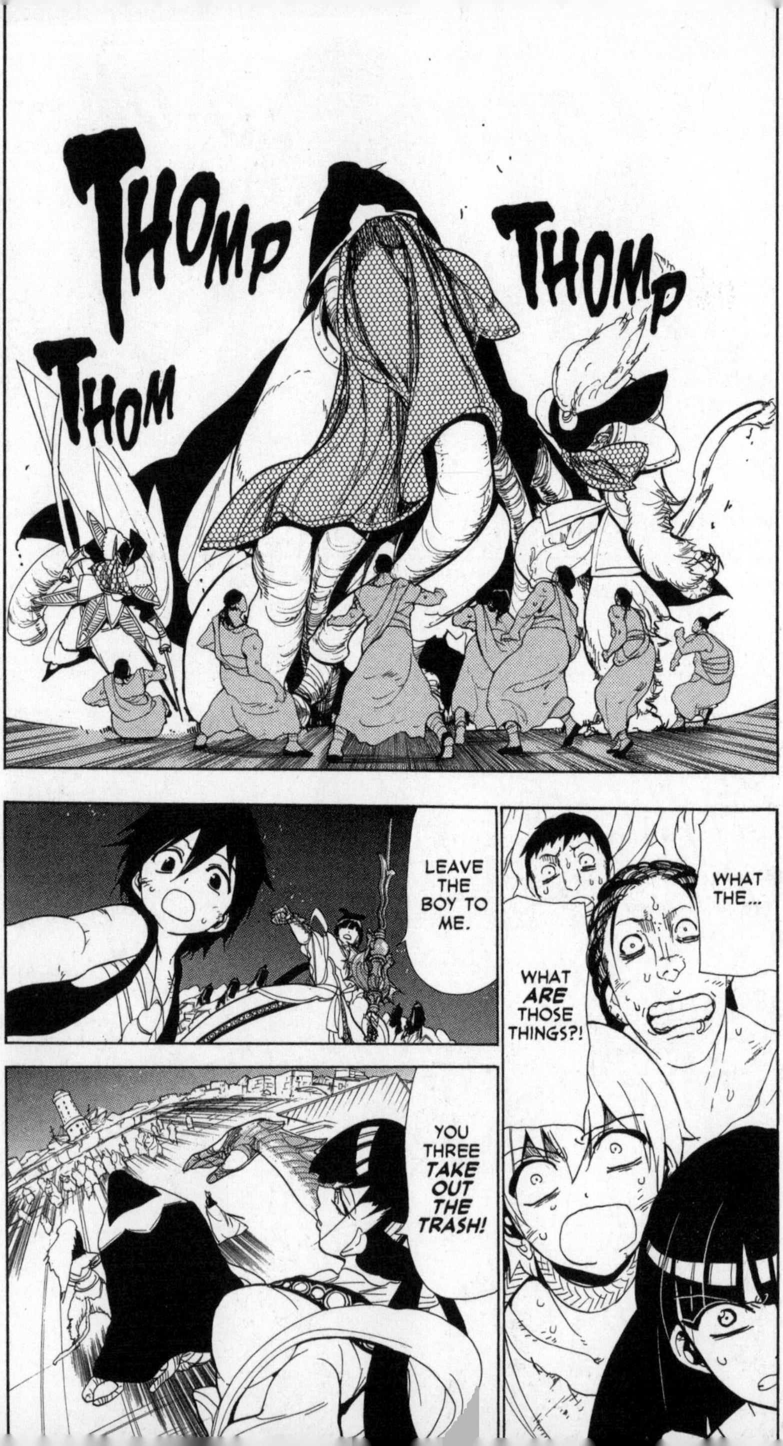
THOMP
THOMP
THOM
WHAT THE...
WHAT ARE THOSE THINGS?!
LEAVE THE BOY TO ME.
YOU THREE TAKE OUT THE TRASH!

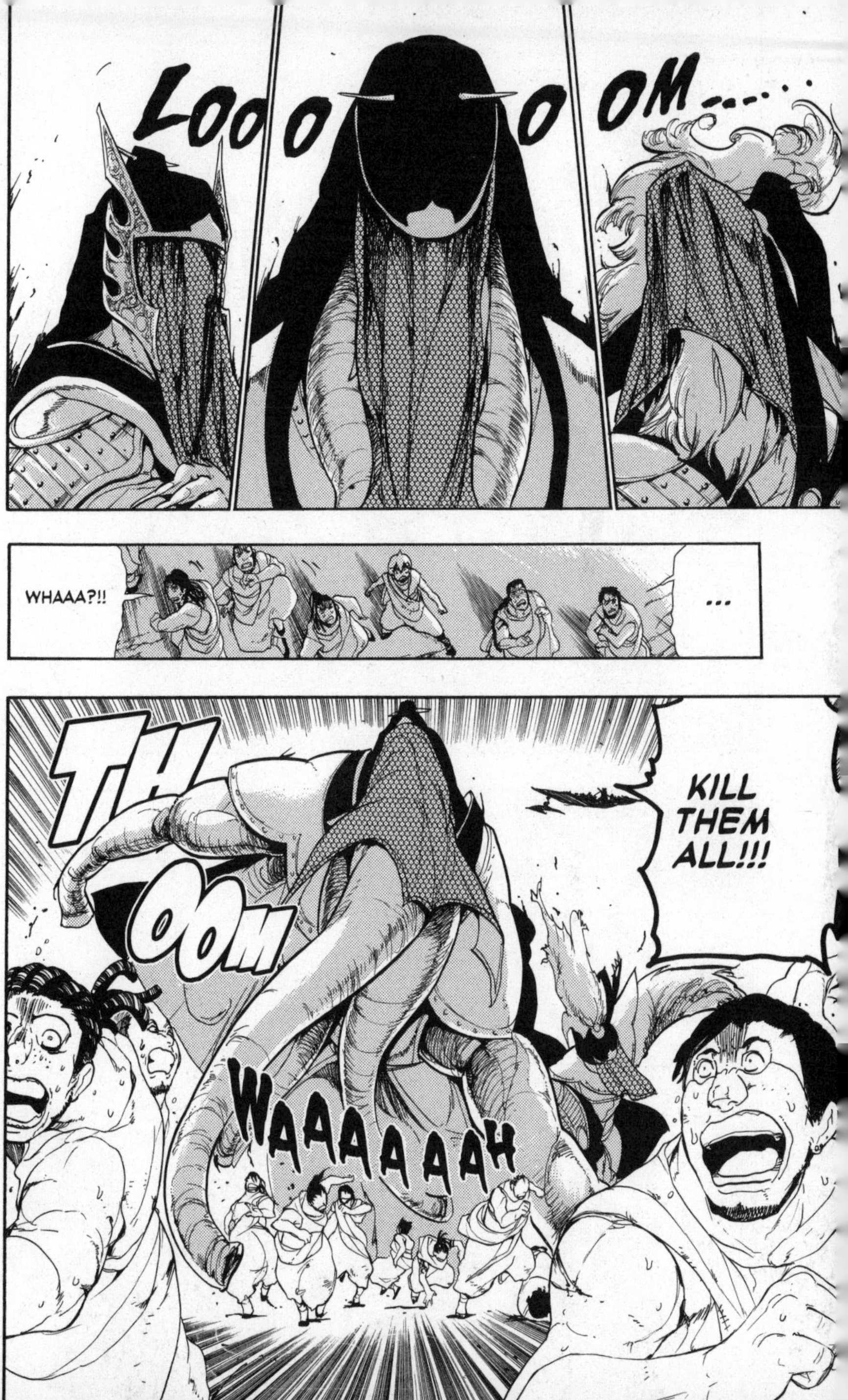
LOOOOOOM......
...
WHAAA?!!
KILL THEM ALL!!!
THOOM
WAAAAAAAH

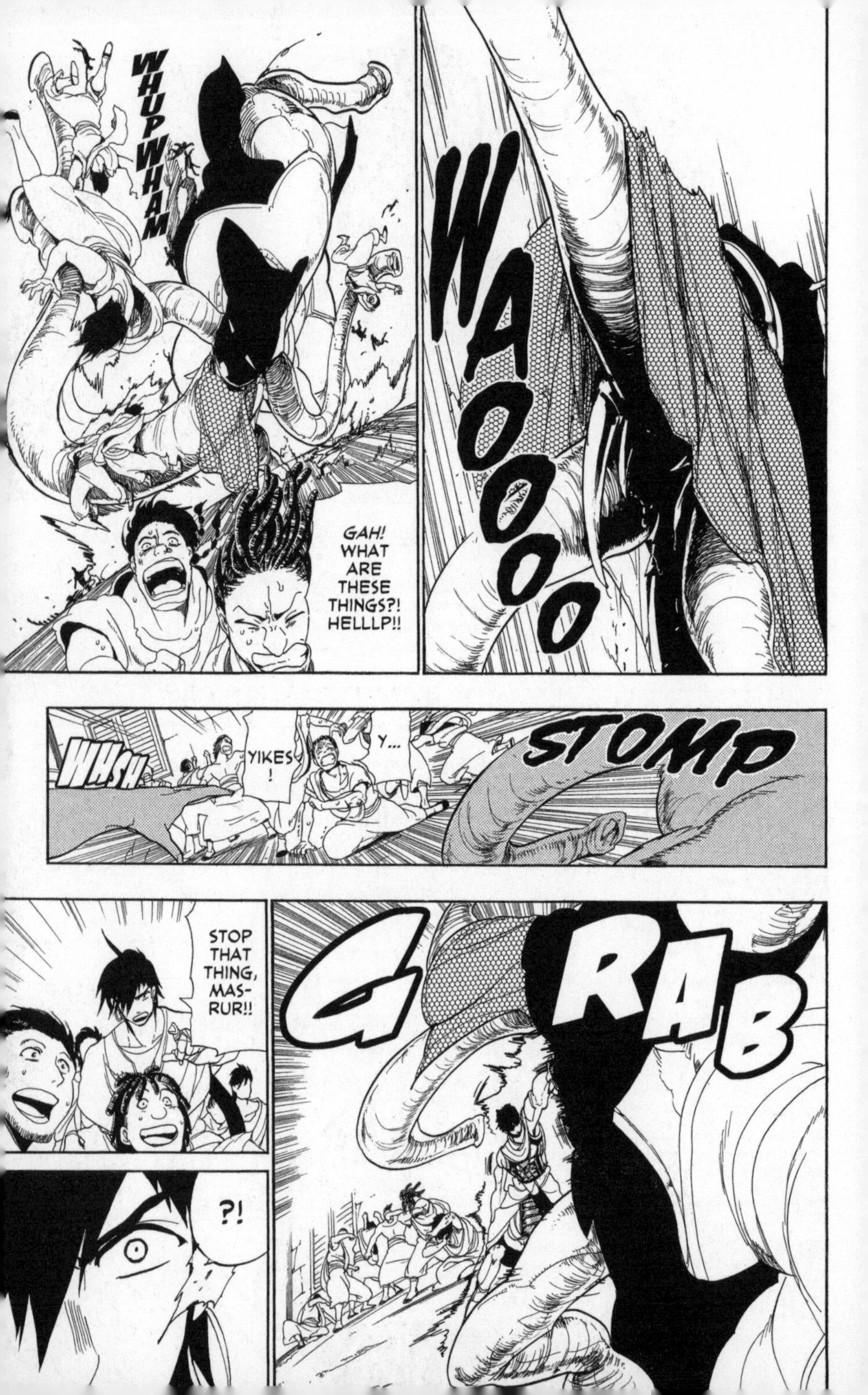
WAOOOOO
WHUPWHAM
GAH! WHAT ARE THESE THINGS?! HELLLP!!
STOMP
Y...
YIKES!
WHSH
GRAB
STOP THAT THING, MASRUR!!
?!

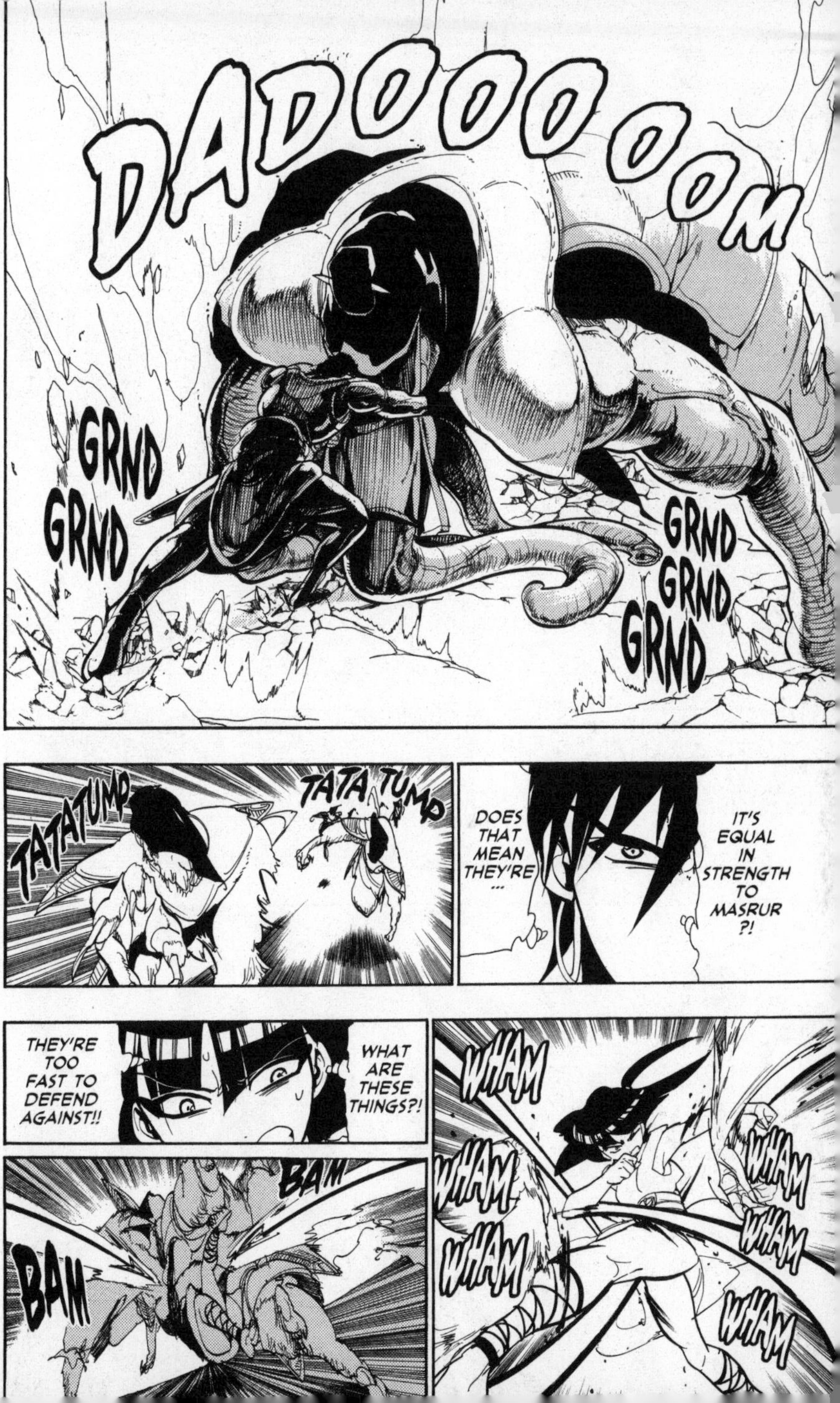
DADOOOOOM
GRND GRND GRND
GRND GRND
IT'S EQUAL IN STRENGTH TO MASRUR?!
DOES THAT MEAN THEY'RE...
TATA TUMP
TATATUMP
WHAM
WHAM
WHAM
WHAM
WHAM
WHAM
WHAT ARE THESE THINGS?!
THEY'RE TOO FAST TO DEFEND AGAINST!!
BAM
BAM

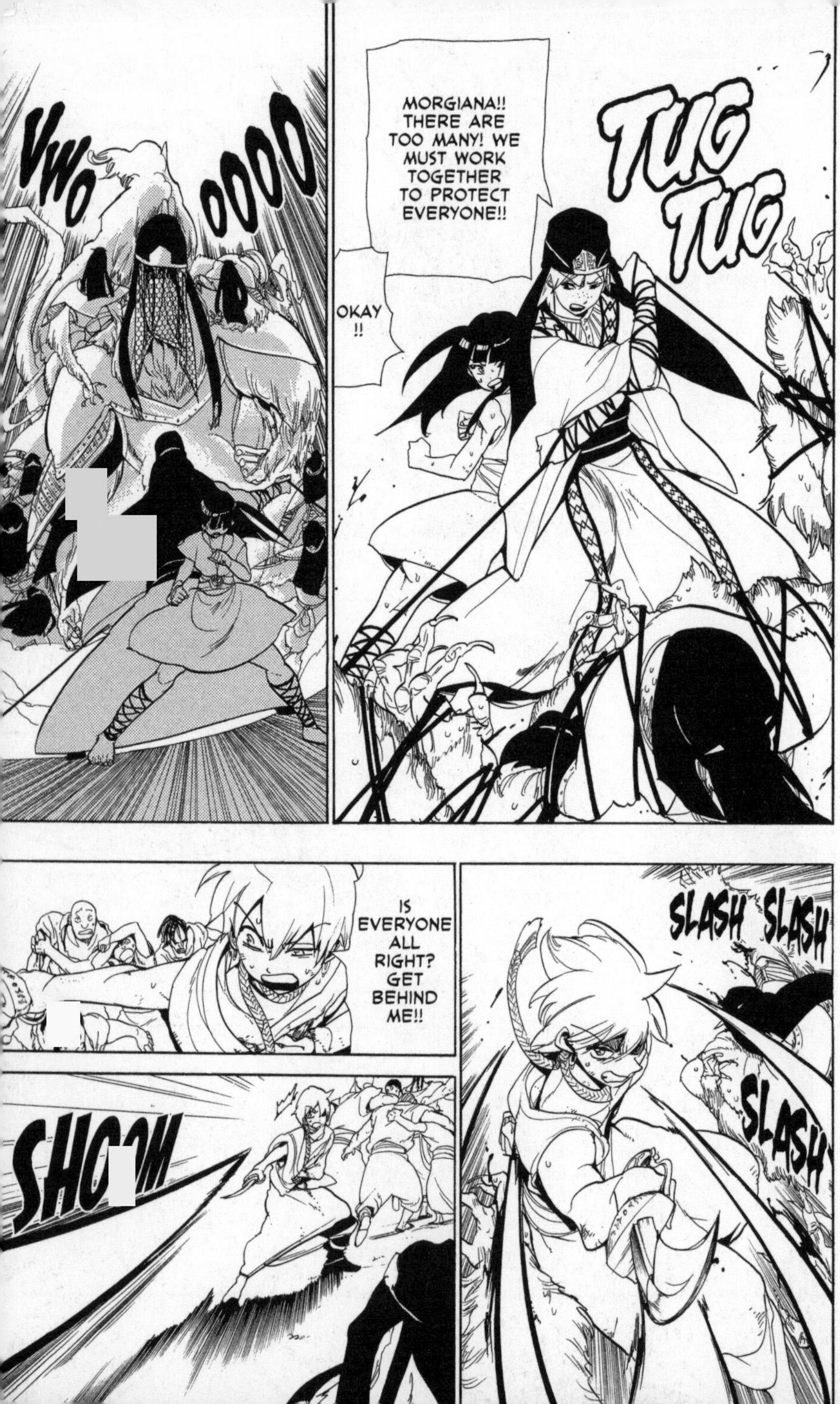
MORGIANA!! THERE ARE TOO MANY! WE MUST WORK TOGETHER TO PROTECT EVERYONE!!
TUG TUG
OKAY !!
VWO OOOO
SLASH SLASH
SLASH
IS EVERYONE ALL RIGHT? GET BEHIND ME!!
SHOOM

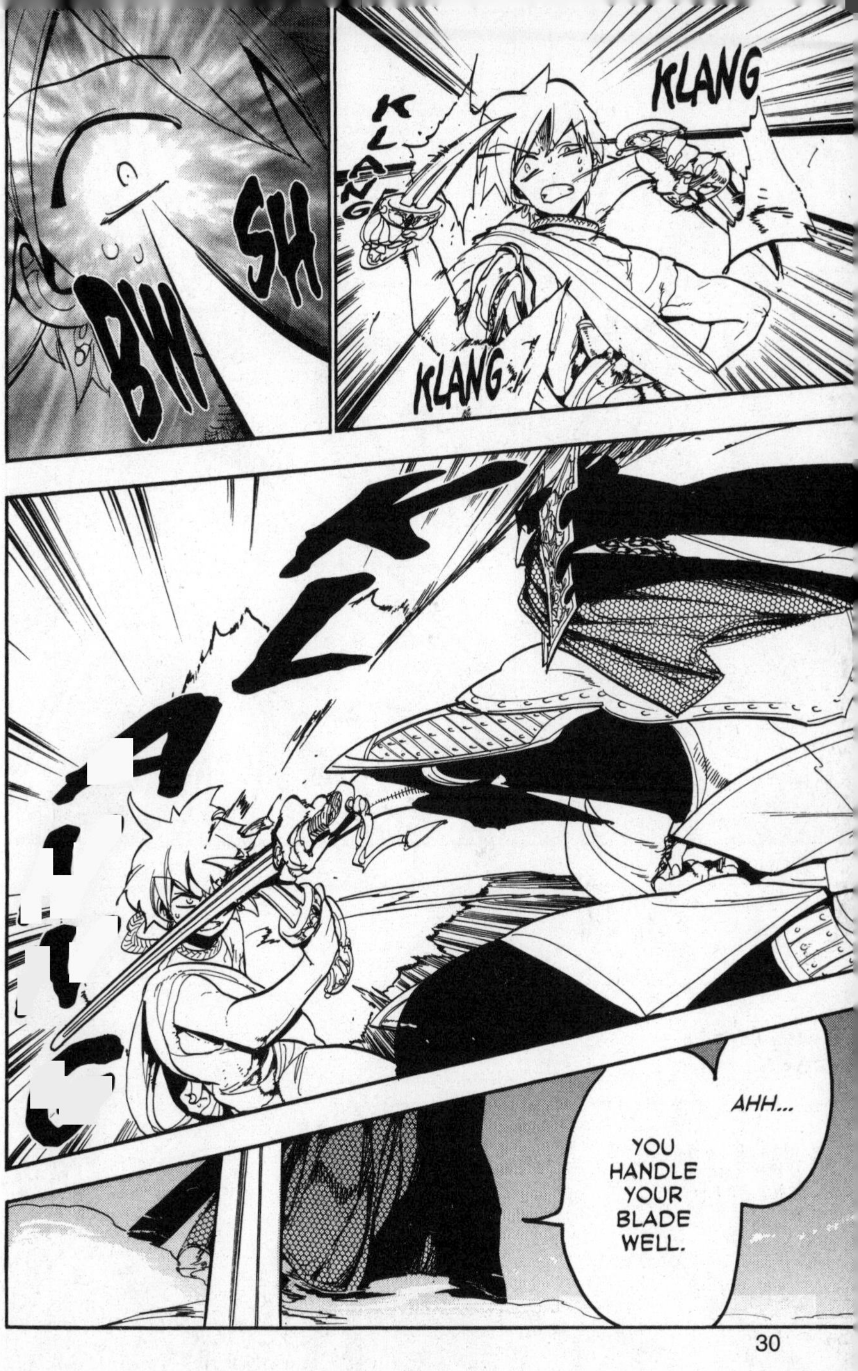
KLANG
KLANG
KLANG
BWSH
AHH...
YOU HANDLE YOUR BLADE WELL.

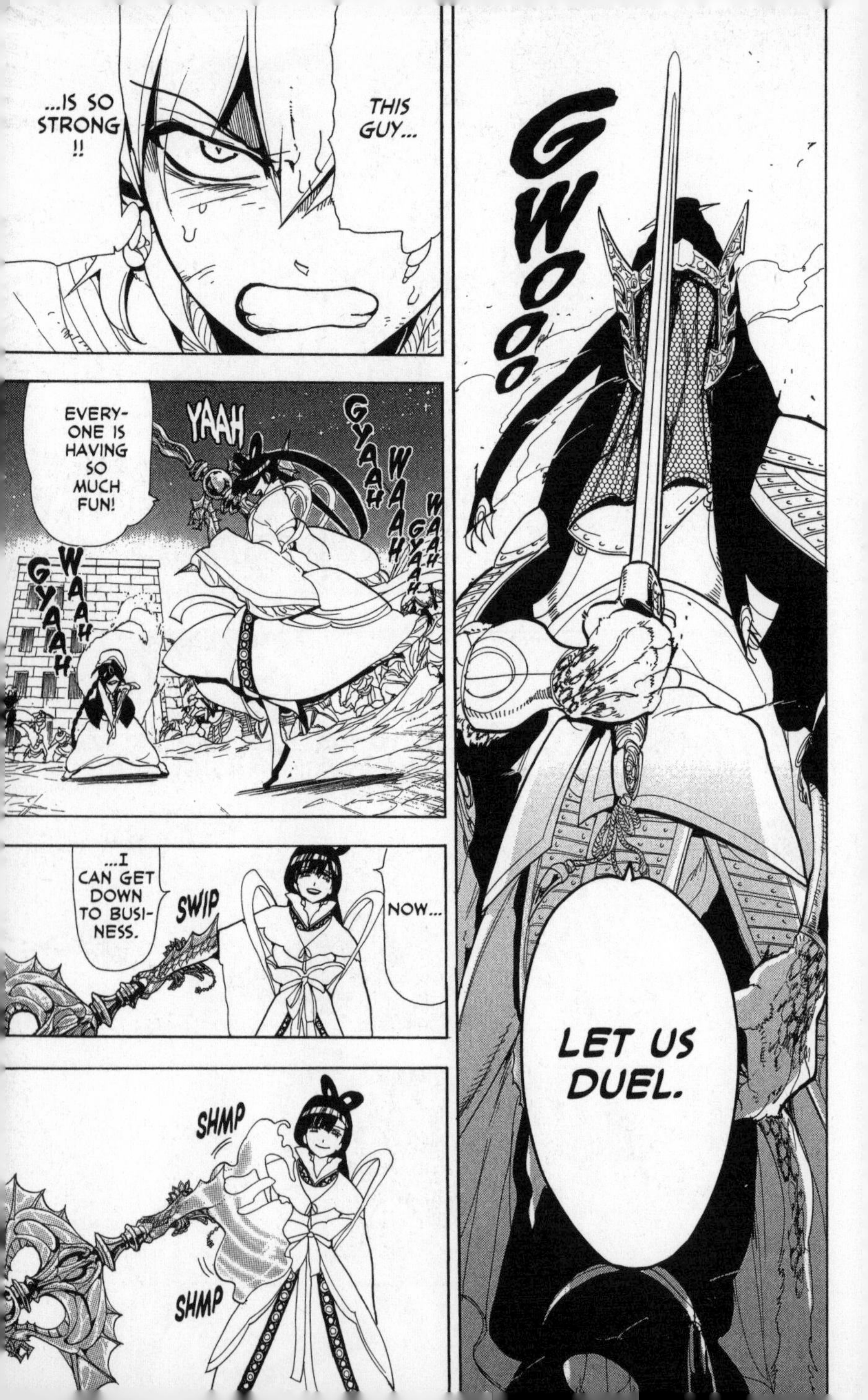
GWOOOO
LET US DUEL.
THIS GUY...
...IS SO STRONG !!
GYAAH
WAAAH
WAAAH
GYAAAH
YAAH
EVERY-ONE IS HAVING SO MUCH FUN!
WAAAH
GYAAAH
NOW...
SWIP
...I CAN GET DOWN TO BUSI-NESS.
SHMP
SHMP

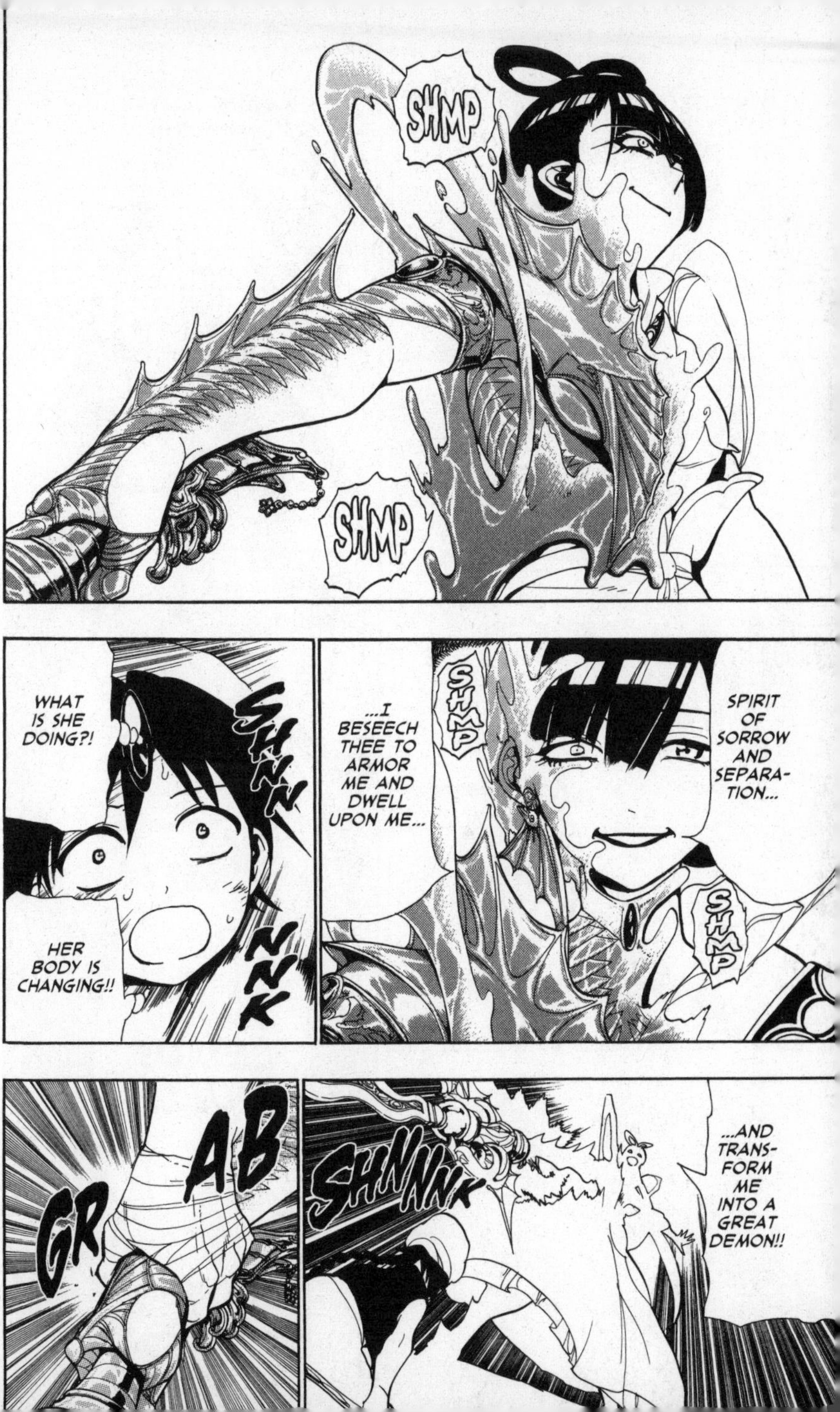
SHMP
SHMP
SPIRIT OF SORROW AND SEPARATION...
SHMP
...I BESEECH THEE TO ARMOR ME AND DWELL UPON ME...
SHMP
WHAT IS SHE DOING?!
SHNNNNK
HER BODY IS CHANGING!!
...AND TRANSFORM ME INTO A GREAT DEMON!!
SHNNNNK
GRAB

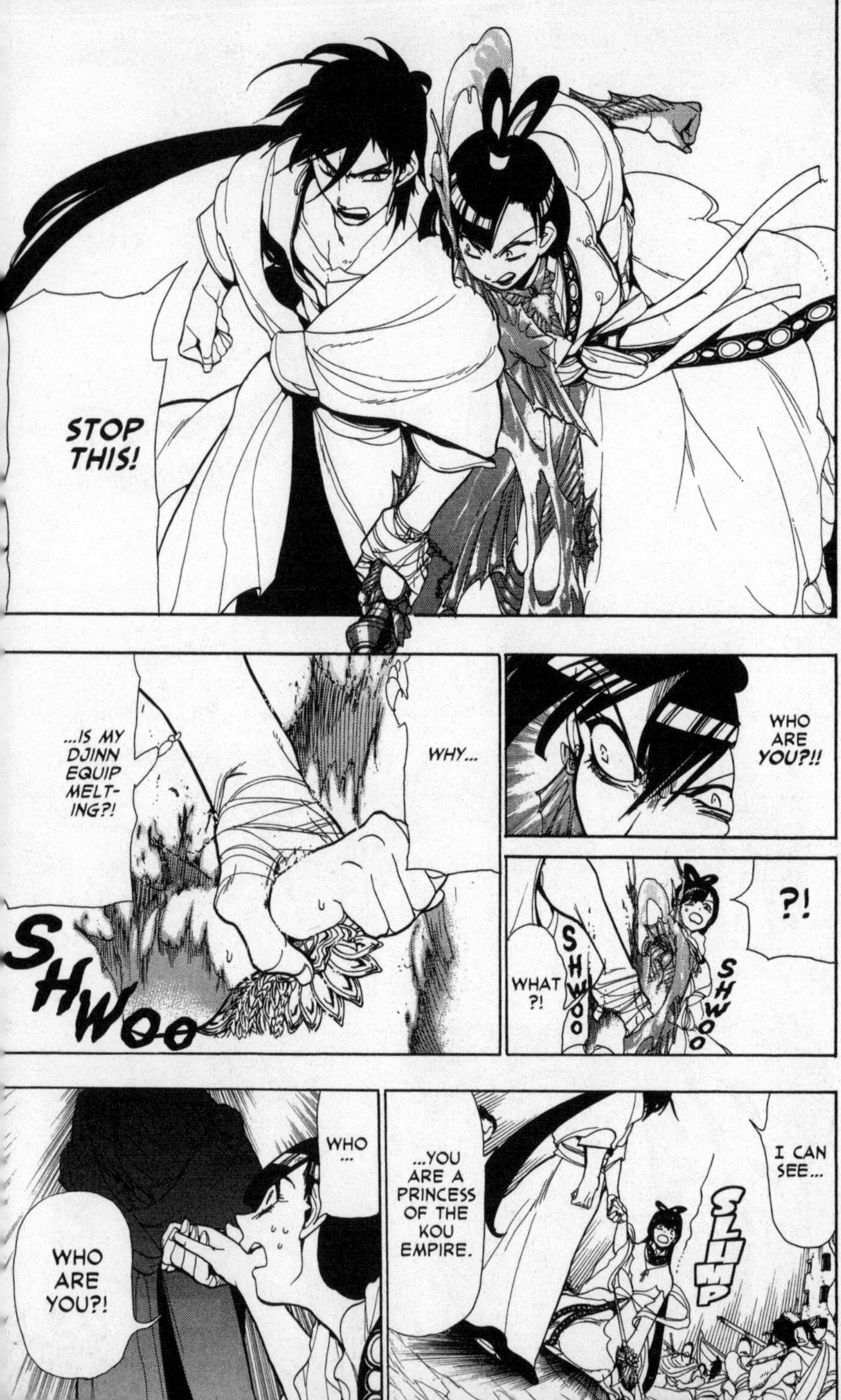
STOP THIS!
WHO ARE YOU?!!
?!
SHWOO
WHAT?!
SHWOO
WHY...
...IS MY DJINN EQUIP MELTING?!
SHWOO
I CAN SEE...
SLUMP
...YOU ARE A PRINCESS OF THE KOU EMPIRE.
WHO...
WHO ARE YOU?!

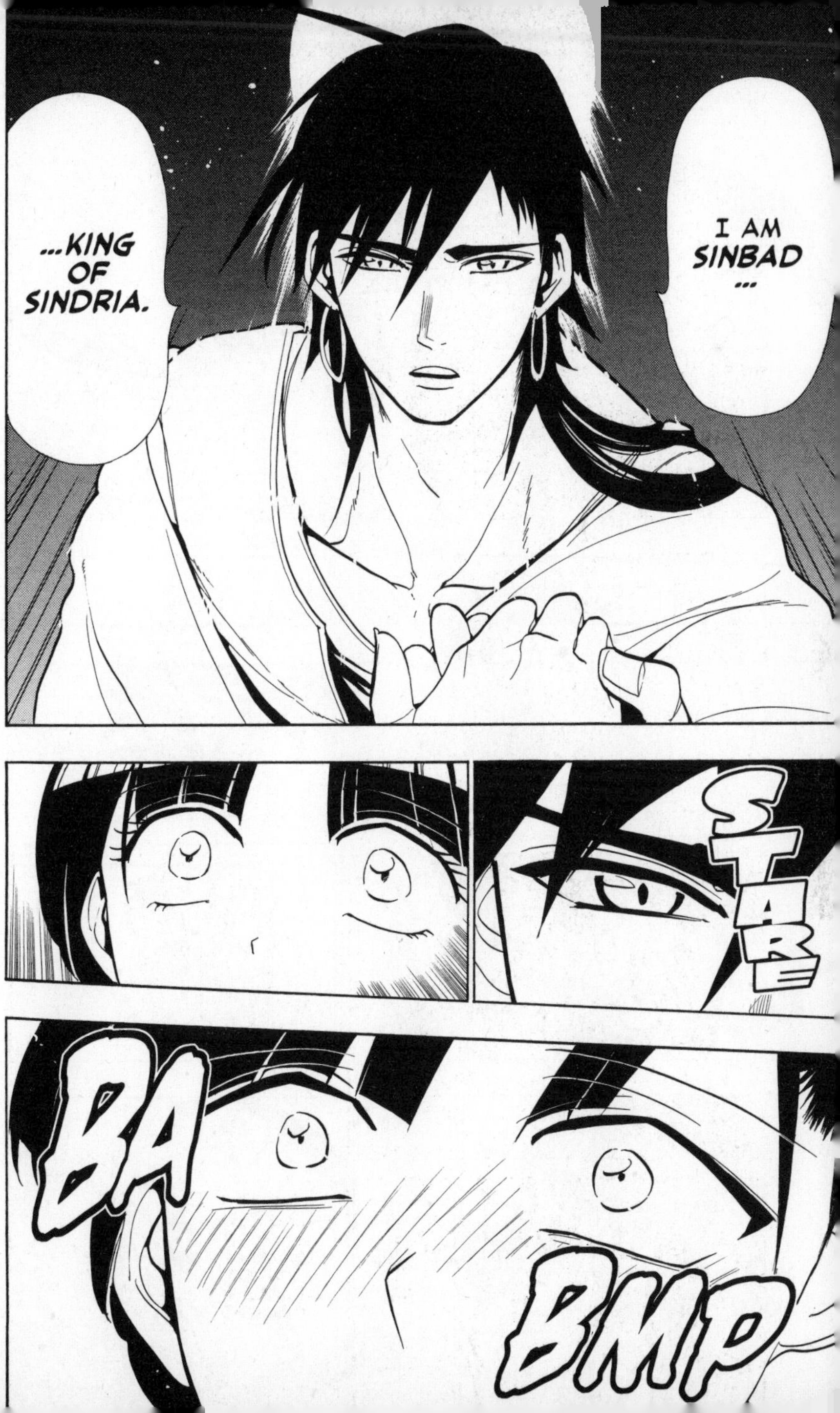
I AM SINBAD ...
...KING OF SINDRIA.
STARE
BA
BMP

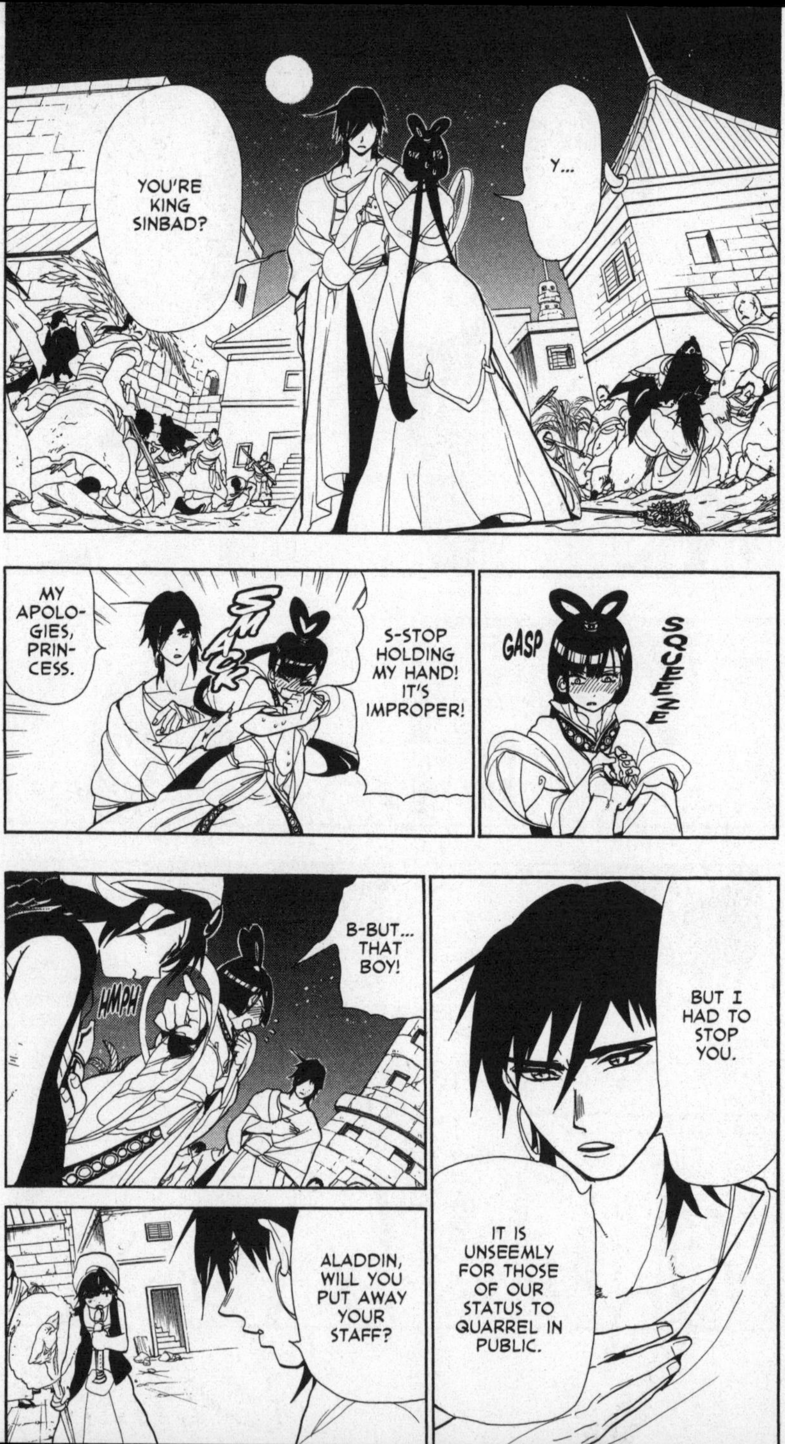
Y...
YOU'RE KING SINBAD?
GASP
SQUEEZE
S-STOP HOLDING MY HAND! IT'S IMPROPER!
SMACK
MY APOLOGIES, PRINCESS.
BUT I HAD TO STOP YOU.
IT IS UNSEEMLY FOR THOSE OF OUR STATUS TO QUARREL IN PUBLIC.
B-BUT... THAT BOY!
HMPH
ALADDIN, WILL YOU PUT AWAY YOUR STAFF?

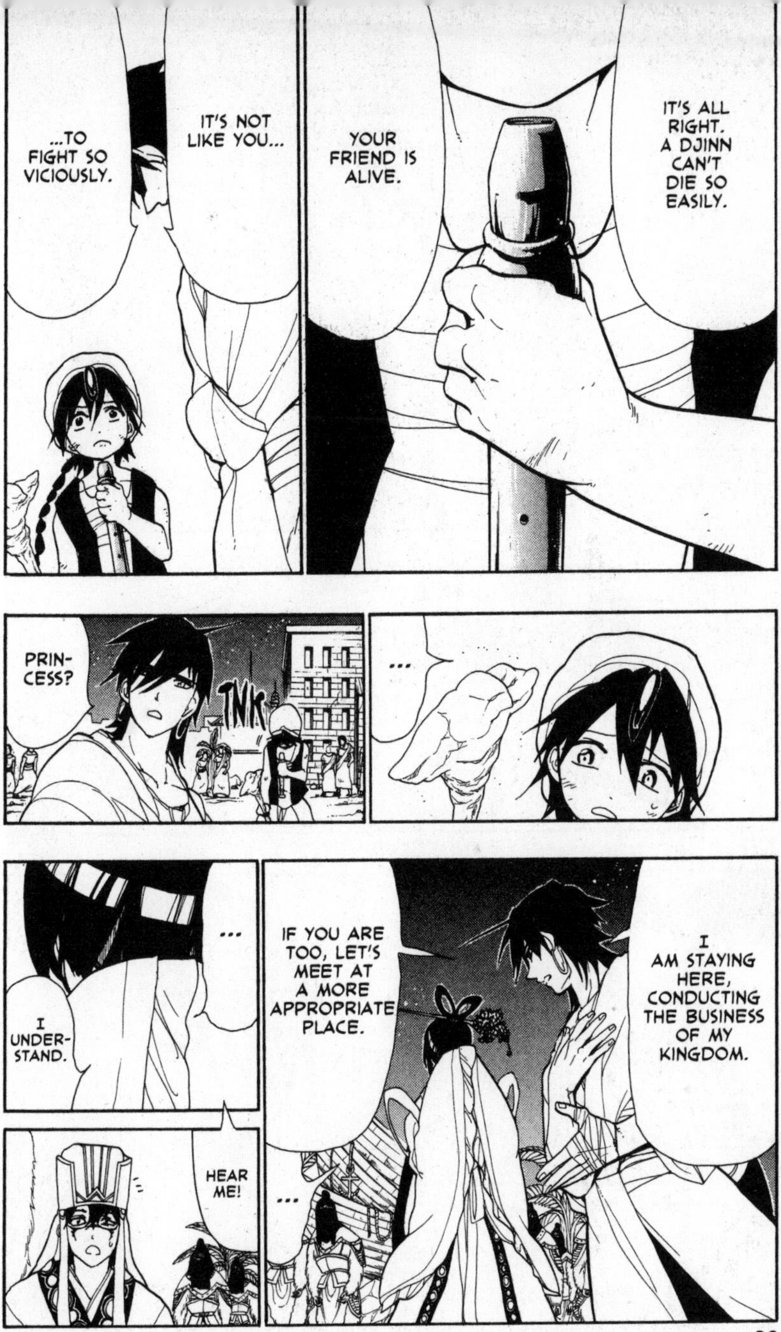
IT'S ALL RIGHT. A DJINN CAN'T DIE SO EASILY.
YOUR FRIEND IS ALIVE.
IT'S NOT LIKE YOU...
...TO FIGHT SO VICIOUSLY.
...
PRIN- CESS?
TNK
I AM STAYING HERE, CONDUCTING THE BUSINESS OF MY KINGDOM.
IF YOU ARE TOO, LET'S MEET AT A MORE APPROPRIATE PLACE.
...
...
I UNDER- STAND.
HEAR ME!

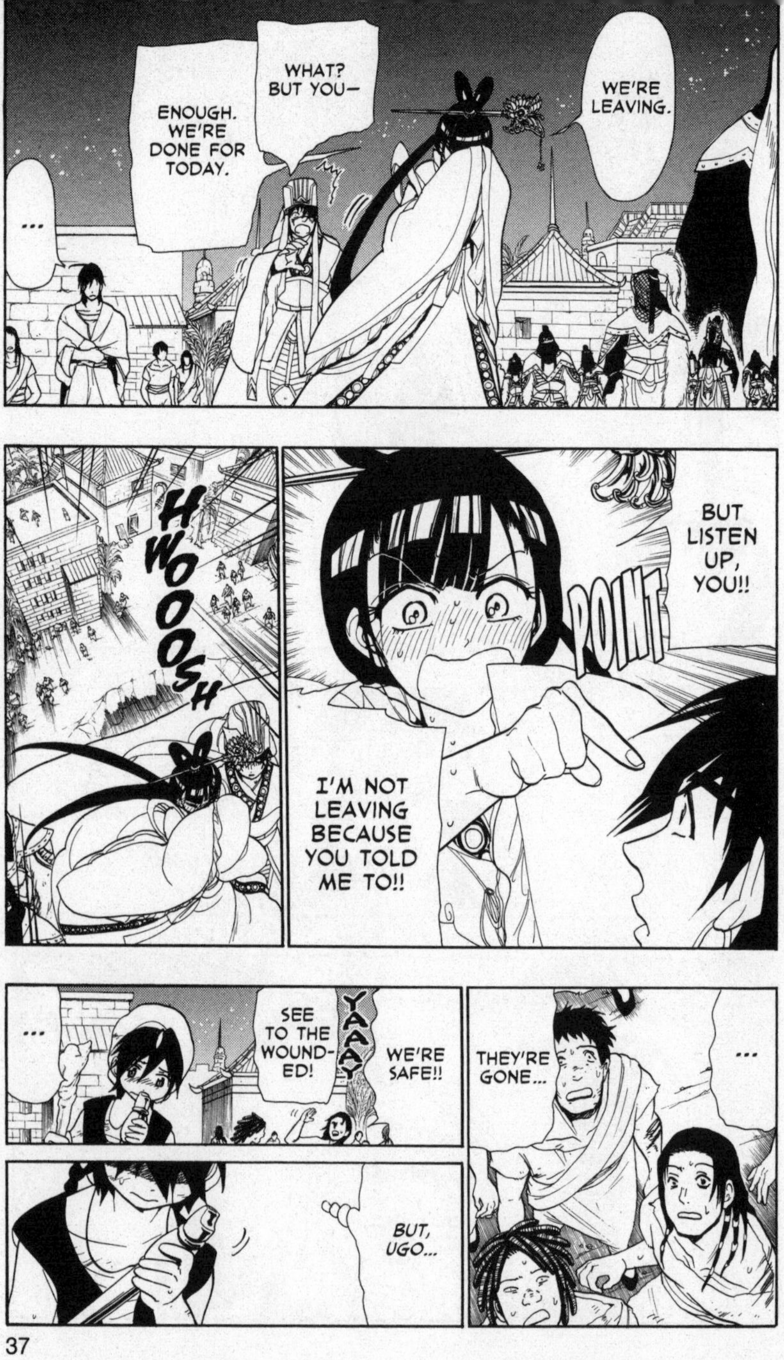
WE'RE LEAVING.
WHAT? BUT YOU—
ENOUGH. WE'RE DONE FOR TODAY.
...
BUT LISTEN UP, YOU!!
POINT
I'M NOT LEAVING BECAUSE YOU TOLD ME TO!!
HWOOOOSH
...
THEY'RE GONE...
WE'RE SAFE!!
YAAAY
SEE TO THE WOUNDED!
...
BUT, UGO...

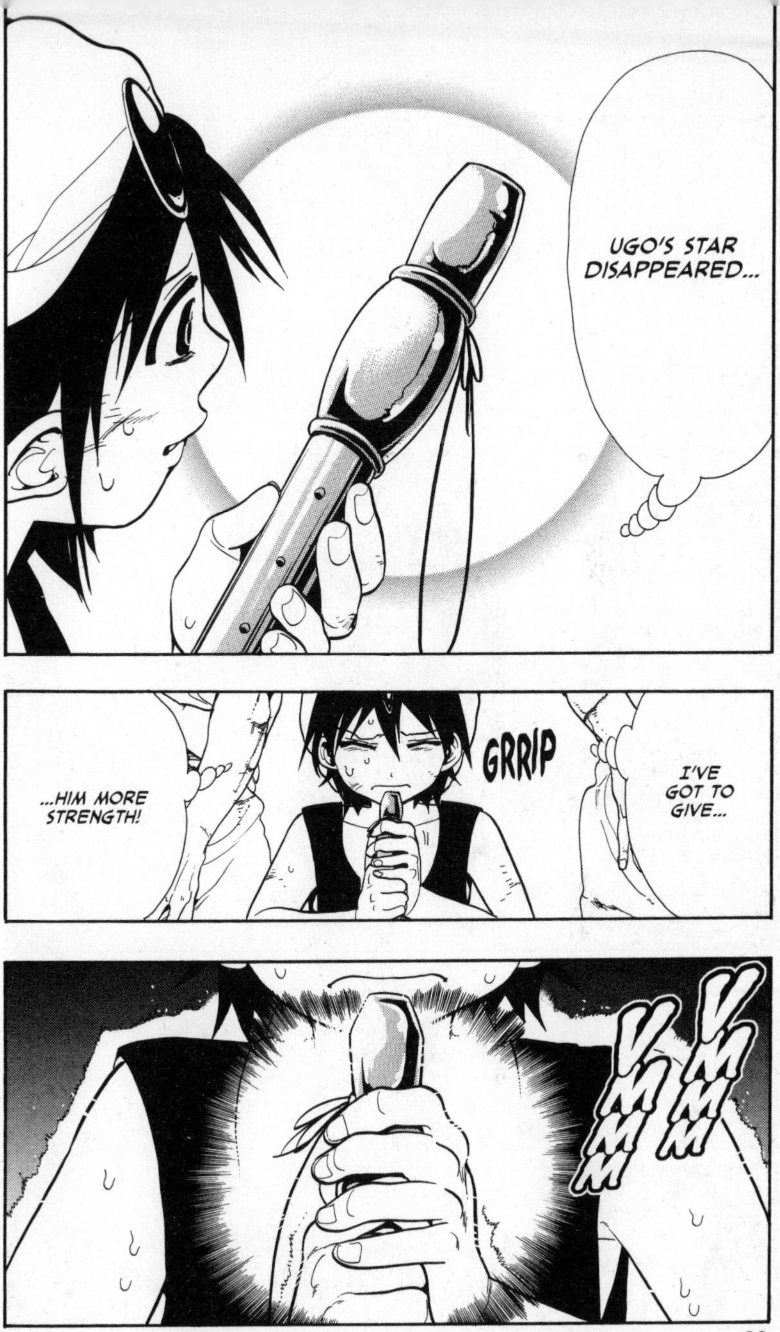
UGO'S STAR DISAPPEARED...
I'VE GOT TO GIVE...
GRRIP
...HIM MORE STRENGTH!
VMMM
VMMM

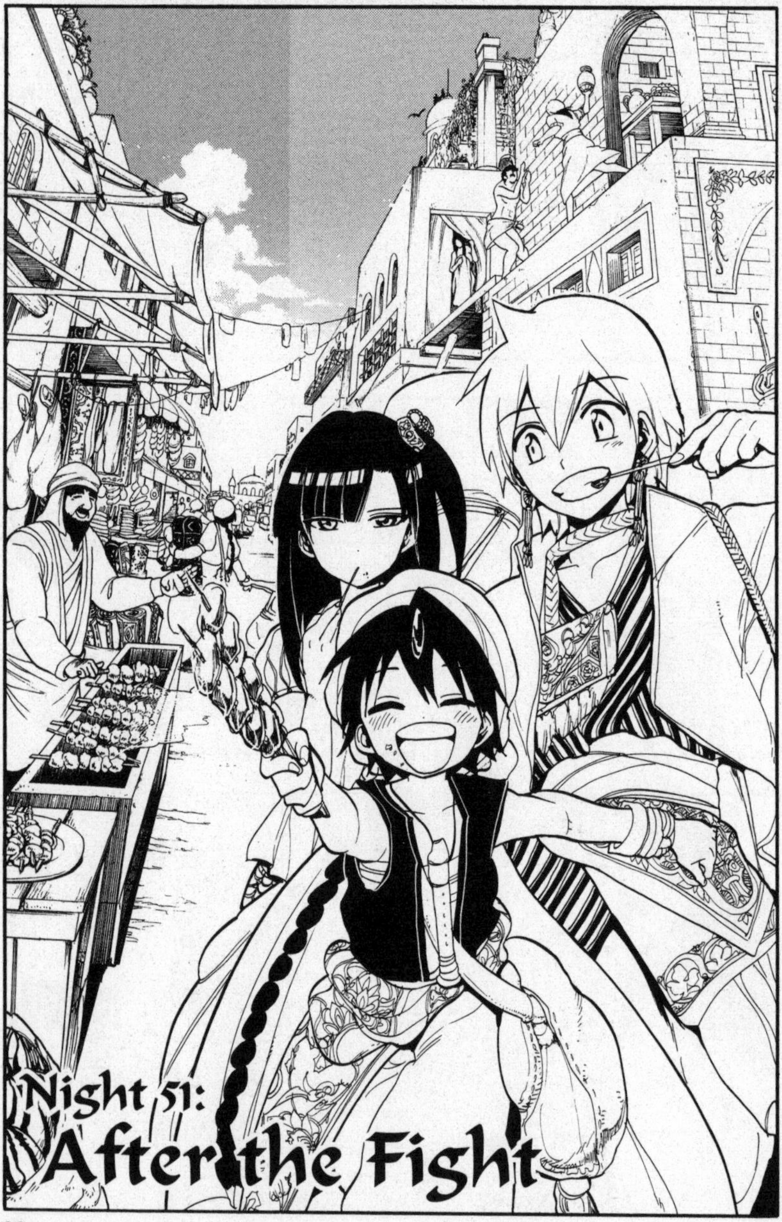
Night 51:
After the Fight

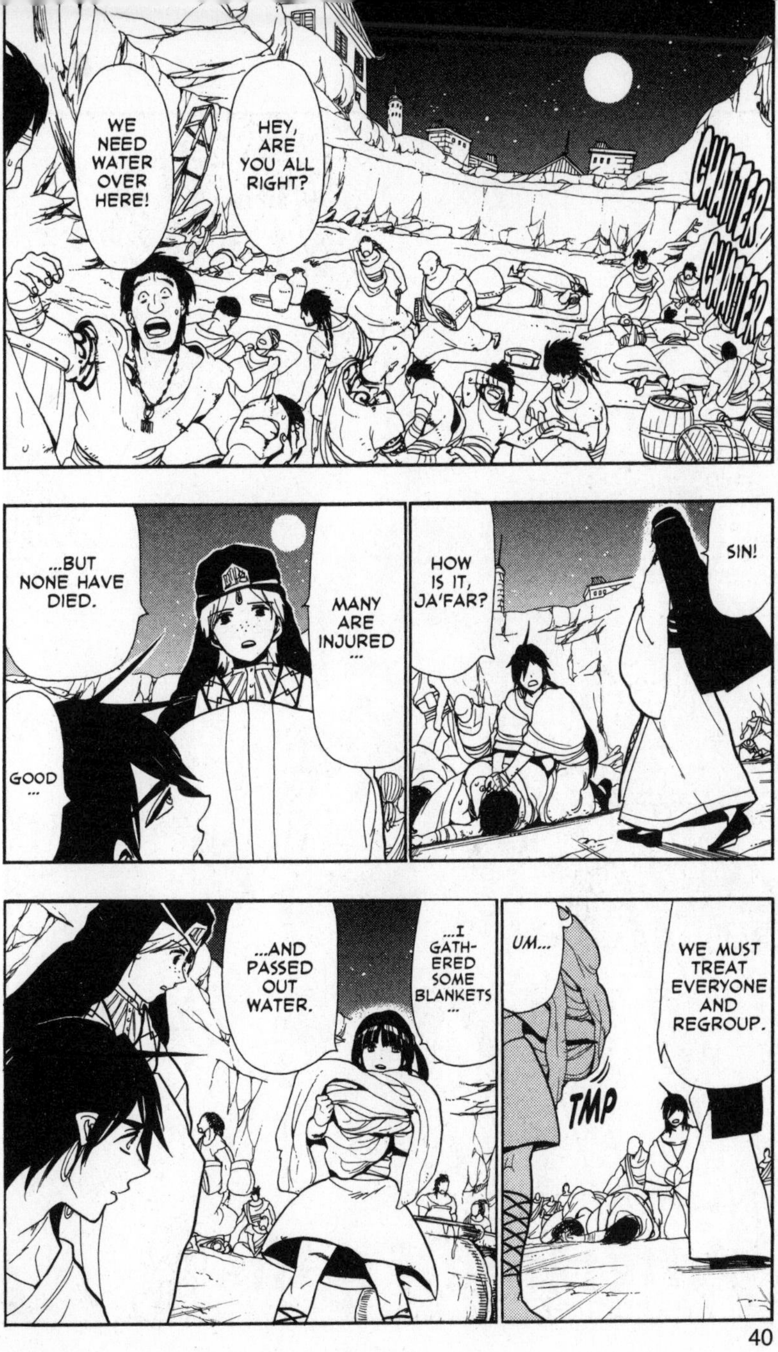
CHATTER CHATTER
HEY, ARE YOU ALL RIGHT?
WE NEED WATER OVER HERE!
SIN!
HOW IS IT, JA'FAR?
MANY ARE INJURED...
...BUT NONE HAVE DIED.
GOOD...
WE MUST TREAT EVERYONE AND REGROUP.
UM...
TMP
...I GATH-ERED SOME BLANKETS...
...AND PASSED OUT WATER.

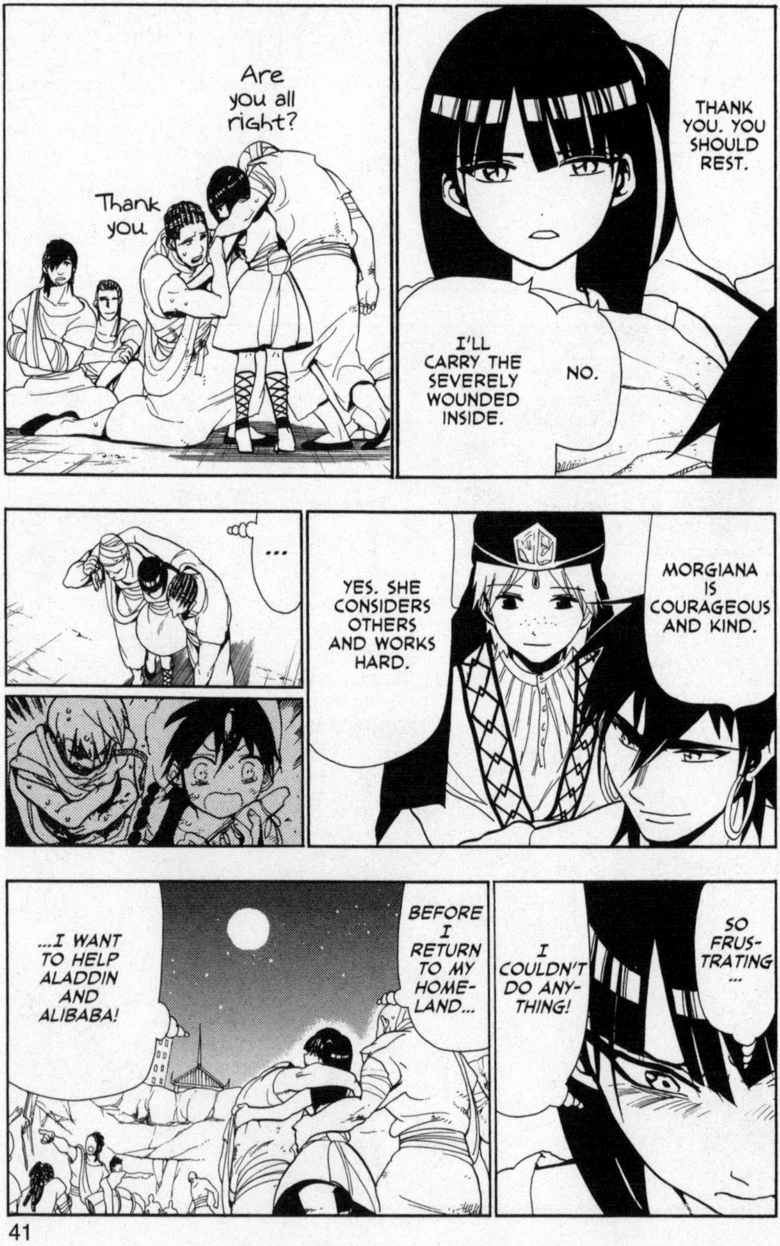
THANK YOU. YOU SHOULD REST.
NO.
I'LL CARRY THE SEVERELY WOUNDED INSIDE.
Are you all right?
Thank you.
MORGIANA IS COURAGEOUS AND KIND.
YES. SHE CONSIDERS OTHERS AND WORKS HARD.
...
SO FRUS-TRATING...
I COULDN'T DO ANY-THING!
BEFORE I RETURN TO MY HOME-LAND...
...I WANT TO HELP ALADDIN AND ALIBABA!

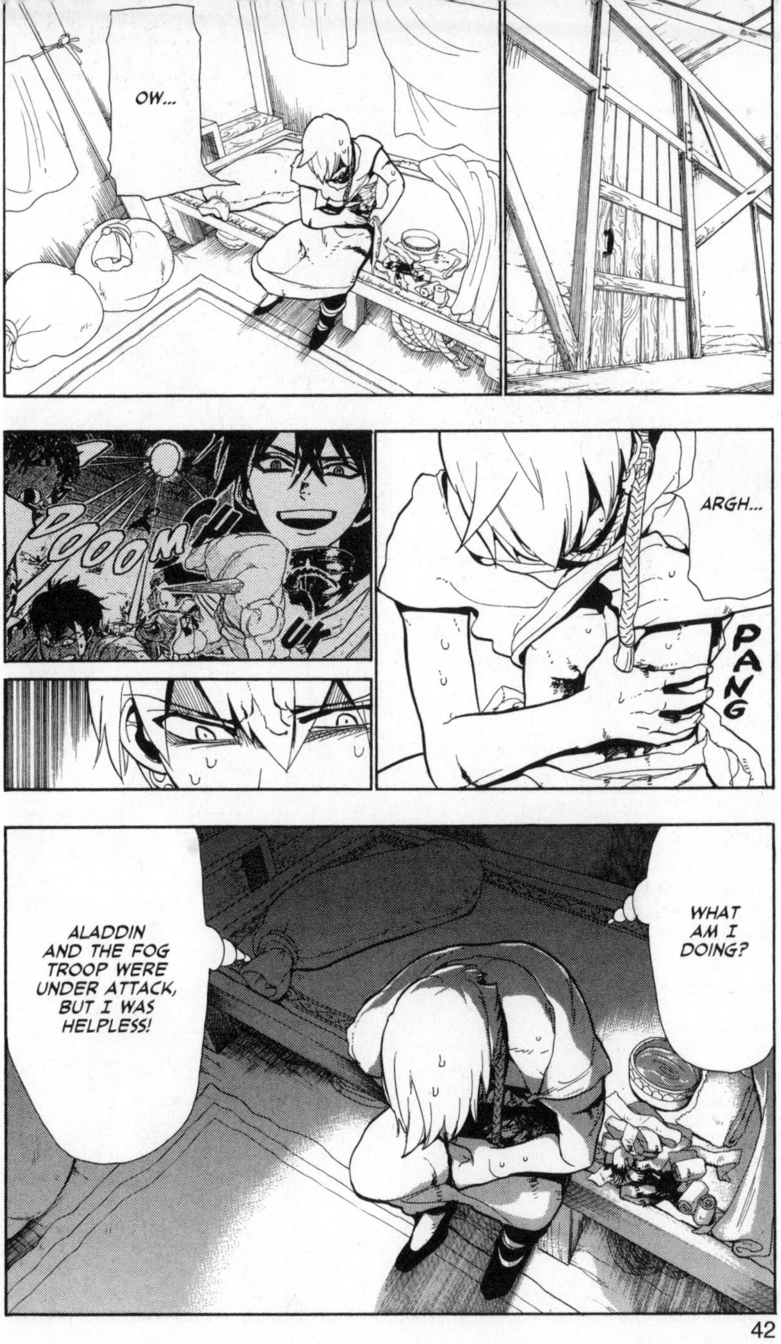
OW...
ARGH...
PANG
DOOOMCH
UK
WHAT AM I DOING?
ALADDIN AND THE FOG TROOP WERE UNDER ATTACK, BUT I WAS HELPLESS!

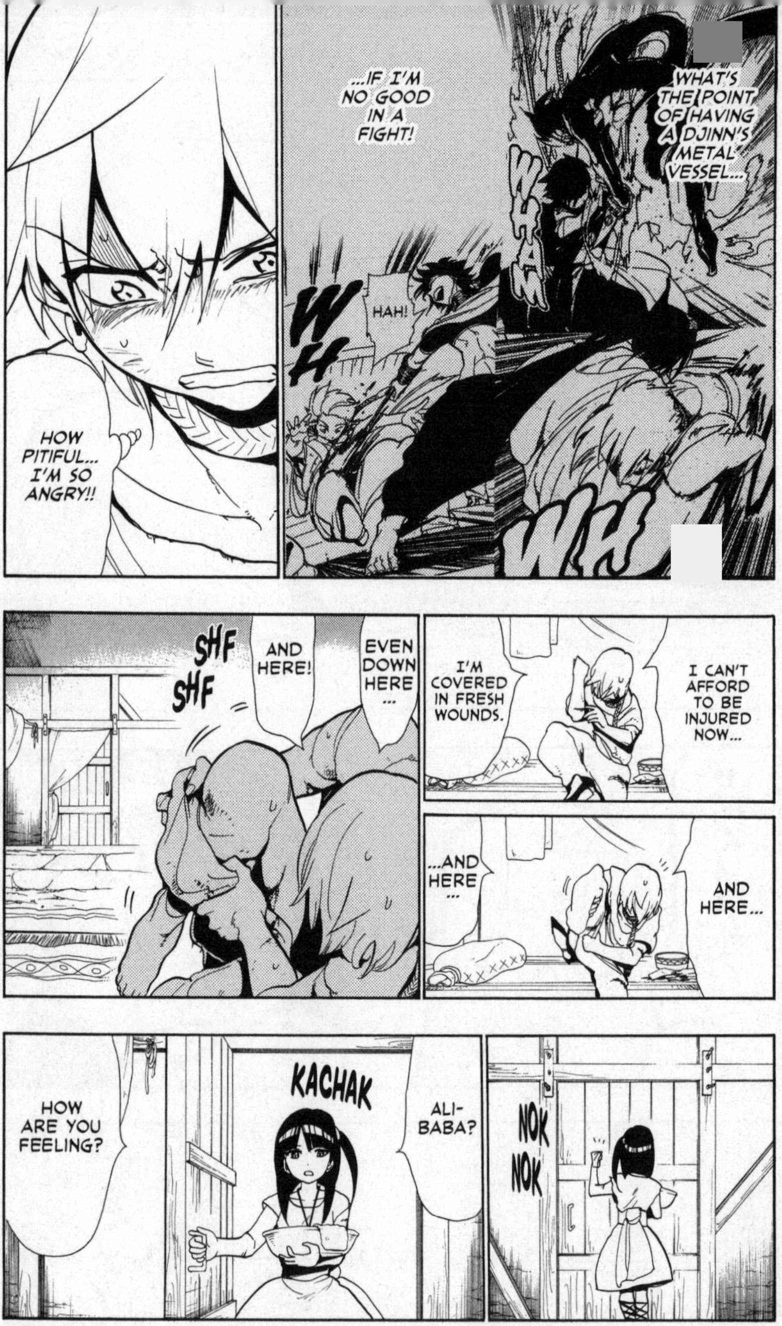
WHAT'S THE POINT OF HAVING A DJINN'S METAL VESSEL...
WH
...IF I'M NO GOOD IN A FIGHT!
HAH!
WH
HOW PITIFUL... I'M SO ANGRY!!
I CAN'T AFFORD TO BE INJURED NOW...
I'M COVERED IN FRESH WOUNDS.
AND HERE...
...AND HERE ...
EVEN DOWN HERE ...
AND HERE!
SHF
SHF
NOK
NOK
ALI-BABA?
KACHAK
HOW ARE YOU FEELING?

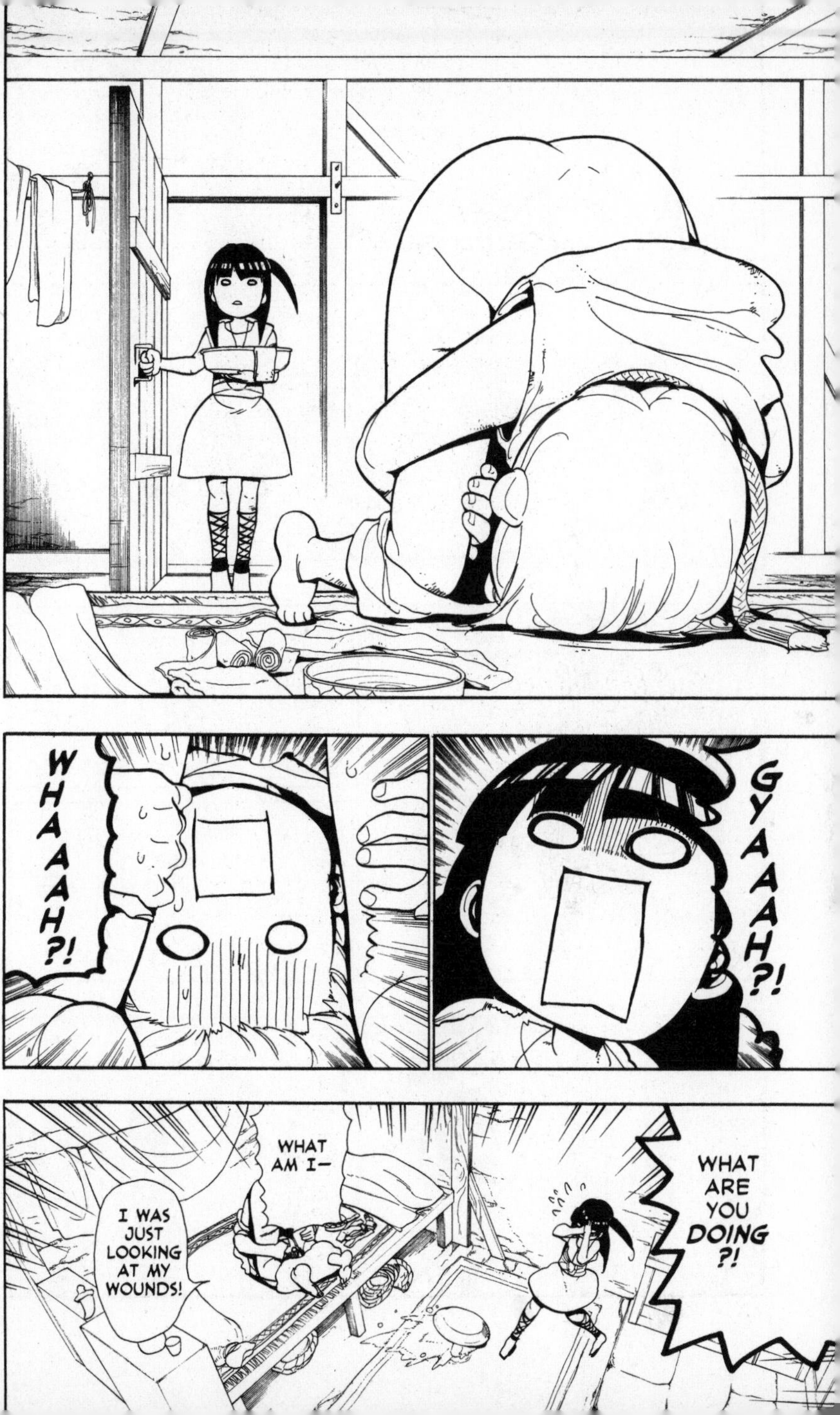
GYAAAAH?!
WHAAAAH?!
WHAT ARE YOU DOING?!
WHAT AM I—
I WAS JUST LOOKING AT MY WOUNDS!

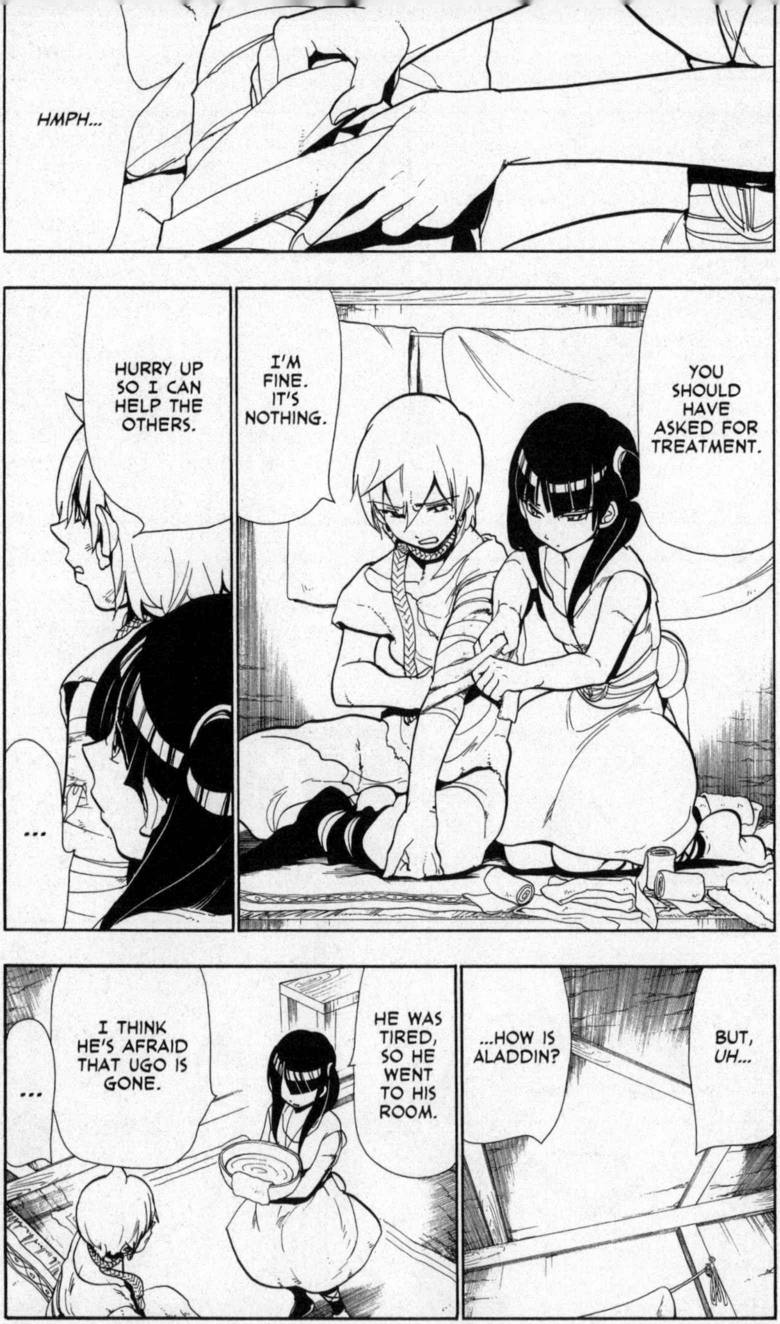
HMPH...
YOU SHOULD HAVE ASKED FOR TREATMENT.
I'M FINE. IT'S NOTHING.
HURRY UP SO I CAN HELP THE OTHERS.
...
BUT, UH...
...HOW IS ALADDIN?
HE WAS TIRED, SO HE WENT TO HIS ROOM.
I THINK HE'S AFRAID THAT UGO IS GONE.
...

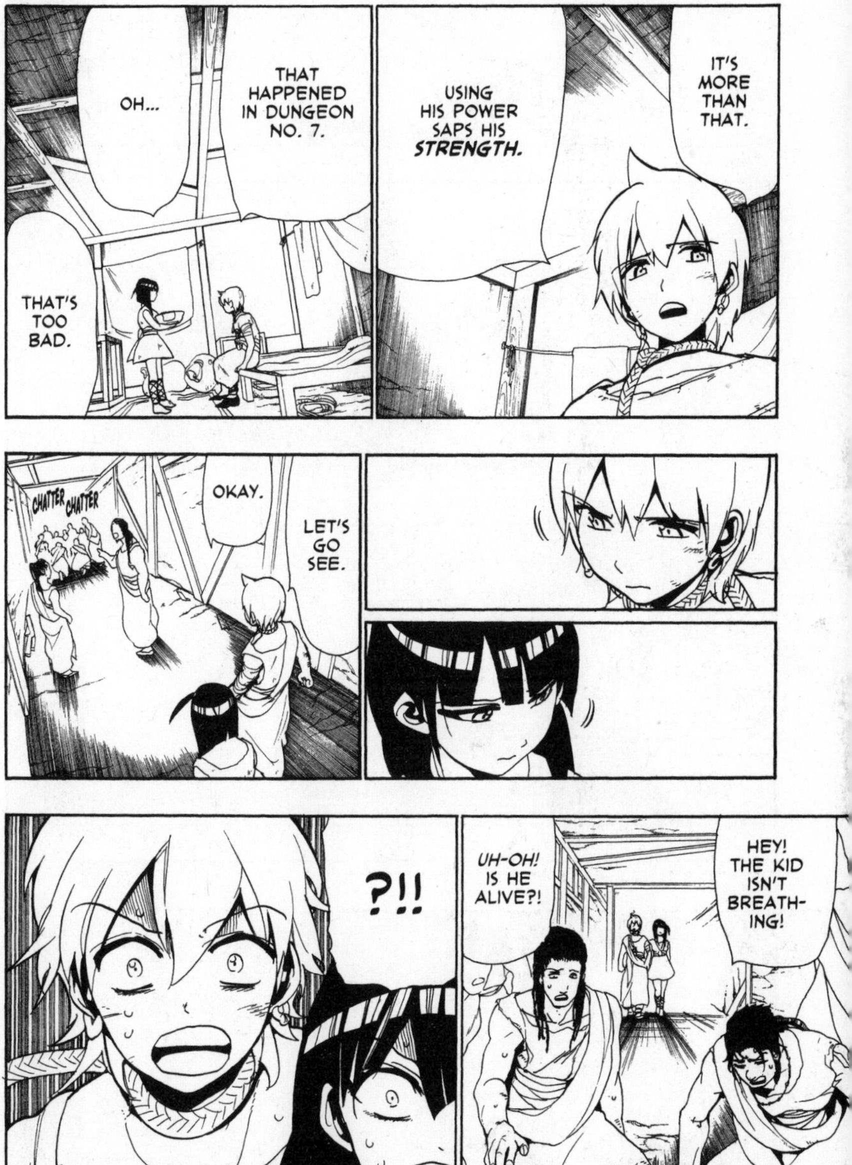
IT'S MORE THAN THAT.
USING HIS POWER SAPS HIS *STRENGTH.*
THAT HAPPENED IN DUNGEON NO. 7.
OH...
THAT'S TOO BAD.
OKAY.
LET'S GO SEE.
CHATTER CHATTER
HEY! THE KID ISN'T BREATHING!
UH-OH! IS HE ALIVE?!
?!!

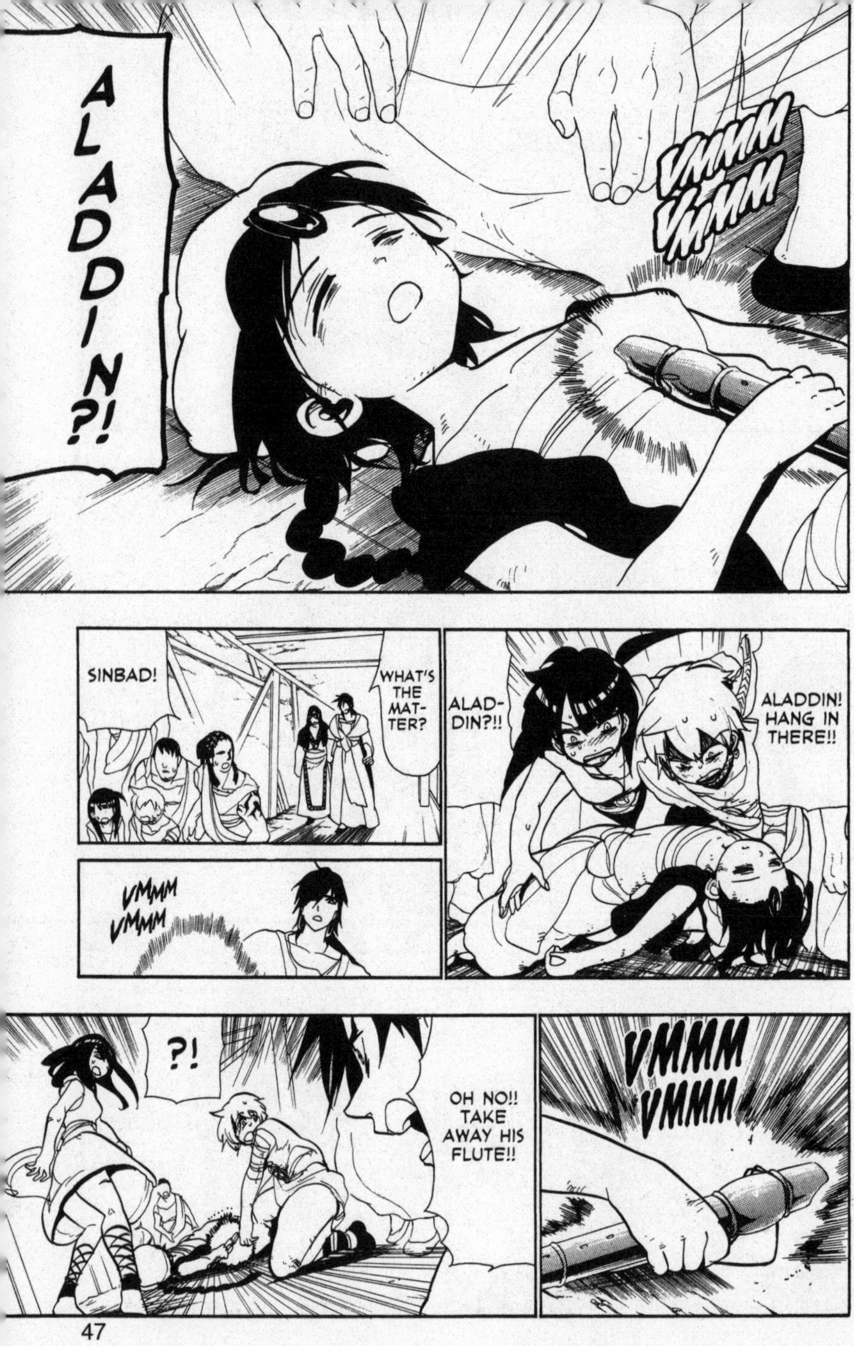
VMMM VMMM
ALADDIN?!
ALADDIN! HANG IN THERE!!
ALAD-DIN?!!
WHAT'S THE MAT-TER?
SINBAD!
VMMM VMMM
VMMM VMMM
OH NO!! TAKE AWAY HIS FLUTE!!
?!

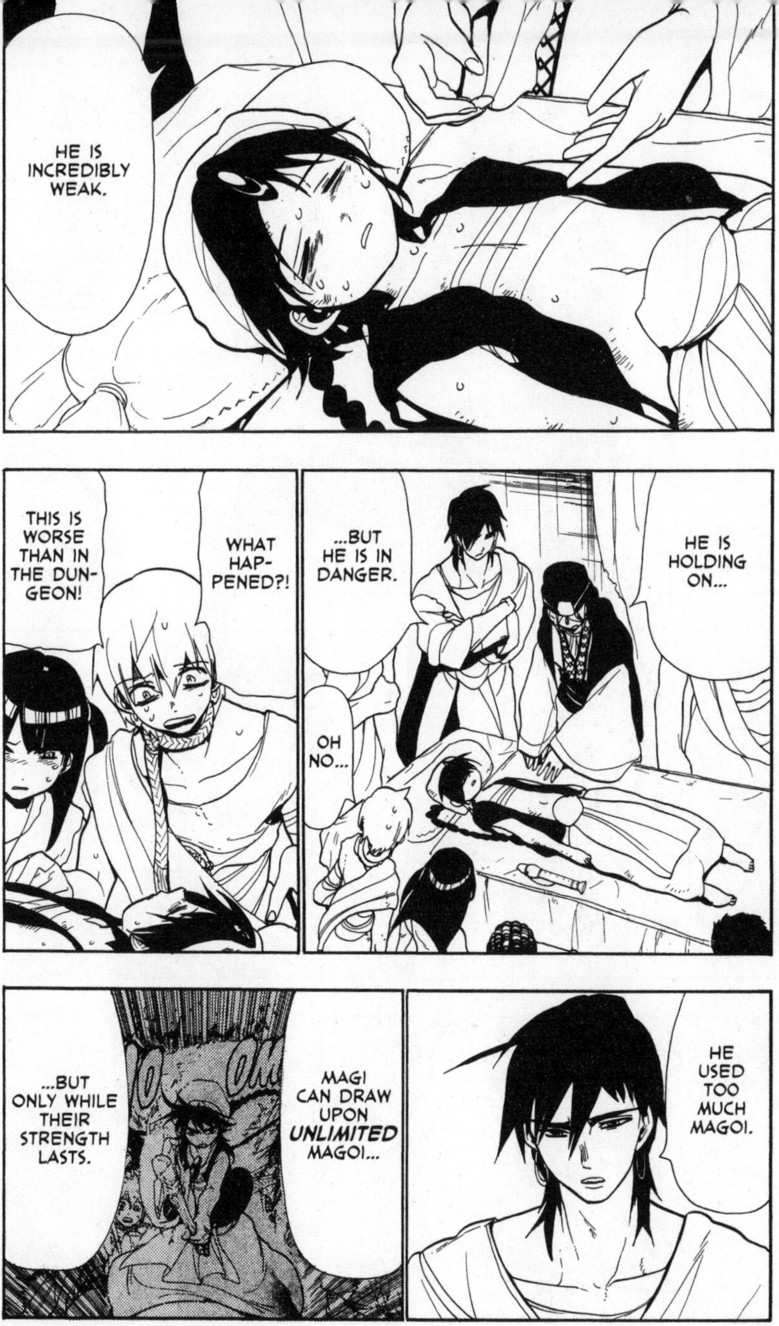
HE IS INCREDIBLY WEAK.
HE IS HOLDING ON...
...BUT HE IS IN DANGER.
OH NO...
WHAT HAP-PENED?!
THIS IS WORSE THAN IN THE DUN-GEON!
HE USED TOO MUCH MAGOI.
MAGI CAN DRAW UPON *UNLIMITED* MAGOI...
...BUT ONLY WHILE THEIR STRENGTH LASTS.

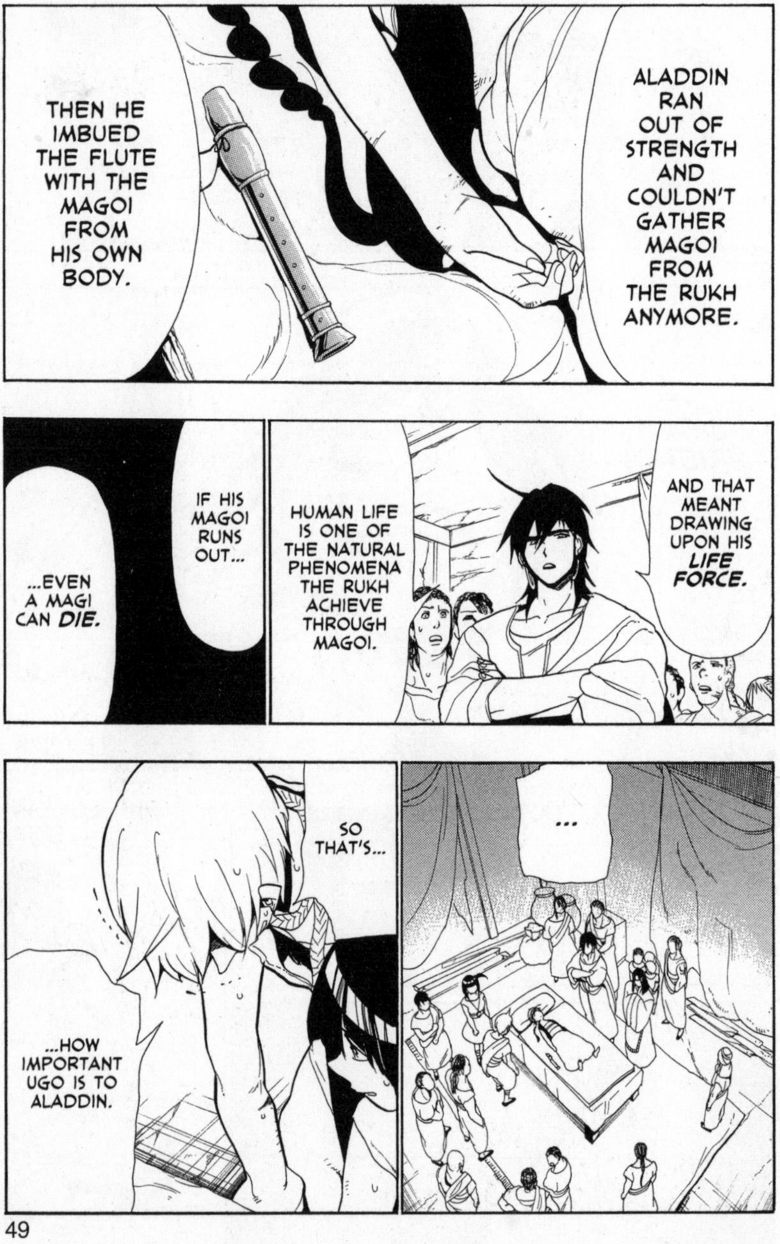
ALADDIN RAN OUT OF STRENGTH AND COULDN'T GATHER MAGOI FROM THE RUKH ANYMORE.
THEN HE IMBUED THE FLUTE WITH THE MAGOI FROM HIS OWN BODY.
AND THAT MEANT DRAWING UPON HIS *LIFE FORCE.*
HUMAN LIFE IS ONE OF THE NATURAL PHENOMENA THE RUKH ACHIEVE THROUGH MAGOI.
IF HIS MAGOI RUNS OUT...
...EVEN A MAGI CAN *DIE.*
...
SO THAT'S...
...HOW IMPORTANT UGO IS TO ALADDIN.

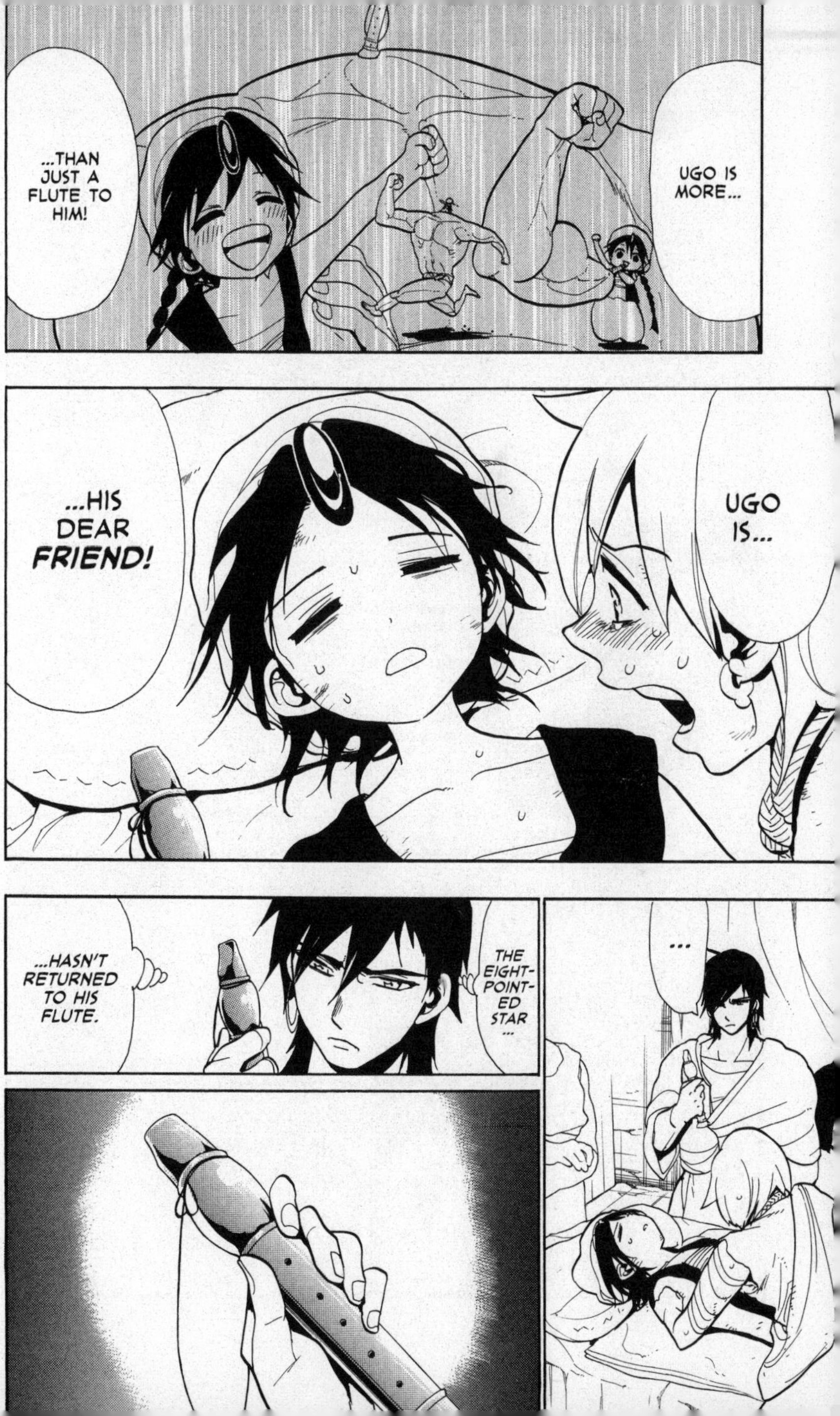
UGO IS MORE...
...THAN JUST A FLUTE TO HIM!
UGO IS...
...HIS DEAR FRIEND!
...
THE EIGHT-POINTED STAR...
...HASN'T RETURNED TO HIS FLUTE.

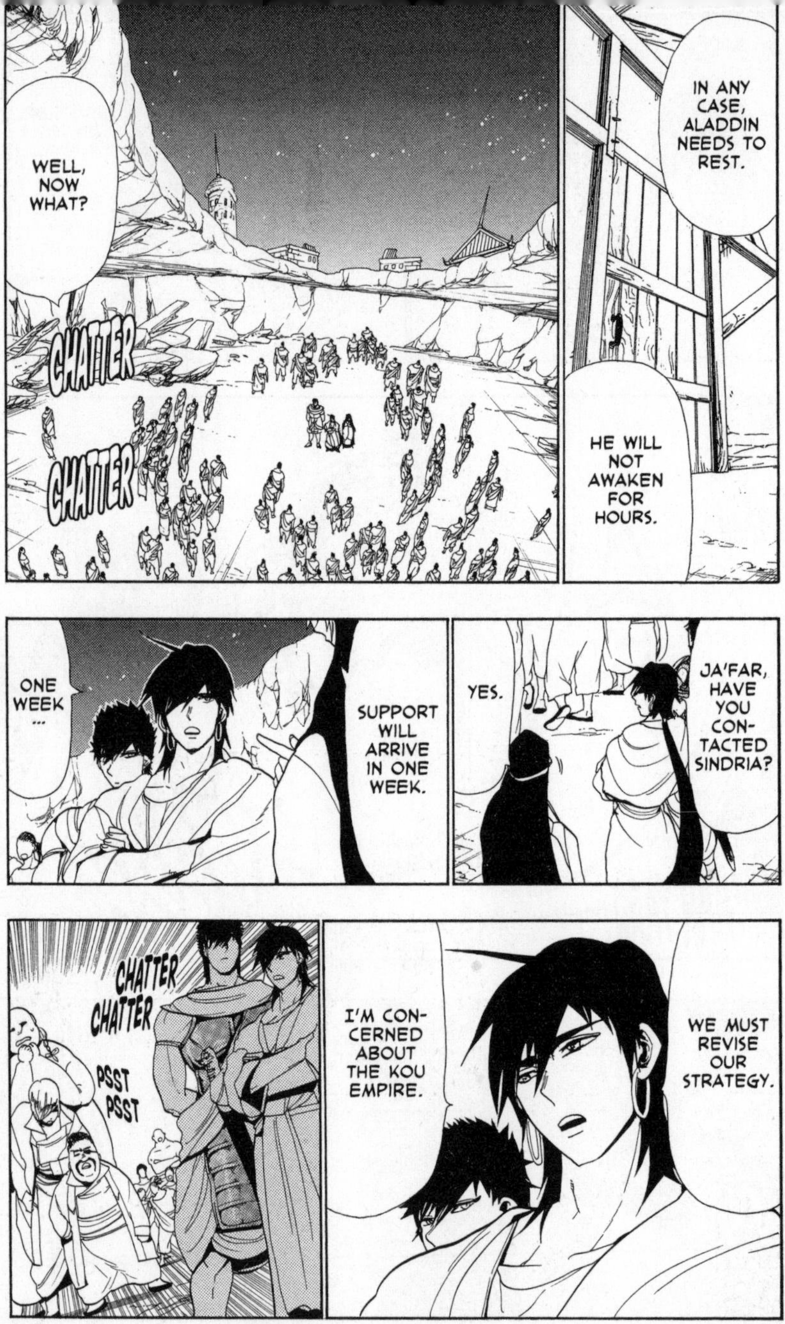
IN ANY CASE, ALADDIN NEEDS TO REST.
HE WILL NOT AWAKEN FOR HOURS.
WELL, NOW WHAT?
CHATTER
CHATTER
JA'FAR, HAVE YOU CON-TACTED SINDRIA?
YES.
SUPPORT WILL ARRIVE IN ONE WEEK.
ONE WEEK ...
WE MUST REVISE OUR STRATEGY.
I'M CON-CERNED ABOUT THE KOU EMPIRE.
CHATTER CHATTER
PSST PSST

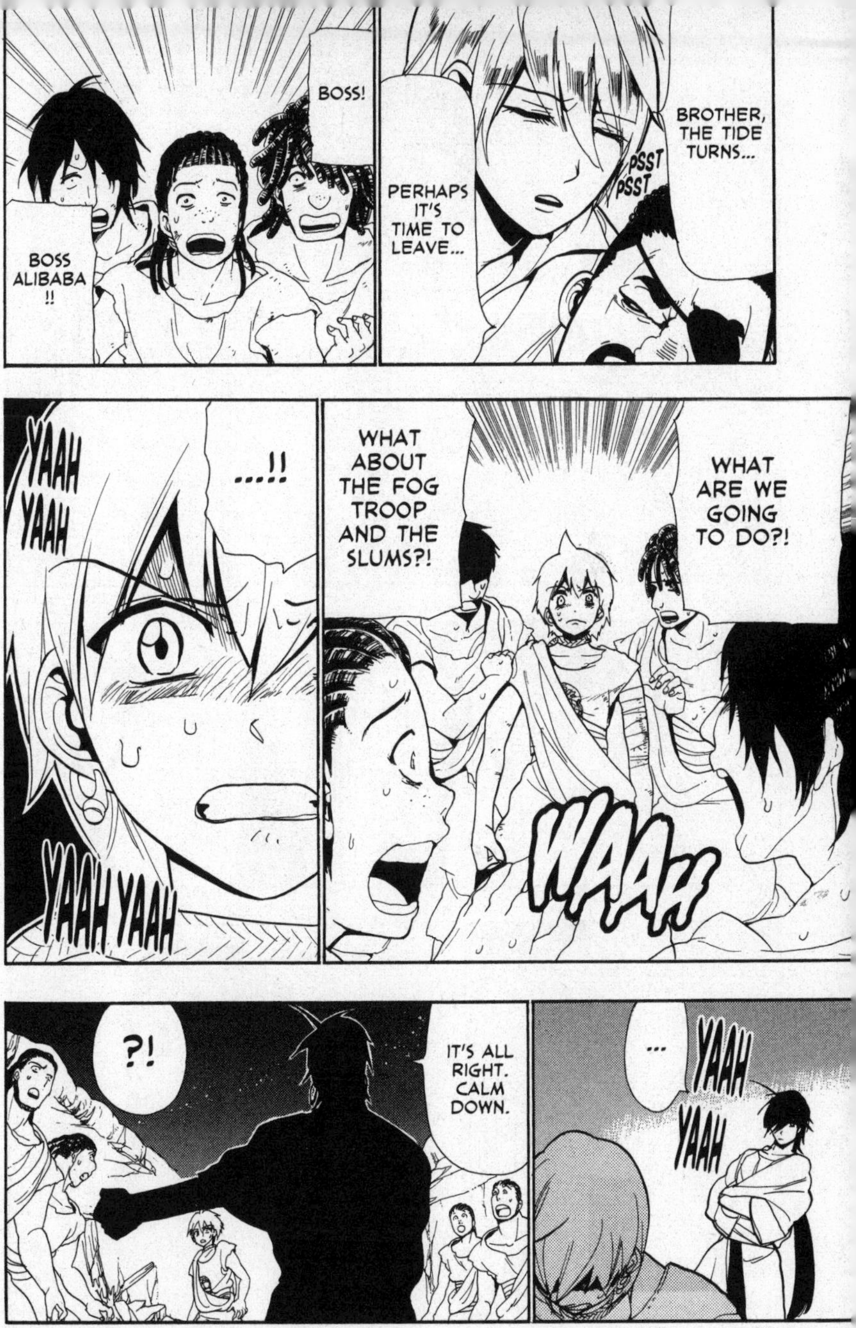
BROTHER, THE TIDE TURNS...
PSST PSST
PERHAPS IT'S TIME TO LEAVE...
BOSS!
BOSS ALIBABA !!
WHAT ARE WE GOING TO DO?!
WHAT ABOUT THE FOG TROOP AND THE SLUMS?!
WAAAH
YAAH YAAH
...!!
YAAH YAAH
YAAH YAAH
...
IT'S ALL RIGHT. CALM DOWN.
?!

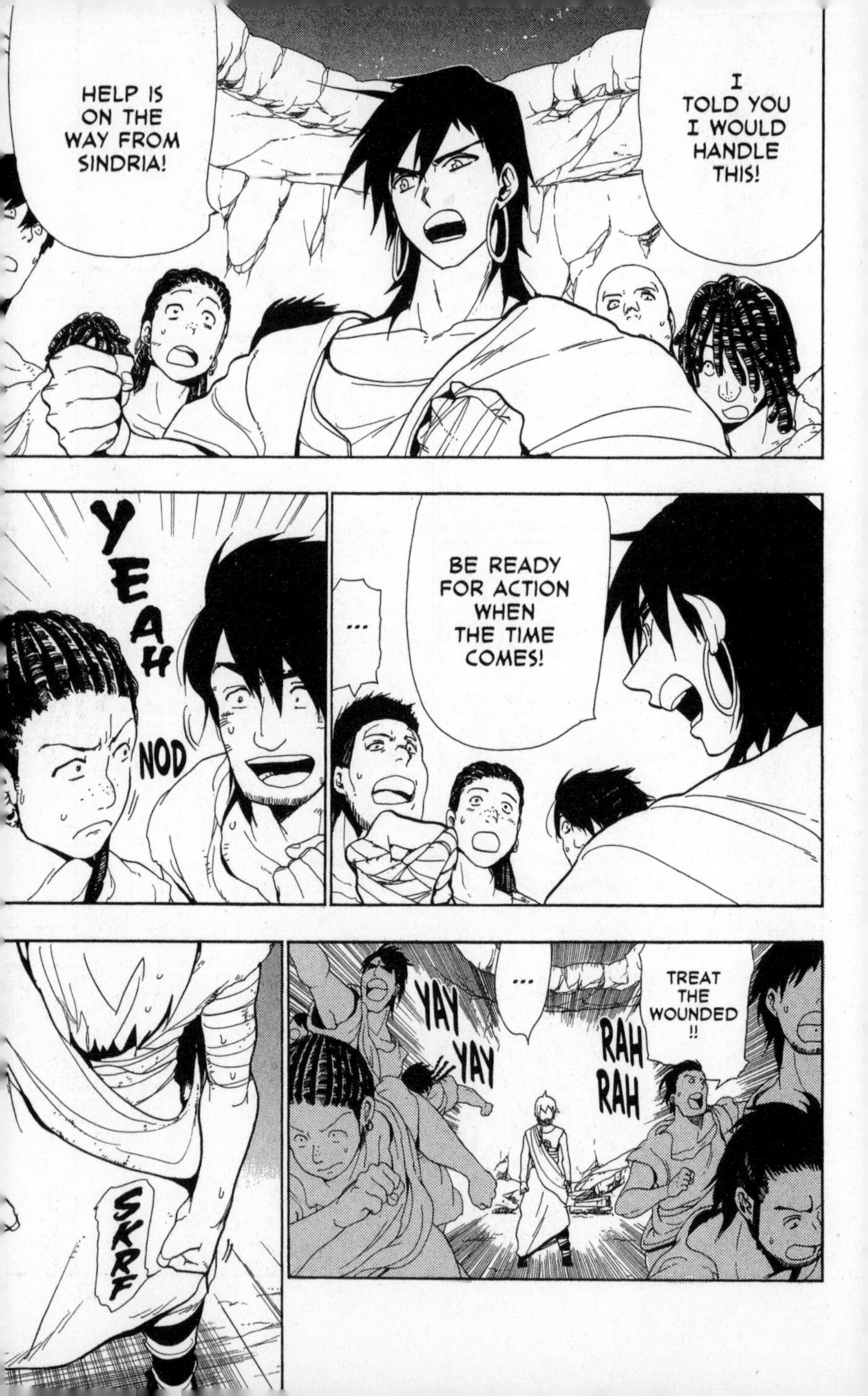
I TOLD YOU I WOULD HANDLE THIS!
HELP IS ON THE WAY FROM SINDRIA!
BE READY FOR ACTION WHEN THE TIME COMES!
...
YEAH
NOD
TREAT THE WOUNDED !!
RAH RAH
...
YAY YAY
SKRF

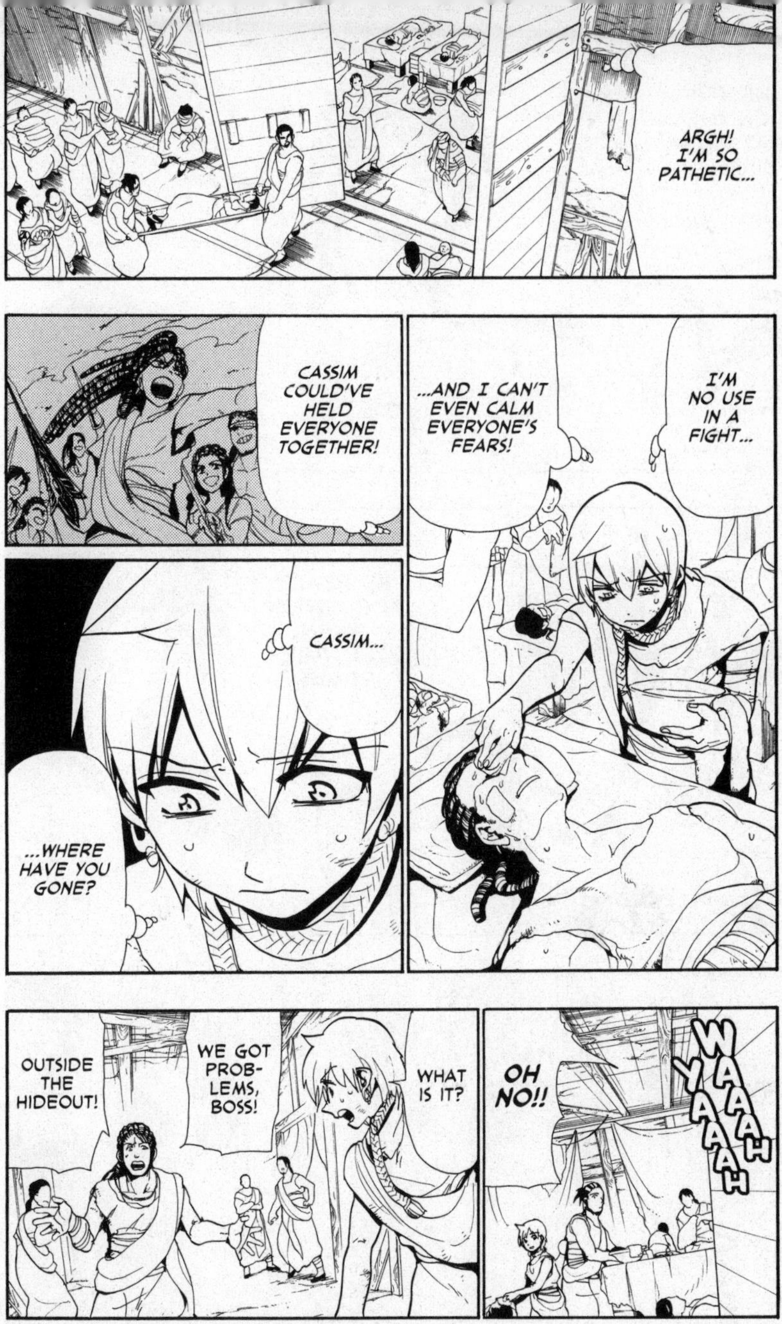
ARGH! I'M SO PATHETIC...
I'M NO USE IN A FIGHT...
...AND I CAN'T EVEN CALM EVERYONE'S FEARS!
CASSIM COULD'VE HELD EVERYONE TOGETHER!
CASSIM...
...WHERE HAVE YOU GONE?
WAAAAH YAAAAH
OH NO!!
WHAT IS IT?
WE GOT PROB-LEMS, BOSS!
OUTSIDE THE HIDEOUT!

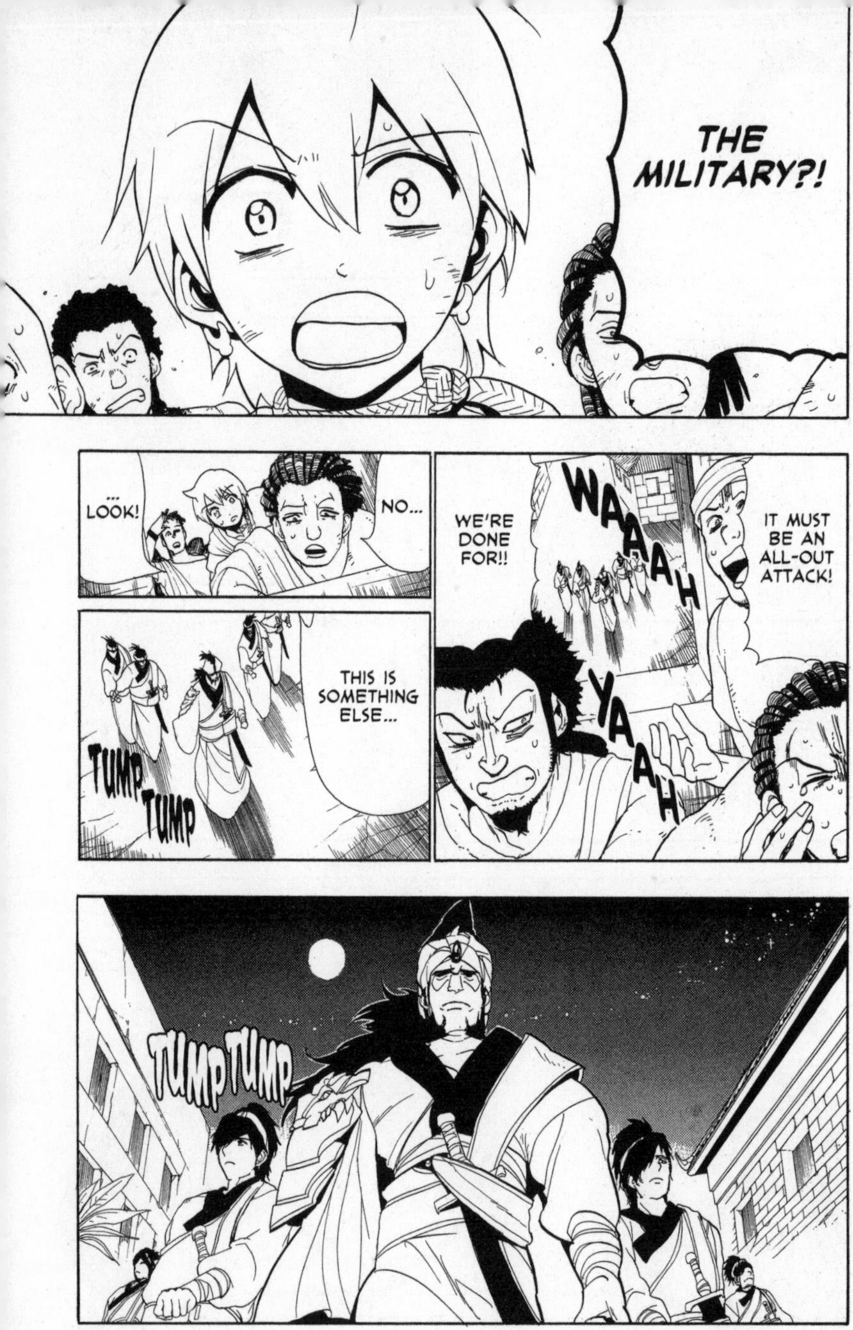
THE MILITARY?!
IT MUST BE AN ALL-OUT ATTACK!
WAAAAH
WE'RE DONE FOR!!
YAAAH
NO...
... LOOK!
THIS IS SOMETHING ELSE...
TUMP TUMP
TUMP TUMP

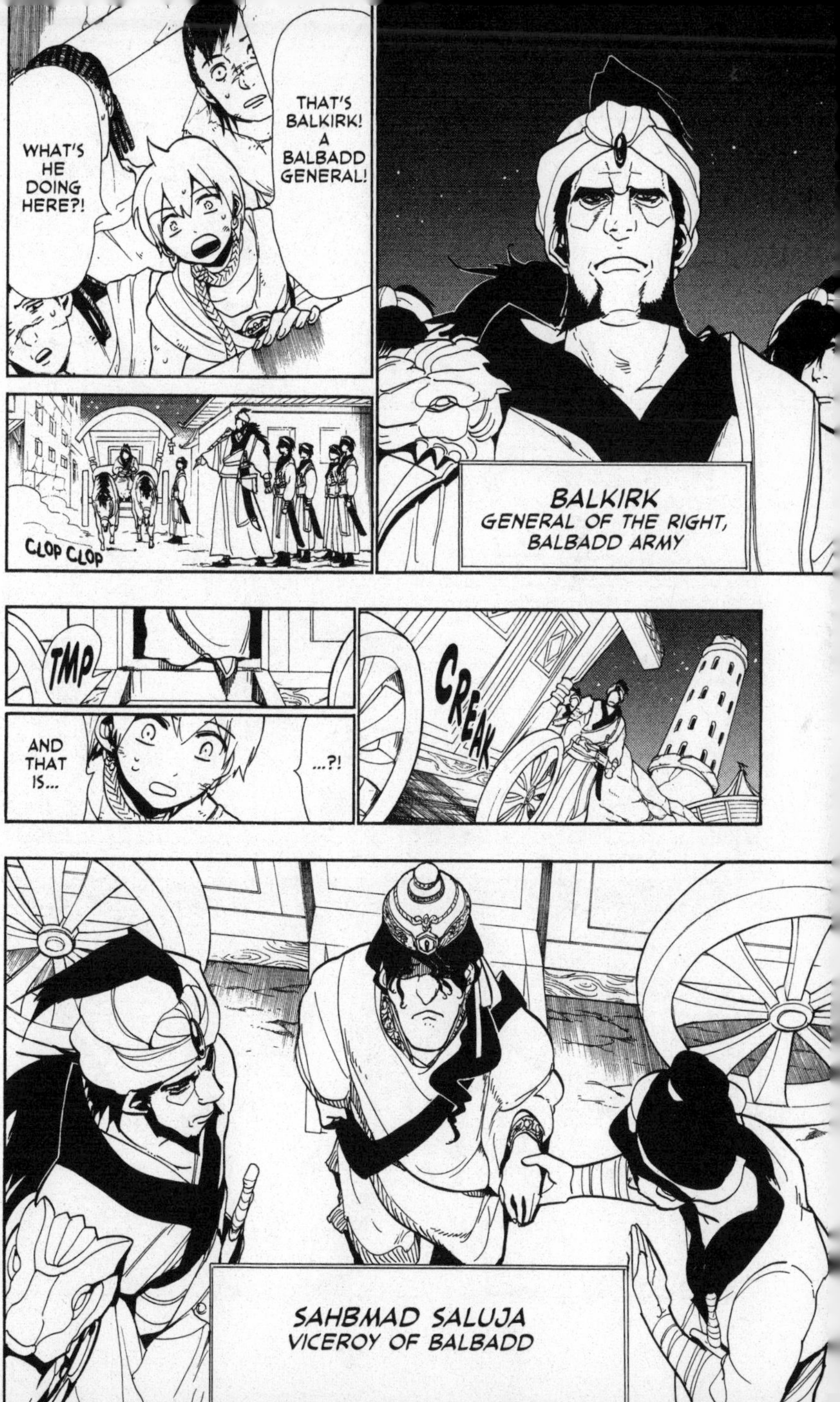
BALKIRK
GENERAL OF THE RIGHT, BALBADD ARMY
THAT'S BALKIRK! A BALBADD GENERAL!
WHAT'S HE DOING HERE?!
CLOP CLOP
CREAK
TMP
...?!
AND THAT IS...
SAHBMAD SALUJA
VICEROY OF BALBADD

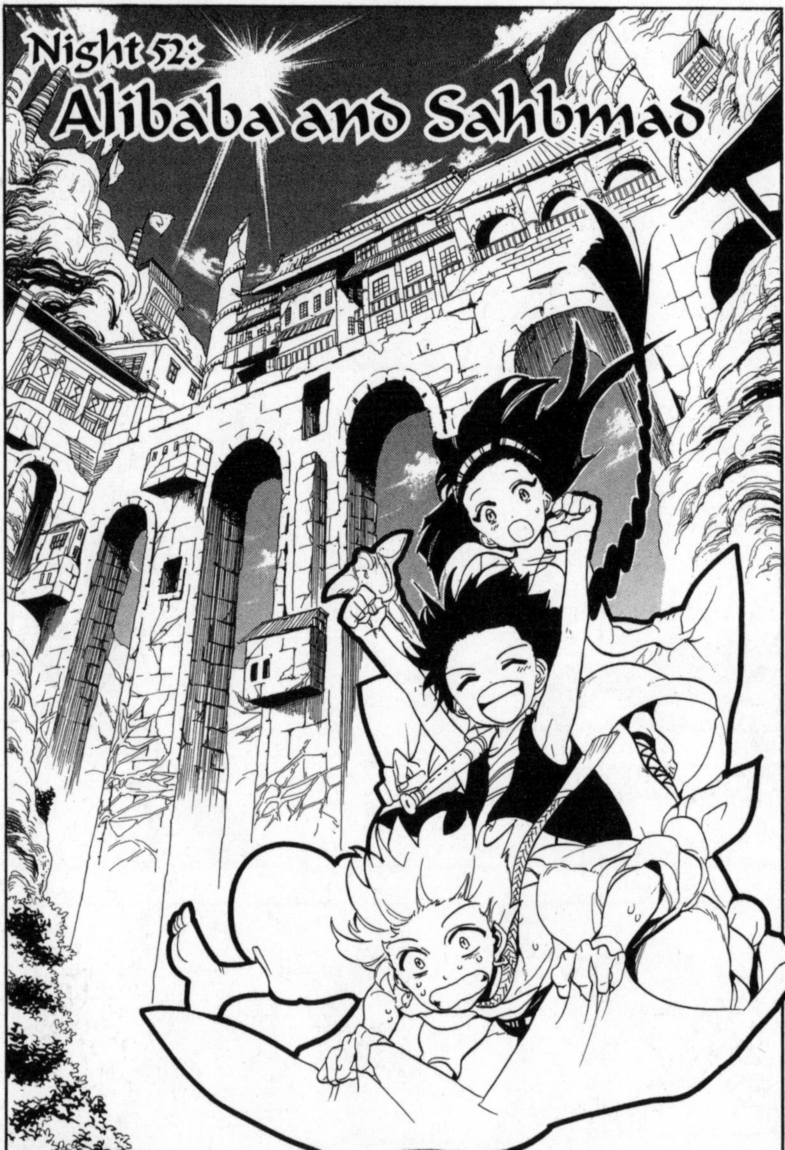
Night 52:
Alibaba and Sahbmad

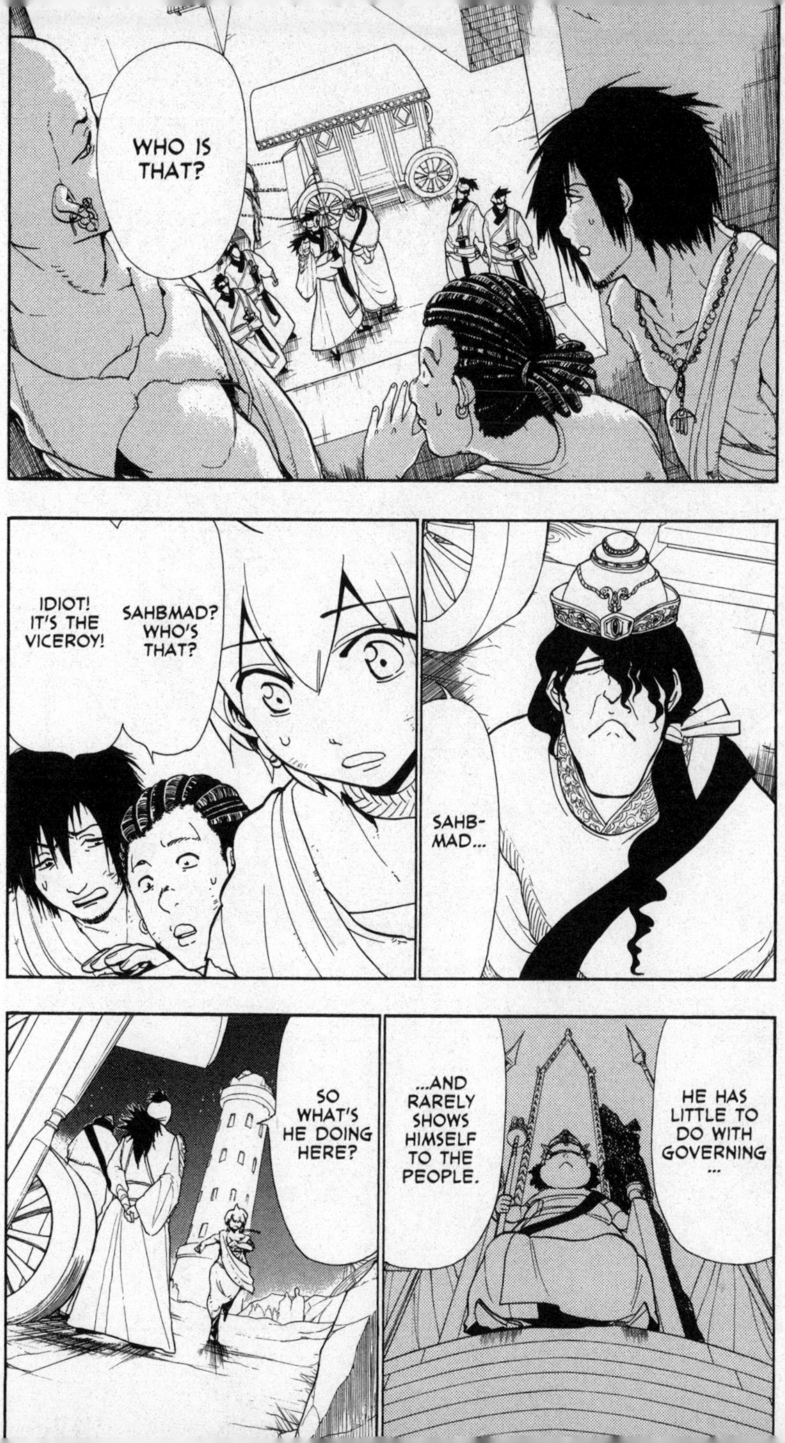
WHO IS THAT?
SAHB-MAD...
SAHBMAD? WHO'S THAT?
IDIOT! IT'S THE VICEROY!
HE HAS LITTLE TO DO WITH GOVERNING ...
...AND RARELY SHOWS HIMSELF TO THE PEOPLE.
SO WHAT'S HE DOING HERE?

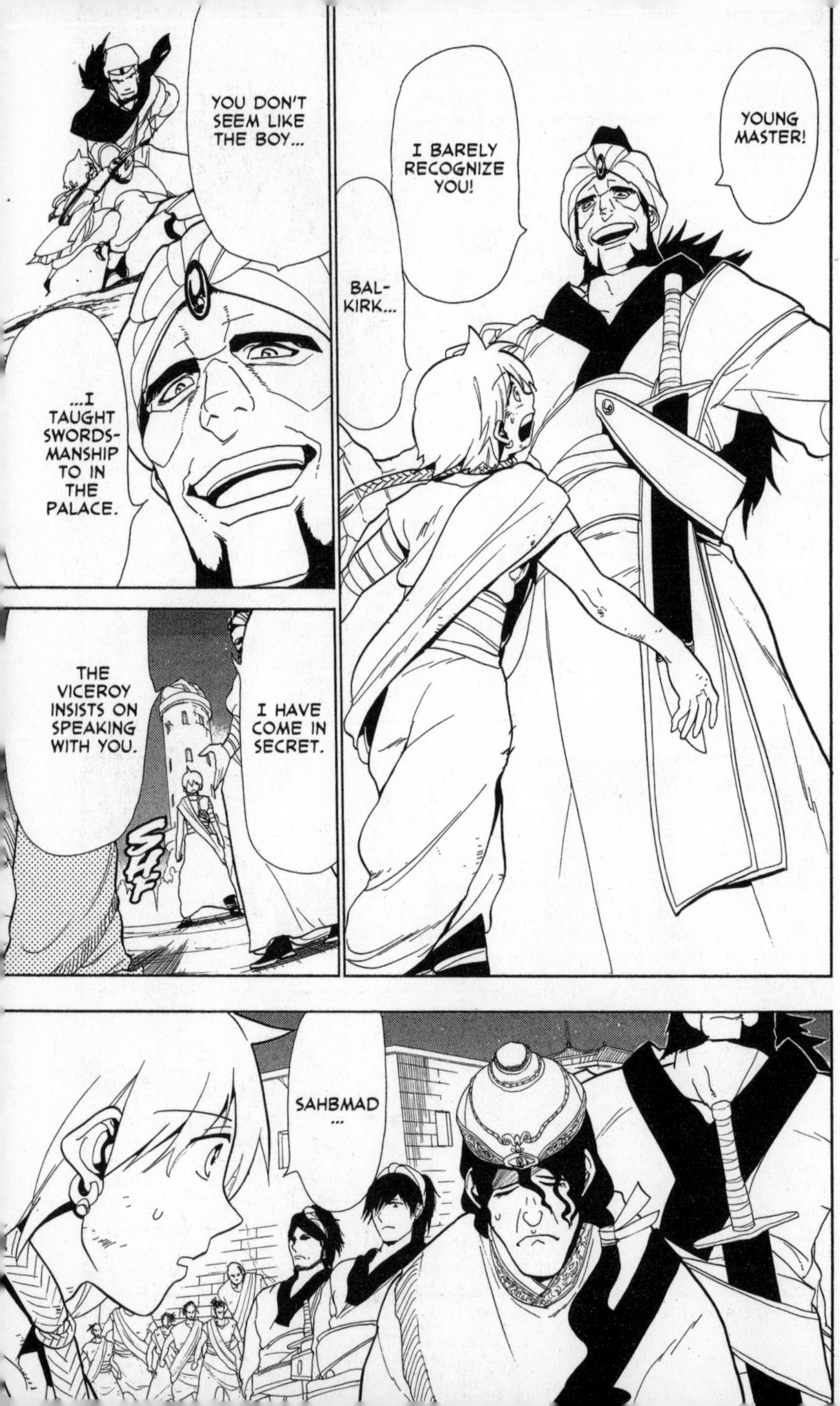
YOUNG MASTER!
I BARELY RECOGNIZE YOU!
BAL-KIRK...
YOU DON'T SEEM LIKE THE BOY...
...I TAUGHT SWORDS-MANSHIP TO IN THE PALACE.
I HAVE COME IN SECRET.
THE VICEROY INSISTS ON SPEAKING WITH YOU.
SHF
SAHBMAD ...

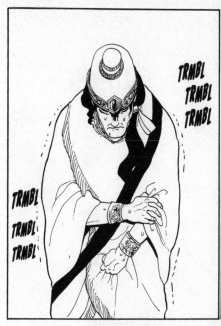

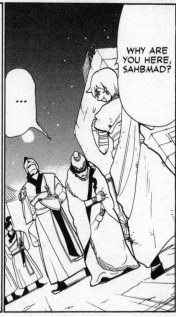

WHY ARE YOU HERE, SAHBMAD?
...
TRMBL TRMBL TRMBL
TRMBL TRMBL TRMBL
FIDGET
SQUIRM
ALIBABA...
...Y-YOU'RE AMAZ-ING.
YOU L-LED...
...ALL TH-THESE PEOPLE.

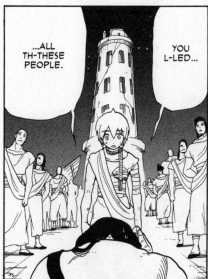

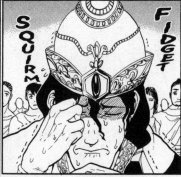

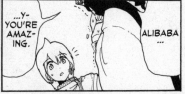

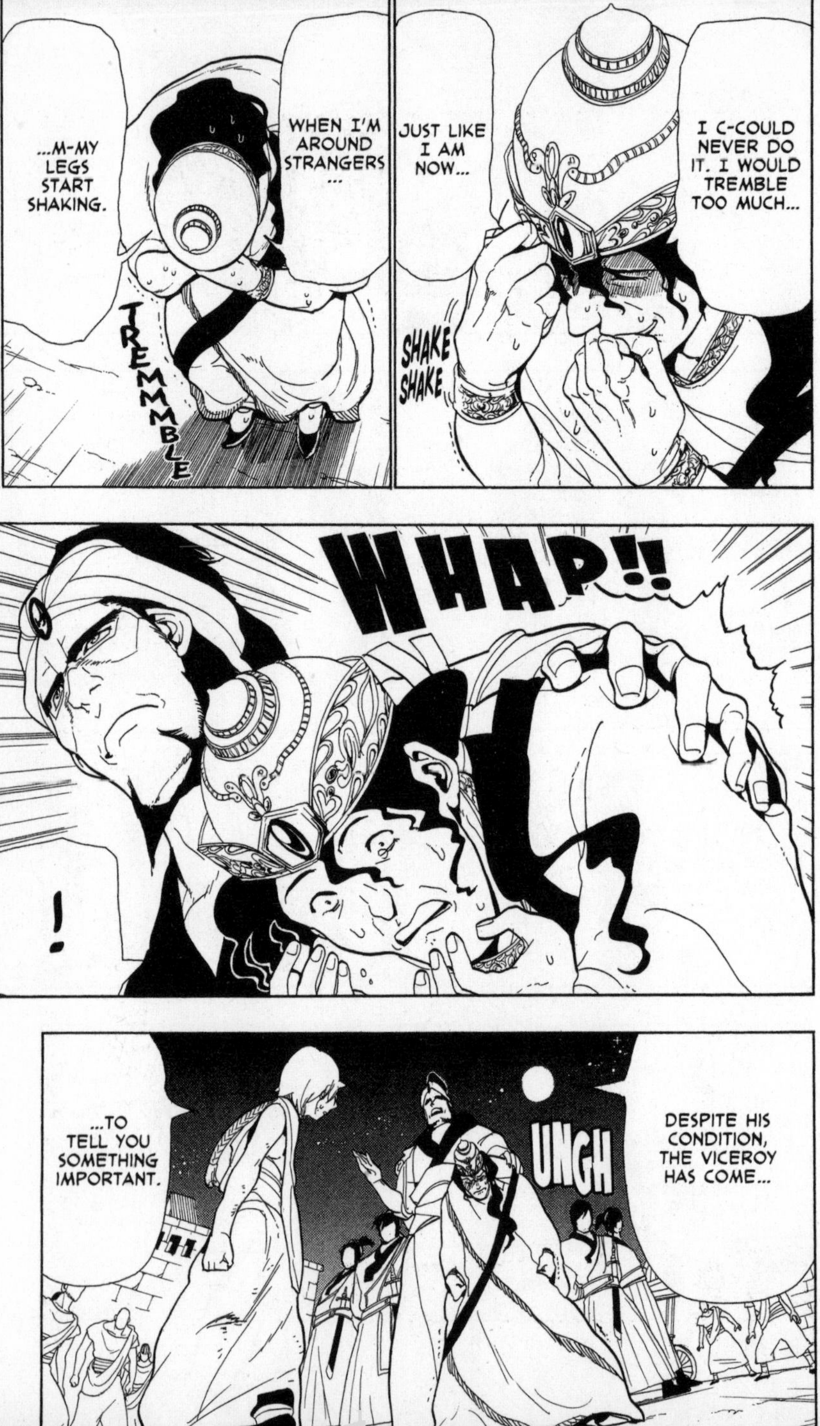
I C-COULD NEVER DO IT. I WOULD TREMBLE TOO MUCH...
JUST LIKE I AM NOW...
SHAKE SHAKE
WHEN I'M AROUND STRANGERS...
...M-MY LEGS START SHAKING.
TREMMMBLE
WHAP!!
!
DESPITE HIS CONDITION, THE VICEROY HAS COME...
UNGH
...TO TELL YOU SOMETHING IMPORTANT.

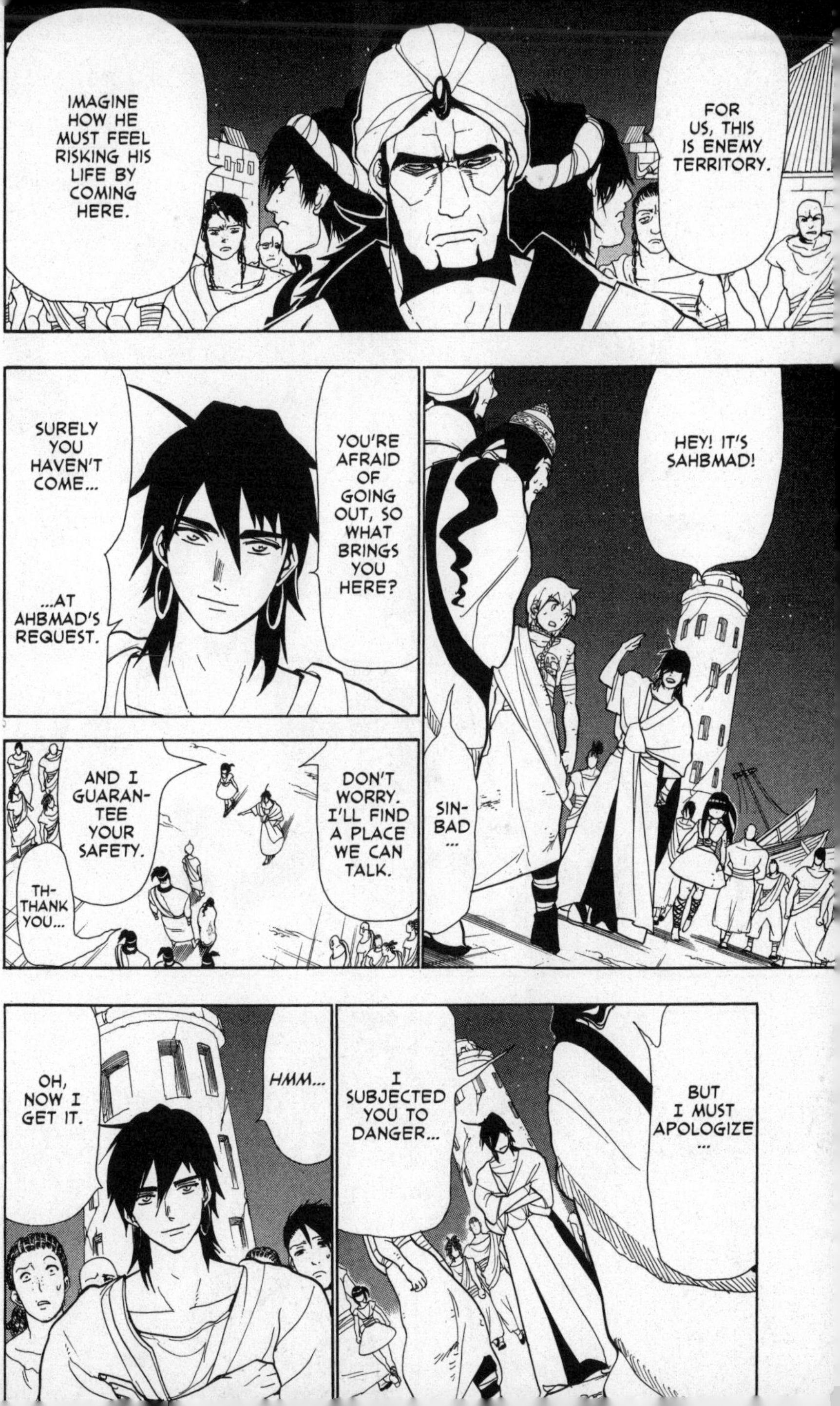
FOR US, THIS IS ENEMY TERRITORY.
IMAGINE HOW HE MUST FEEL RISKING HIS LIFE BY COMING HERE.
HEY! IT'S SAHBMAD!
SIN-BAD...
YOU'RE AFRAID OF GOING OUT, SO WHAT BRINGS YOU HERE?
SURELY YOU HAVEN'T COME...
...AT AHBMAD'S REQUEST.
DON'T WORRY. I'LL FIND A PLACE WE CAN TALK.
AND I GUARAN-TEE YOUR SAFETY.
TH-THANK YOU...
BUT I MUST APOLOGIZE...
I SUBJECTED YOU TO DANGER...
HMM...
OH, NOW I GET IT.

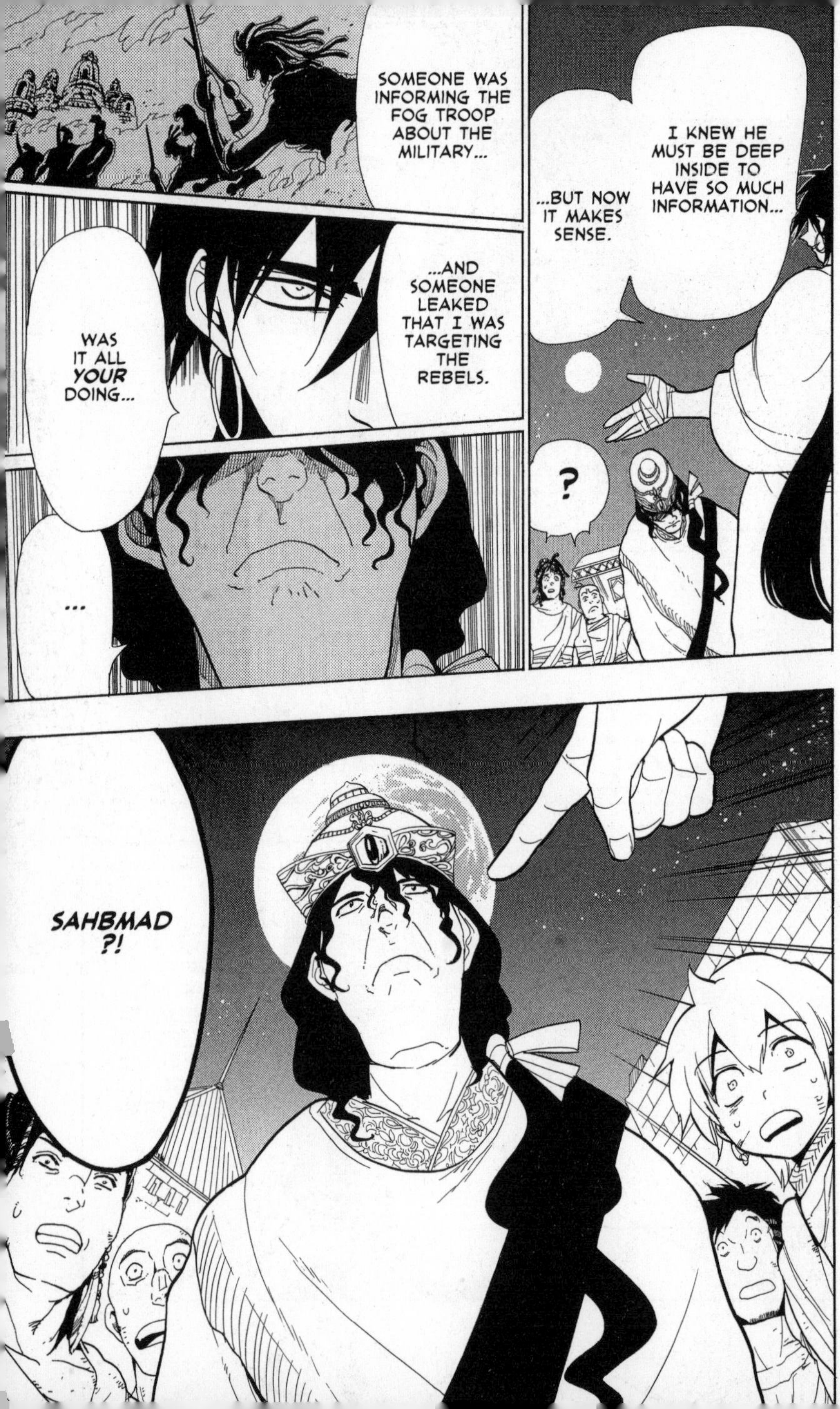
I KNEW HE MUST BE DEEP INSIDE TO HAVE SO MUCH INFORMATION...
...BUT NOW IT MAKES SENSE.
?
SOMEONE WAS INFORMING THE FOG TROOP ABOUT THE MILITARY...
...AND SOMEONE LEAKED THAT I WAS TARGETING THE REBELS.
WAS IT ALL YOUR DOING...
...
SAHBMAD ?!

I HAD TO...
I DIDN'T THINK YOU COULD REALLY CRUSH THEM.
ARE YOU ONE OF THE FOG TROOP?
N-NO...
I'VE NEVER EVEN MET THEM.
BUT I LEAKED INFORMATION TO HELP THEM...
...BECAUSE OF ALIBABA.
!
IF HE WAS WITH THEM, I BELIEVED THEY COULD CHANGE THIS COUNTRY!
HE COULD ALWAYS DO WHAT I COULDN'T!

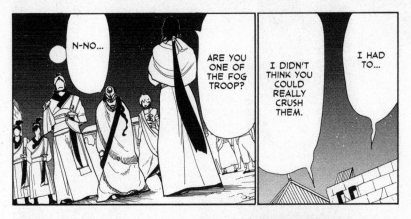

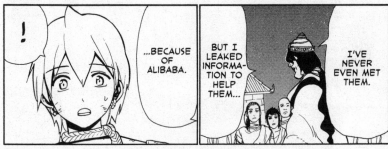

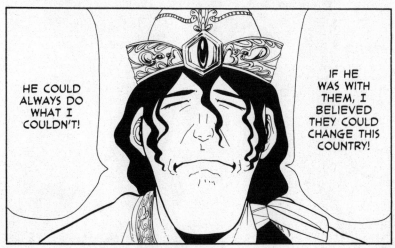

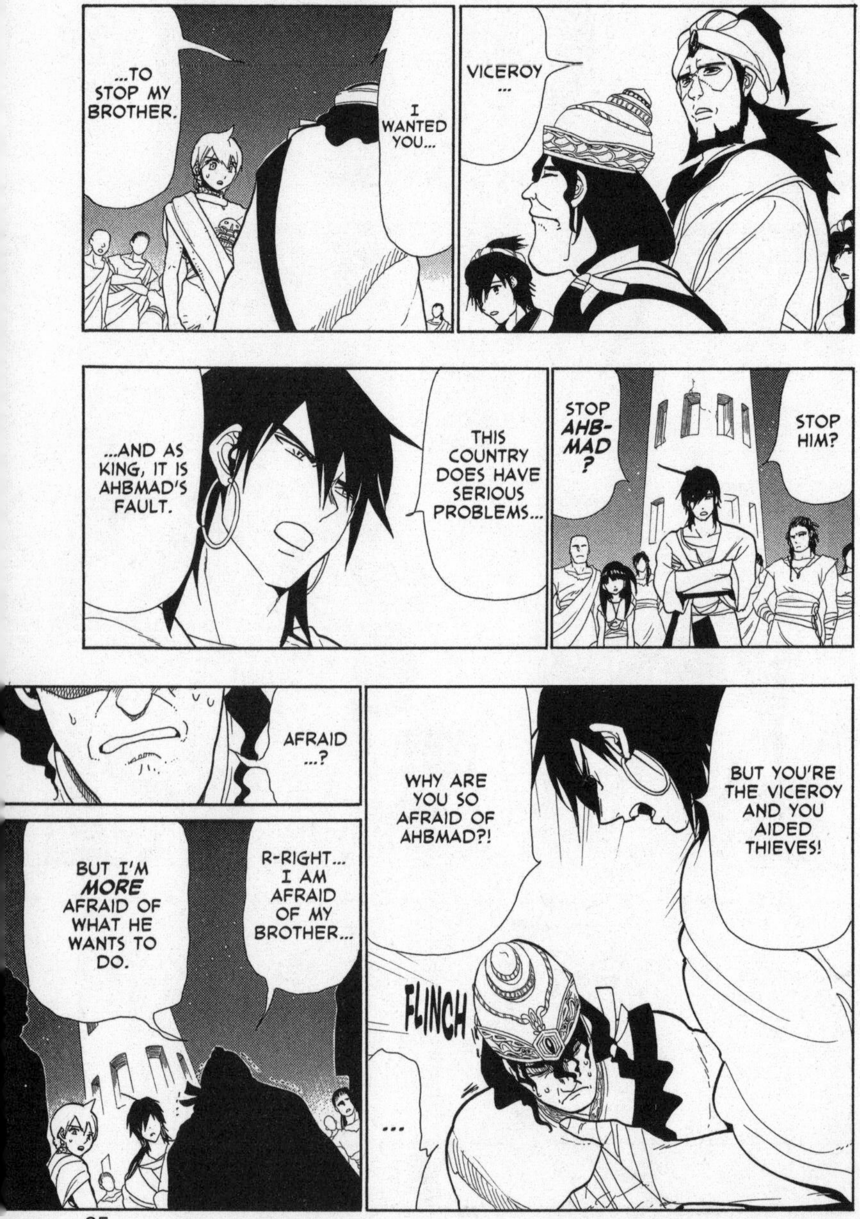
VICEROY ...
I WANTED YOU...
...TO STOP MY BROTHER.
STOP HIM?
STOP AHBMAD?
THIS COUNTRY DOES HAVE SERIOUS PROBLEMS...
...AND AS KING, IT IS AHBMAD'S FAULT.
BUT YOU'RE THE VICEROY AND YOU AIDED THIEVES!
WHY ARE YOU SO AFRAID OF AHBMAD?!
FLINCH
...
AFRAID ...?
R-RIGHT... I AM AFRAID OF MY BROTHER...
BUT I'M MORE AFRAID OF WHAT HE WANTS TO DO.

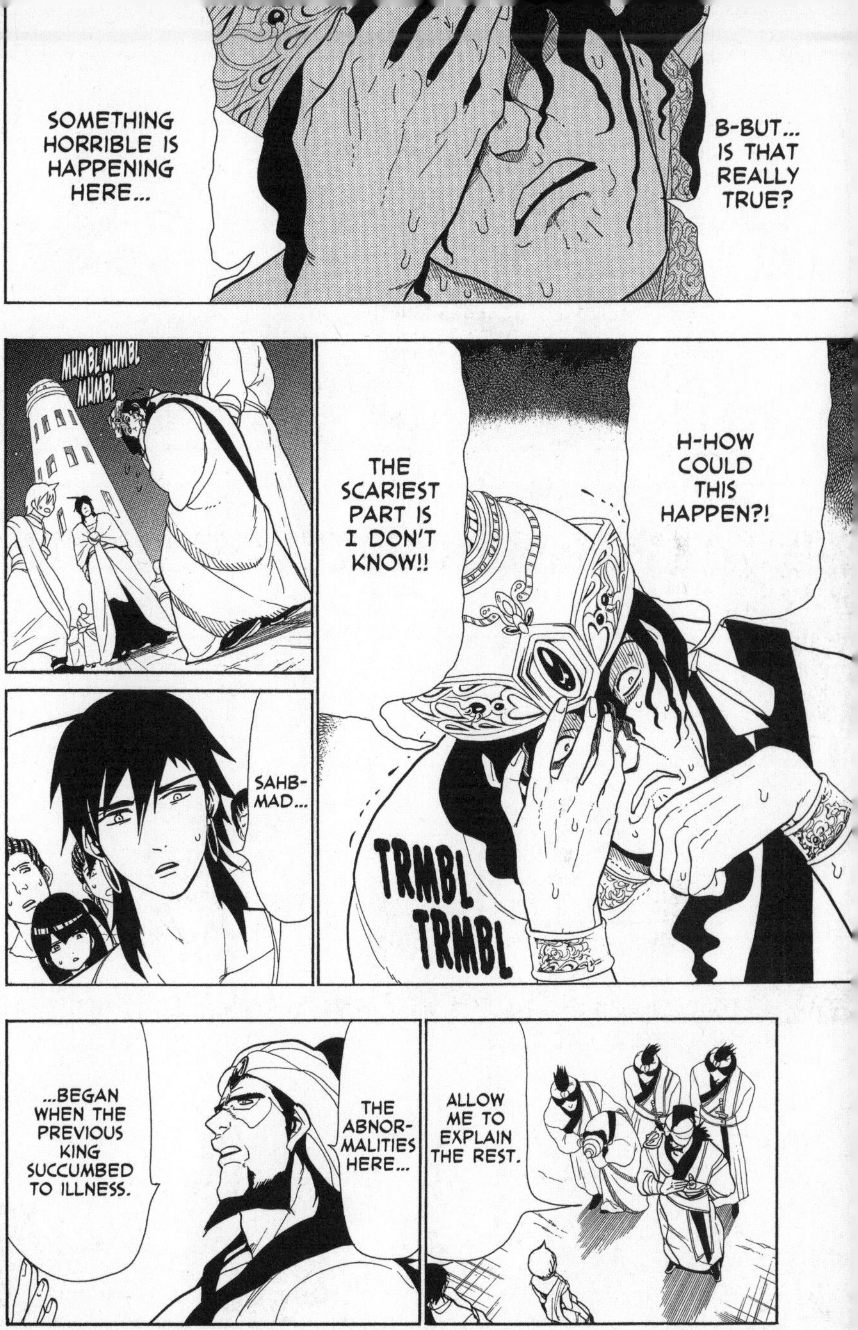
B-BUT... IS THAT REALLY TRUE?
SOMETHING HORRIBLE IS HAPPENING HERE...
H-HOW COULD THIS HAPPEN?!
THE SCARIEST PART IS I DON'T KNOW!!
TRMBL TRMBL
MUMBL MUMBL MUMBL
SAHB-MAD...
ALLOW ME TO EXPLAIN THE REST.
THE ABNOR-MALITIES HERE...
...BEGAN WHEN THE PREVIOUS KING SUCCUMBED TO ILLNESS.

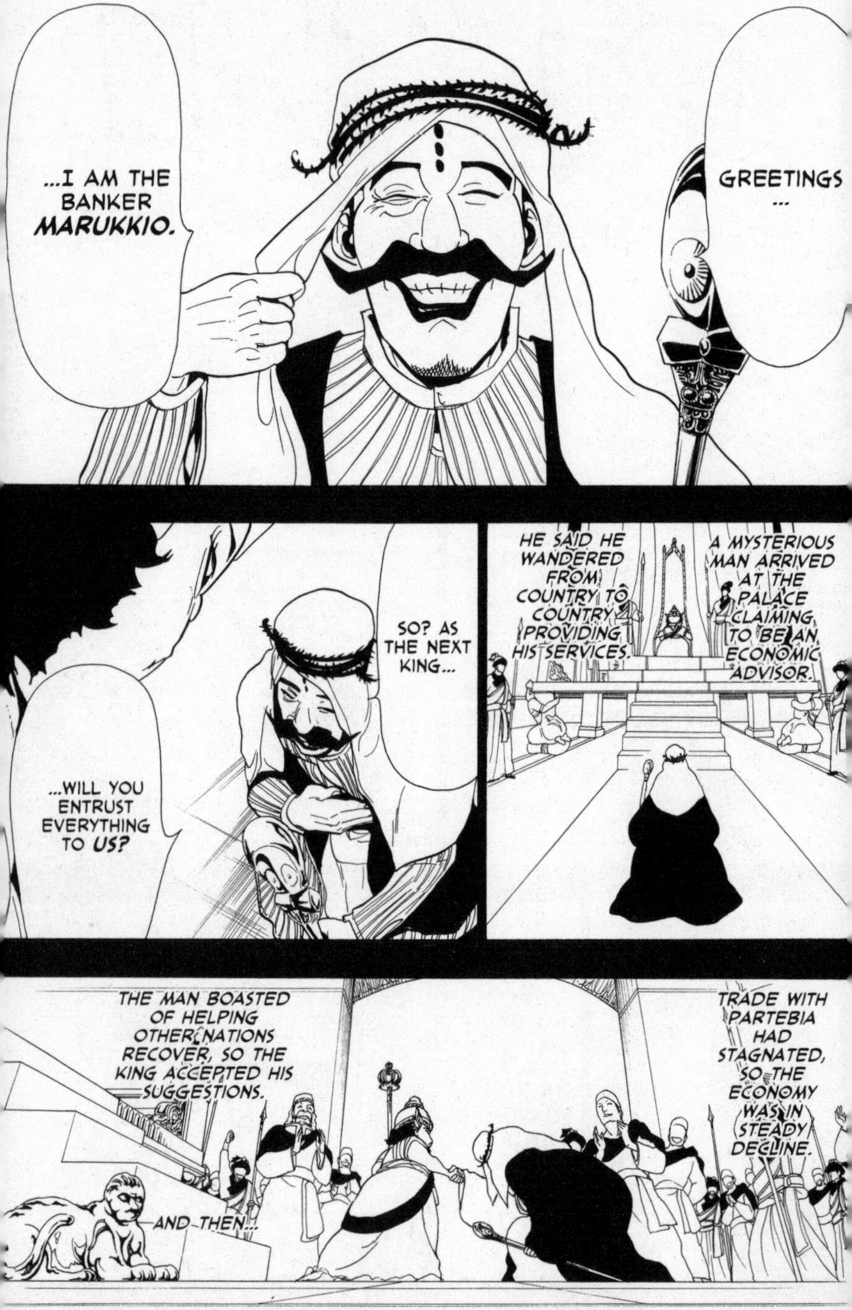
GREETINGS ...
...I AM THE BANKER MARUKKIO.
A MYSTERIOUS MAN ARRIVED AT THE PALACE CLAIMING TO BE AN ECONOMIC ADVISOR.
HE SAID HE WANDERED FROM COUNTRY TO COUNTRY PROVIDING HIS SERVICES.
SO? AS THE NEXT KING...
...WILL YOU ENTRUST EVERYTHING TO US?
TRADE WITH PARTEBIA HAD STAGNATED, SO THE ECONOMY WAS IN STEADY DECLINE.
THE MAN BOASTED OF HELPING OTHER NATIONS RECOVER, SO THE KING ACCEPTED HIS SUGGESTIONS.
AND THEN...

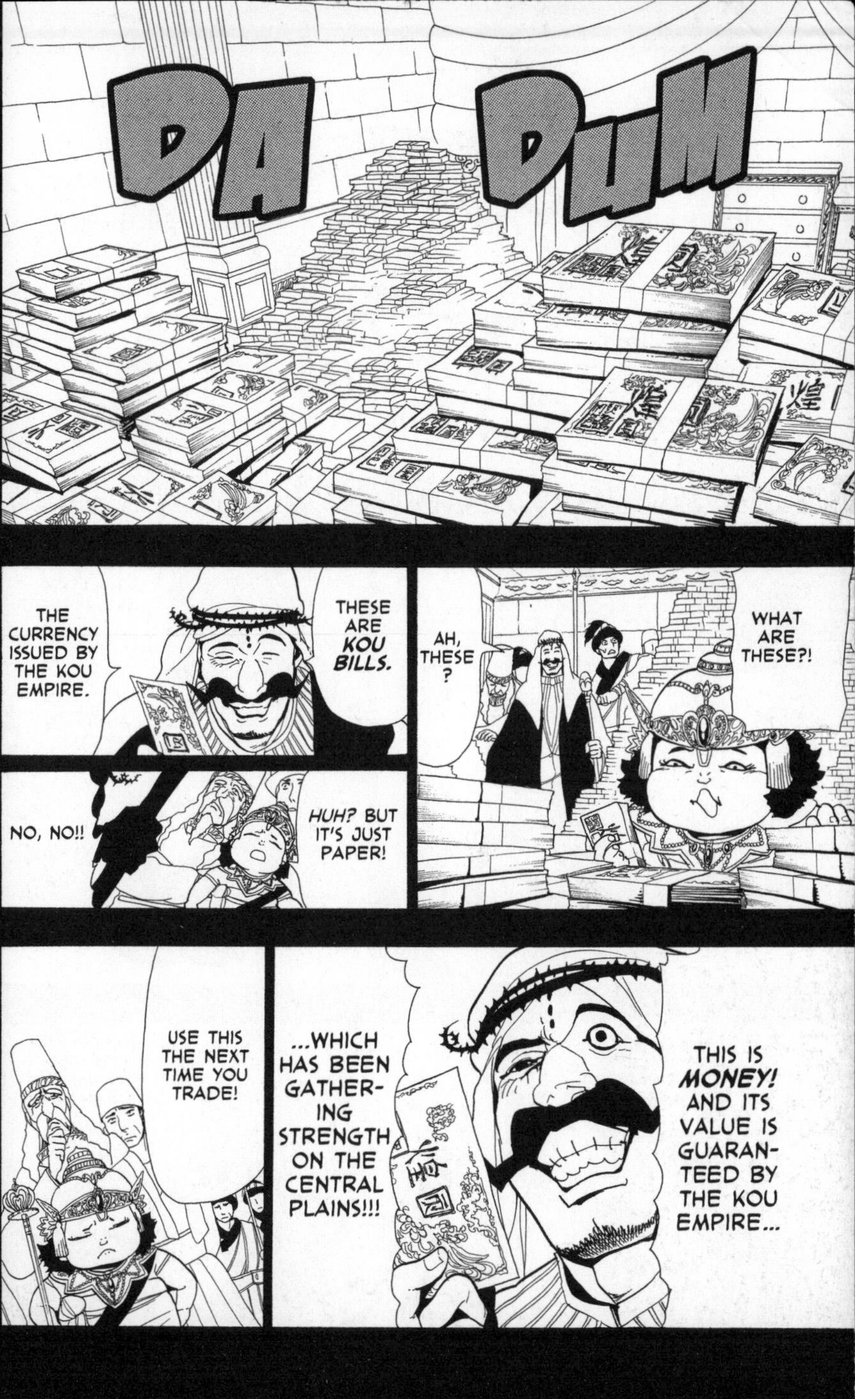
DA DUM
WHAT ARE THESE?!
AH, THESE?
THESE ARE *KOU BILLS.*
THE CURRENCY ISSUED BY THE KOU EMPIRE.
HUH? BUT IT'S JUST PAPER!
NO, NO!!
THIS IS *MONEY!* AND ITS VALUE IS GUARAN-TEED BY THE KOU EMPIRE...
...WHICH HAS BEEN GATHER-ING STRENGTH ON THE CENTRAL PLAINS!!!
USE THIS THE NEXT TIME YOU TRADE!

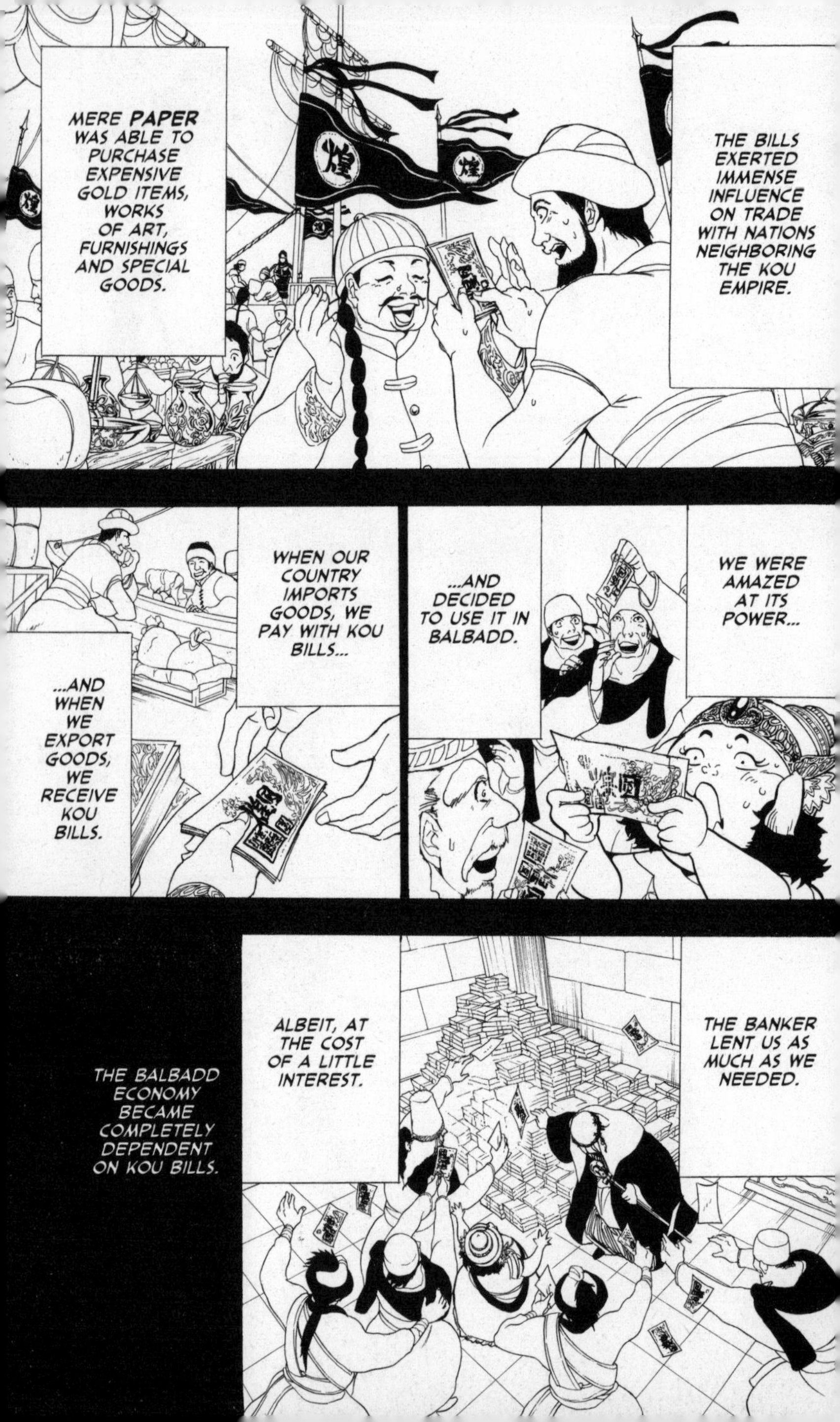
THE BILLS EXERTED IMMENSE INFLUENCE ON TRADE WITH NATIONS NEIGHBORING THE KOU EMPIRE.
MERE **PAPER** WAS ABLE TO PURCHASE EXPENSIVE GOLD ITEMS, WORKS OF ART, FURNISHINGS AND SPECIAL GOODS.
WE WERE AMAZED AT ITS POWER...
...AND DECIDED TO USE IT IN BALBADD.
WHEN OUR COUNTRY IMPORTS GOODS, WE PAY WITH KOU BILLS...
...AND WHEN WE EXPORT GOODS, WE RECEIVE KOU BILLS.
THE BANKER LENT US AS MUCH AS WE NEEDED.
ALBEIT, AT THE COST OF A LITTLE INTEREST.
THE BALBADD ECONOMY BECAME COMPLETELY DEPENDENT ON KOU BILLS.

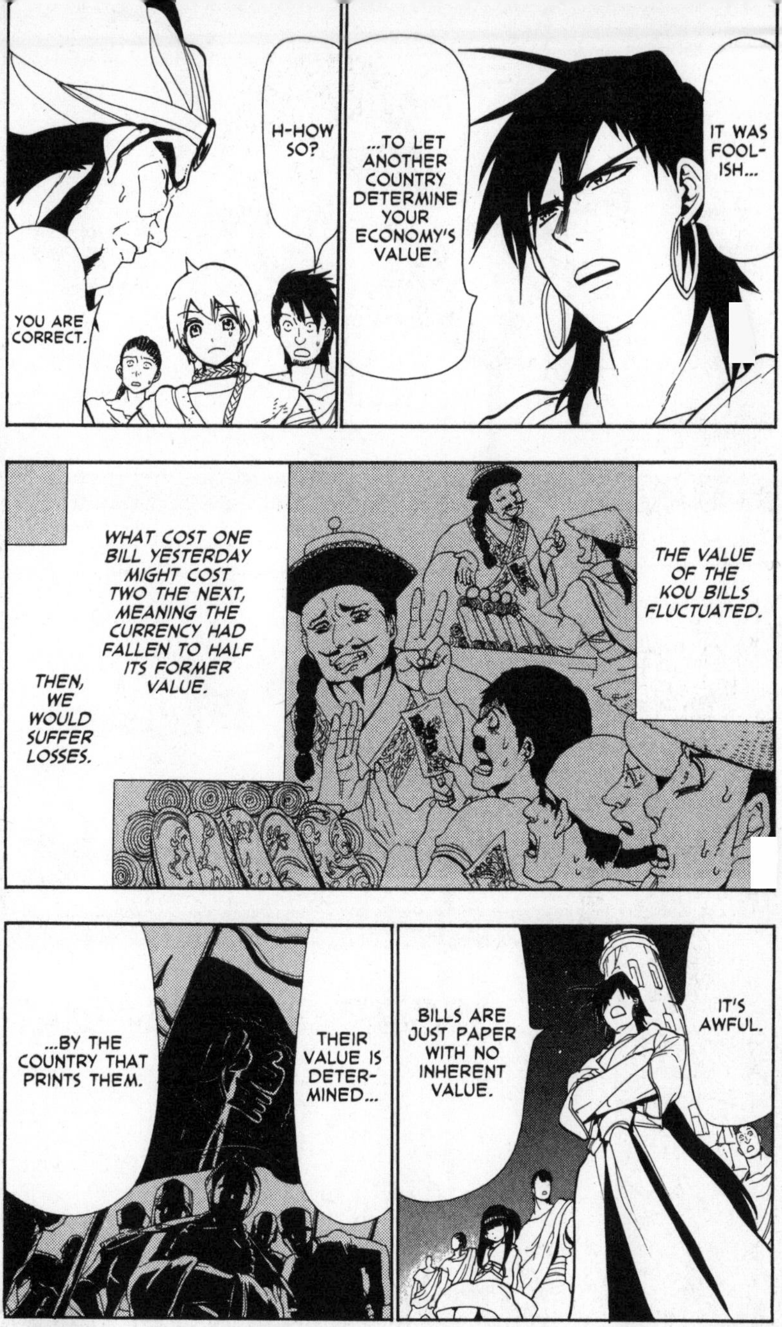
IT WAS FOOLISH...
...TO LET ANOTHER COUNTRY DETERMINE YOUR ECONOMY'S VALUE.
H-HOW SO?
YOU ARE CORRECT.
THE VALUE OF THE KOU BILLS FLUCTUATED.
WHAT COST ONE BILL YESTERDAY MIGHT COST TWO THE NEXT, MEANING THE CURRENCY HAD FALLEN TO HALF ITS FORMER VALUE.
THEN, WE WOULD SUFFER LOSSES.
IT'S AWFUL.
BILLS ARE JUST PAPER WITH NO INHERENT VALUE.
THEIR VALUE IS DETERMINED...
...BY THE COUNTRY THAT PRINTS THEM.

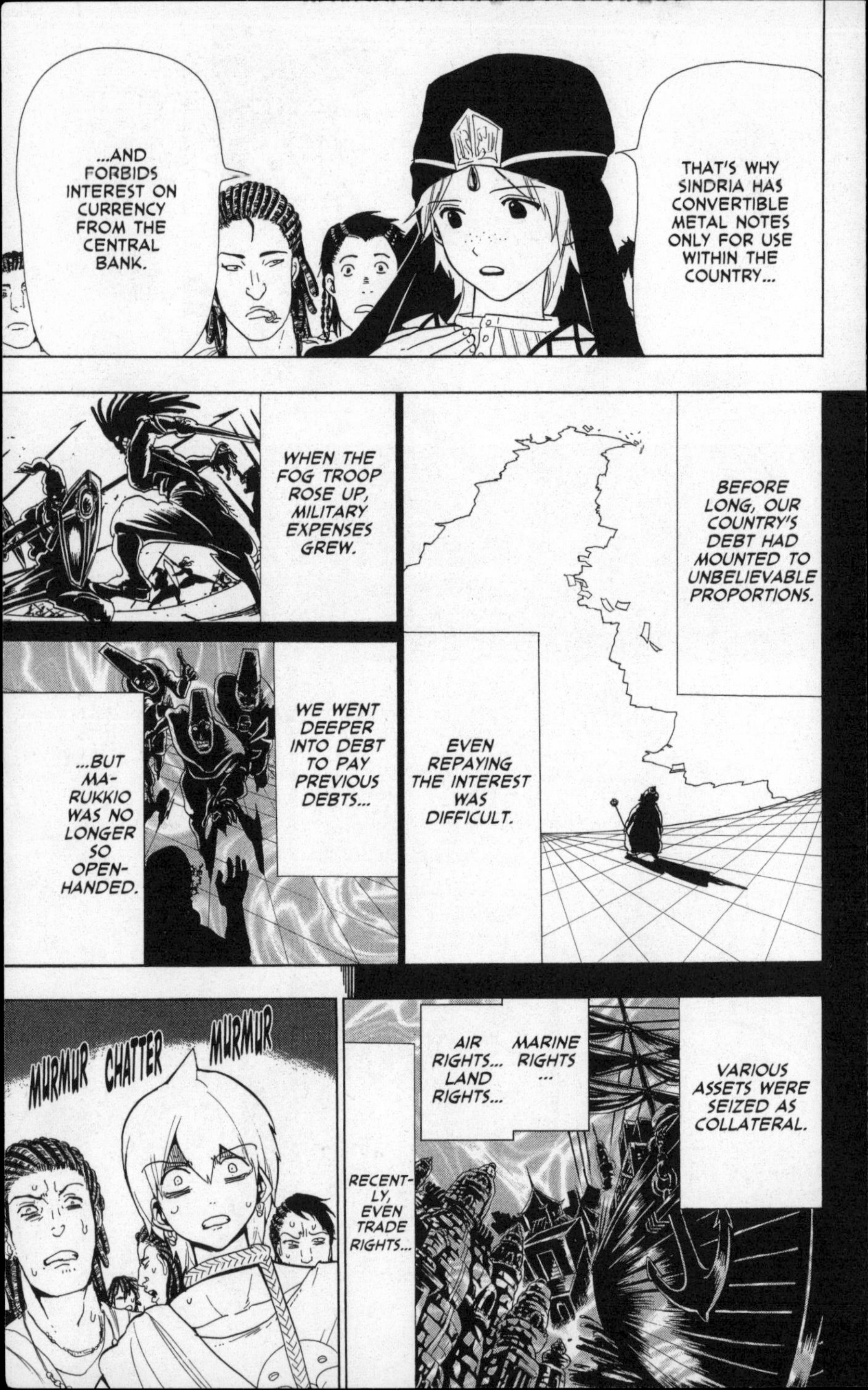
THAT'S WHY SINDRIA HAS CONVERTIBLE METAL NOTES ONLY FOR USE WITHIN THE COUNTRY...
...AND FORBIDS INTEREST ON CURRENCY FROM THE CENTRAL BANK.
BEFORE LONG, OUR COUNTRY'S DEBT HAD MOUNTED TO UNBELIEVABLE PROPORTIONS.
EVEN REPAYING THE INTEREST WAS DIFFICULT.
WHEN THE FOG TROOP ROSE UP, MILITARY EXPENSES GREW.
WE WENT DEEPER INTO DEBT TO PAY PREVIOUS DEBTS...
...BUT MA-RUKKIO WAS NO LONGER SO OPEN-HANDED.
VARIOUS ASSETS WERE SEIZED AS COLLATERAL.
MARINE RIGHTS...
AIR RIGHTS... LAND RIGHTS...
RECENT-LY, EVEN TRADE RIGHTS...
MURMUR
CHATTER
MURMUR

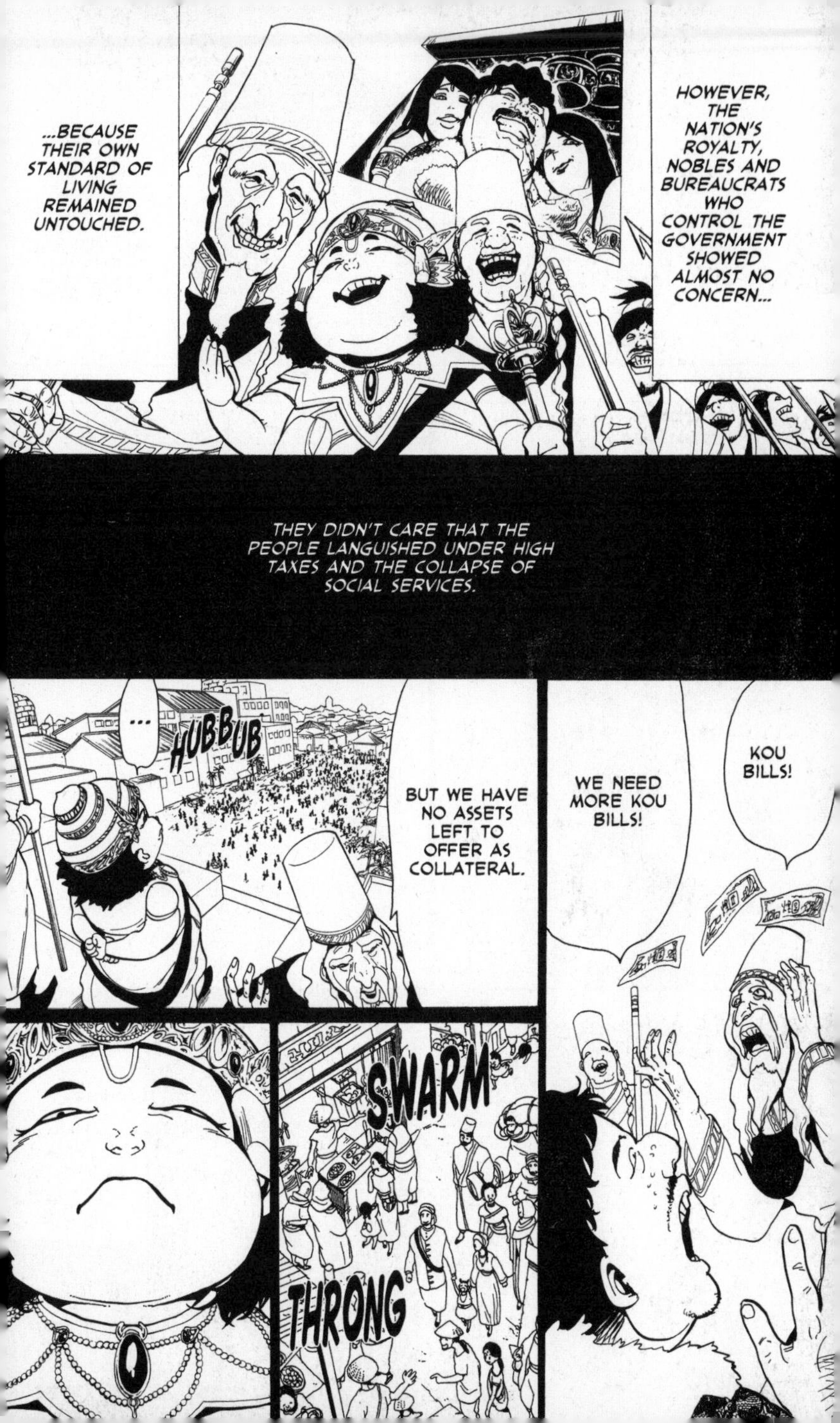
HOWEVER, THE NATION'S ROYALTY, NOBLES AND BUREAUCRATS WHO CONTROL THE GOVERNMENT SHOWED ALMOST NO CONCERN...
...BECAUSE THEIR OWN STANDARD OF LIVING REMAINED UNTOUCHED.
THEY DIDN'T CARE THAT THE PEOPLE LANGUISHED UNDER HIGH TAXES AND THE COLLAPSE OF SOCIAL SERVICES.
KOU BILLS!
WE NEED MORE KOU BILLS!
BUT WE HAVE NO ASSETS LEFT TO OFFER AS COLLATERAL.
...
HUBBUB
SWARM
THRONG

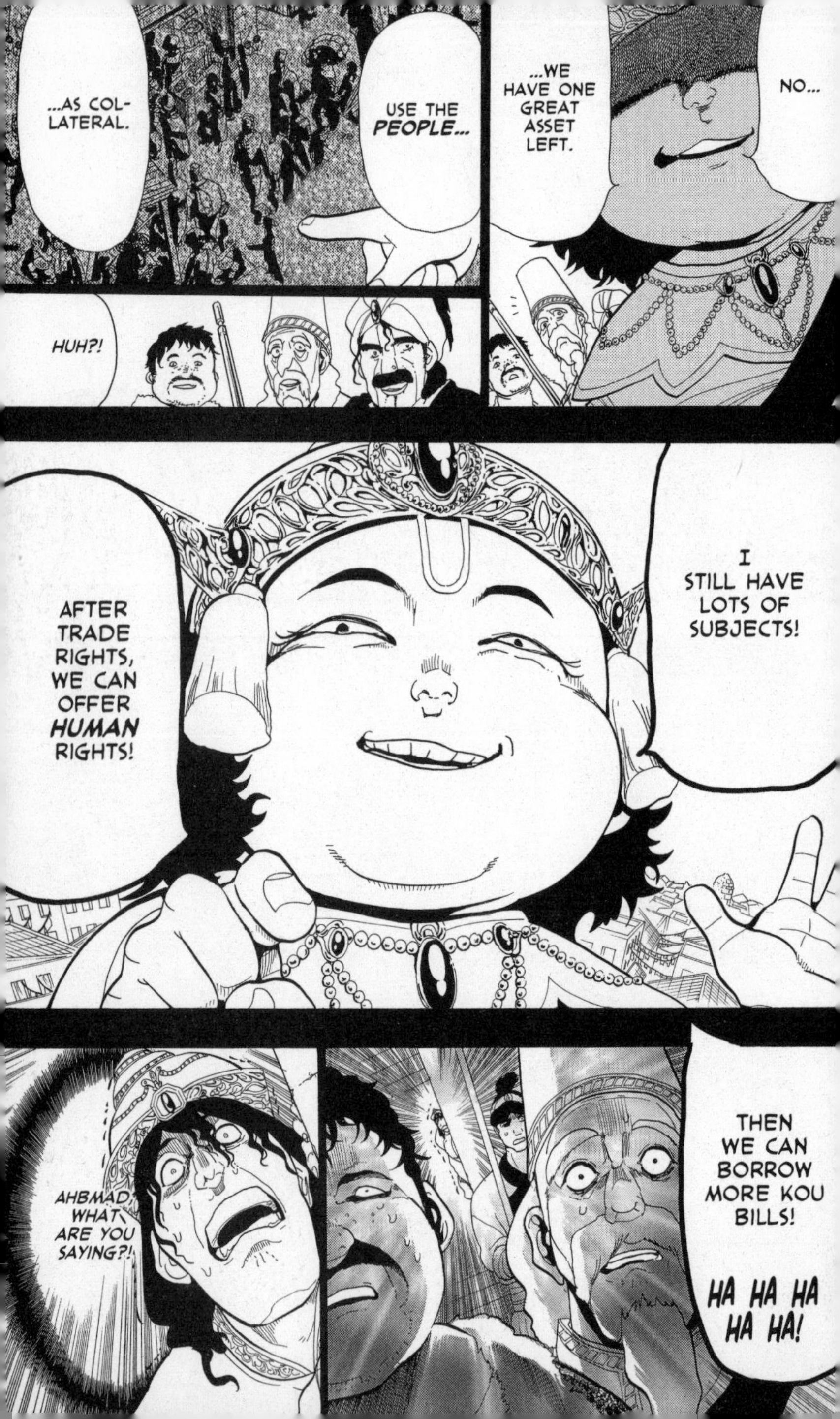
NO...
...WE HAVE ONE GREAT ASSET LEFT.
USE THE *PEOPLE...*
...AS COL-LATERAL.
HUH?!
I STILL HAVE LOTS OF SUBJECTS!
AFTER TRADE RIGHTS, WE CAN OFFER *HUMAN* RIGHTS!
THEN WE CAN BORROW MORE KOU BILLS!
HA HA HA HA HA!
AHBMAD, WHAT ARE YOU SAYING?!

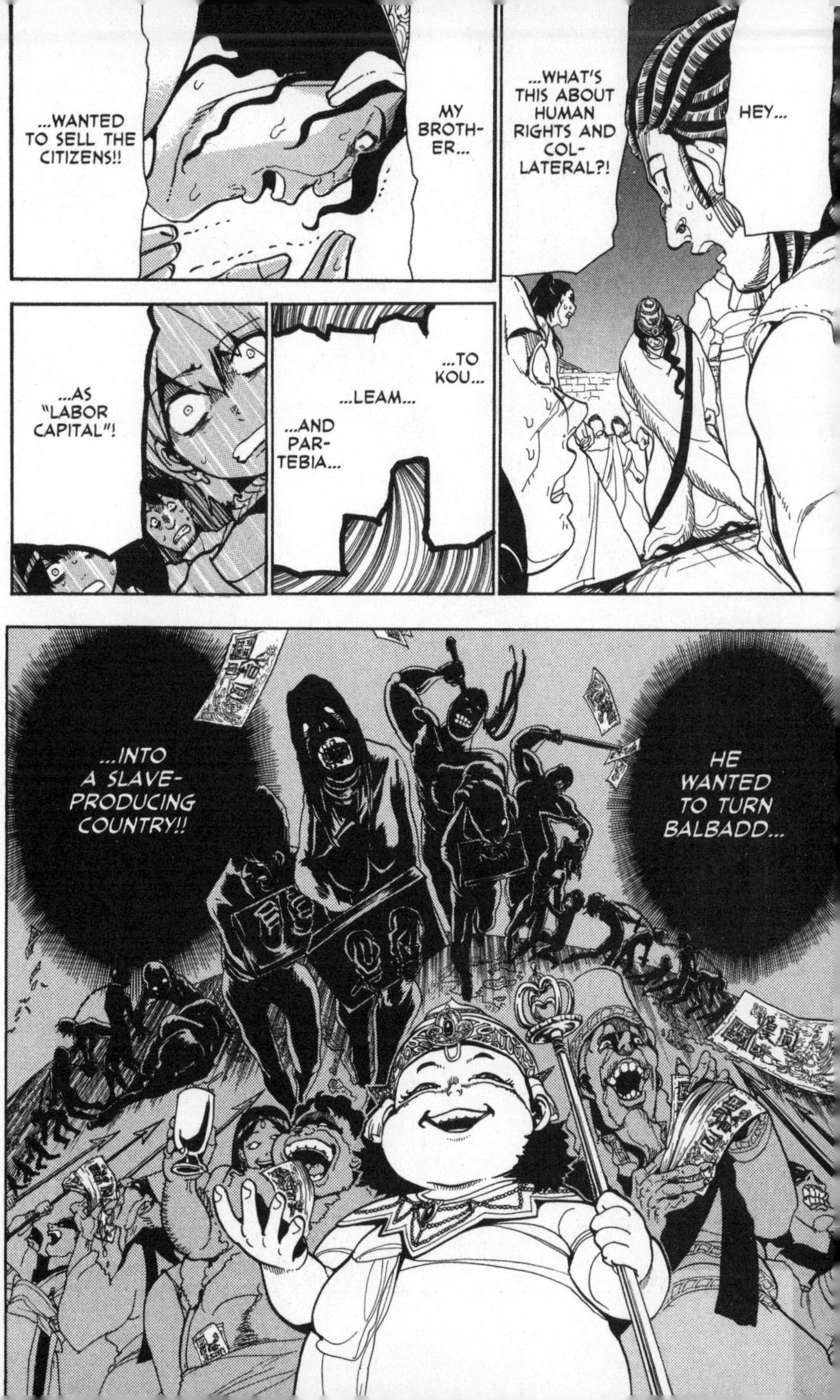
HEY...
...WHAT'S THIS ABOUT HUMAN RIGHTS AND COL-LATERAL?!
MY BROTH-ER...
...WANTED TO SELL THE CITIZENS!!
...TO KOU...
...LEAM...
...AND PAR-TEBIA...
...AS "LABOR CAPITAL"!
HE WANTED TO TURN BALBADD...
...INTO A SLAVE-PRODUCING COUNTRY!!

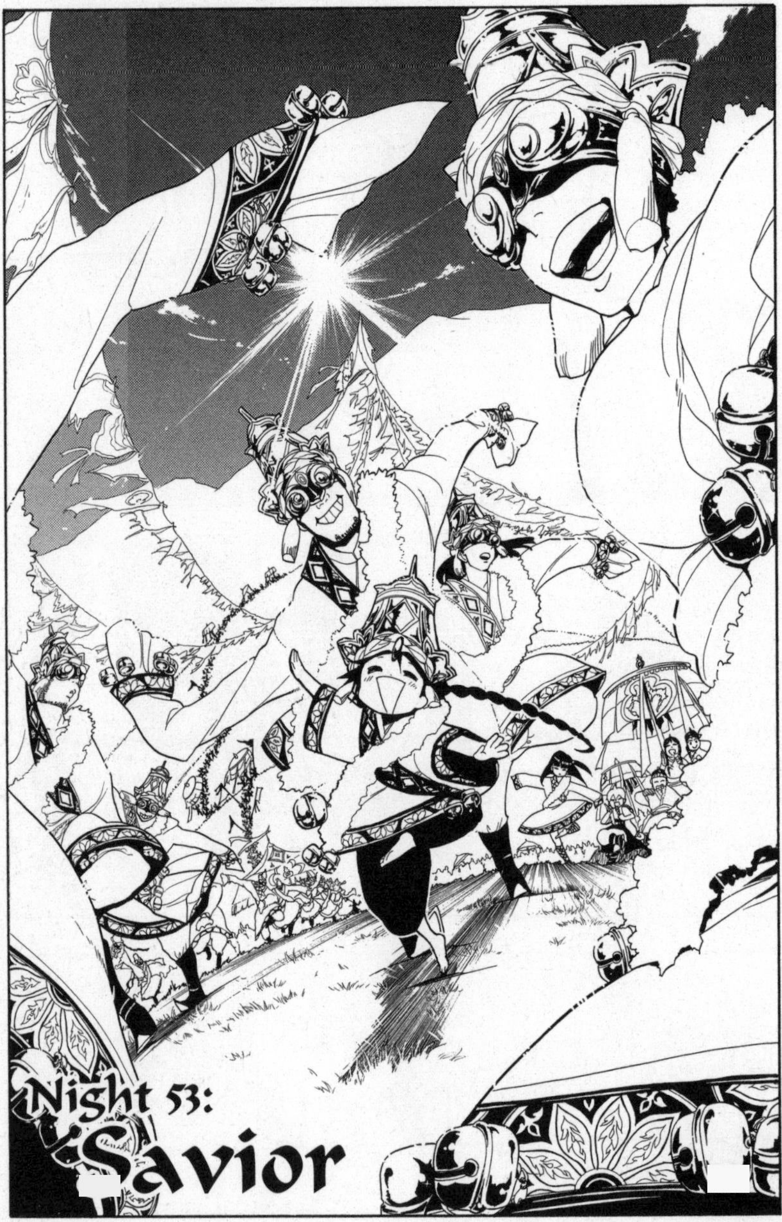
Night 53:
Savior

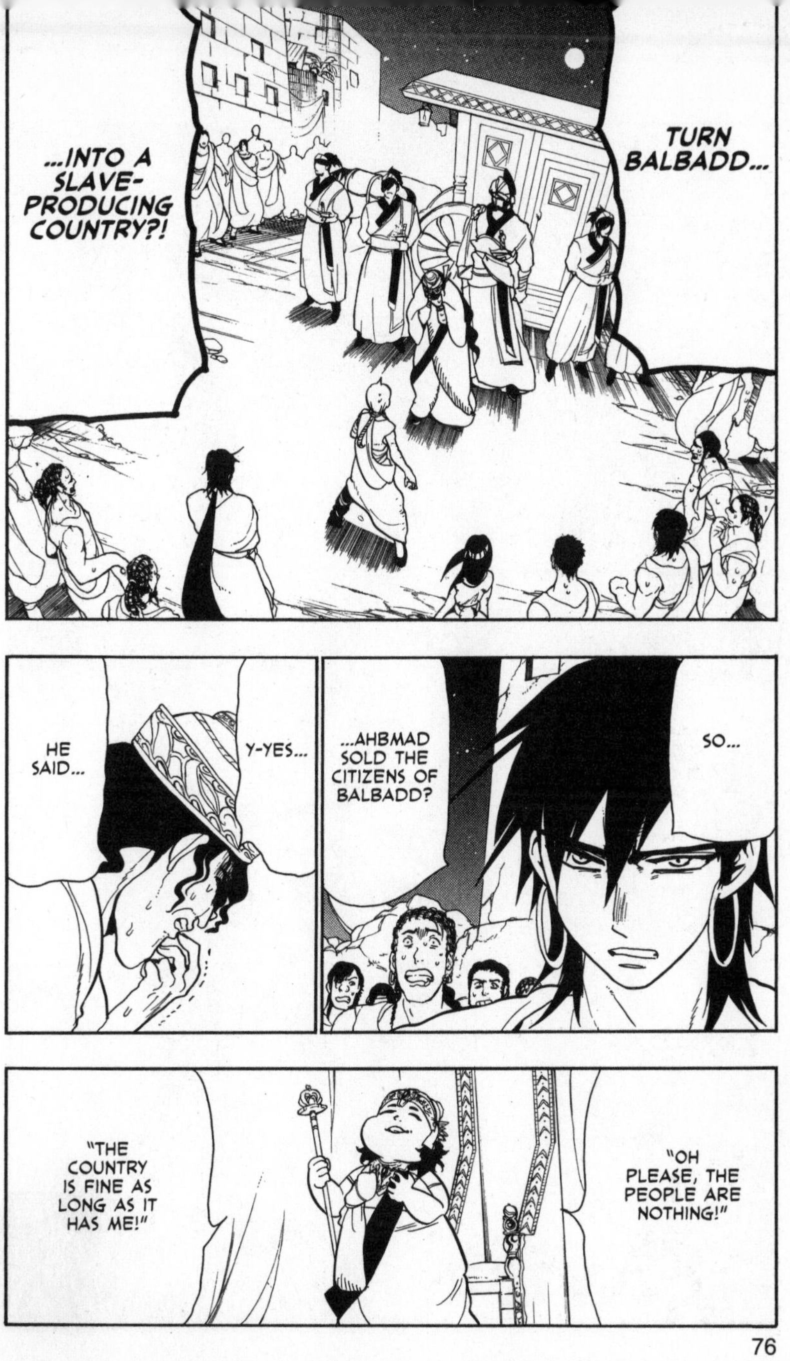
TURN BALBADD...
...INTO A SLAVE-PRODUCING COUNTRY?!
SO...
...AHBMAD SOLD THE CITIZENS OF BALBADD?
Y-YES...
HE SAID...
"OH PLEASE, THE PEOPLE ARE NOTHING!"
"THE COUNTRY IS FINE AS LONG AS IT HAS ME!"

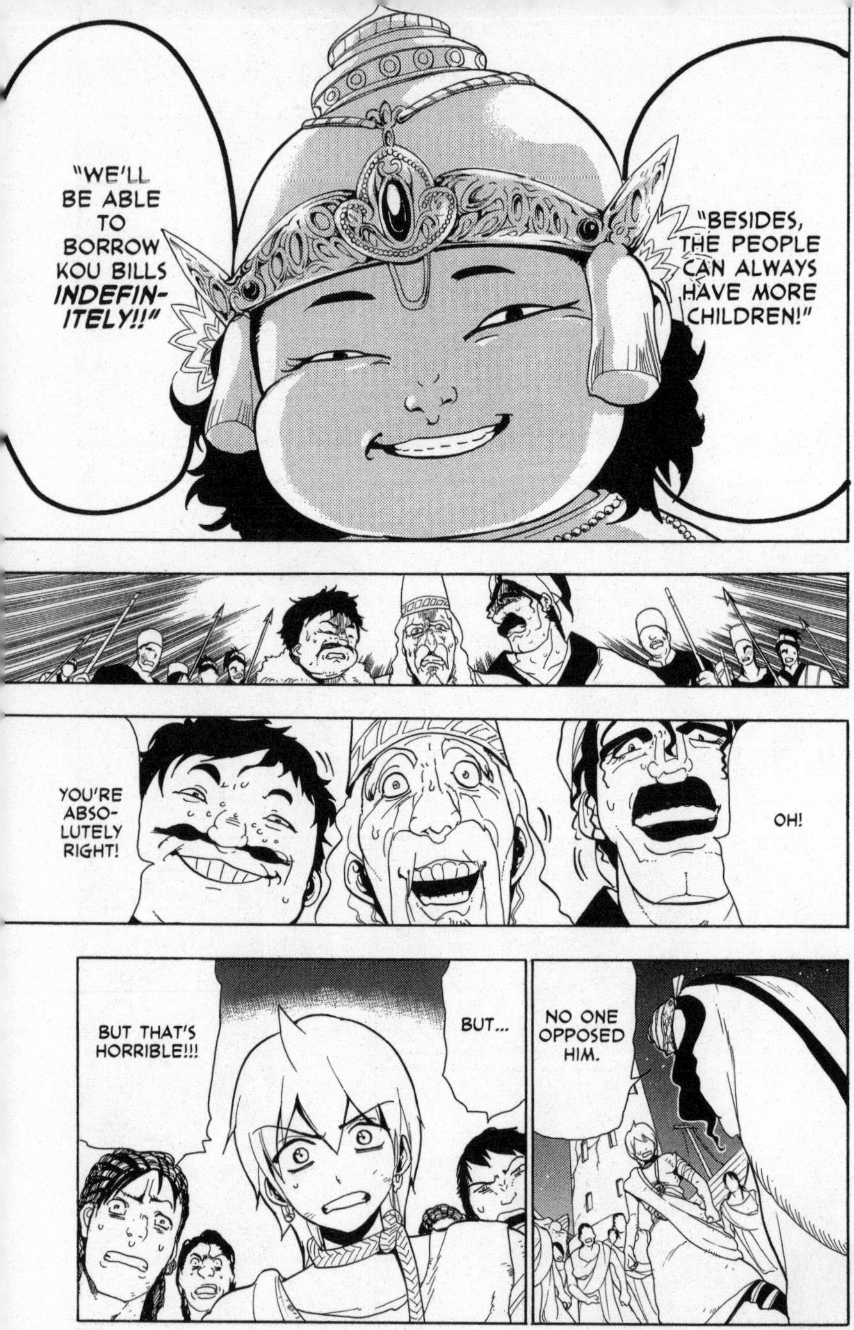
"WE'LL BE ABLE TO BORROW KOU BILLS *INDEFINITELY!!*"
"BESIDES, THE PEOPLE CAN ALWAYS HAVE MORE CHILDREN!"
OH!
YOU'RE ABSOLUTELY RIGHT!
NO ONE OPPOSED HIM.
BUT...
BUT THAT'S HORRIBLE!!!

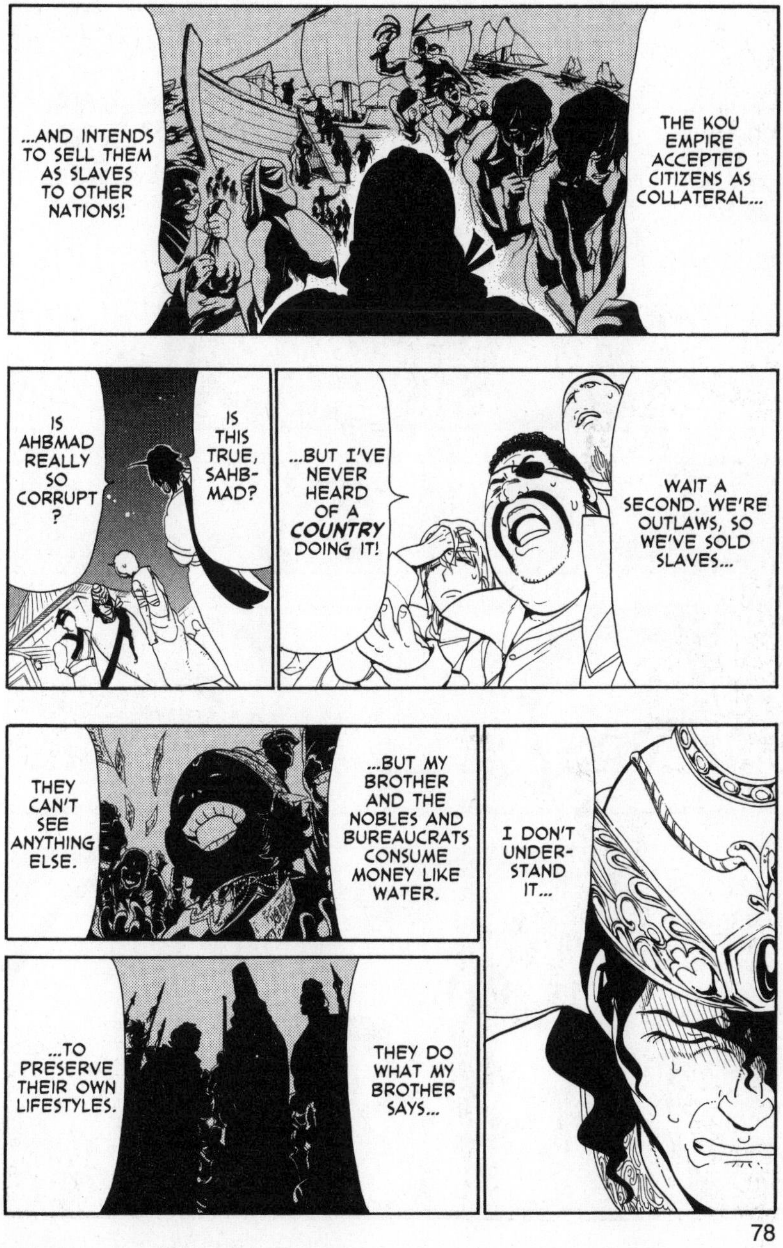
THE KOU EMPIRE ACCEPTED CITIZENS AS COLLATERAL...
...AND INTENDS TO SELL THEM AS SLAVES TO OTHER NATIONS!
WAIT A SECOND. WE'RE OUTLAWS, SO WE'VE SOLD SLAVES...
...BUT I'VE NEVER HEARD OF A *COUNTRY* DOING IT!
IS THIS TRUE, SAHBMAD?
IS AHBMAD REALLY SO CORRUPT?
I DON'T UNDERSTAND IT...
...BUT MY BROTHER AND THE NOBLES AND BUREAUCRATS CONSUME MONEY LIKE WATER.
THEY CAN'T SEE ANYTHING ELSE.
THEY DO WHAT MY BROTHER SAYS...
...TO PRESERVE THEIR OWN LIFESTYLES.

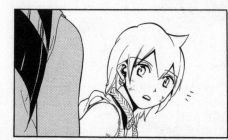

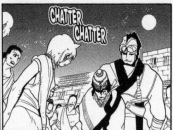

CHATTER CHATTER

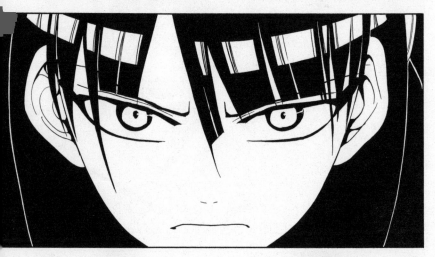

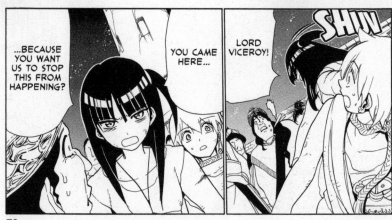

...BECAUSE YOU WANT US TO STOP THIS FROM HAPPENING?

YOU CAME HERE...

LORD VICEROY!

SHIN

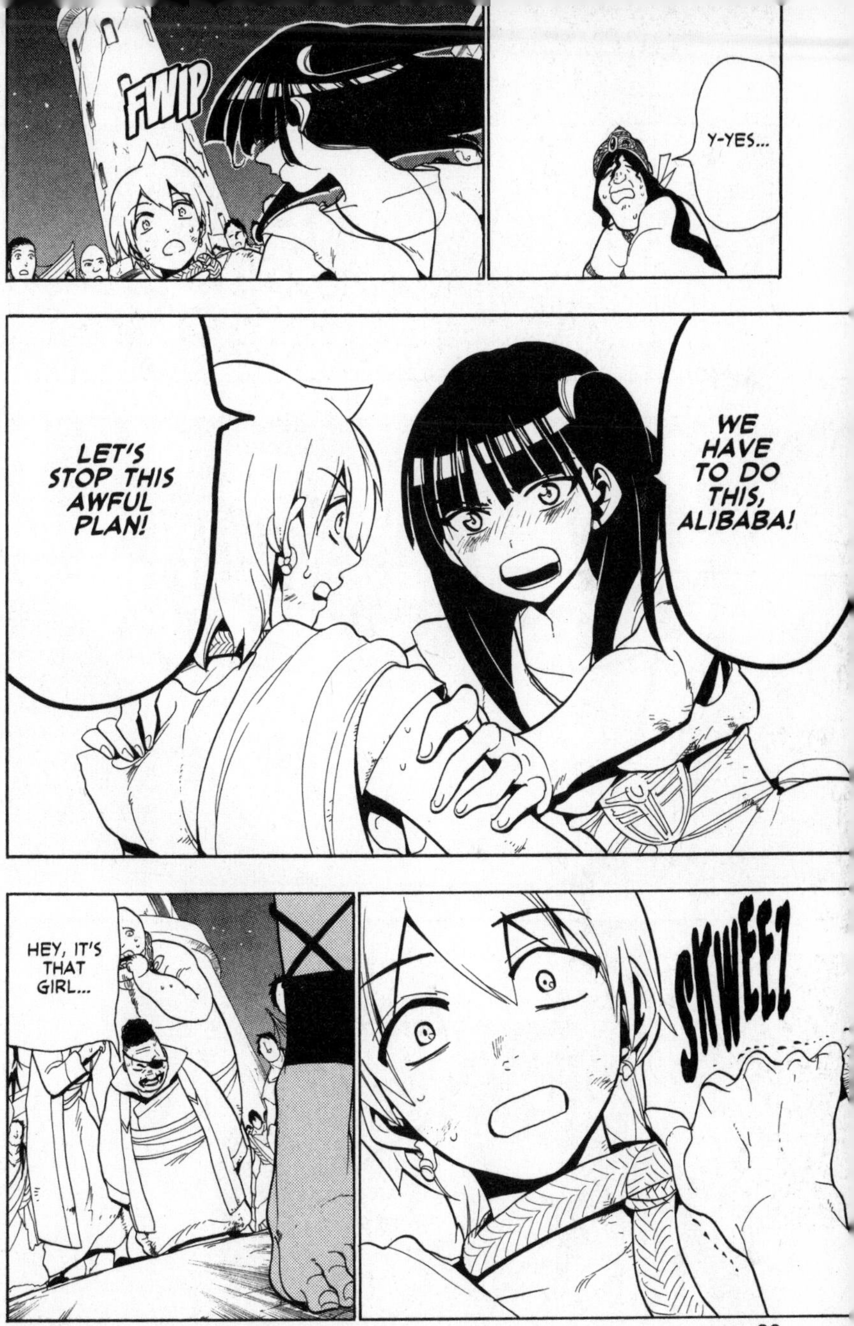
Y-YES...
FWIP
WE HAVE TO DO THIS, ALIBABA!
LET'S STOP THIS AWFUL PLAN!
SKWEEZ
HEY, IT'S THAT GIRL...

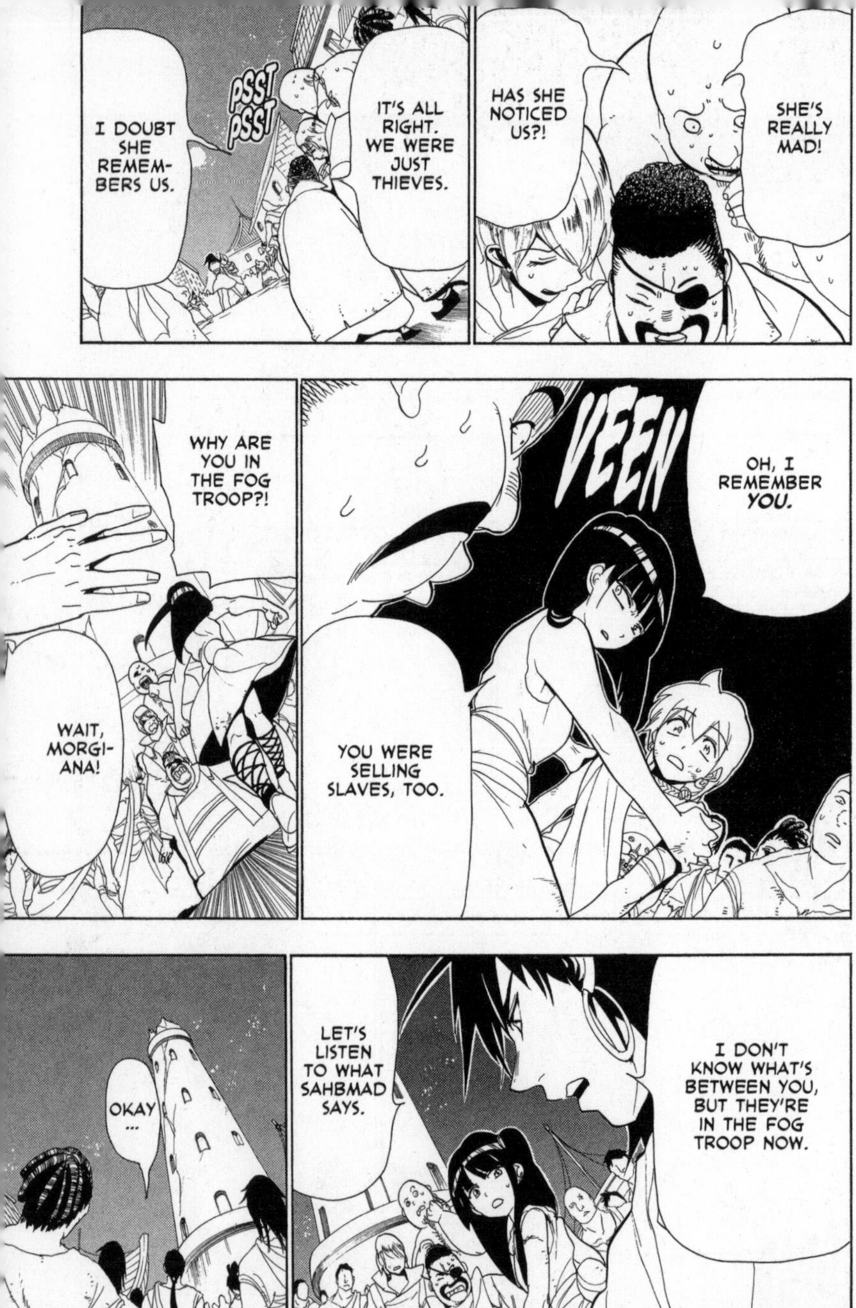
SHE'S REALLY MAD!
HAS SHE NOTICED US?!
IT'S ALL RIGHT. WE WERE JUST THIEVES.
PSST PSST
I DOUBT SHE REMEM-BERS US.
OH, I REMEMBER *YOU.*
VEEN
YOU WERE SELLING SLAVES, TOO.
WHY ARE YOU IN THE FOG TROOP?!
WAIT, MORGI-ANA!
I DON'T KNOW WHAT'S BETWEEN YOU, BUT THEY'RE IN THE FOG TROOP NOW.
LET'S LISTEN TO WHAT SAHBMAD SAYS.
OKAY ...

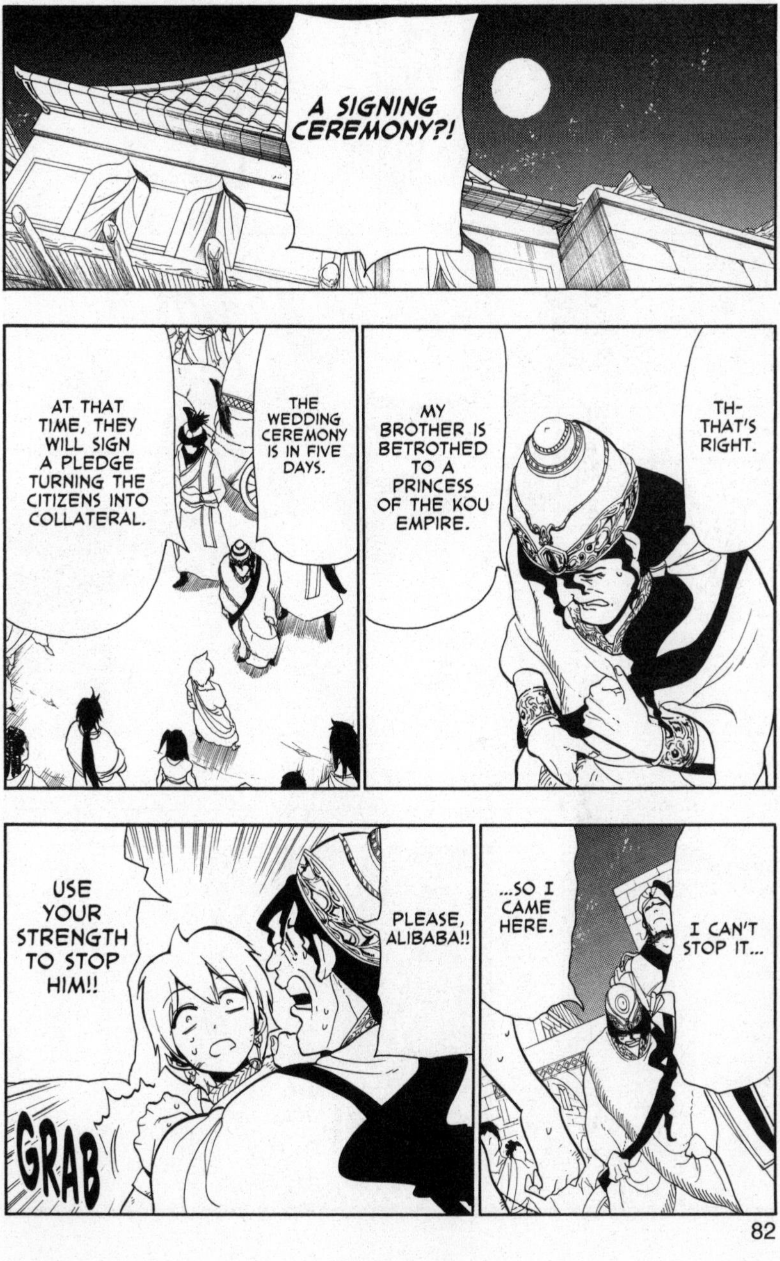
A SIGNING CEREMONY?!
TH- THAT'S RIGHT.
MY BROTHER IS BETROTHED TO A PRINCESS OF THE KOU EMPIRE.
THE WEDDING CEREMONY IS IN FIVE DAYS.
AT THAT TIME, THEY WILL SIGN A PLEDGE TURNING THE CITIZENS INTO COLLATERAL.
I CAN'T STOP IT...
...SO I CAME HERE.
PLEASE, ALIBABA!!
USE YOUR STRENGTH TO STOP HIM!!
GRAB

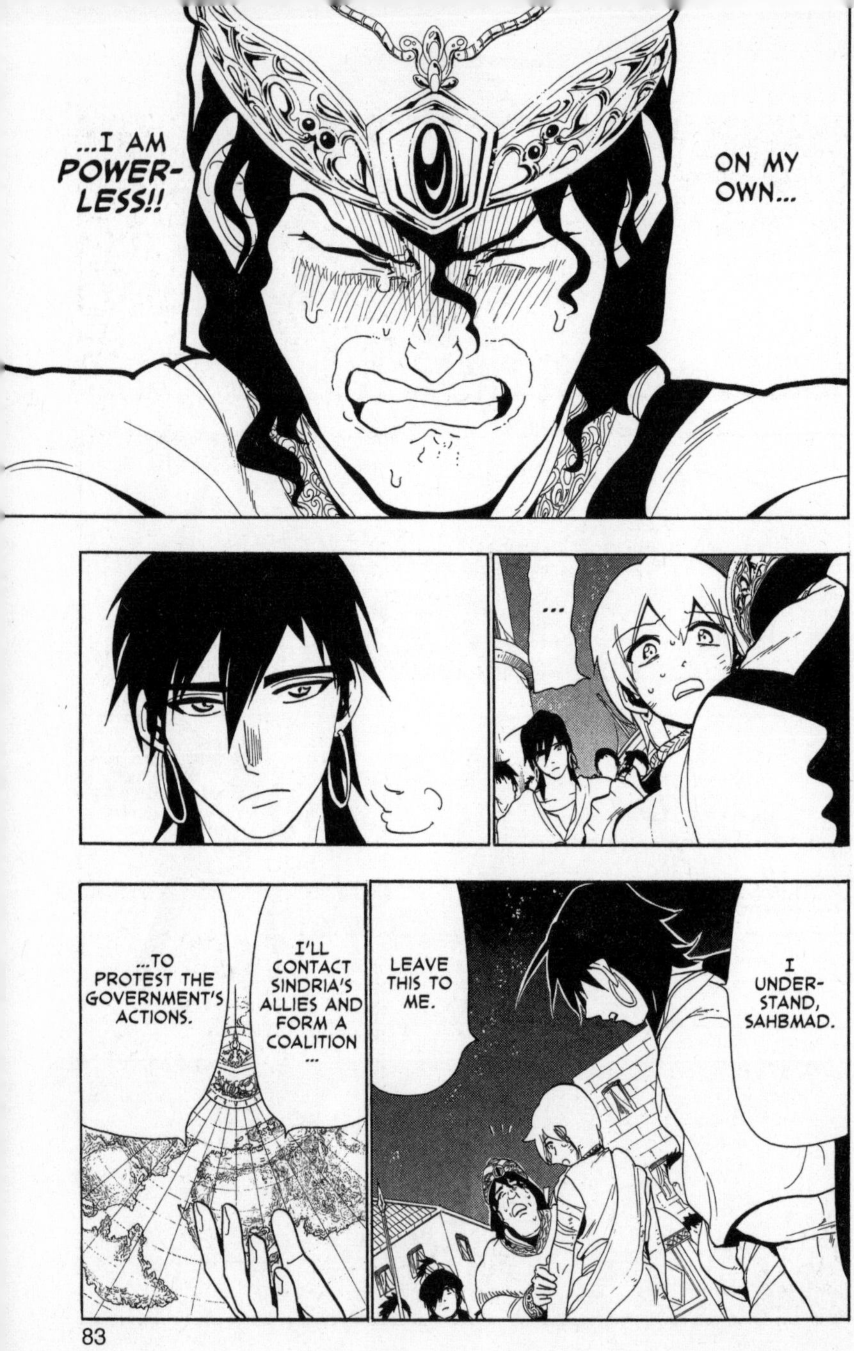

ON MY OWN...
...I AM POWERLESS!!
...
I UNDERSTAND, SAHBMAD.
LEAVE THIS TO ME.
I'LL CONTACT SINDRIA'S ALLIES AND FORM A COALITION ...
...TO PROTEST THE GOVERNMENT'S ACTIONS.

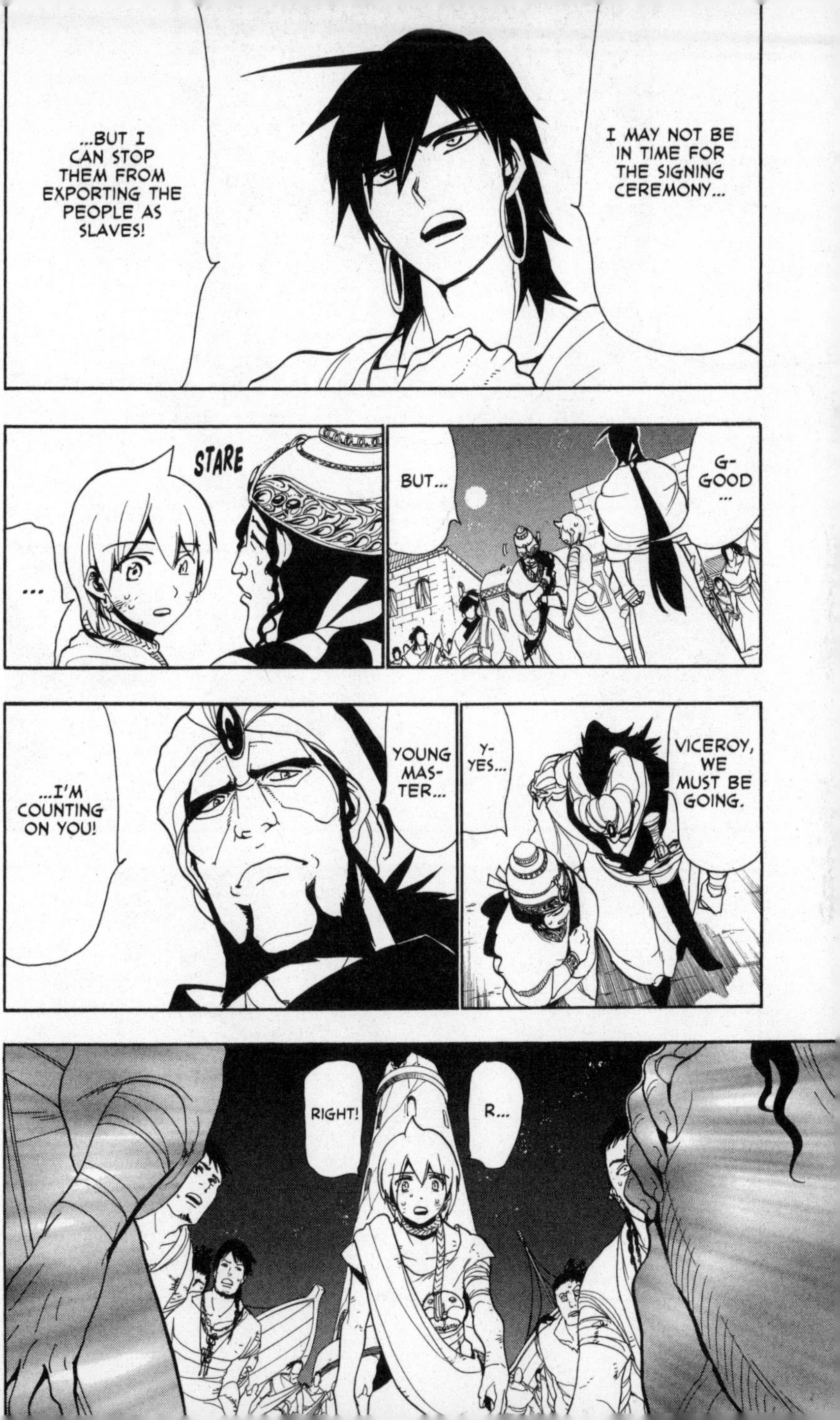
I MAY NOT BE IN TIME FOR THE SIGNING CEREMONY...
...BUT I CAN STOP THEM FROM EXPORTING THE PEOPLE AS SLAVES!
G-GOOD ...
BUT...
STARE
...
VICEROY, WE MUST BE GOING.
Y-YES...
YOUNG MAS-TER...
...I'M COUNTING ON YOU!
R...
RIGHT!

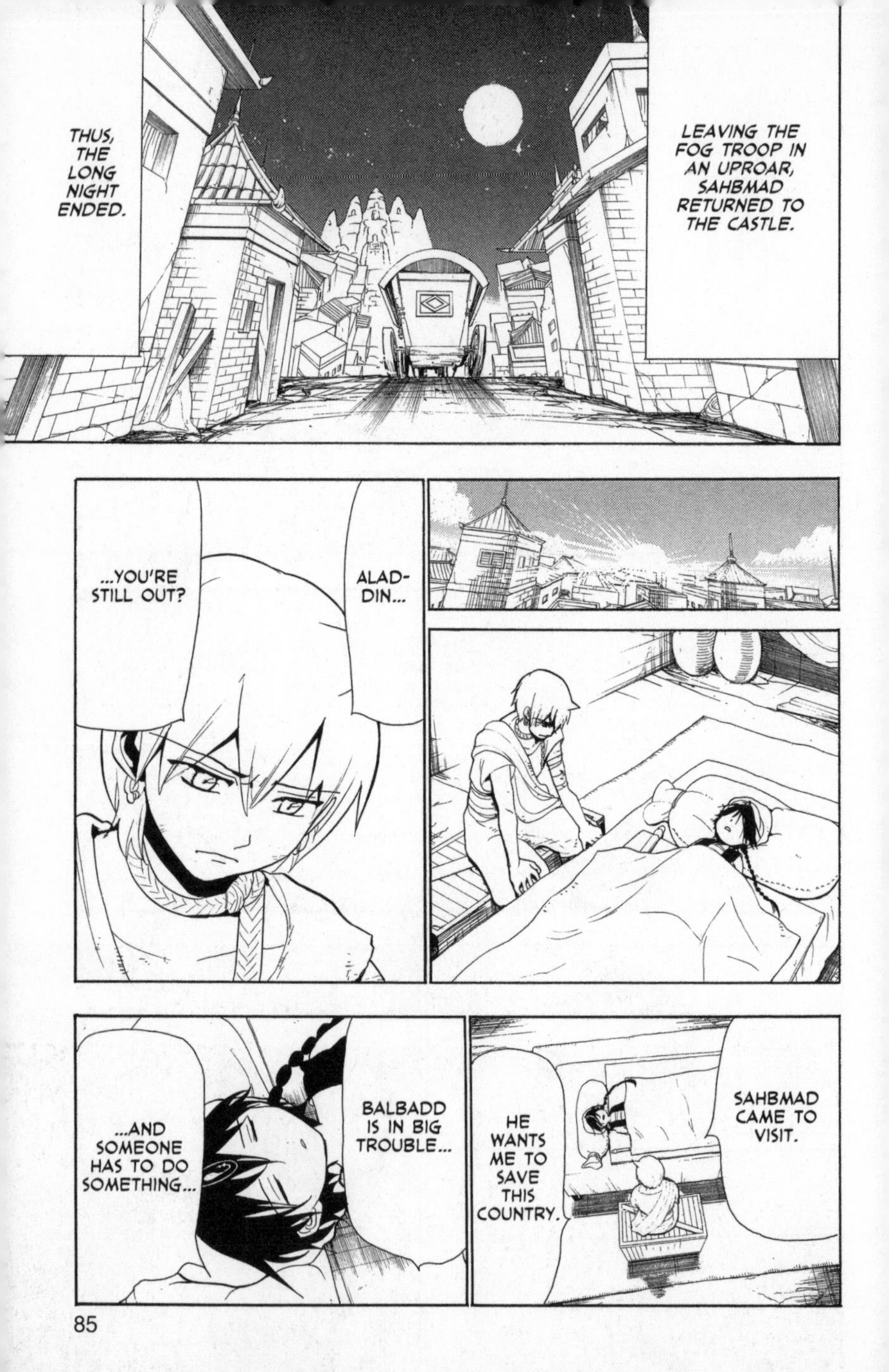

LEAVING THE FOG TROOP IN AN UPROAR, SAHBMAD RETURNED TO THE CASTLE.
THUS, THE LONG NIGHT ENDED.
ALAD-DIN...
...YOU'RE STILL OUT?
SAHBMAD CAME TO VISIT.
HE WANTS ME TO SAVE THIS COUNTRY.
BALBADD IS IN BIG TROUBLE...
...AND SOMEONE HAS TO DO SOMETHING...

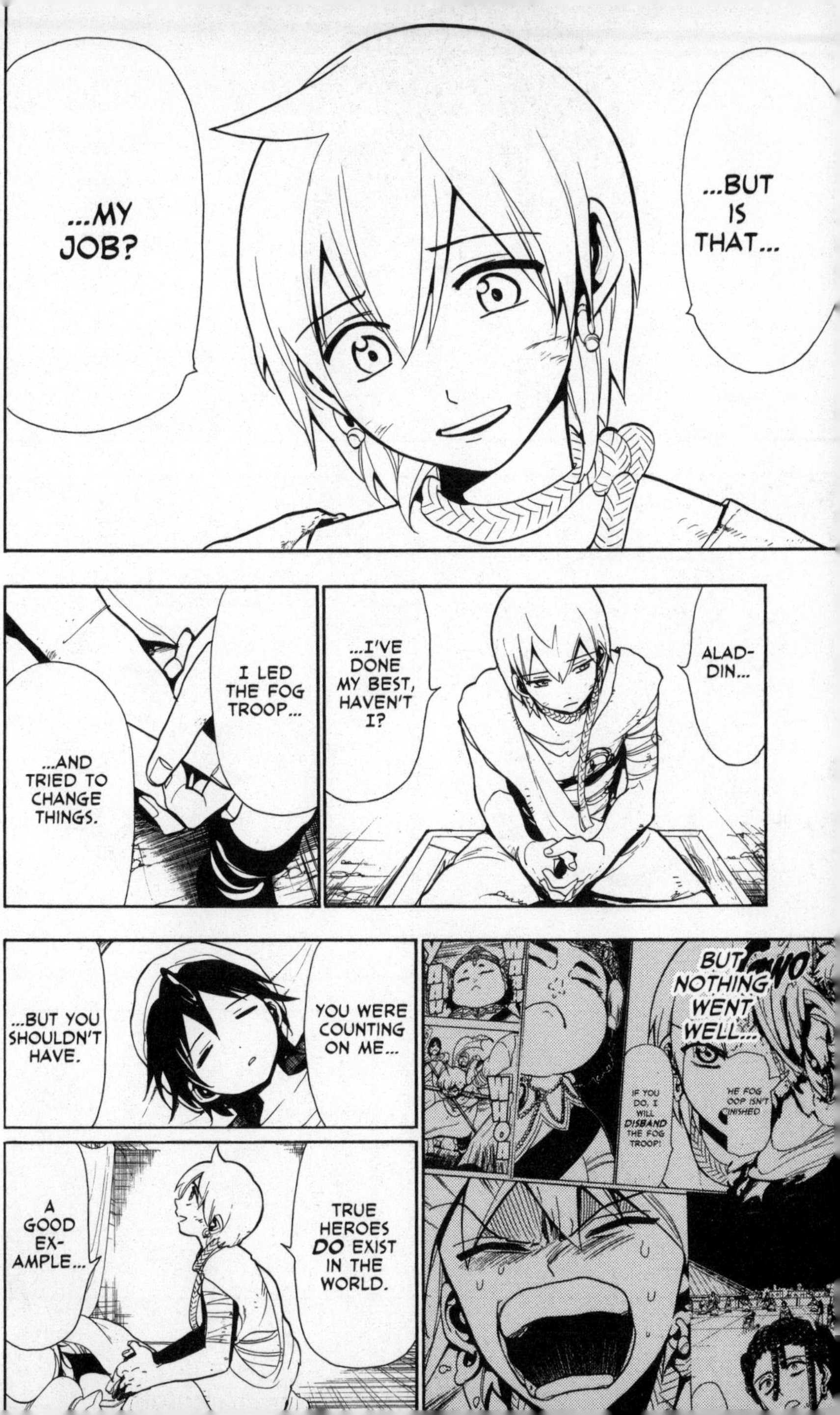
...BUT IS THAT...
...MY JOB?
ALAD-DIN...
...I'VE DONE MY BEST, HAVEN'T I?
I LED THE FOG TROOP...
...AND TRIED TO CHANGE THINGS.
BUT NOTHING WENT WELL...
IF YOU DO, I WILL *DISBAND* THE FOG TROOP!
YOU WERE COUNTING ON ME...
...BUT YOU SHOULDN'T HAVE.
TRUE HEROES *DO* EXIST IN THE WORLD.
A GOOD EX-AMPLE...

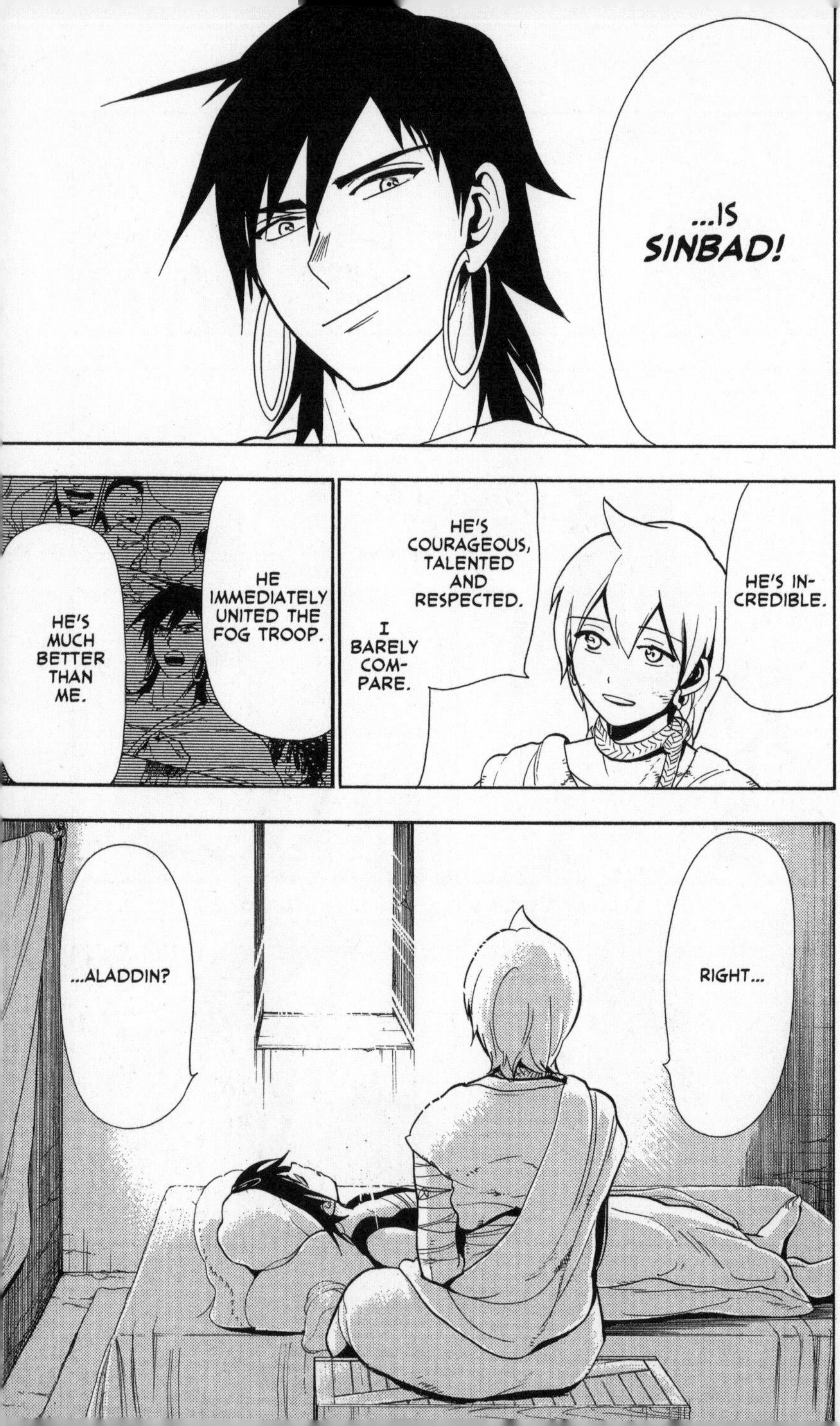
...IS SINBAD!
HE'S IN-CREDIBLE.
HE'S COURAGEOUS, TALENTED AND RESPECTED.
I BARELY COM-PARE.
HE IMMEDIATELY UNITED THE FOG TROOP.
HE'S MUCH BETTER THAN ME.
RIGHT...
...ALADDIN?

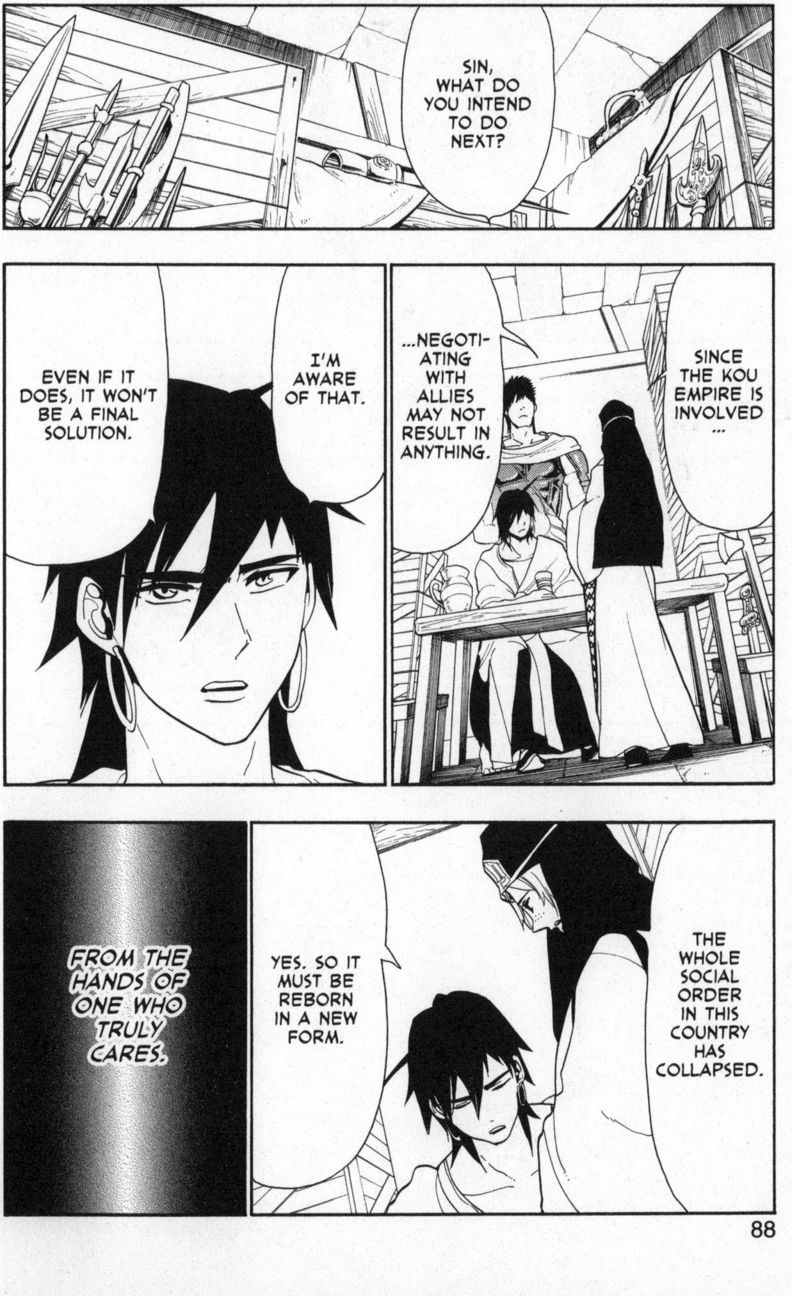
SIN, WHAT DO YOU INTEND TO DO NEXT?
SINCE THE KOU EMPIRE IS INVOLVED ...
...NEGOTIATING WITH ALLIES MAY NOT RESULT IN ANYTHING.
I'M AWARE OF THAT.
EVEN IF IT DOES, IT WON'T BE A FINAL SOLUTION.
THE WHOLE SOCIAL ORDER IN THIS COUNTRY HAS COLLAPSED.
YES. SO IT MUST BE REBORN IN A NEW FORM.
FROM THE HANDS OF ONE WHO TRULY CARES.

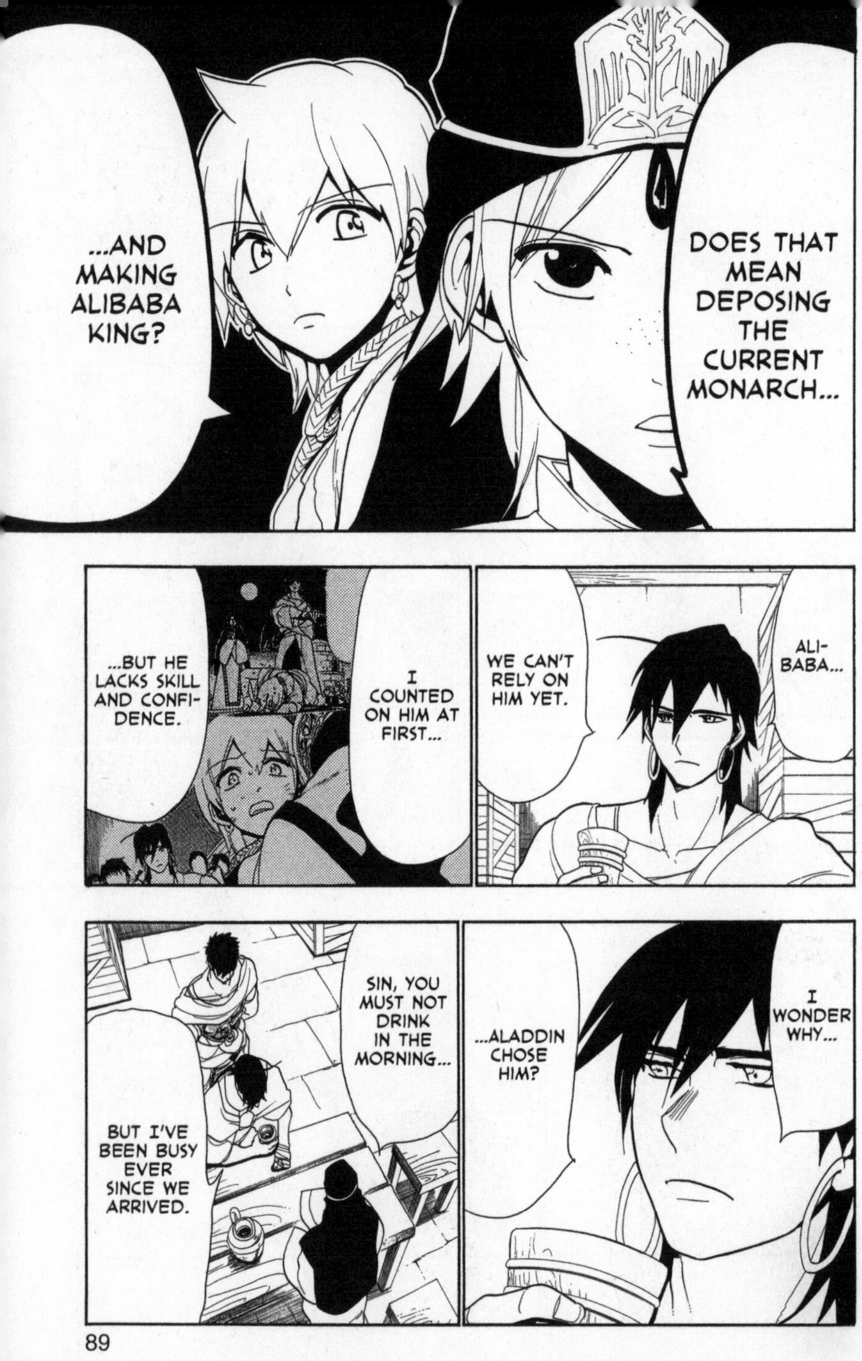
DOES THAT MEAN DEPOSING THE CURRENT MONARCH...
...AND MAKING ALIBABA KING?
ALI-BABA...
WE CAN'T RELY ON HIM YET.
I COUNTED ON HIM AT FIRST...
...BUT HE LACKS SKILL AND CONFI-DENCE.
I WONDER WHY...
...ALADDIN CHOSE HIM?
SIN, YOU MUST NOT DRINK IN THE MORNING...
BUT I'VE BEEN BUSY EVER SINCE WE ARRIVED.

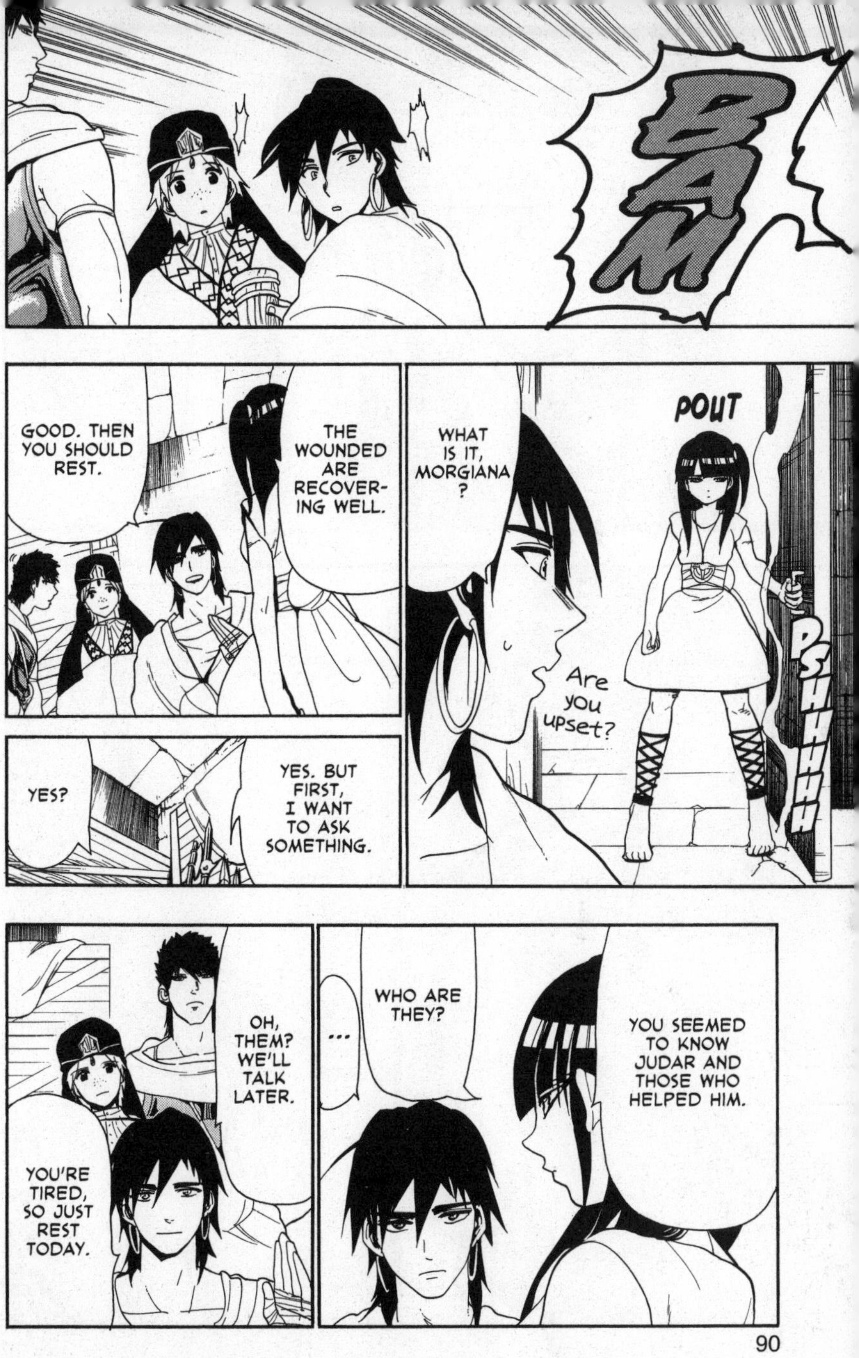
BAM
POUT
WHAT IS IT, MORGIANA?
PSHHHHHH
Are you upset?
THE WOUNDED ARE RECOVERING WELL.
GOOD. THEN YOU SHOULD REST.
YES. BUT FIRST, I WANT TO ASK SOMETHING.
YES?
YOU SEEMED TO KNOW JUDAR AND THOSE WHO HELPED HIM.
WHO ARE THEY?
...
OH, THEM? WE'LL TALK LATER.
YOU'RE TIRED, SO JUST REST TODAY.

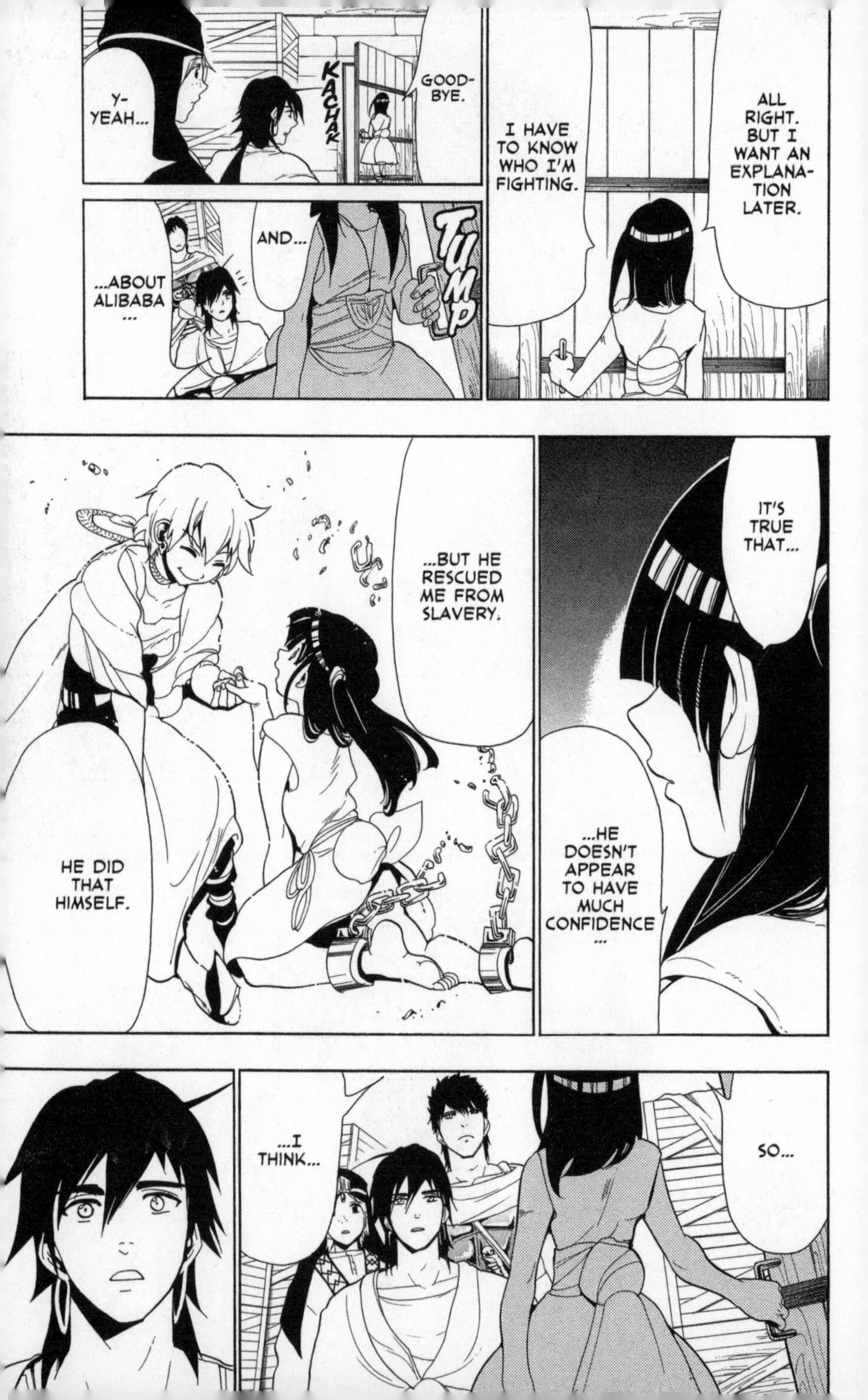
ALL RIGHT. BUT I WANT AN EXPLANA-TION LATER.
I HAVE TO KNOW WHO I'M FIGHTING.
GOOD-BYE.
KACHAK
Y-YEAH...
TUMP
AND...
...ABOUT ALIBABA...
IT'S TRUE THAT...
...HE DOESN'T APPEAR TO HAVE MUCH CONFIDENCE...
...BUT HE RESCUED ME FROM SLAVERY.
HE DID THAT HIMSELF.
SO...
...I THINK...

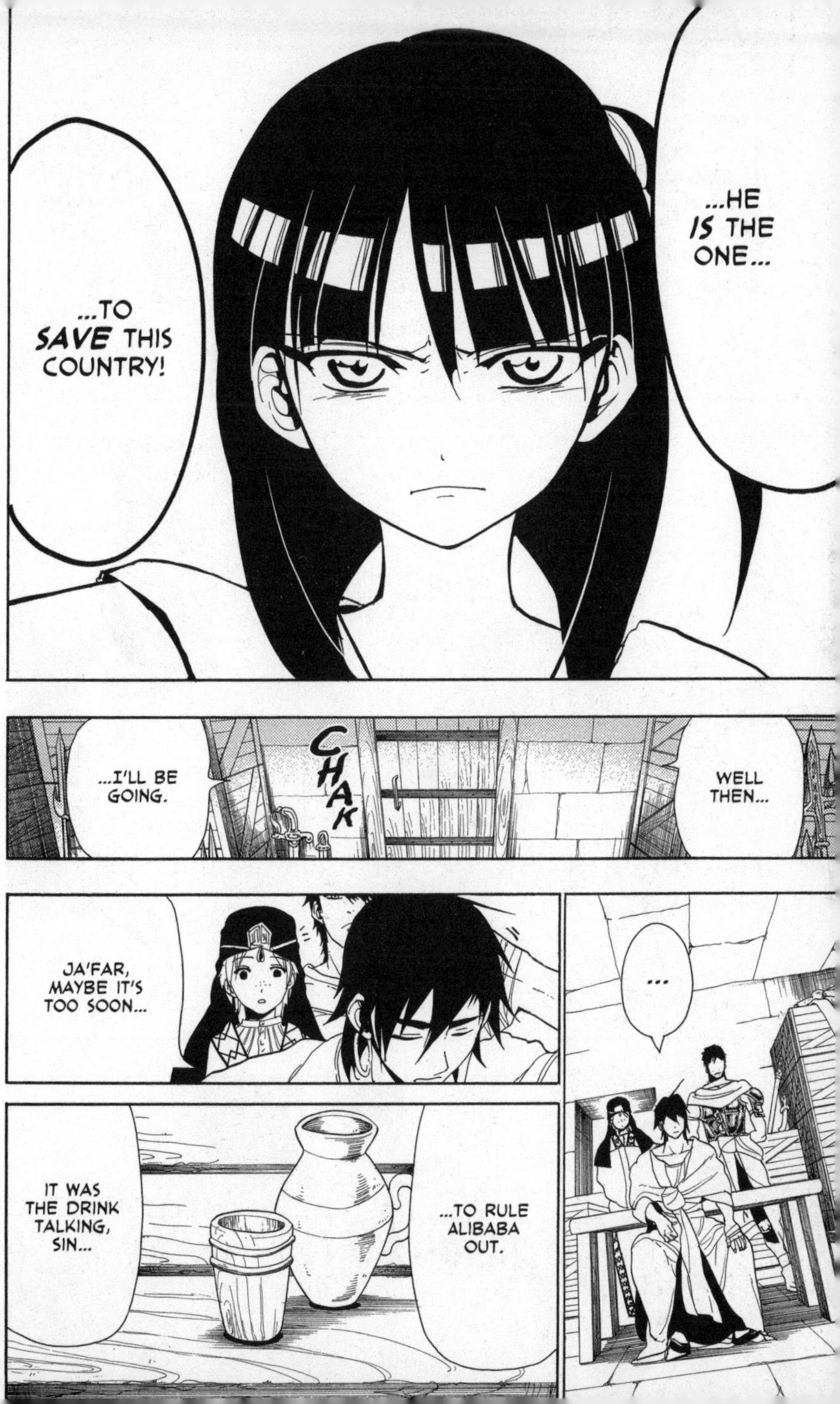
...HE IS THE ONE...
...TO SAVE THIS COUNTRY!
WELL THEN...
CHAK
...I'LL BE GOING.
...
JA'FAR, MAYBE IT'S TOO SOON...
...TO RULE ALIBABA OUT.
IT WAS THE DRINK TALKING, SIN...

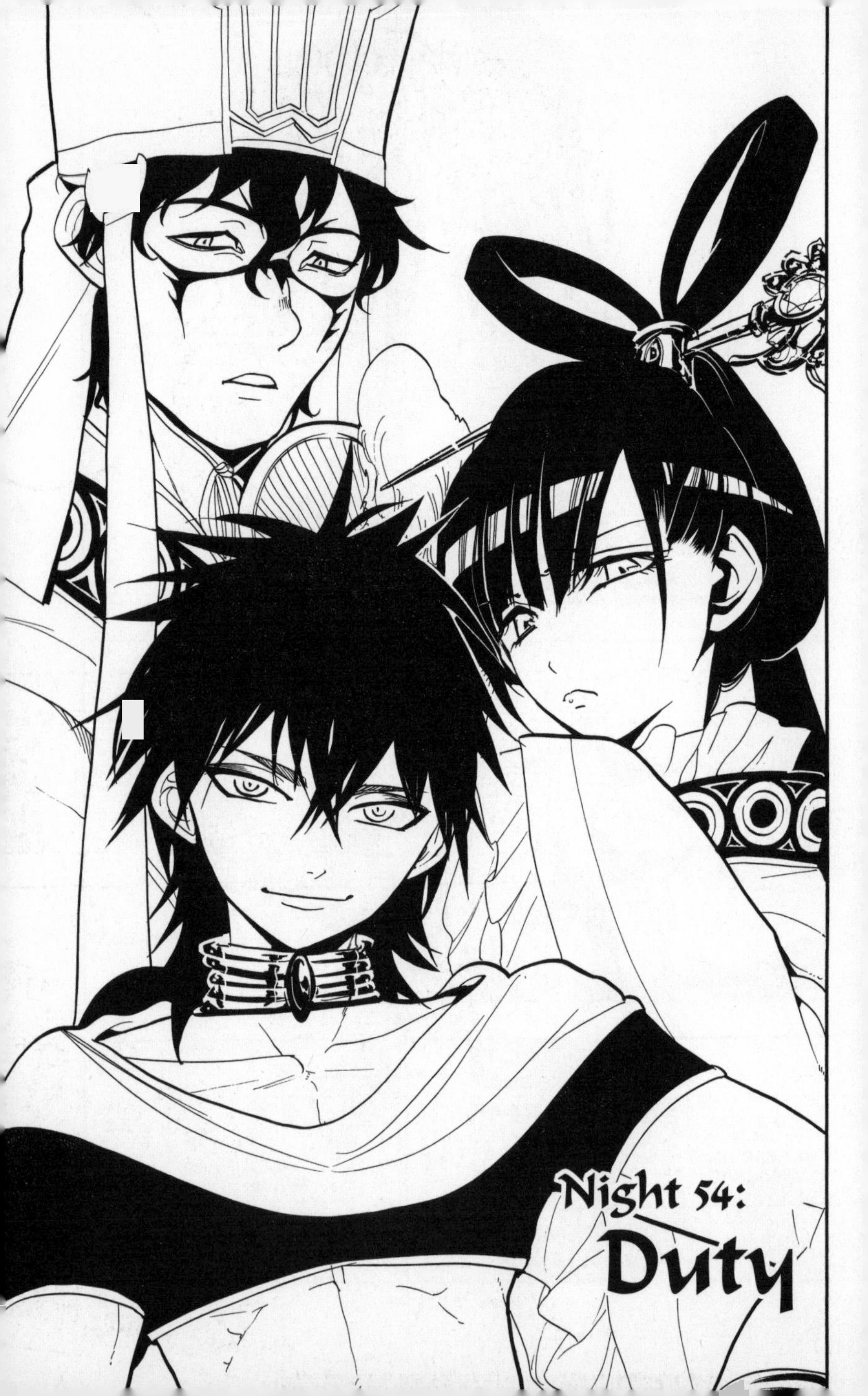
Night 54:
Duty

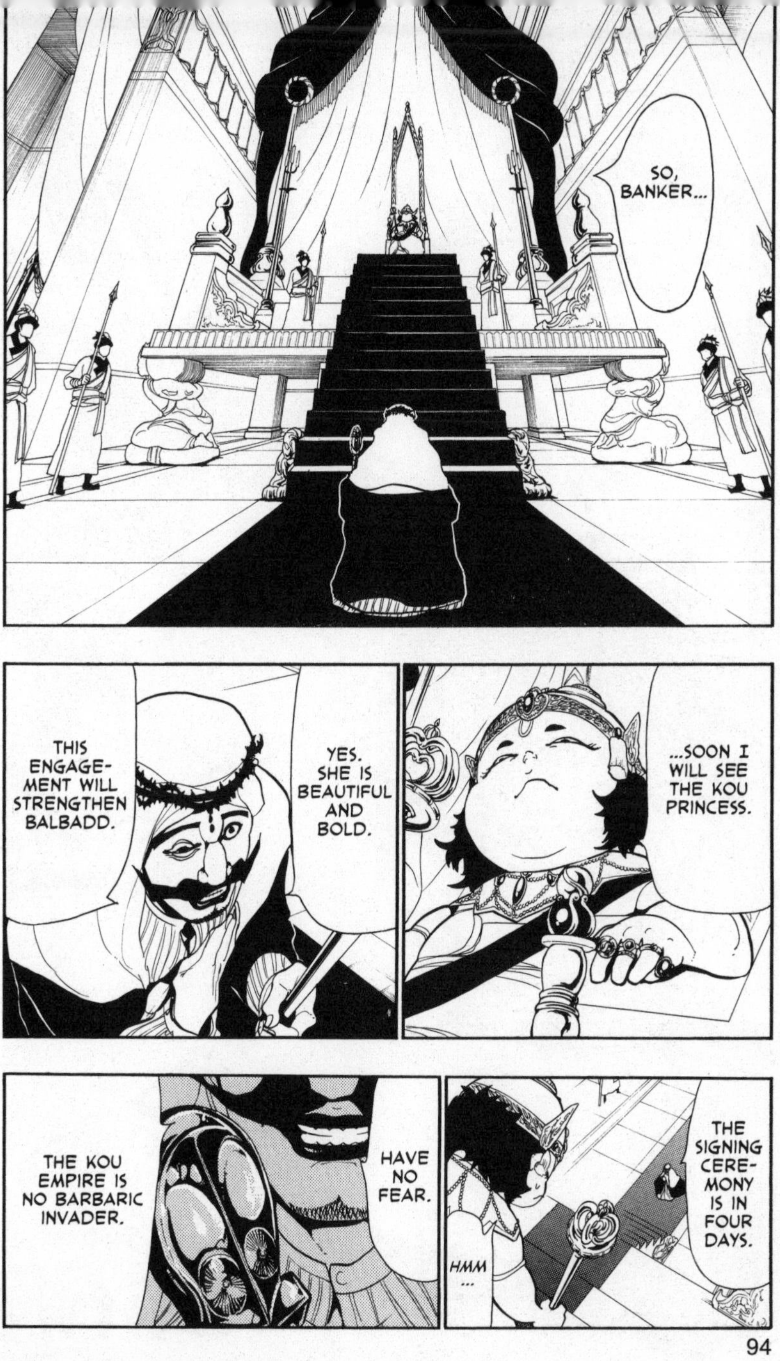
SO, BANKER...
...SOON I WILL SEE THE KOU PRINCESS.
YES. SHE IS BEAUTIFUL AND BOLD.
THIS ENGAGEMENT WILL STRENGTHEN BALBADD.
THE SIGNING CEREMONY IS IN FOUR DAYS.
HMM...
HAVE NO FEAR.
THE KOU EMPIRE IS NO BARBARIC INVADER.

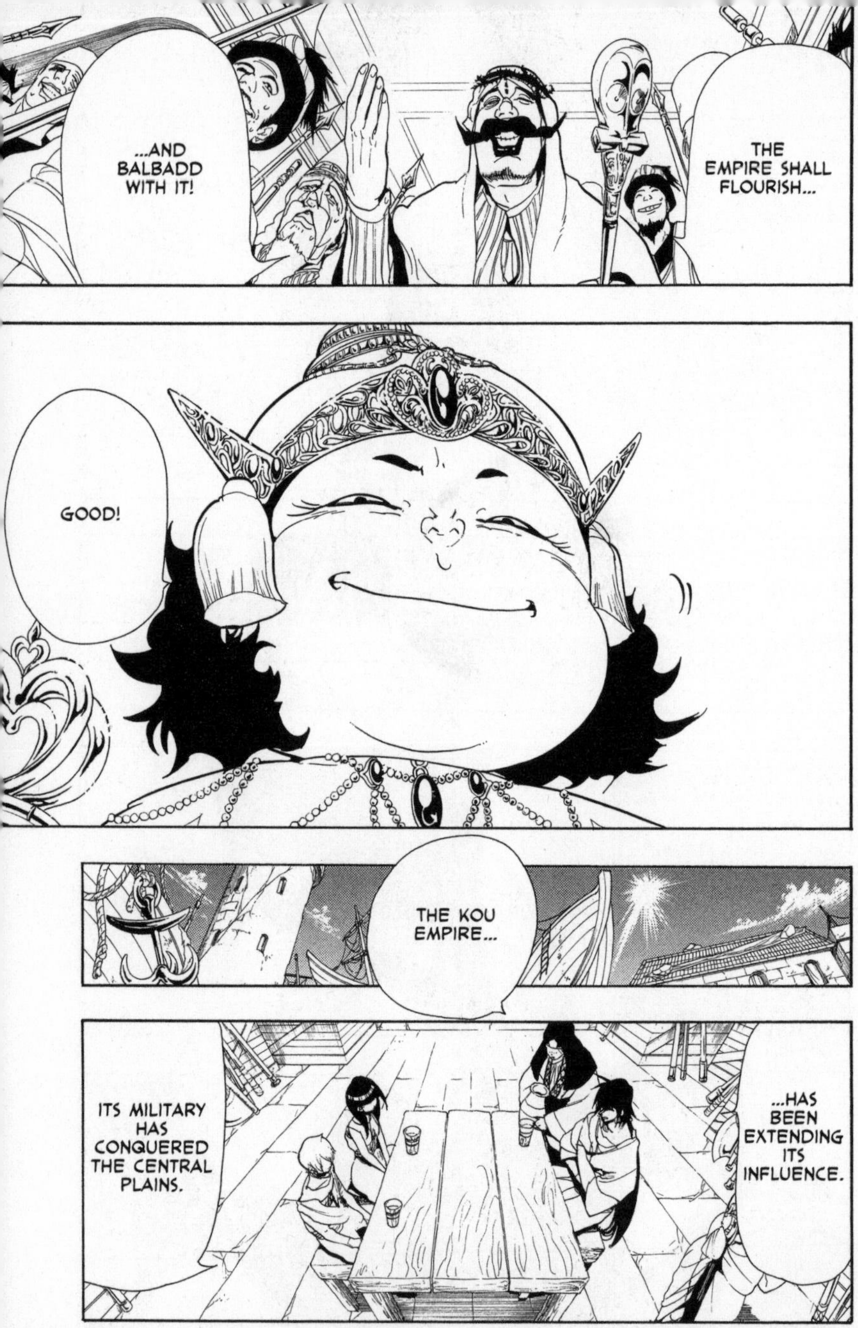
THE EMPIRE SHALL FLOURISH...
...AND BALBADD WITH IT!
GOOD!
THE KOU EMPIRE...
...HAS BEEN EXTENDING ITS INFLUENCE.
ITS MILITARY HAS CONQUERED THE CENTRAL PLAINS.

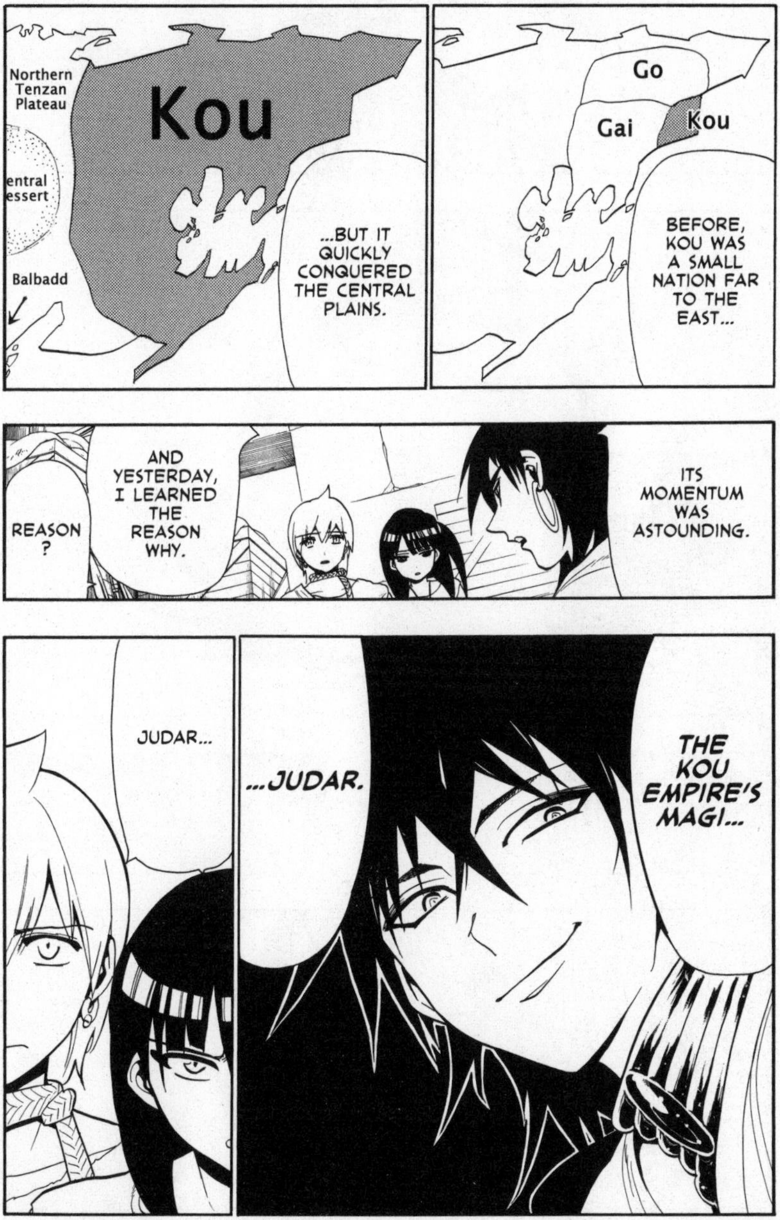
Go
Gai
Kou
BEFORE, KOU WAS A SMALL NATION FAR TO THE EAST...
Northern Tenzan Plateau
Kou
entral essert
Balbadd
...BUT IT QUICKLY CONQUERED THE CENTRAL PLAINS.
ITS MOMENTUM WAS ASTOUNDING.
AND YESTERDAY, I LEARNED THE REASON WHY.
REASON?
THE KOU EMPIRE'S MAGI...
...JUDAR.
JUDAR...

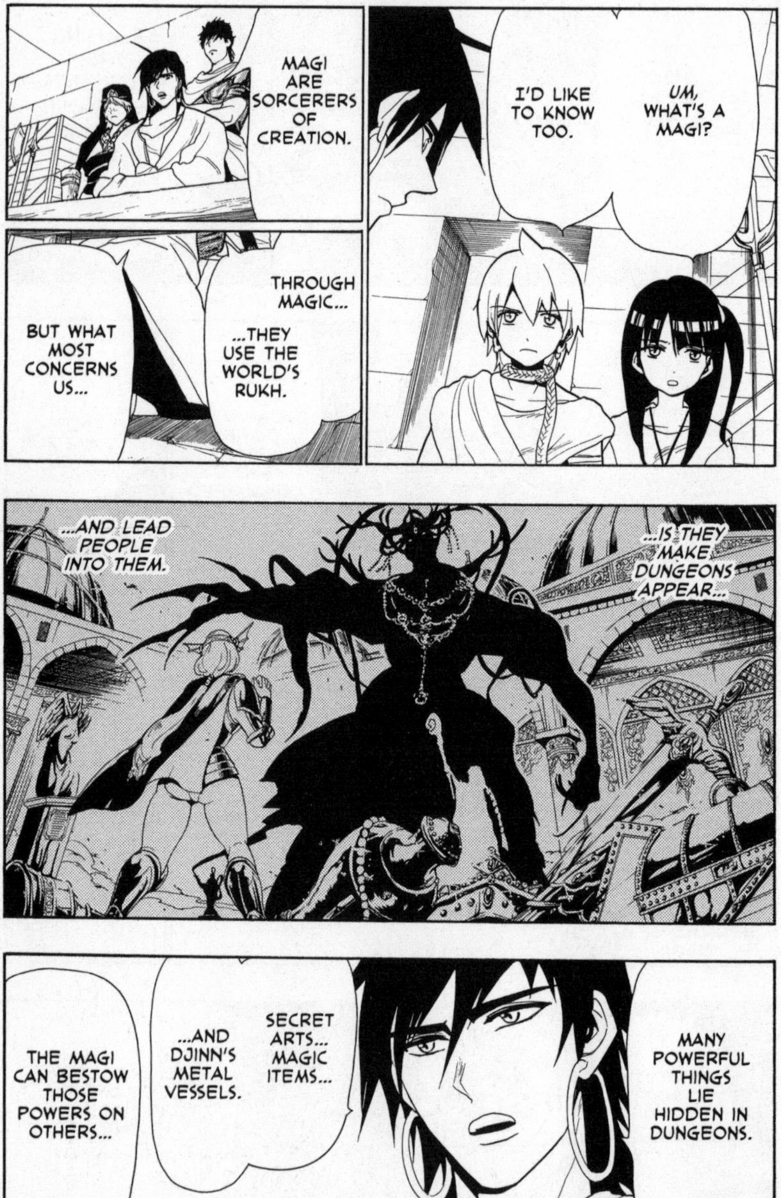
UM, WHAT'S A MAGI?
I'D LIKE TO KNOW TOO.
MAGI ARE SORCERERS OF CREATION.
THROUGH MAGIC...
...THEY USE THE WORLD'S RUKH.
BUT WHAT MOST CONCERNS US...
...IS THEY MAKE DUNGEONS APPEAR...
...AND LEAD PEOPLE INTO THEM.
MANY POWERFUL THINGS LIE HIDDEN IN DUNGEONS.
SECRET ARTS... MAGIC ITEMS...
...AND DJINN'S METAL VESSELS.
THE MAGI CAN BESTOW THOSE POWERS ON OTHERS...

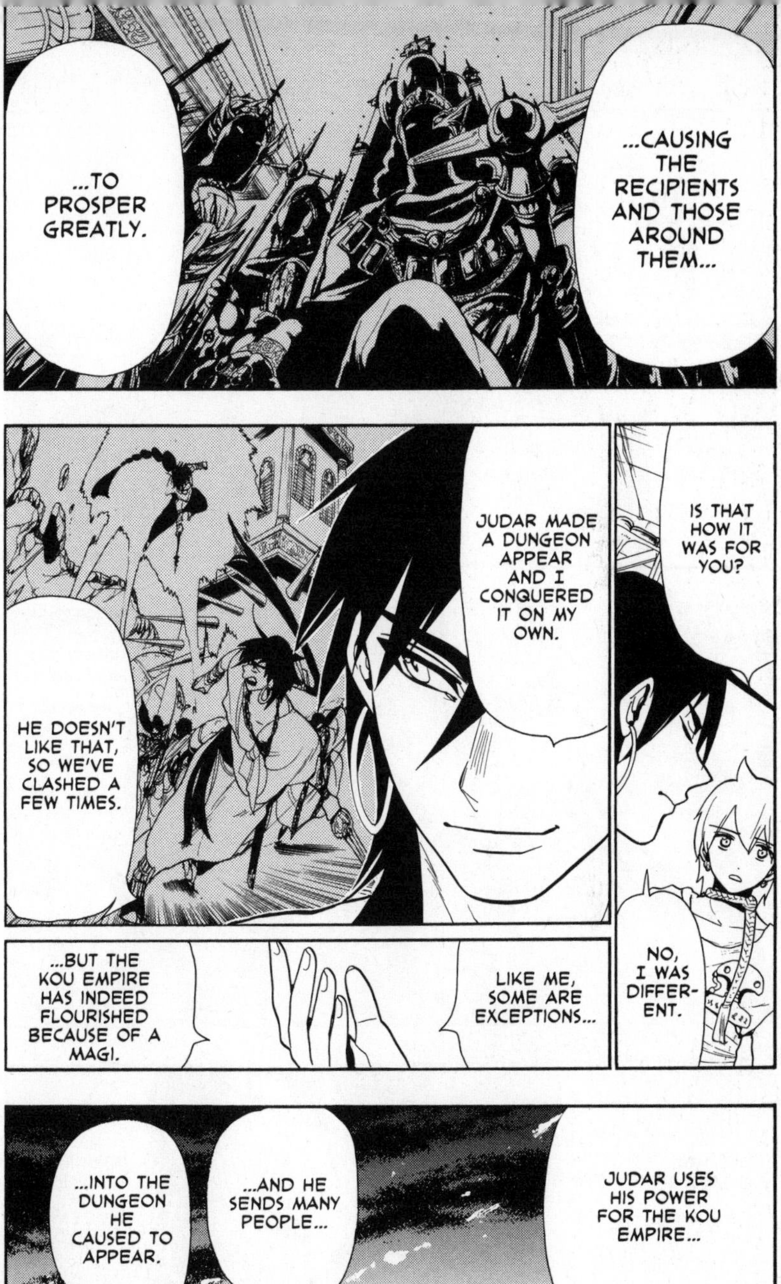
...CAUSING THE RECIPIENTS AND THOSE AROUND THEM...
...TO PROSPER GREATLY.
IS THAT HOW IT WAS FOR YOU?
NO, I WAS DIFFER-ENT.
JUDAR MADE A DUNGEON APPEAR AND I CONQUERED IT ON MY OWN.
HE DOESN'T LIKE THAT, SO WE'VE CLASHED A FEW TIMES.
LIKE ME, SOME ARE EXCEPTIONS...
...BUT THE KOU EMPIRE HAS INDEED FLOURISHED BECAUSE OF A MAGI.
JUDAR USES HIS POWER FOR THE KOU EMPIRE...
...AND HE SENDS MANY PEOPLE...
...INTO THE DUNGEON HE CAUSED TO APPEAR.

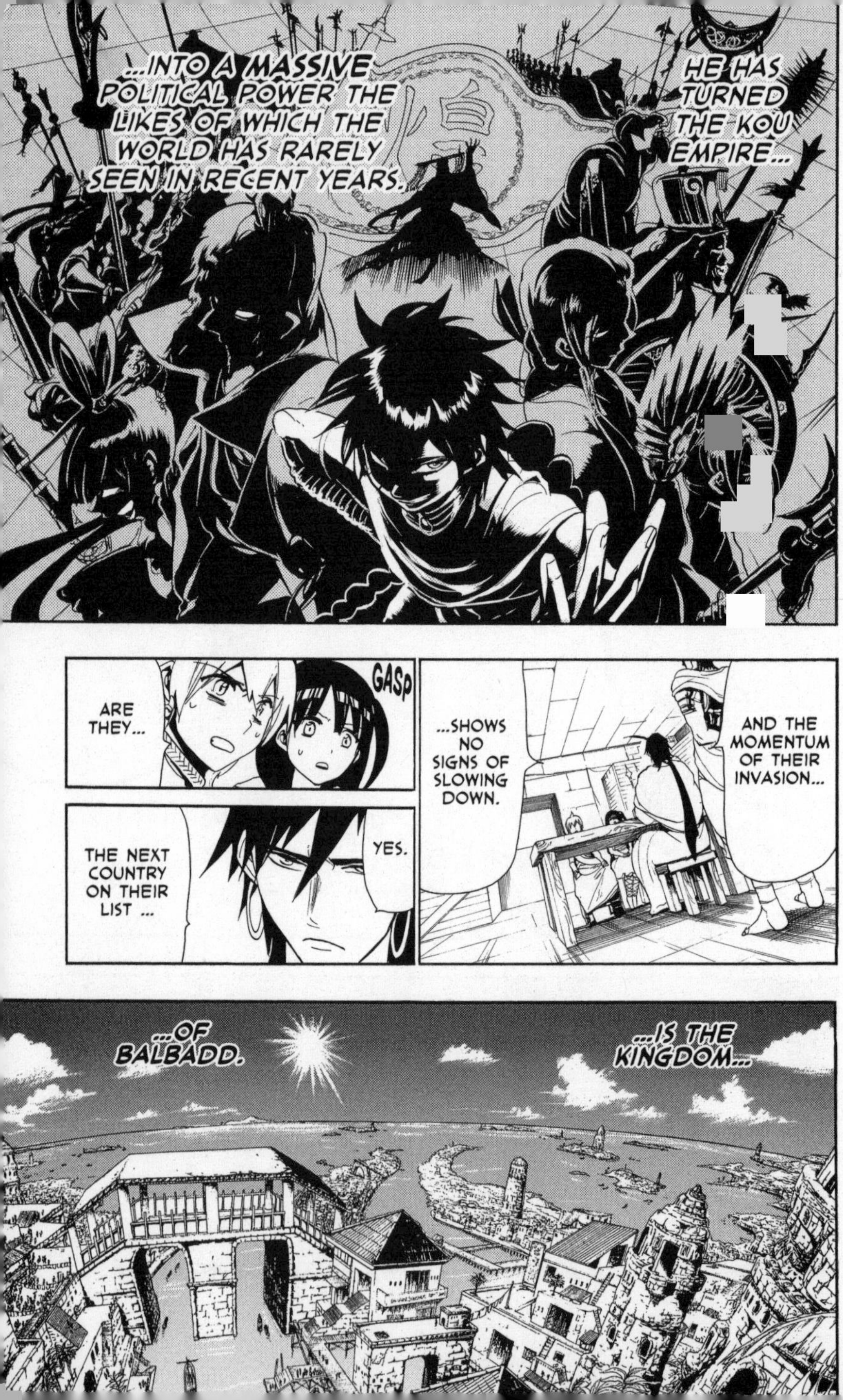
HE HAS TURNED THE KOU EMPIRE...
...INTO A MASSIVE POLITICAL POWER THE LIKES OF WHICH THE WORLD HAS RARELY SEEN IN RECENT YEARS.
AND THE MOMENTUM OF THEIR INVASION...
...SHOWS NO SIGNS OF SLOWING DOWN.
GASP
ARE THEY...
YES.
THE NEXT COUNTRY ON THEIR LIST ...
...IS THE KINGDOM...
...OF BALBADD.

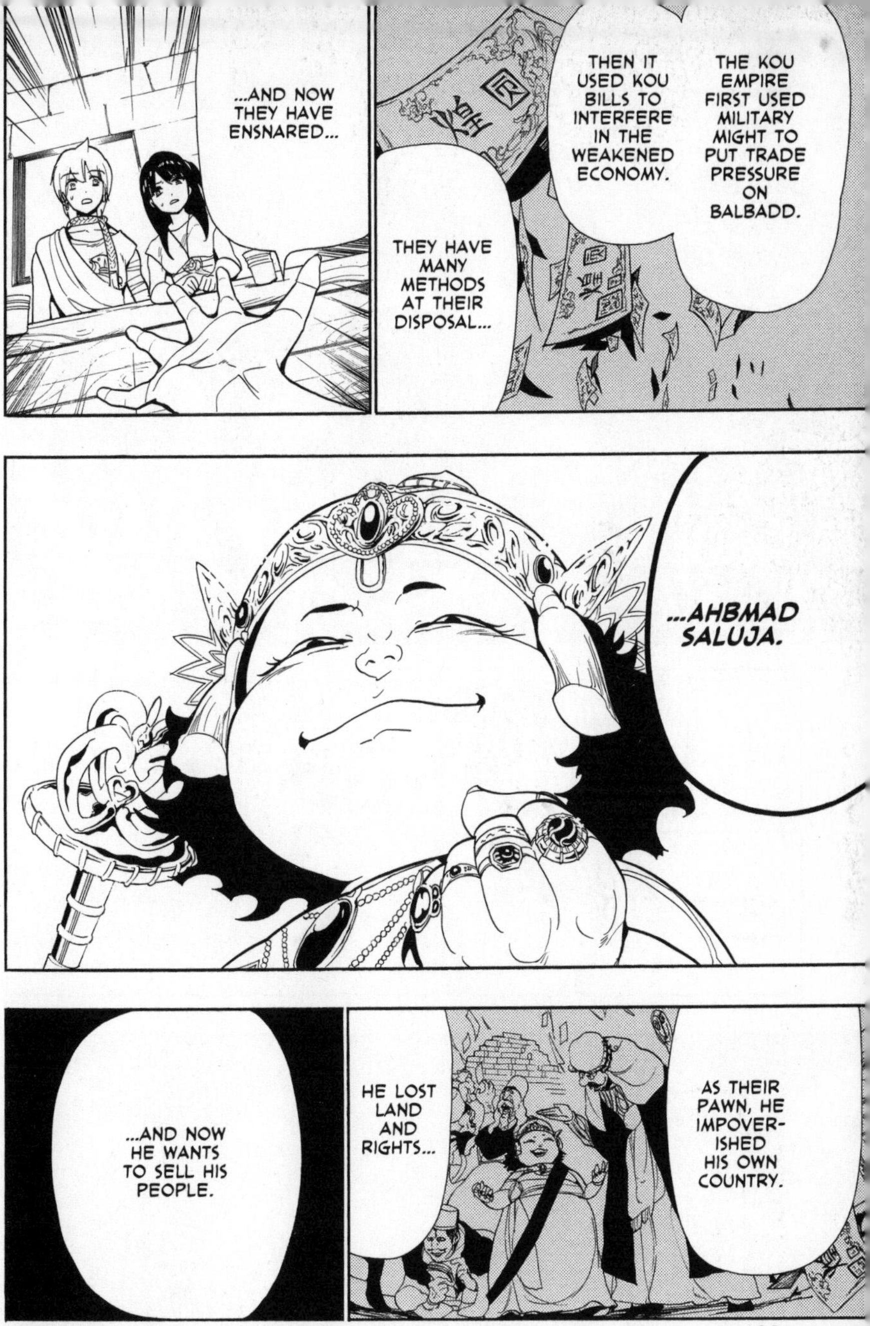
THE KOU EMPIRE FIRST USED MILITARY MIGHT TO PUT TRADE PRESSURE ON BALBADD.
THEN IT USED KOU BILLS TO INTERFERE IN THE WEAKENED ECONOMY.
THEY HAVE MANY METHODS AT THEIR DISPOSAL...
...AND NOW THEY HAVE ENSNARED...
...AHBMAD SALUJA.
AS THEIR PAWN, HE IMPOVERISHED HIS OWN COUNTRY.
HE LOST LAND AND RIGHTS...
...AND NOW HE WANTS TO SELL HIS PEOPLE.

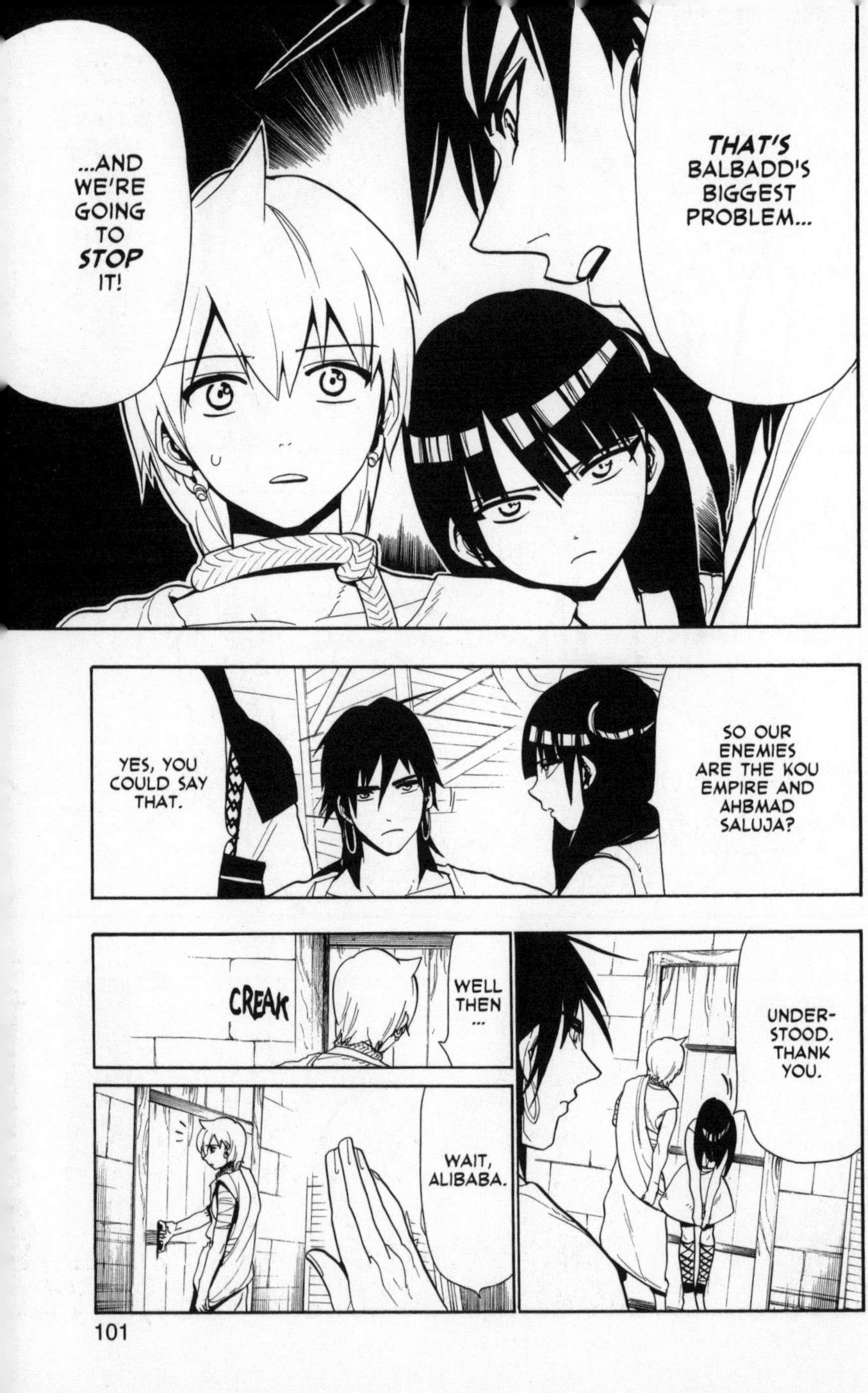
THAT'S BALBADD'S BIGGEST PROBLEM...
...AND WE'RE GOING TO STOP IT!
SO OUR ENEMIES ARE THE KOU EMPIRE AND AHBMAD SALUJA?
YES, YOU COULD SAY THAT.
UNDER-STOOD. THANK YOU.
WELL THEN ...
CREAK
WAIT, ALIBABA.

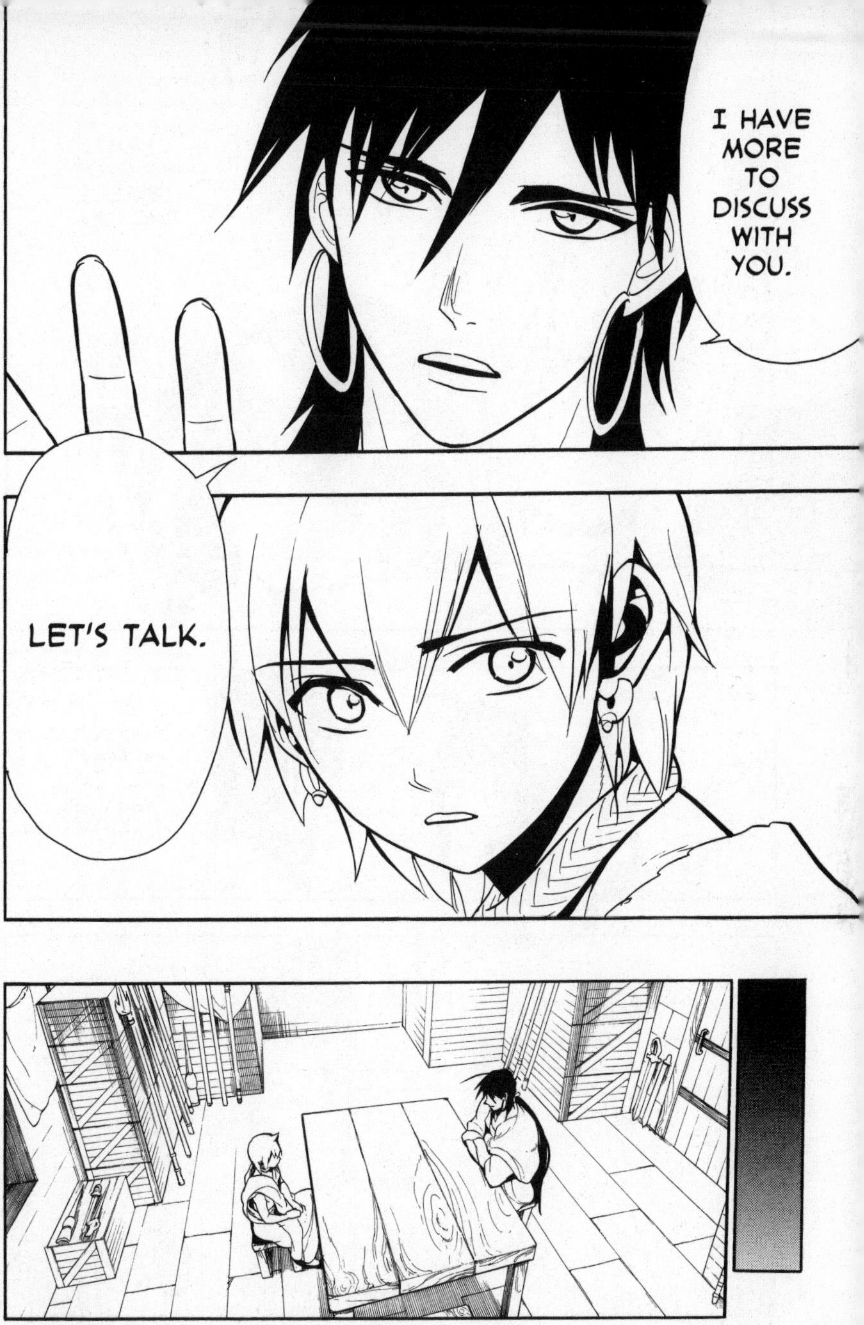
I HAVE MORE TO DISCUSS WITH YOU.
LET'S TALK.

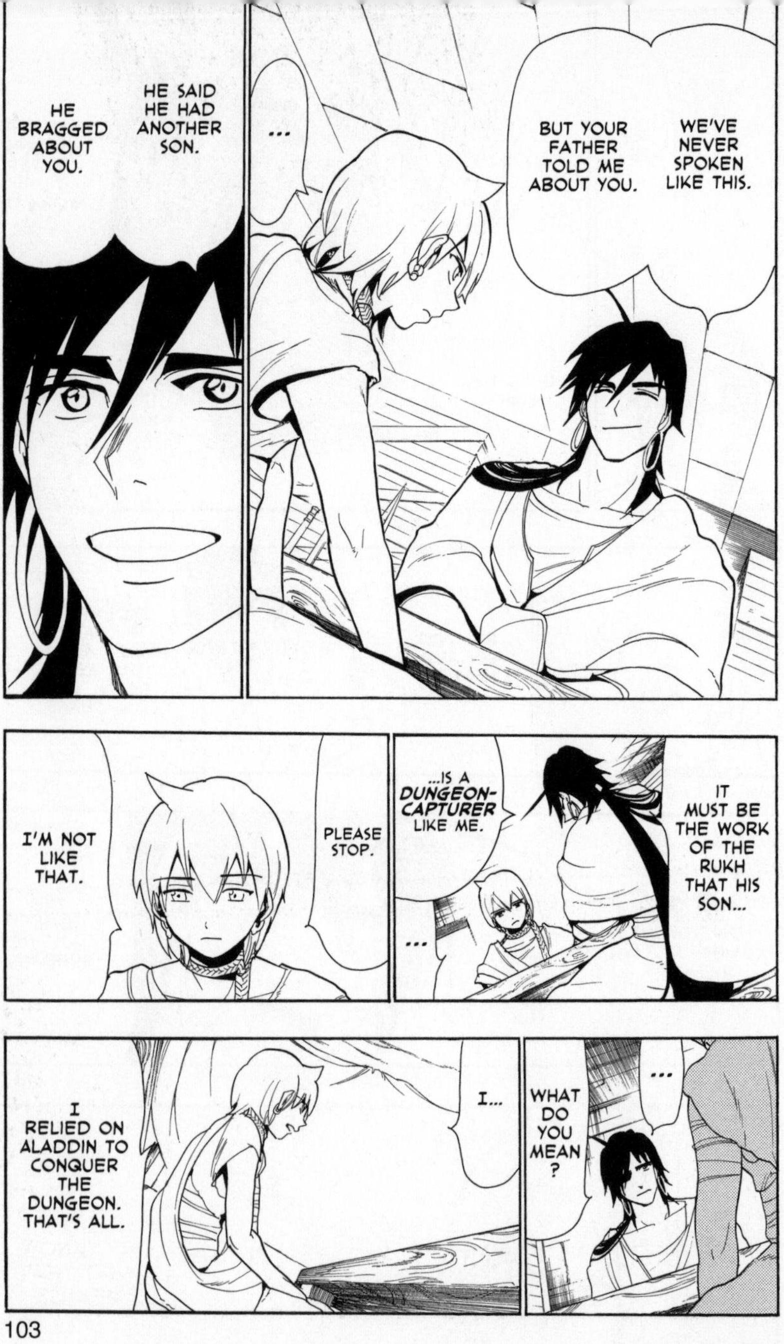
WE'VE NEVER SPOKEN LIKE THIS.
BUT YOUR FATHER TOLD ME ABOUT YOU.
...
HE SAID HE HAD ANOTHER SON.
HE BRAGGED ABOUT YOU.
IT MUST BE THE WORK OF THE RUKH THAT HIS SON...
...IS A *DUNGEON-CAPTURER* LIKE ME.
...
PLEASE STOP.
I'M NOT LIKE THAT.
...
WHAT DO YOU MEAN?
I...
I RELIED ON ALADDIN TO CONQUER THE DUNGEON. THAT'S ALL.

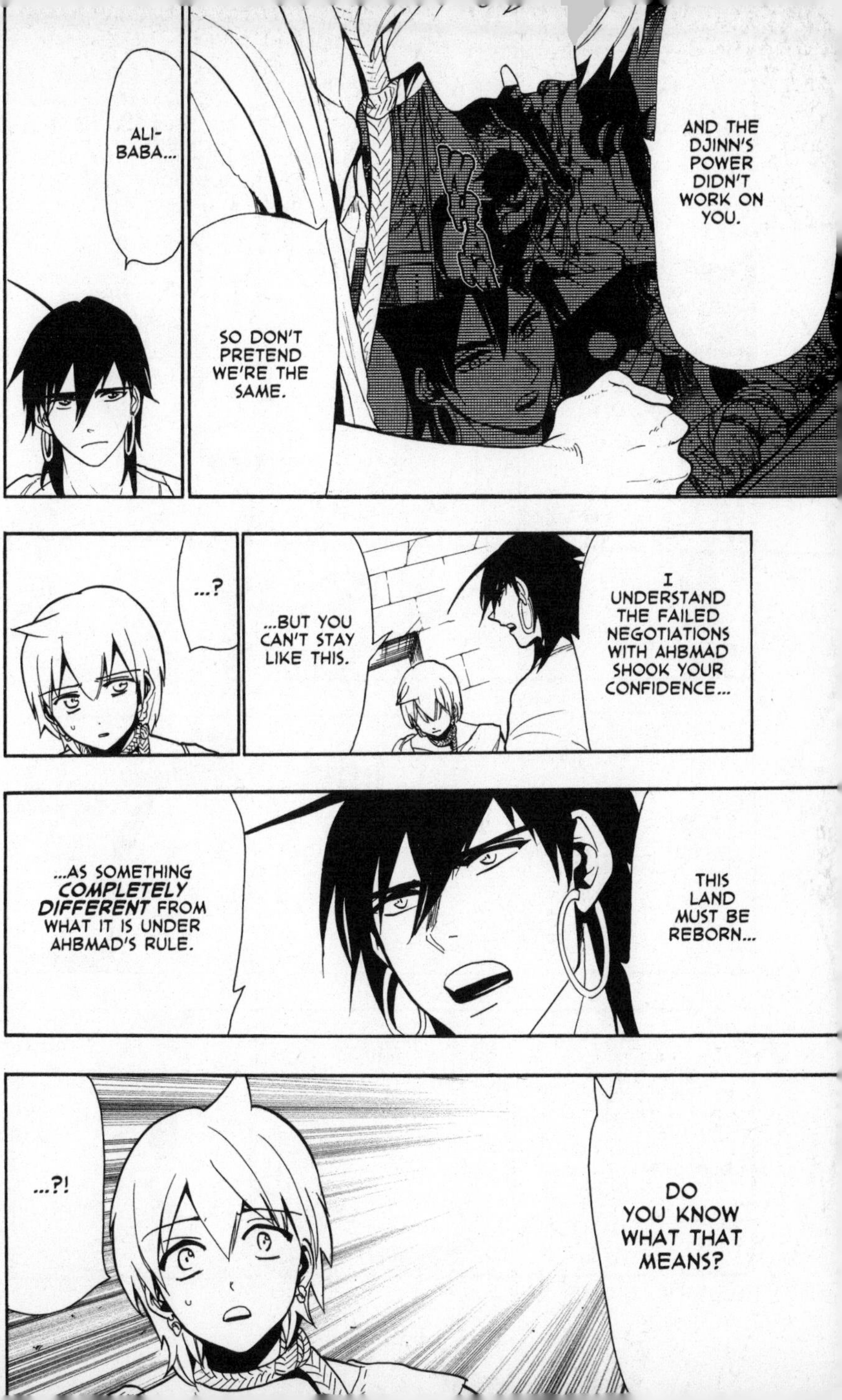
AND THE DJINN'S POWER DIDN'T WORK ON YOU.
SO DON'T PRETEND WE'RE THE SAME.
ALI-BABA...
I UNDERSTAND THE FAILED NEGOTIATIONS WITH AHBMAD SHOOK YOUR CONFIDENCE...
...BUT YOU CAN'T STAY LIKE THIS.
...?
THIS LAND MUST BE REBORN...
...AS SOMETHING *COMPLETELY DIFFERENT* FROM WHAT IT IS UNDER AHBMAD'S RULE.
DO YOU KNOW WHAT THAT MEANS?
...?!

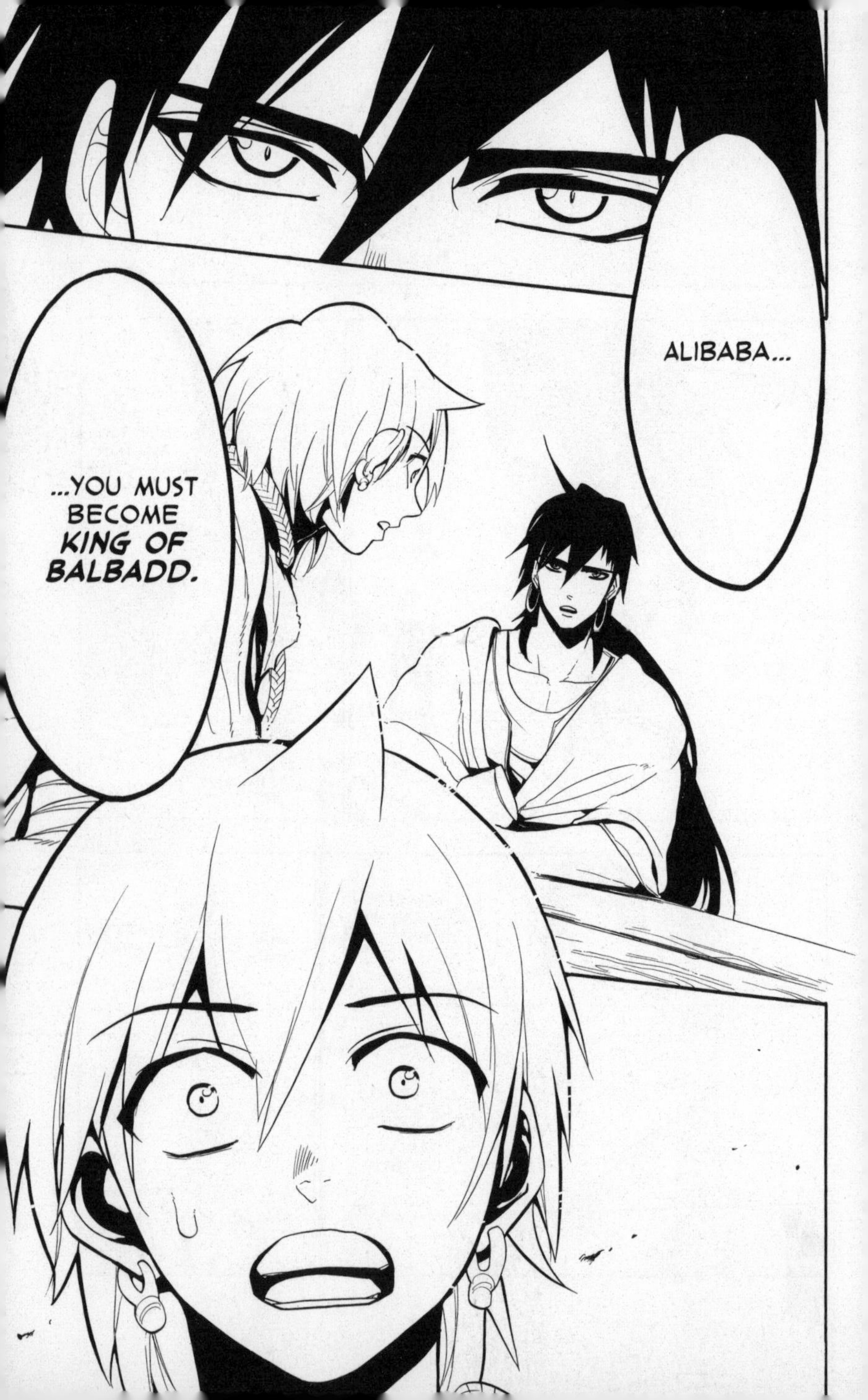
ALIBABA...
...YOU MUST BECOME KING OF BALBADD.

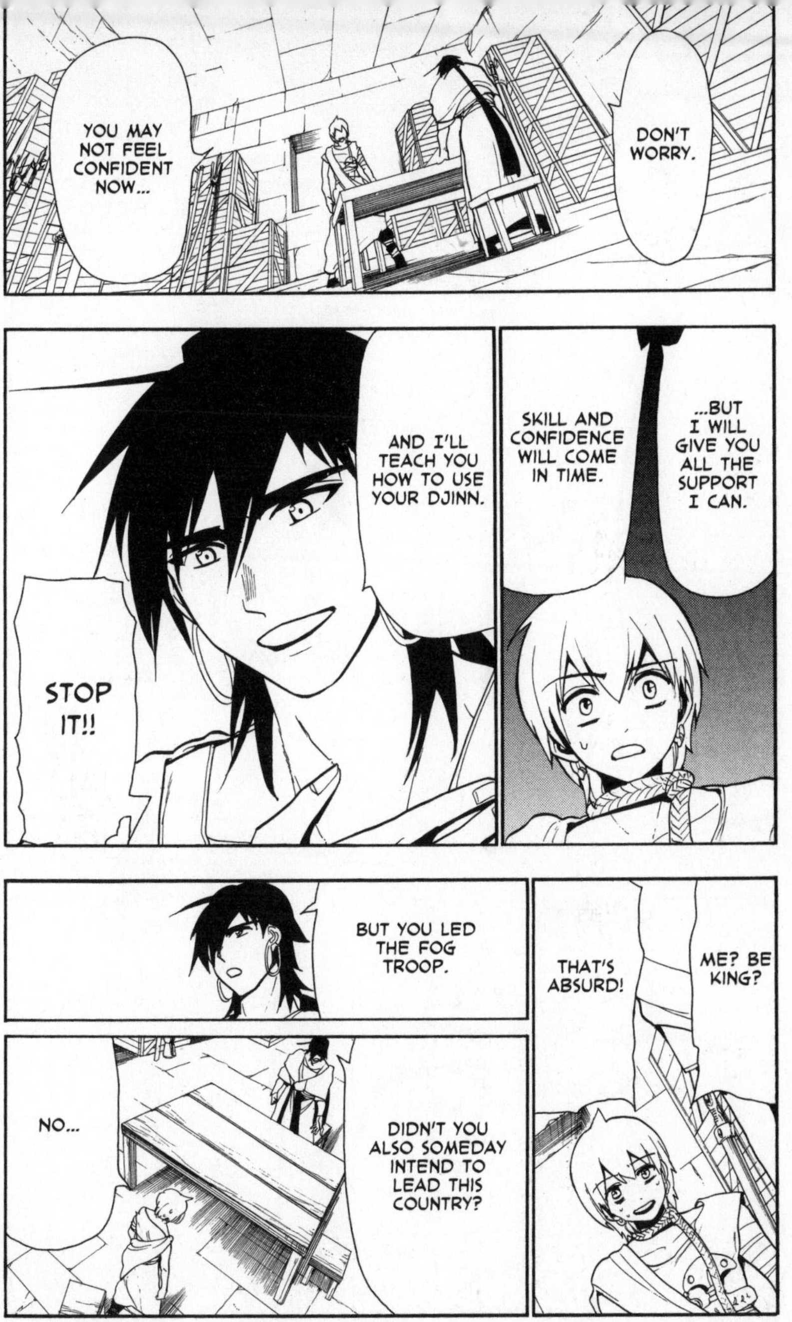
DON'T WORRY.
YOU MAY NOT FEEL CONFIDENT NOW...
...BUT I WILL GIVE YOU ALL THE SUPPORT I CAN.
SKILL AND CONFIDENCE WILL COME IN TIME.
AND I'LL TEACH YOU HOW TO USE YOUR DJINN.
STOP IT!!
ME? BE KING?
THAT'S ABSURD!
BUT YOU LED THE FOG TROOP.
DIDN'T YOU ALSO SOMEDAY INTEND TO LEAD THIS COUNTRY?
NO...

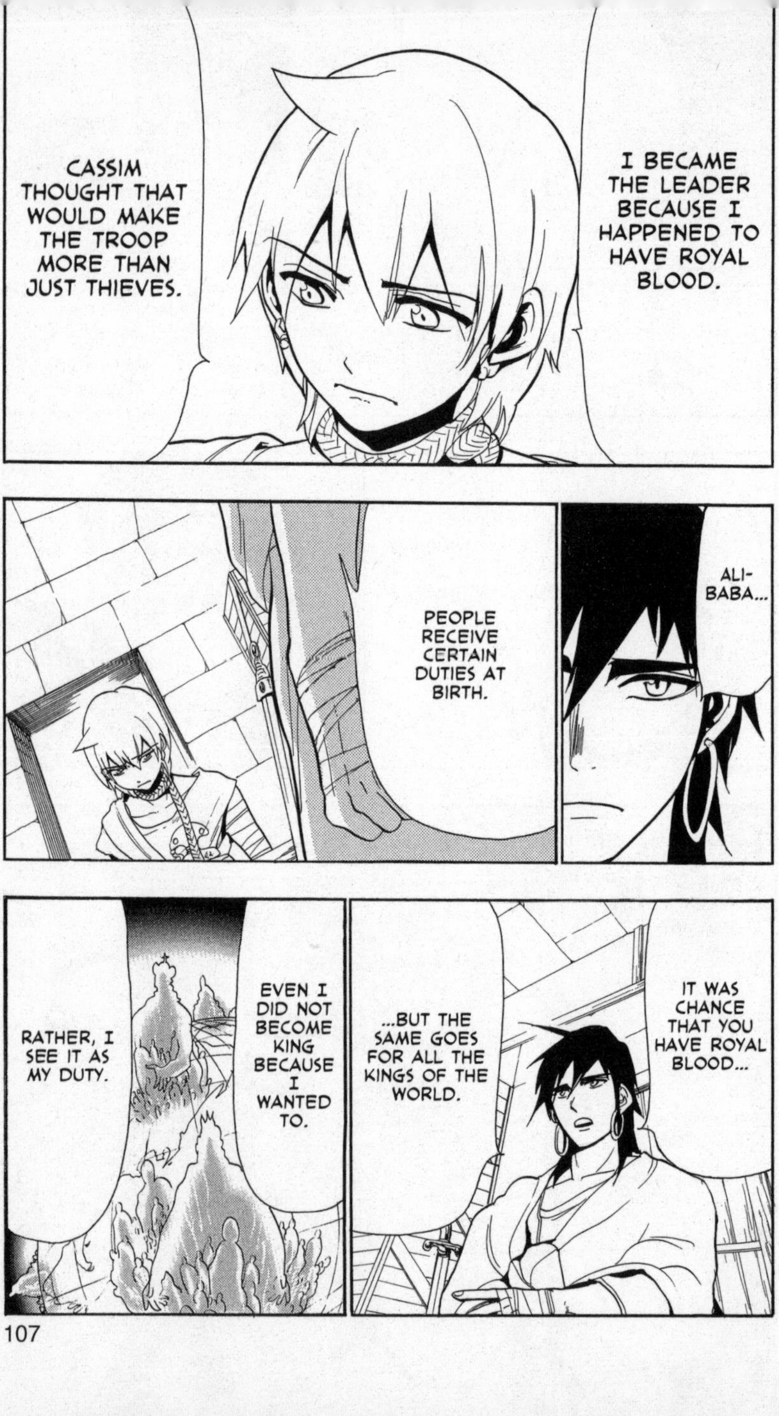
I BECAME THE LEADER BECAUSE I HAPPENED TO HAVE ROYAL BLOOD.
CASSIM THOUGHT THAT WOULD MAKE THE TROOP MORE THAN JUST THIEVES.
ALI-BABA...
PEOPLE RECEIVE CERTAIN DUTIES AT BIRTH.
IT WAS CHANCE THAT YOU HAVE ROYAL BLOOD...
...BUT THE SAME GOES FOR ALL THE KINGS OF THE WORLD.
EVEN I DID NOT BECOME KING BECAUSE I WANTED TO.
RATHER, I SEE IT AS MY DUTY.

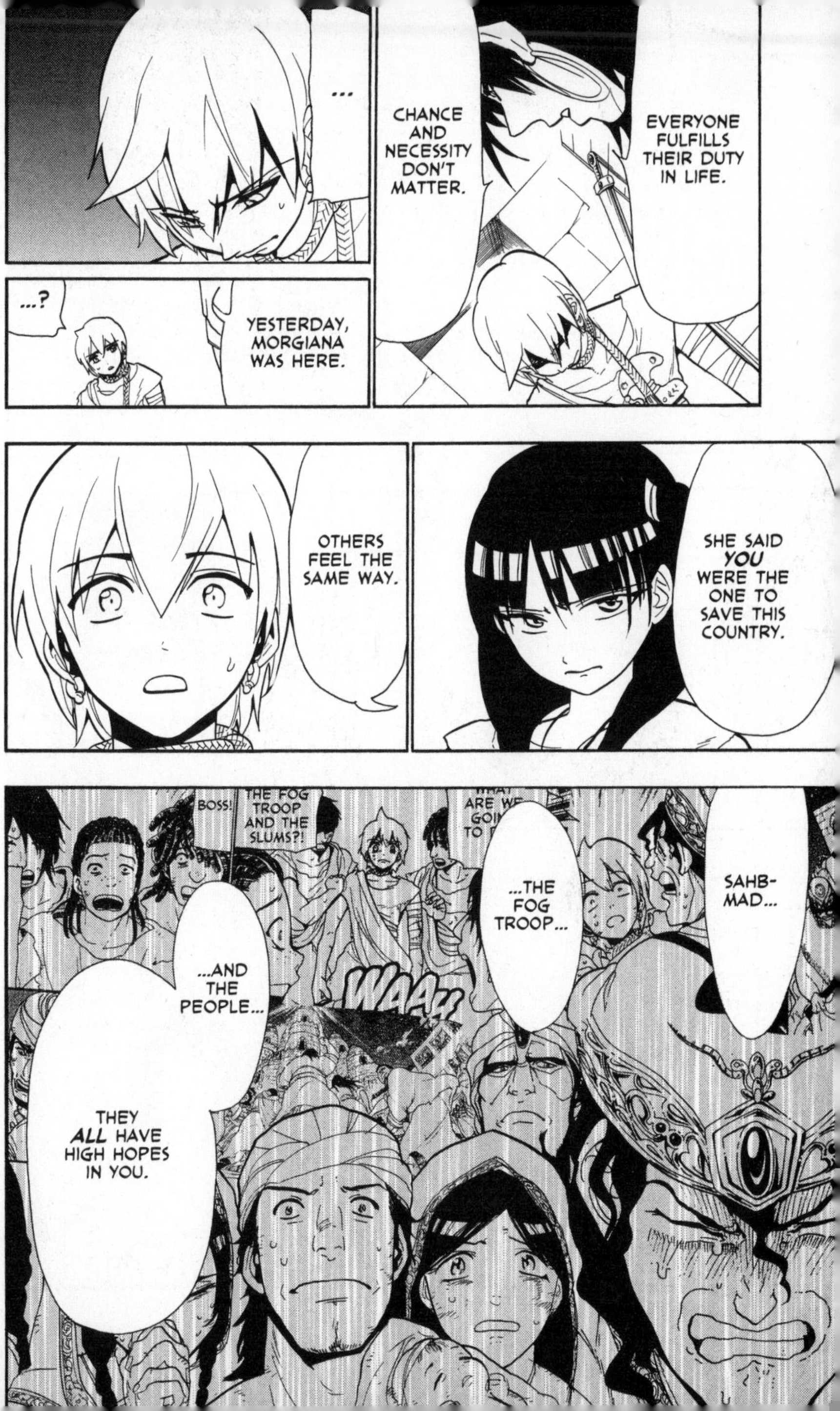
EVERYONE FULFILLS THEIR DUTY IN LIFE.
CHANCE AND NECESSITY DON'T MATTER.
...
...?
YESTERDAY, MORGIANA WAS HERE.
SHE SAID YOU WERE THE ONE TO SAVE THIS COUNTRY.
OTHERS FEEL THE SAME WAY.
SAHB-MAD...
THE FOG TROOP AND THE SLUMS?!
BOSS!
...THE FOG TROOP...
WAAH
...AND THE PEOPLE...
THEY ALL HAVE HIGH HOPES IN YOU.

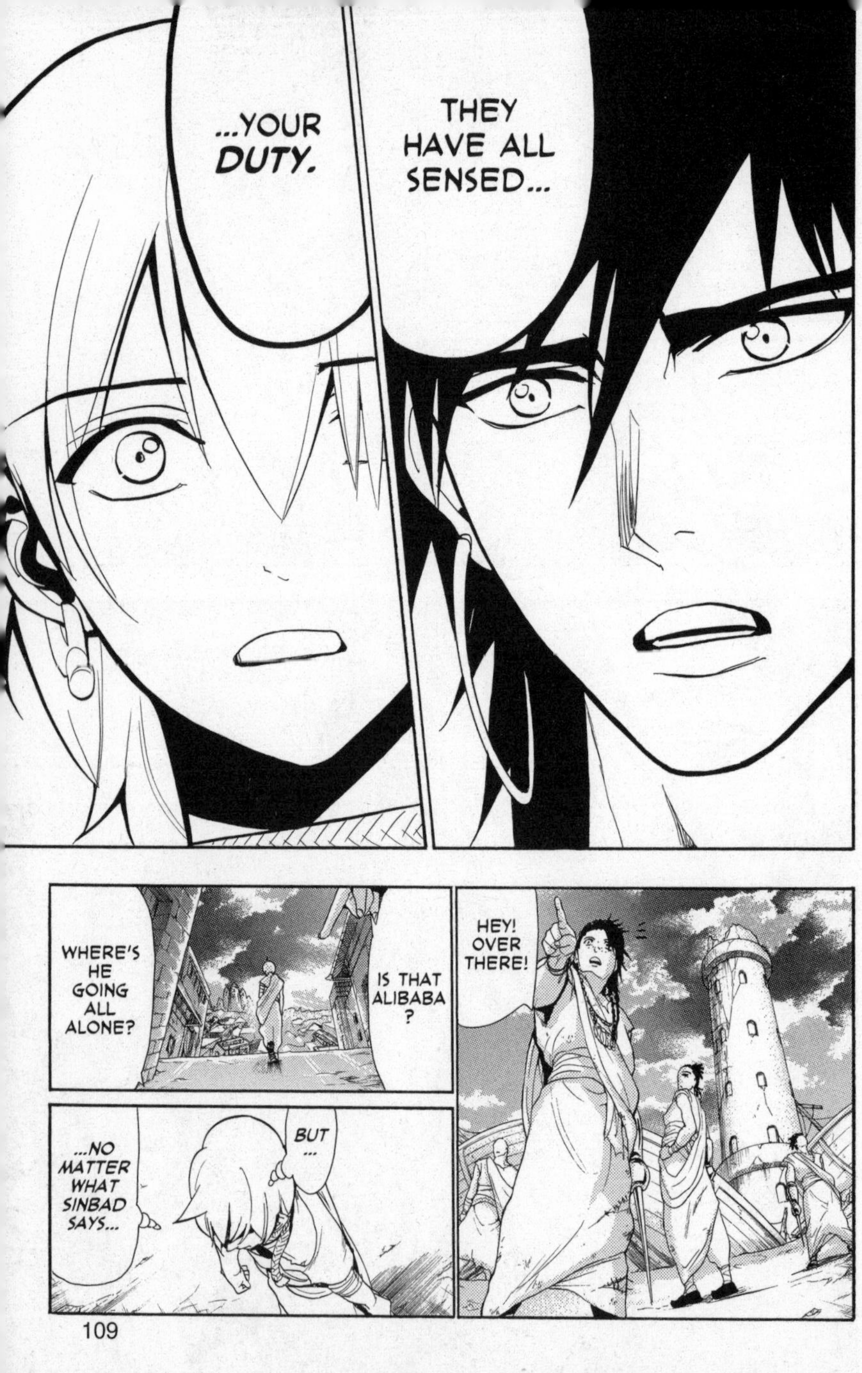
THEY HAVE ALL SENSED...
...YOUR DUTY.
HEY! OVER THERE!
IS THAT ALIBABA ?
WHERE'S HE GOING ALL ALONE?
BUT ...
...NO MATTER WHAT SINBAD SAYS...

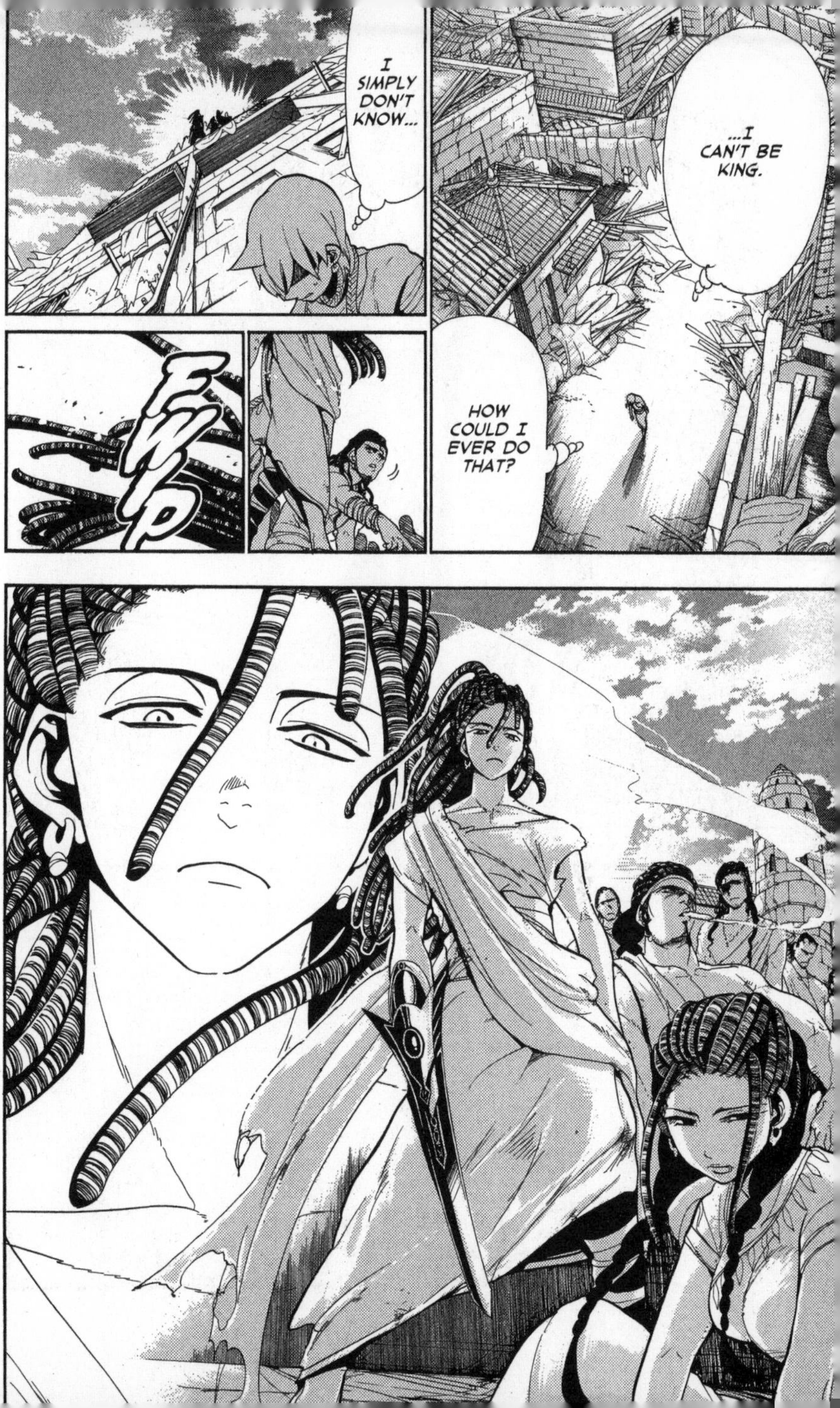
...I CAN'T BE KING.
HOW COULD I EVER DO THAT?
I SIMPLY DON'T KNOW...
FWIP

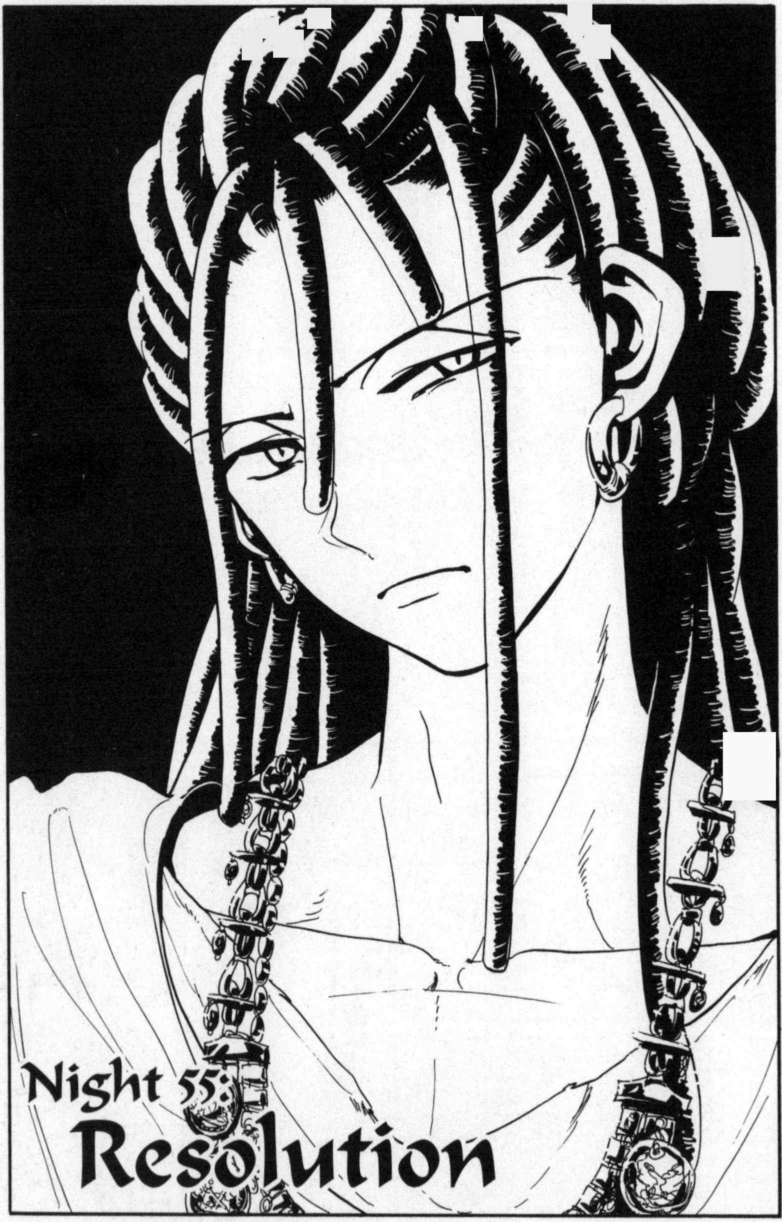
Night 55:
Resolution

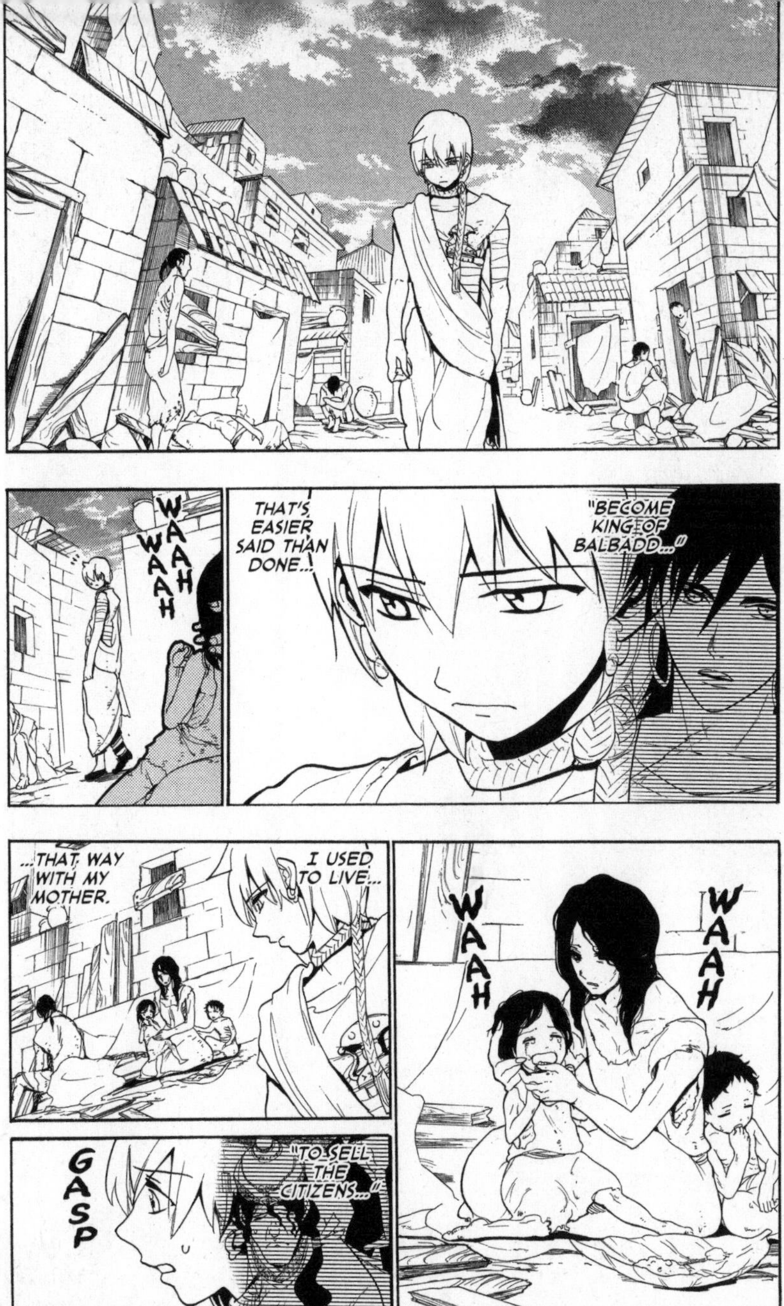
"BECOME KING OF BALBADD..."
THAT'S EASIER SAID THAN DONE...
WAAH WAAH
WAAH
WAAH
I USED TO LIVE...
...THAT WAY WITH MY MOTHER.
"TO SELL THE CITIZENS..."
GASP

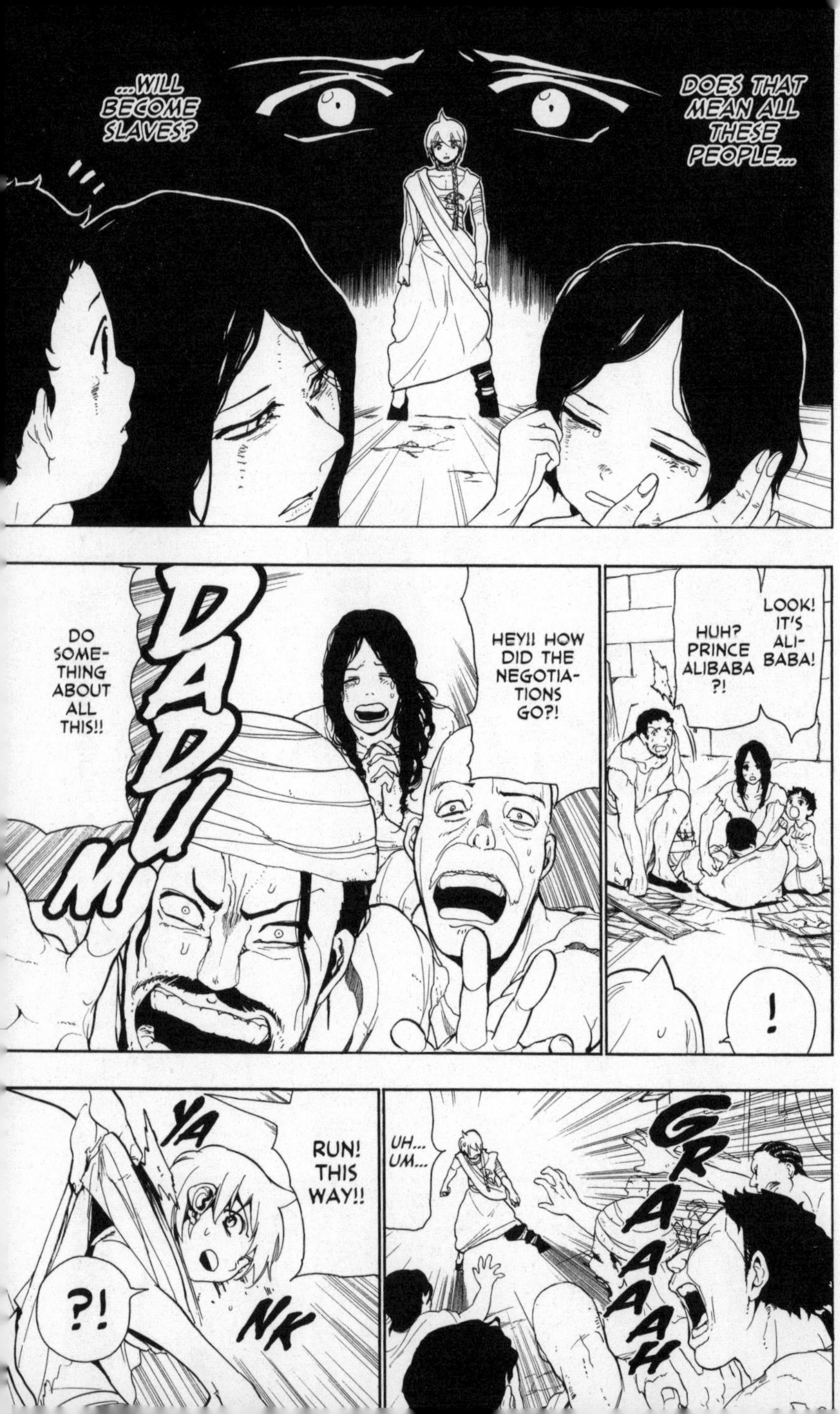
DOES THAT MEAN ALL THESE PEOPLE...
...WILL BECOME SLAVES?
LOOK! IT'S ALI-BABA!
HUH? PRINCE ALIBABA ?!
!
HEY!! HOW DID THE NEGOTIA-TIONS GO?!
DADUM
DO SOME-THING ABOUT ALL THIS!!
GRAAAAAH
UH... UM...
RUN! THIS WAY!!
YANK
?!

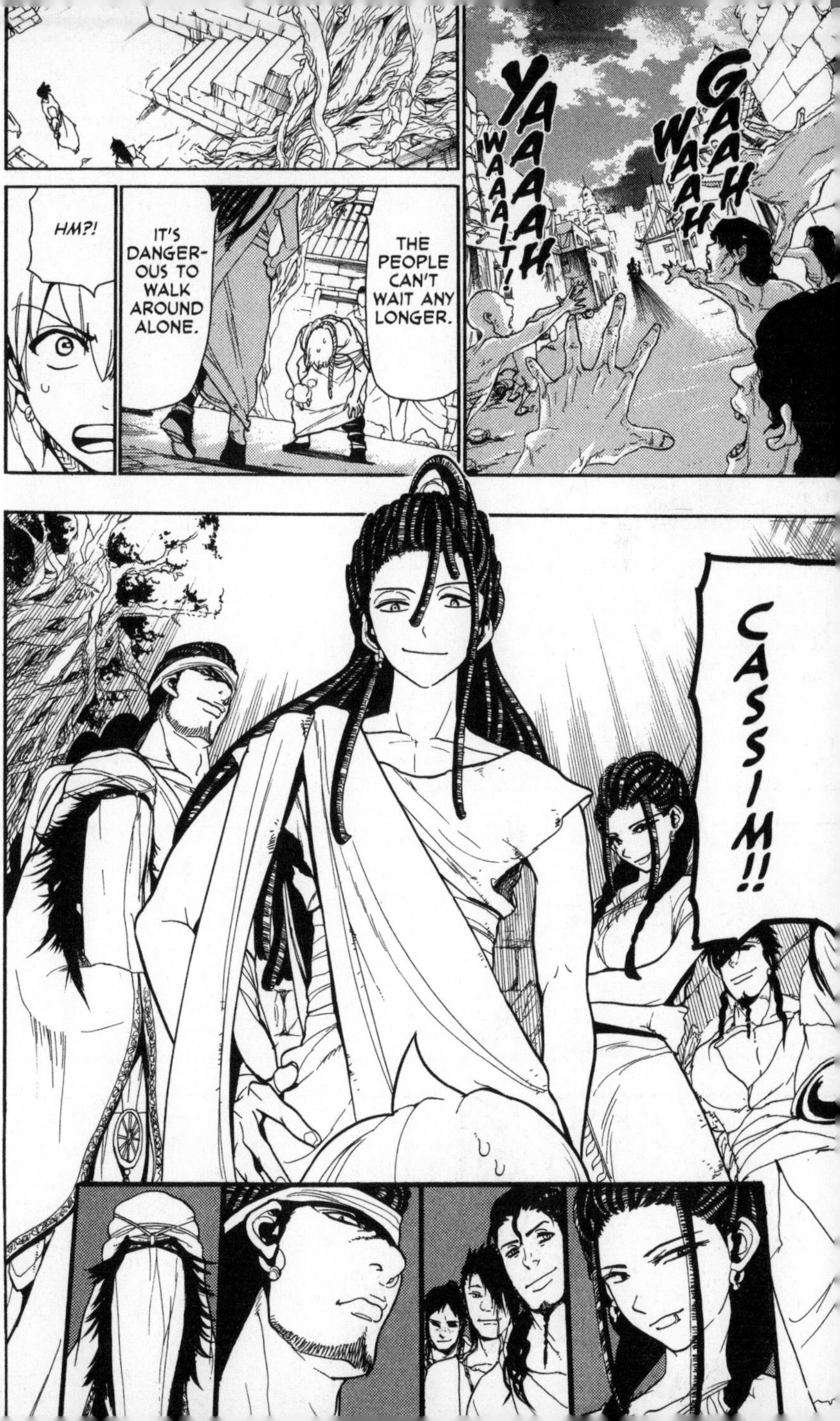
GAAH
WAAH
YAAAAAH
WAAAIT!
THE PEOPLE CAN'T WAIT ANY LONGER.
IT'S DANGER-OUS TO WALK AROUND ALONE.
HM?!
CASSIM!!

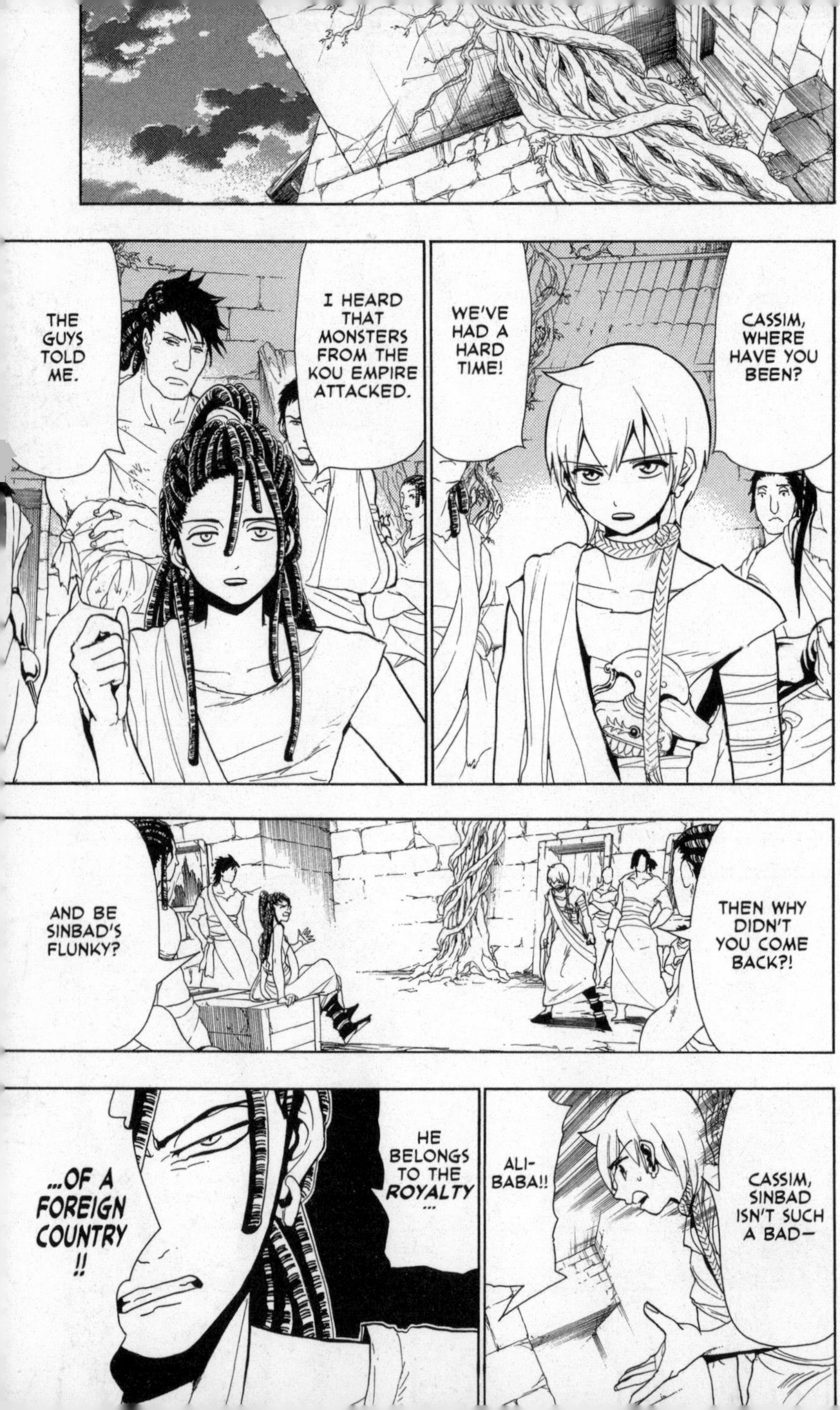

CASSIM, WHERE HAVE YOU BEEN?
WE'VE HAD A HARD TIME!
I HEARD THAT MONSTERS FROM THE KOU EMPIRE ATTACKED.
THE GUYS TOLD ME.
THEN WHY DIDN'T YOU COME BACK?!
AND BE SINBAD'S FLUNKY?
CASSIM, SINBAD ISN'T SUCH A BAD—
ALI-BABA!!
HE BELONGS TO THE *ROYALTY*...
...OF A FOREIGN COUNTRY!!

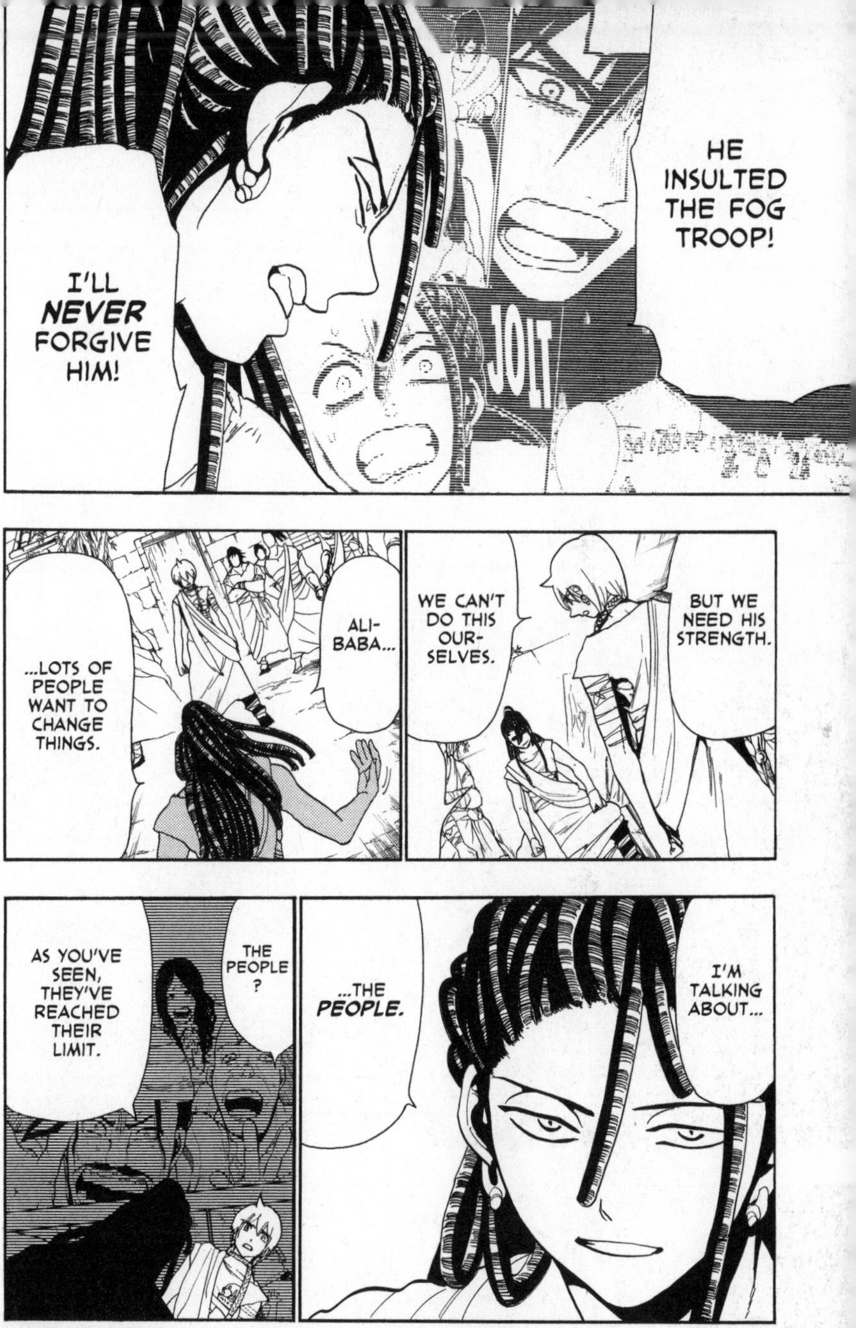
HE INSULTED THE FOG TROOP!
JOLT
I'LL *NEVER* FORGIVE HIM!
BUT WE NEED HIS STRENGTH.
WE CAN'T DO THIS OUR-SELVES.
ALI-BABA...
...LOTS OF PEOPLE WANT TO CHANGE THINGS.
I'M TALKING ABOUT...
...THE *PEOPLE.*
THE PEOPLE?
AS YOU'VE SEEN, THEY'VE REACHED THEIR LIMIT.

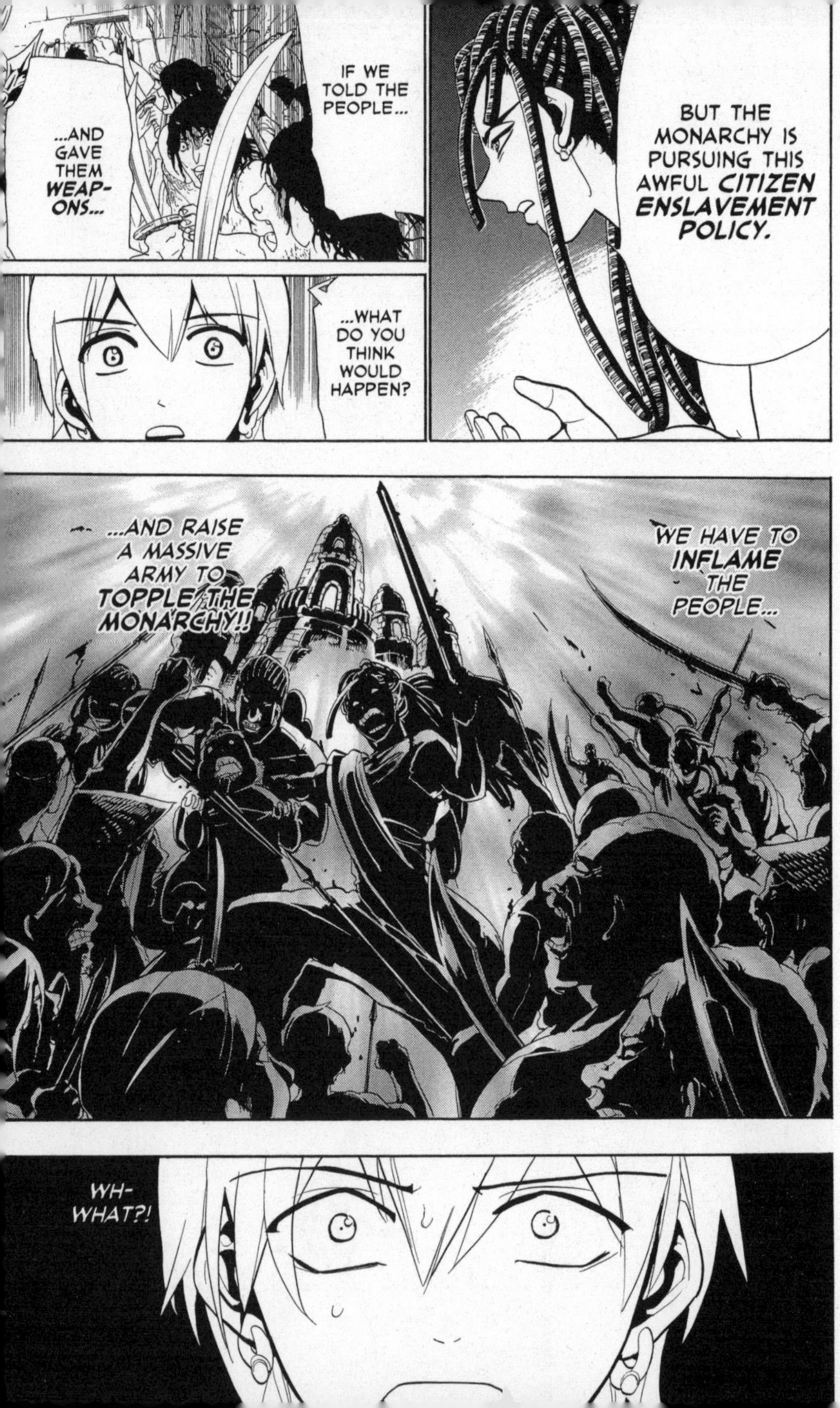
BUT THE MONARCHY IS PURSUING THIS AWFUL CITIZEN ENSLAVEMENT POLICY.
IF WE TOLD THE PEOPLE...
...AND GAVE THEM WEAPONS...
...WHAT DO YOU THINK WOULD HAPPEN?
WE HAVE TO INFLAME THE PEOPLE...
...AND RAISE A MASSIVE ARMY TO TOPPLE THE MONARCHY!!
WH-WHAT?!

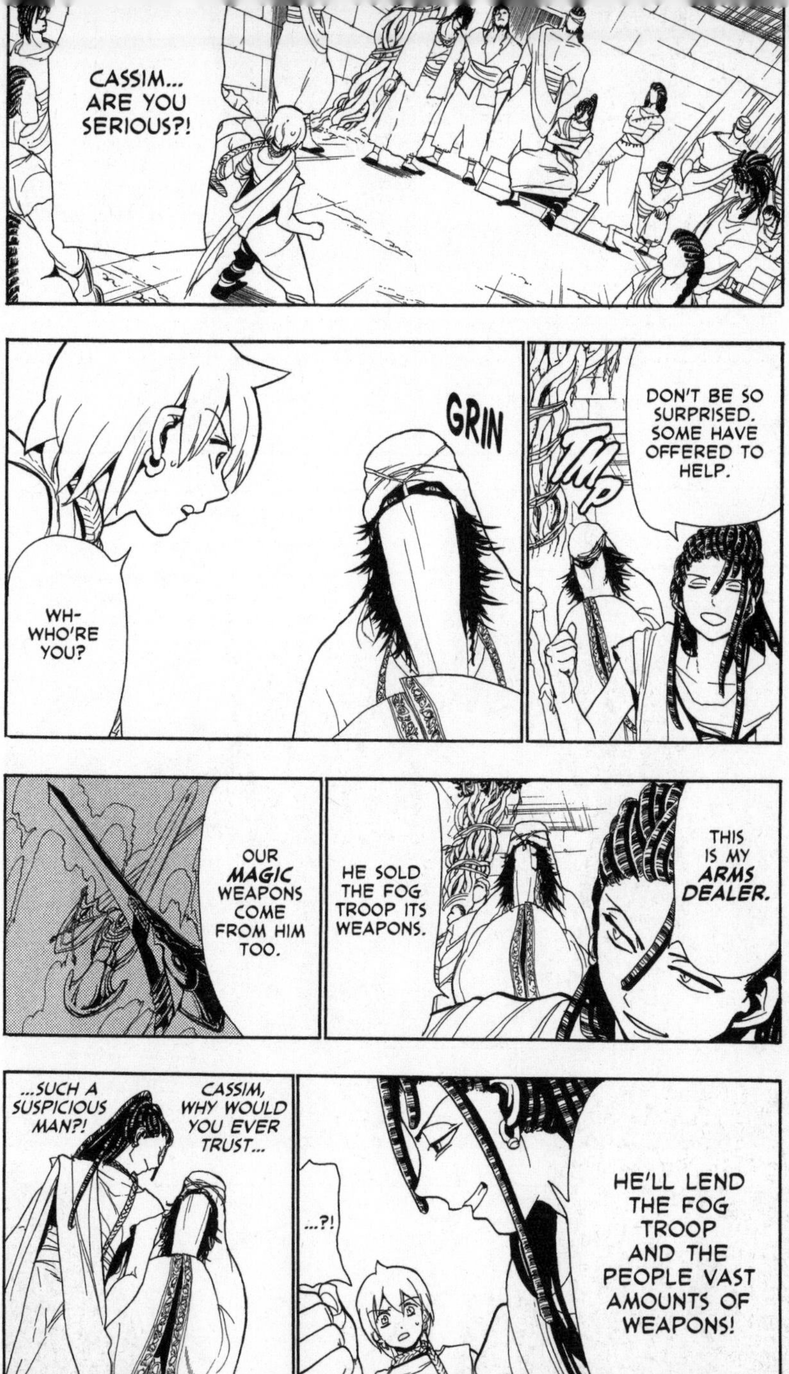
CASSIM... ARE YOU SERIOUS?!
DON'T BE SO SURPRISED. SOME HAVE OFFERED TO HELP.
TMP
GRIN
WH- WHO'RE YOU?
THIS IS MY *ARMS DEALER.*
HE SOLD THE FOG TROOP ITS WEAPONS.
OUR *MAGIC* WEAPONS COME FROM HIM TOO.
HE'LL LEND THE FOG TROOP AND THE PEOPLE VAST AMOUNTS OF WEAPONS!
...?!
CASSIM, WHY WOULD YOU EVER TRUST...
...SUCH A SUSPICIOUS MAN?!

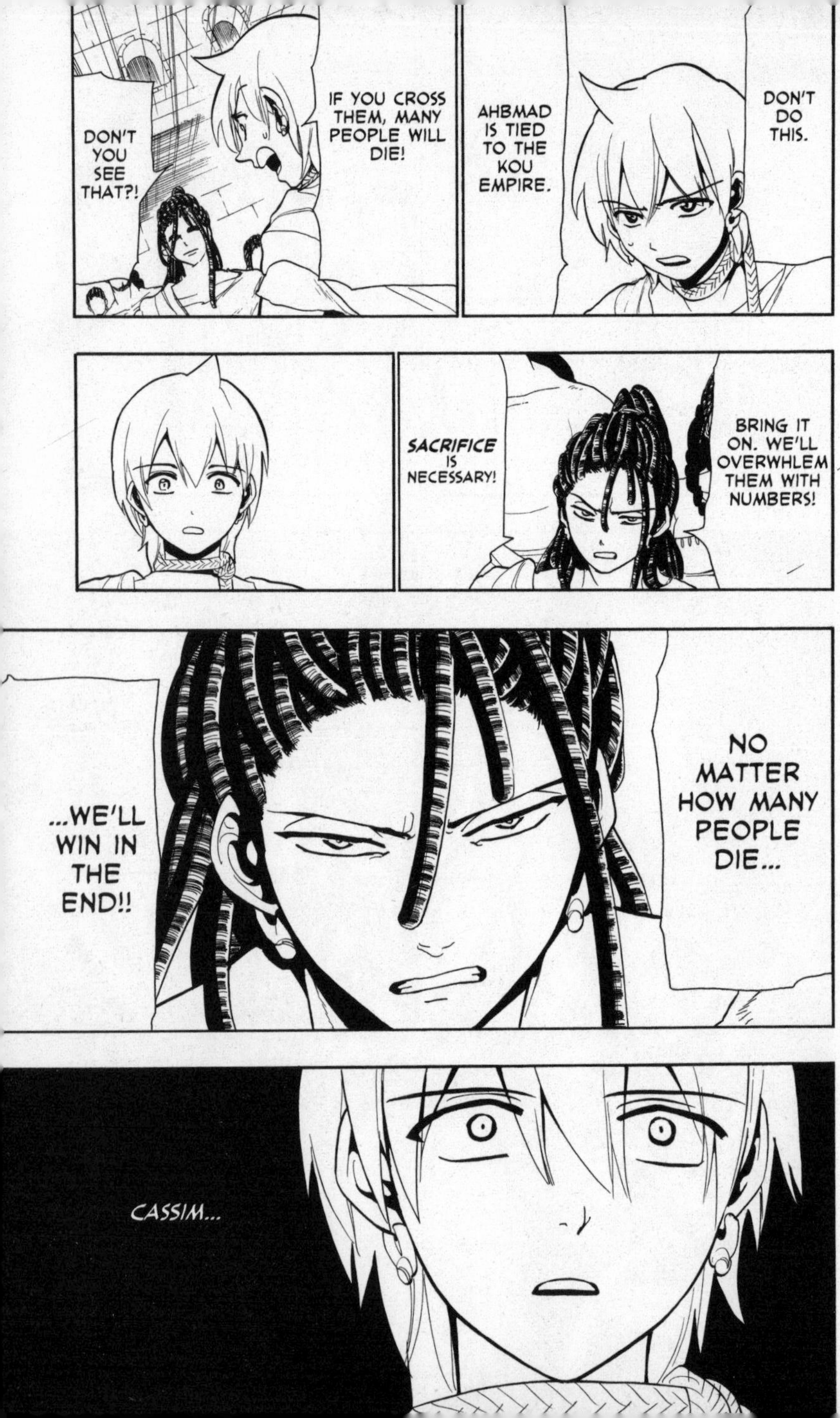
DON'T DO THIS.
AHBMAD IS TIED TO THE KOU EMPIRE.
IF YOU CROSS THEM, MANY PEOPLE WILL DIE!
DON'T YOU SEE THAT?!
BRING IT ON. WE'LL OVERWHLEM THEM WITH NUMBERS!
SACRIFICE IS NECESSARY!
NO MATTER HOW MANY PEOPLE DIE...
...WE'LL WIN IN THE END!!
CASSIM...

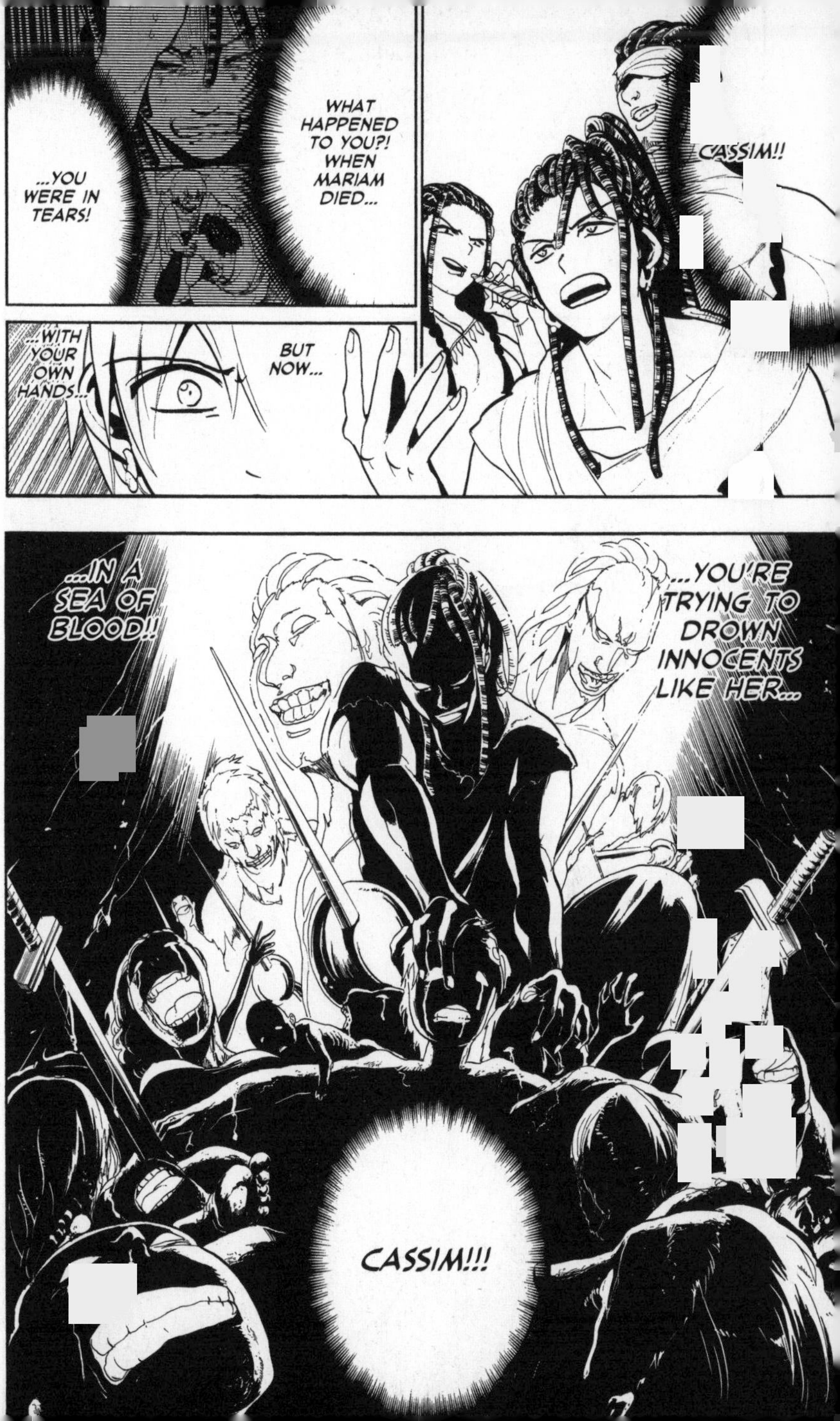
CASSIM!!
WHAT HAPPENED TO YOU?! WHEN MARIAM DIED...
...YOU WERE IN TEARS!
BUT NOW...
...WITH YOUR OWN HANDS...
...YOU'RE TRYING TO DROWN INNOCENTS LIKE HER...
...IN A SEA OF BLOOD!!
CASSIM!!!

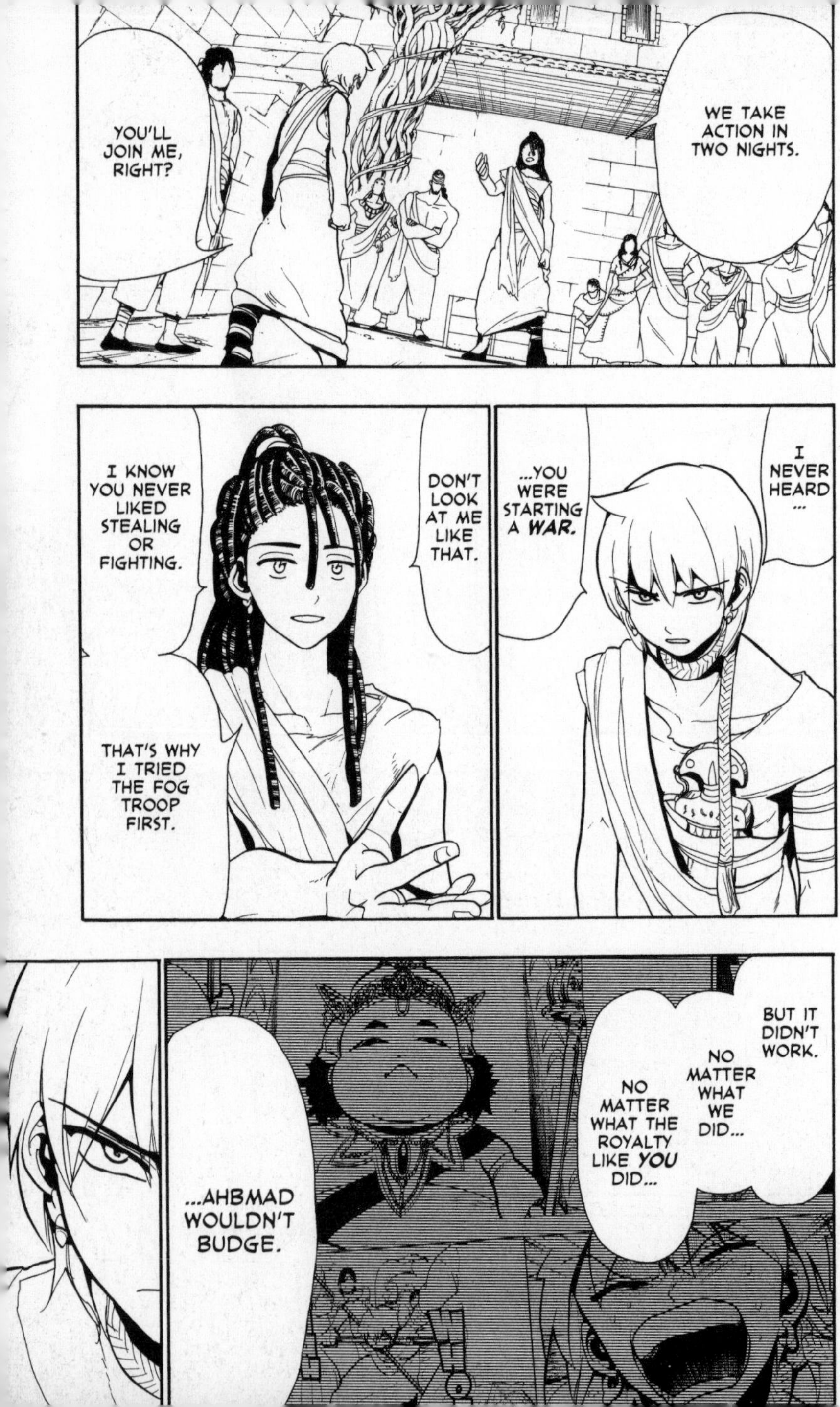
WE TAKE ACTION IN TWO NIGHTS.
YOU'LL JOIN ME, RIGHT?
I NEVER HEARD...
...YOU WERE STARTING A *WAR.*
DON'T LOOK AT ME LIKE THAT.
I KNOW YOU NEVER LIKED STEALING OR FIGHTING.
THAT'S WHY I TRIED THE FOG TROOP FIRST.
BUT IT DIDN'T WORK.
NO MATTER WHAT WE DID...
NO MATTER WHAT THE ROYALTY LIKE *YOU* DID...
...AHBMAD WOULDN'T BUDGE.

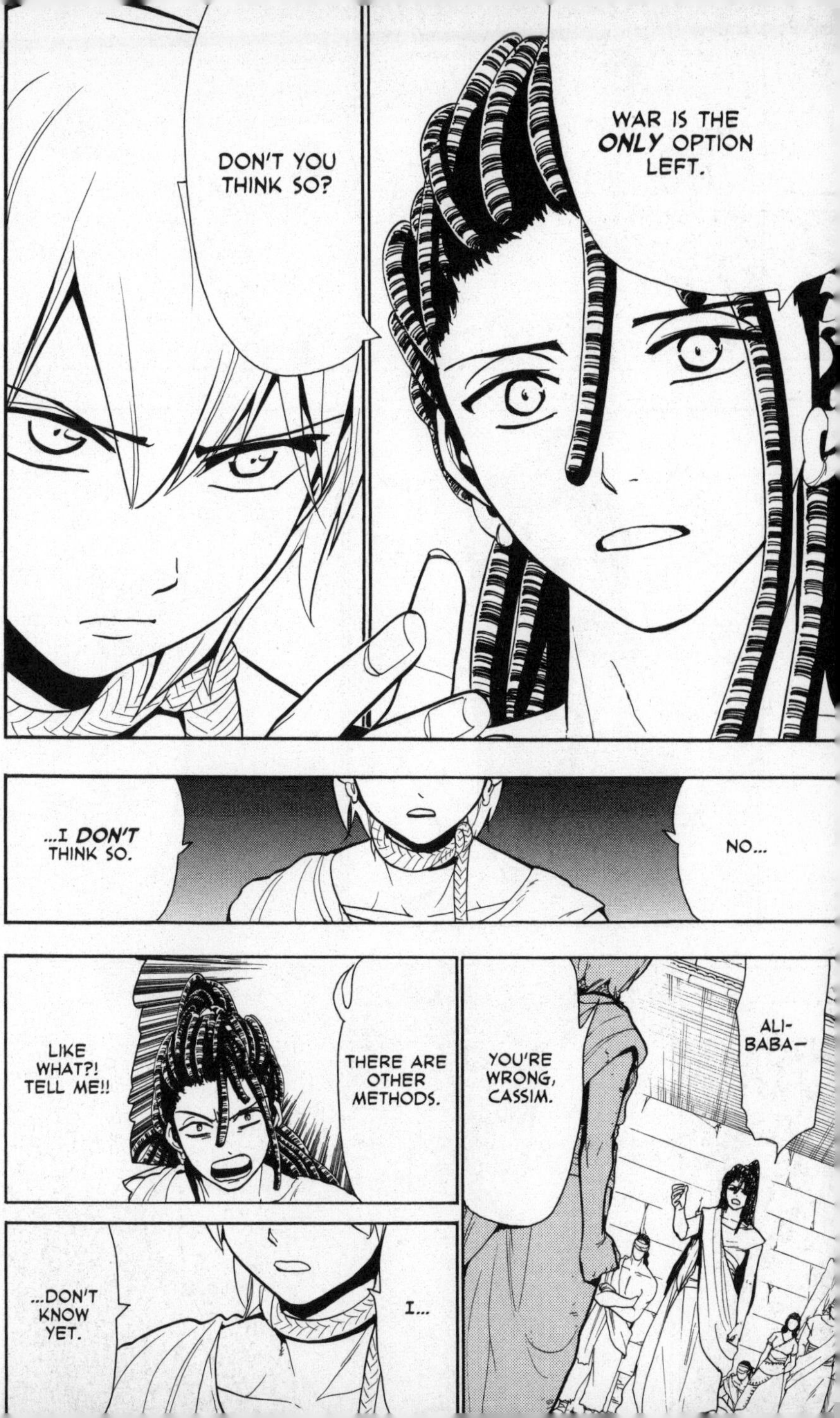
WAR IS THE *ONLY* OPTION LEFT.
DON'T YOU THINK SO?
NO...
...I *DON'T* THINK SO.
ALI-BABA—
YOU'RE WRONG, CASSIM.
THERE ARE OTHER METHODS.
LIKE WHAT?! TELL ME!!
I...
...DON'T KNOW YET.

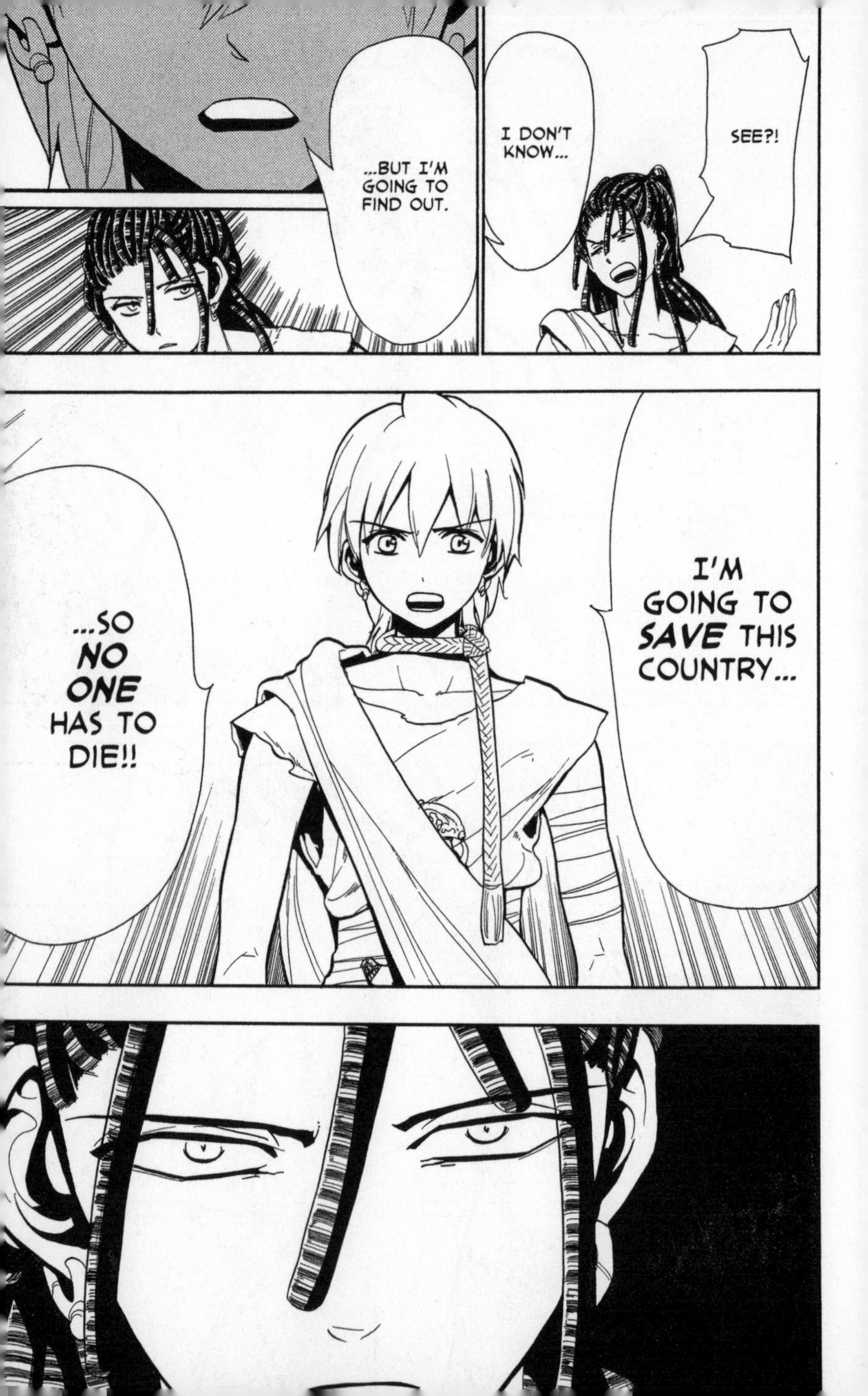
SEE?!
I DON'T KNOW...
...BUT I'M GOING TO FIND OUT.
I'M GOING TO *SAVE* THIS COUNTRY...
...SO **NO ONE** HAS TO DIE!!

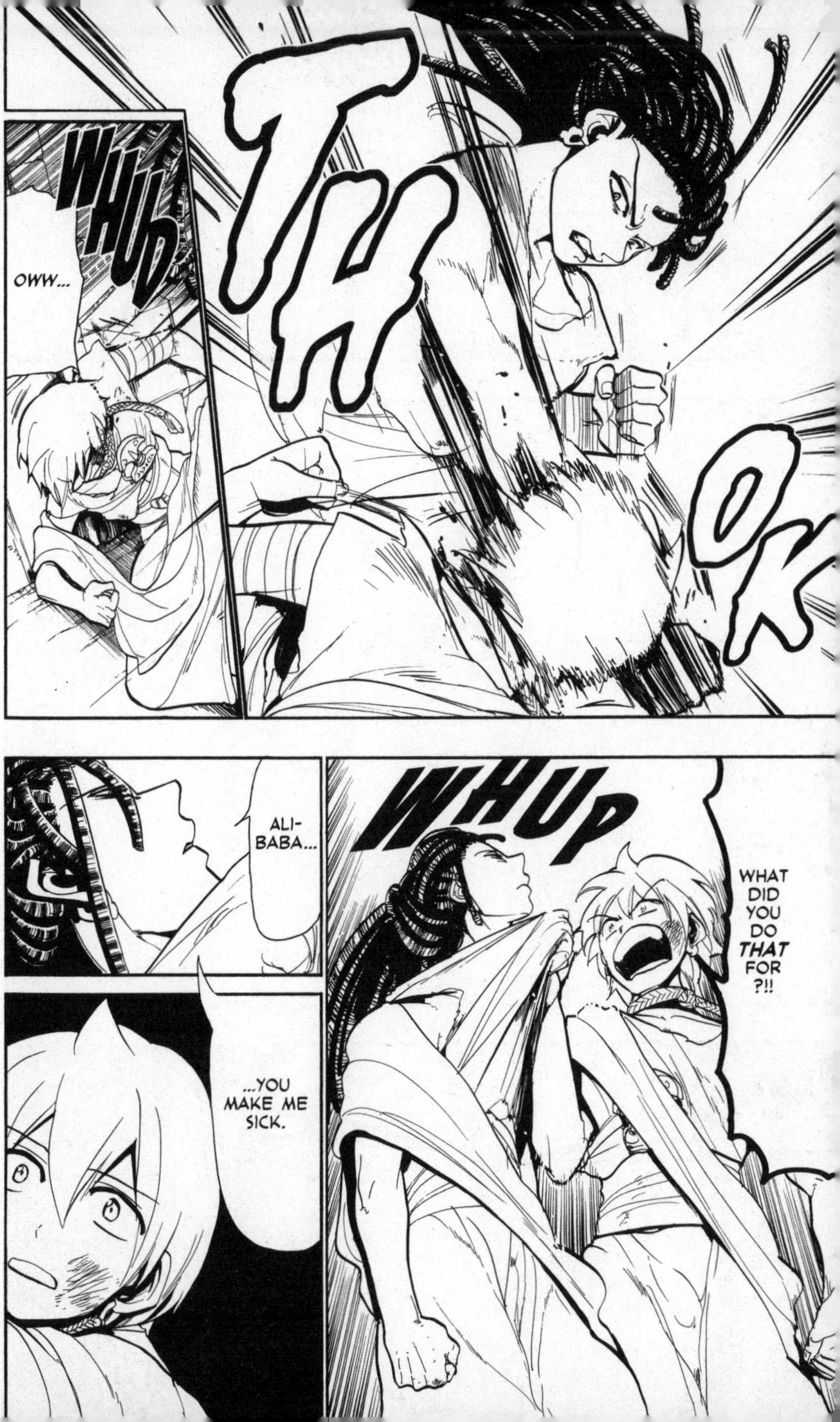
TH
OK
WHUD
OWW...
WHUP
WHAT DID YOU DO *THAT* FOR?!!
ALI-BABA...
...YOU MAKE ME SICK.

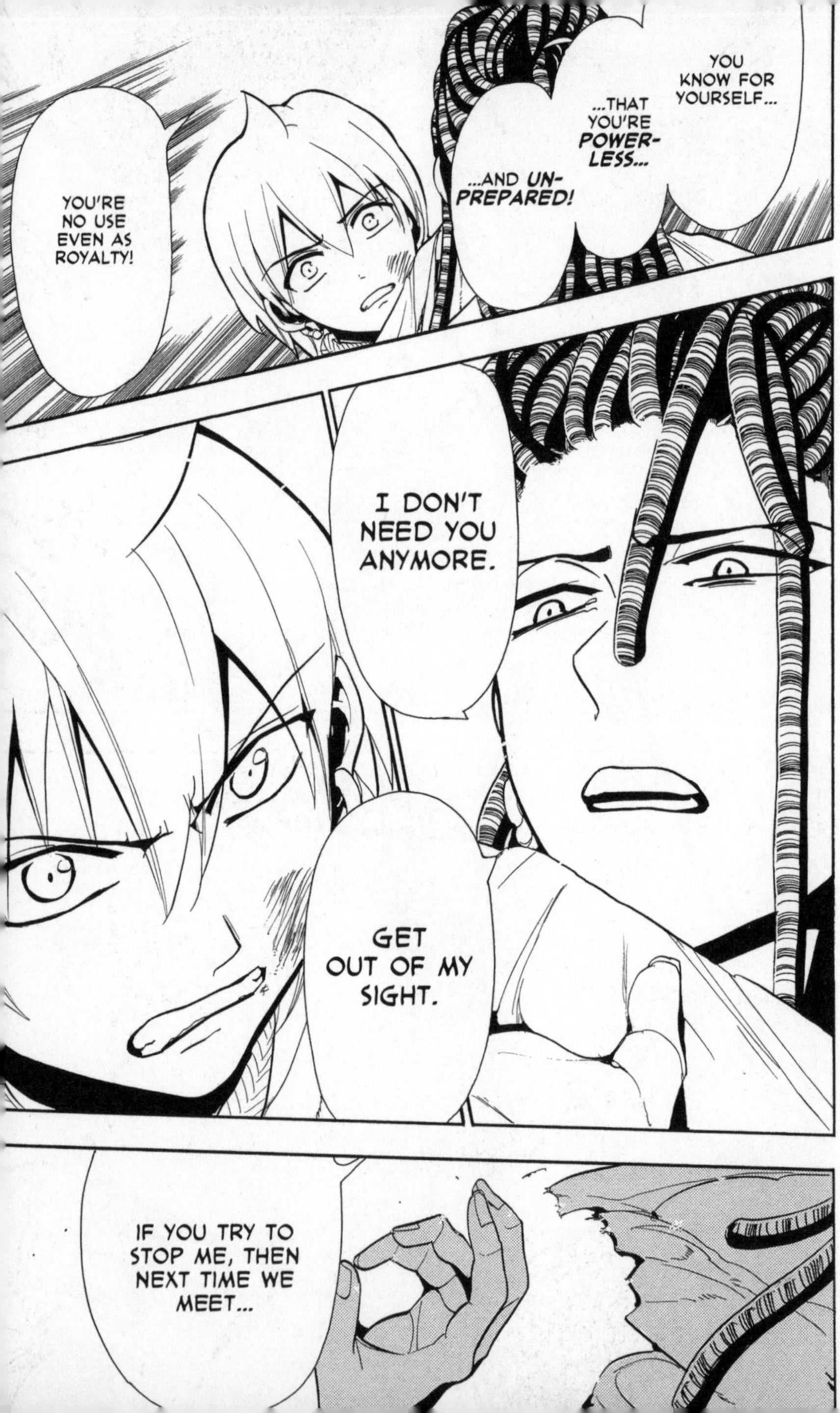
YOU KNOW FOR YOURSELF...
...THAT YOU'RE POWERLESS...
...AND UNPREPARED!
YOU'RE NO USE EVEN AS ROYALTY!
I DON'T NEED YOU ANYMORE.
GET OUT OF MY SIGHT.
IF YOU TRY TO STOP ME, THEN NEXT TIME WE MEET...

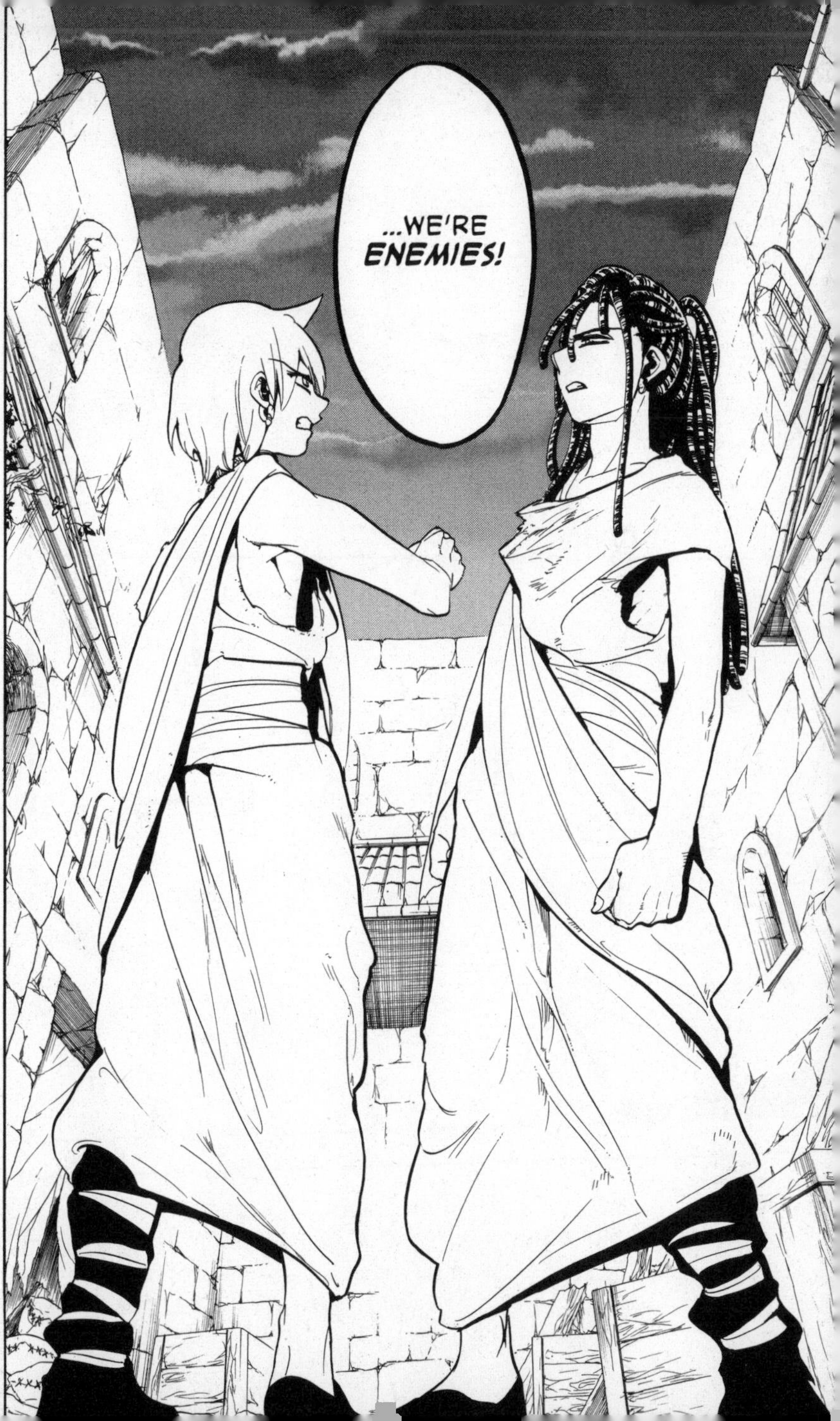
...WE'RE ENEMIES!

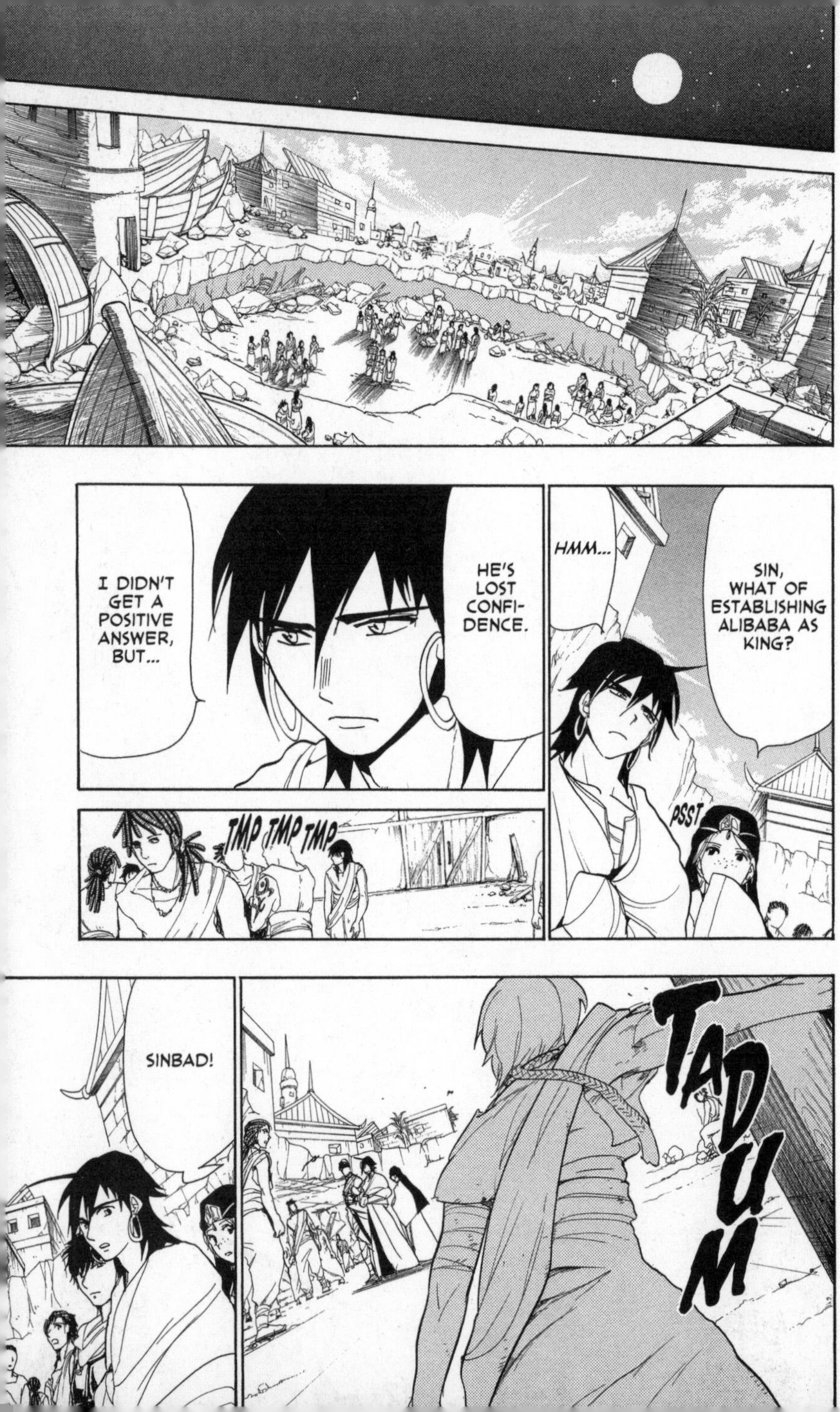
SIN, WHAT OF ESTABLISHING ALIBABA AS KING?
HMM...
PSST
HE'S LOST CONFIDENCE.
I DIDN'T GET A POSITIVE ANSWER, BUT...
TMP TMP TMP
TADUM
SINBAD!

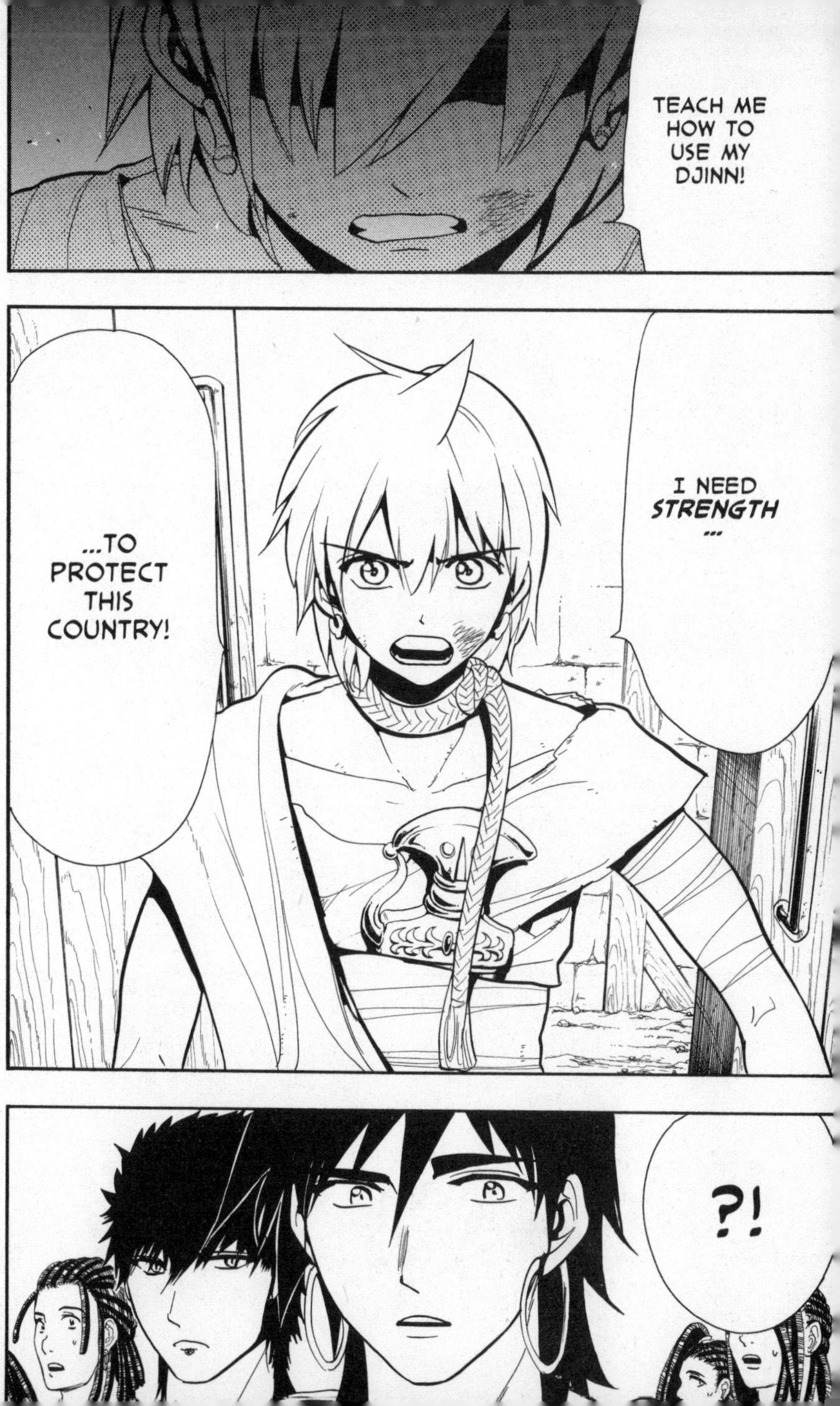
TEACH ME HOW TO USE MY DJINN!
I NEED *STRENGTH*...
...TO PROTECT THIS COUNTRY!
?!

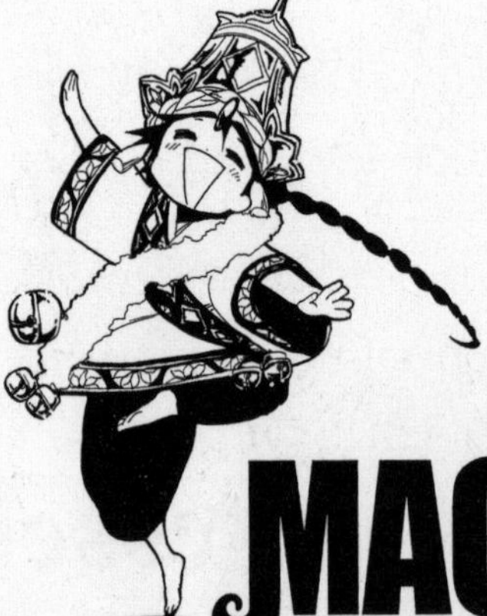

MAGI

The labyrinth of magic

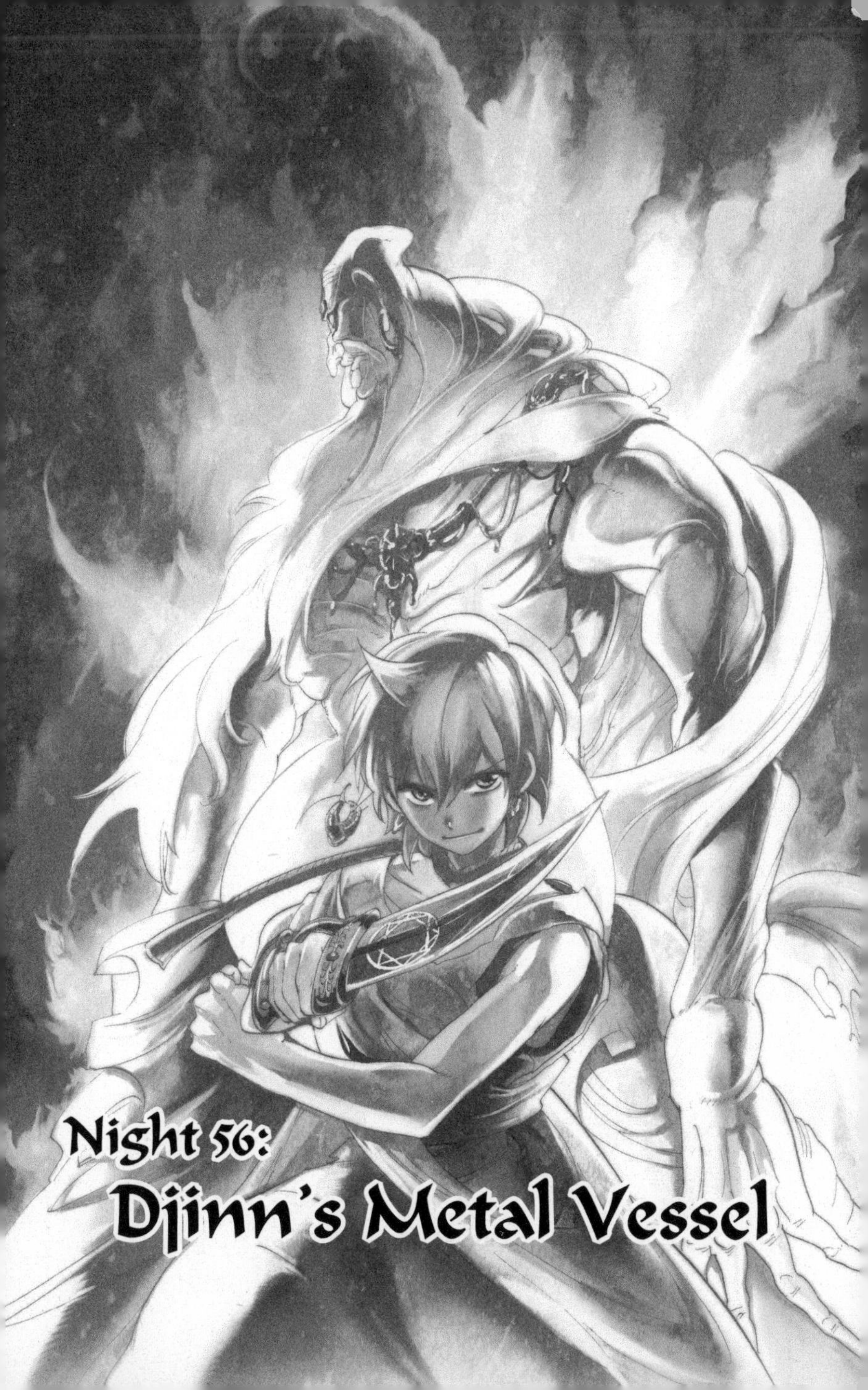
Night 56:
Djinn's Metal Vessel

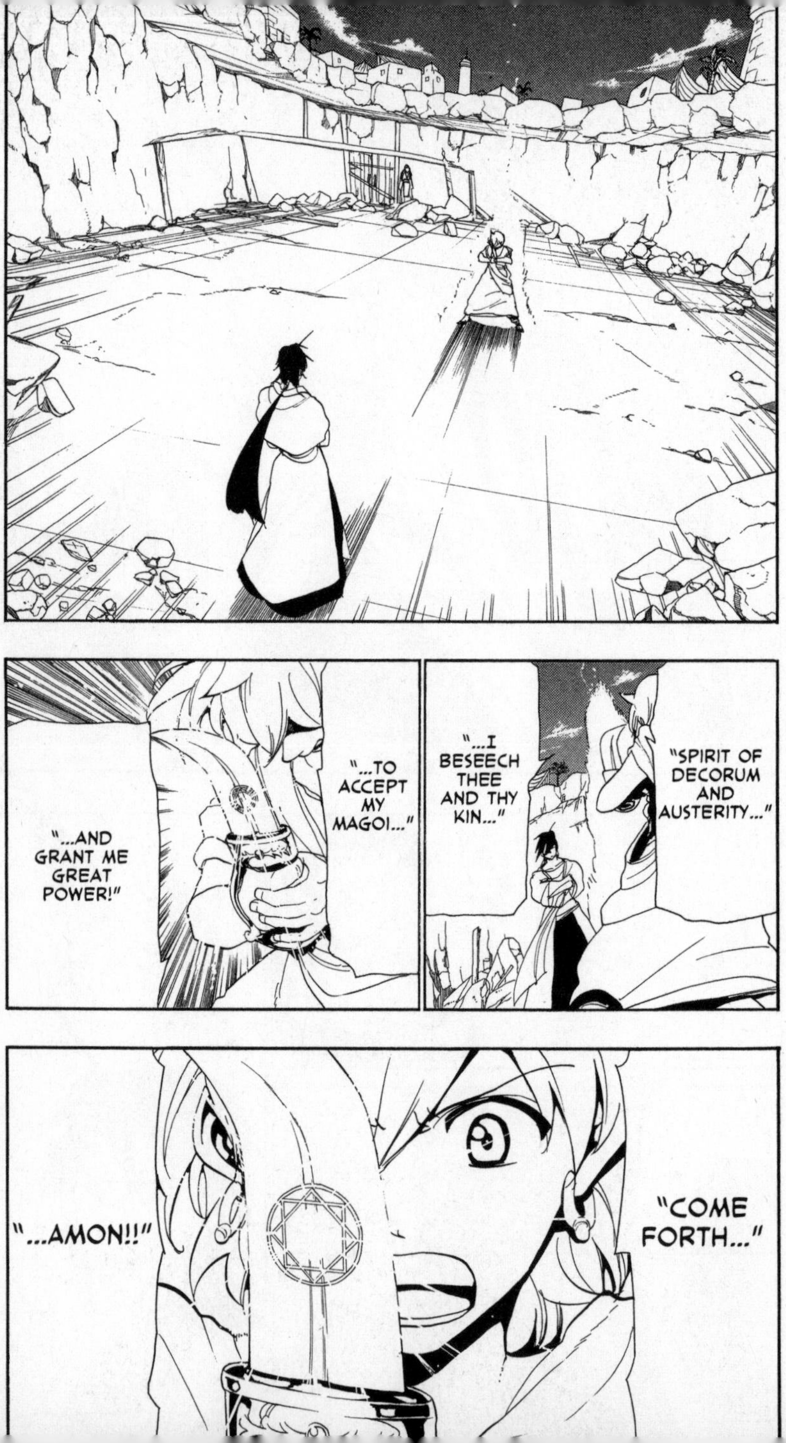
"SPIRIT OF DECORUM AND AUSTERITY..."
"...I BESEECH THEE AND THY KIN..."
"...TO ACCEPT MY MAGOI..."
"...AND GRANT ME GREAT POWER!"
"COME FORTH..."
"...AMON!!"

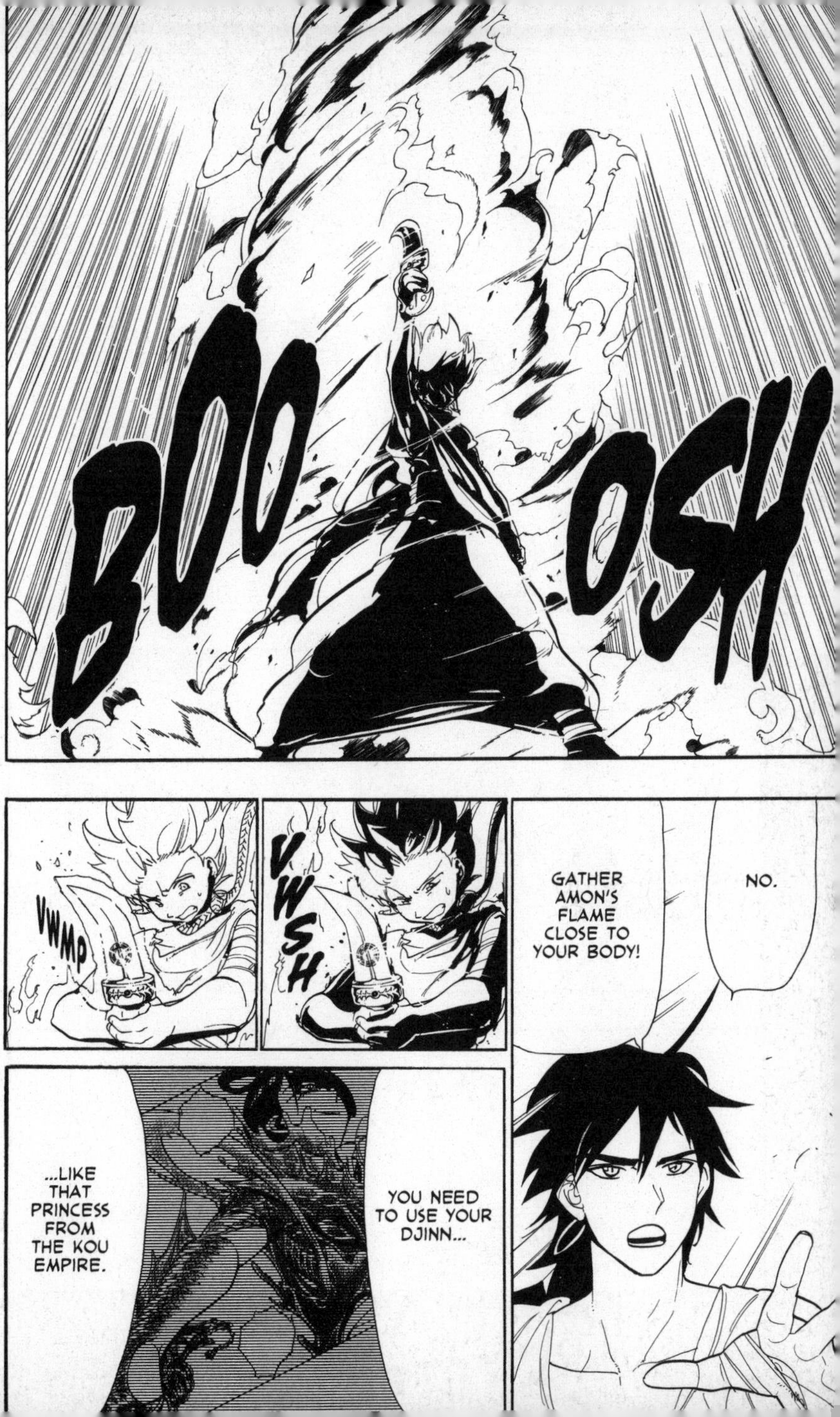
BOO-OSH
NO.
GATHER AMON'S FLAME CLOSE TO YOUR BODY!
VWSH
VWMP
YOU NEED TO USE YOUR DJINN...
...LIKE THAT PRINCESS FROM THE KOU EMPIRE.

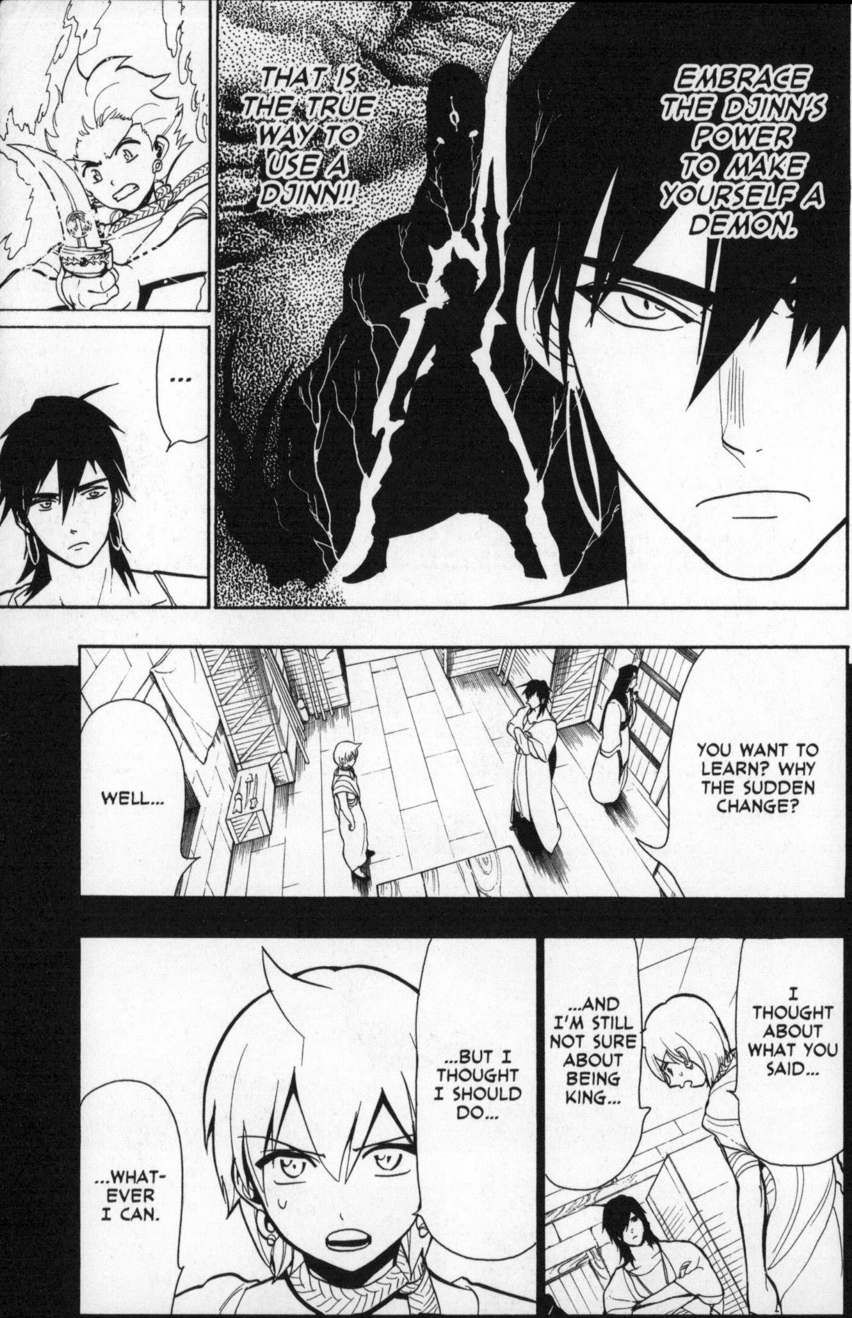
EMBRACE THE DJINN'S POWER TO MAKE YOURSELF A DEMON.
THAT IS THE TRUE WAY TO USE A DJINN!!
...
YOU WANT TO LEARN? WHY THE SUDDEN CHANGE?
WELL...
I THOUGHT ABOUT WHAT YOU SAID...
...AND I'M STILL NOT SURE ABOUT BEING KING...
...BUT I THOUGHT I SHOULD DO...
...WHAT-EVER I CAN.

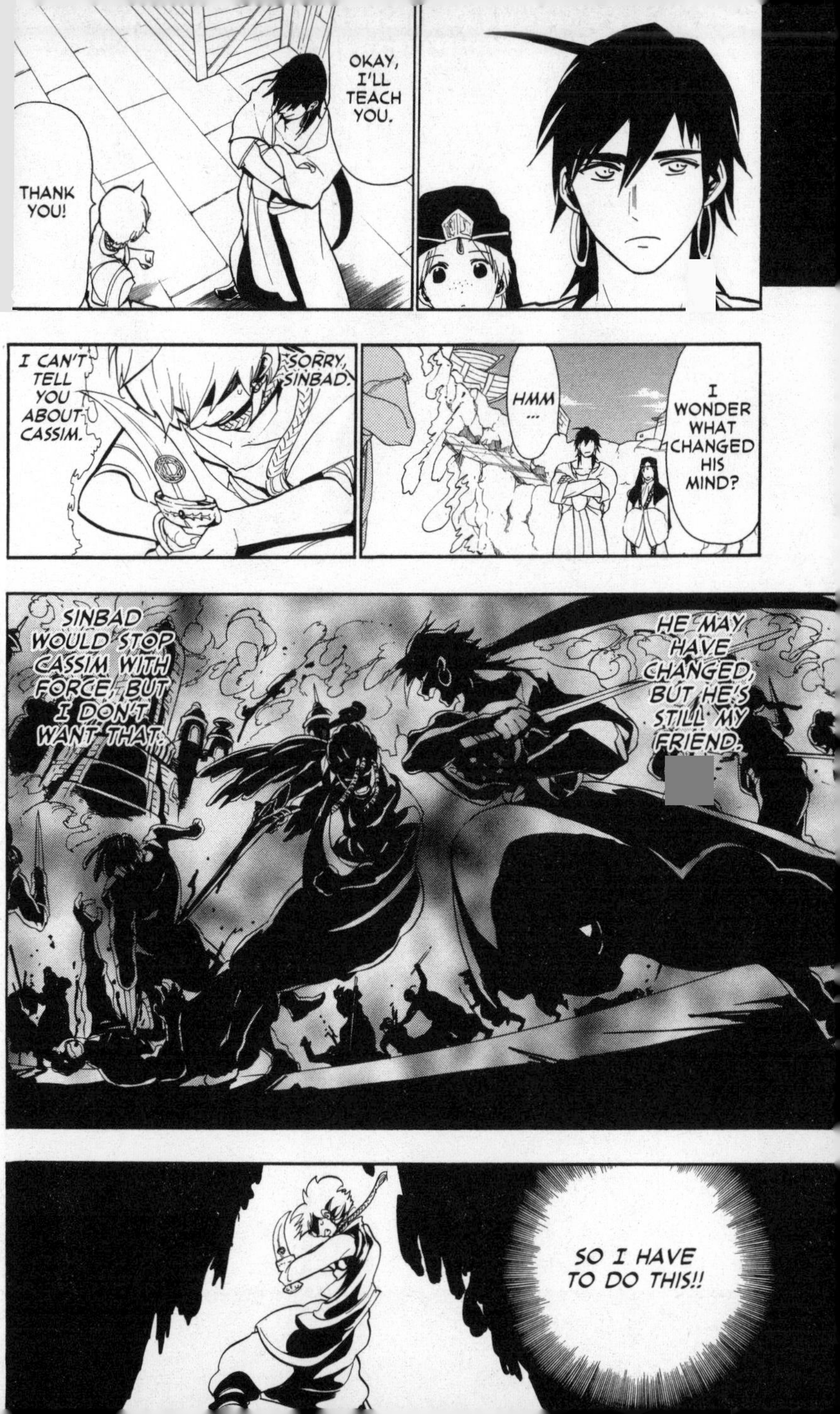
OKAY, I'LL TEACH YOU.
THANK YOU!
I WONDER WHAT CHANGED HIS MIND?
HMM ...
SORRY, SINBAD.
I CAN'T TELL YOU ABOUT CASSIM.
HE MAY HAVE CHANGED, BUT HE'S STILL MY FRIEND.
SINBAD WOULD STOP CASSIM WITH FORCE, BUT I DON'T WANT THAT.
SO I HAVE TO DO THIS!!

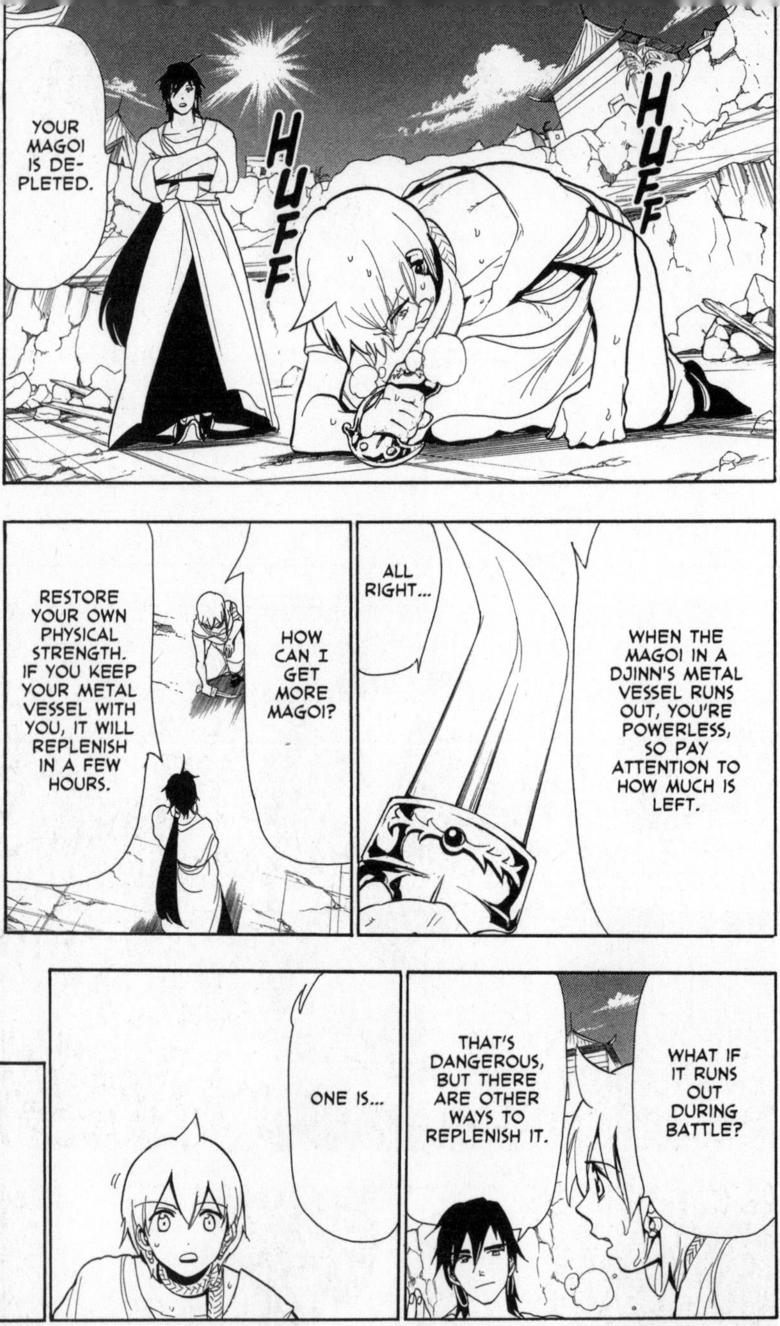
HUFF
HUFF
YOUR MAGOI IS DE-PLETED.
WHEN THE MAGOI IN A DJINN'S METAL VESSEL RUNS OUT, YOU'RE POWERLESS, SO PAY ATTENTION TO HOW MUCH IS LEFT.
ALL RIGHT...
HOW CAN I GET MORE MAGOI?
RESTORE YOUR OWN PHYSICAL STRENGTH. IF YOU KEEP YOUR METAL VESSEL WITH YOU, IT WILL REPLENISH IN A FEW HOURS.
WHAT IF IT RUNS OUT DURING BATTLE?
THAT'S DANGEROUS, BUT THERE ARE OTHER WAYS TO REPLENISH IT.
ONE IS...

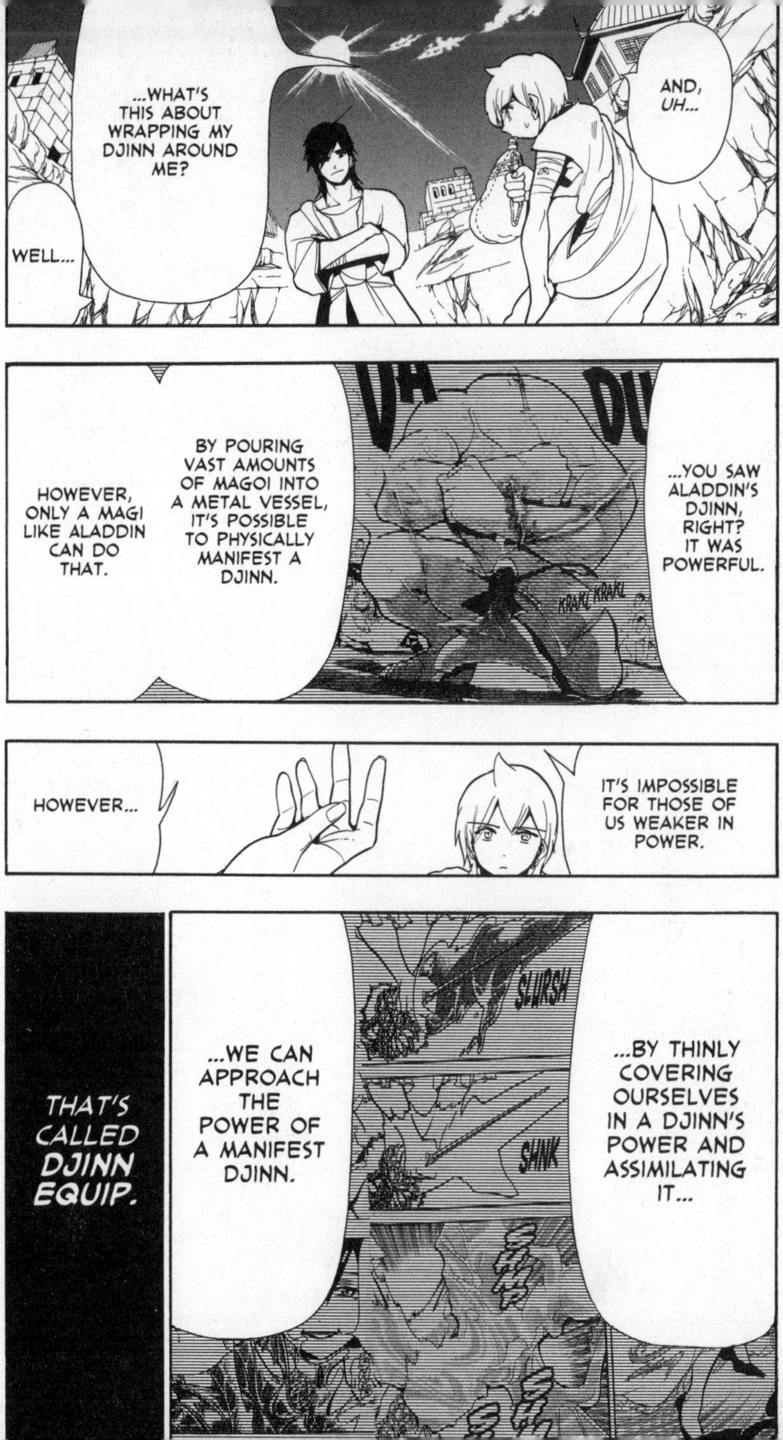

AND, UH...
...WHAT'S THIS ABOUT WRAPPING MY DJINN AROUND ME?
WELL...
DU
DA
...YOU SAW ALADDIN'S DJINN, RIGHT? IT WAS POWERFUL.
KRAKL KRAKL
BY POURING VAST AMOUNTS OF MAGOI INTO A METAL VESSEL, IT'S POSSIBLE TO PHYSICALLY MANIFEST A DJINN.
HOWEVER, ONLY A MAGI LIKE ALADDIN CAN DO THAT.
IT'S IMPOSSIBLE FOR THOSE OF US WEAKER IN POWER.
HOWEVER...
...BY THINLY COVERING OURSELVES IN A DJINN'S POWER AND ASSIMILATING IT...
SLURSH
SHNK
...WE CAN APPROACH THE POWER OF A MANIFEST DJINN.
THAT'S CALLED DJINN EQUIP.

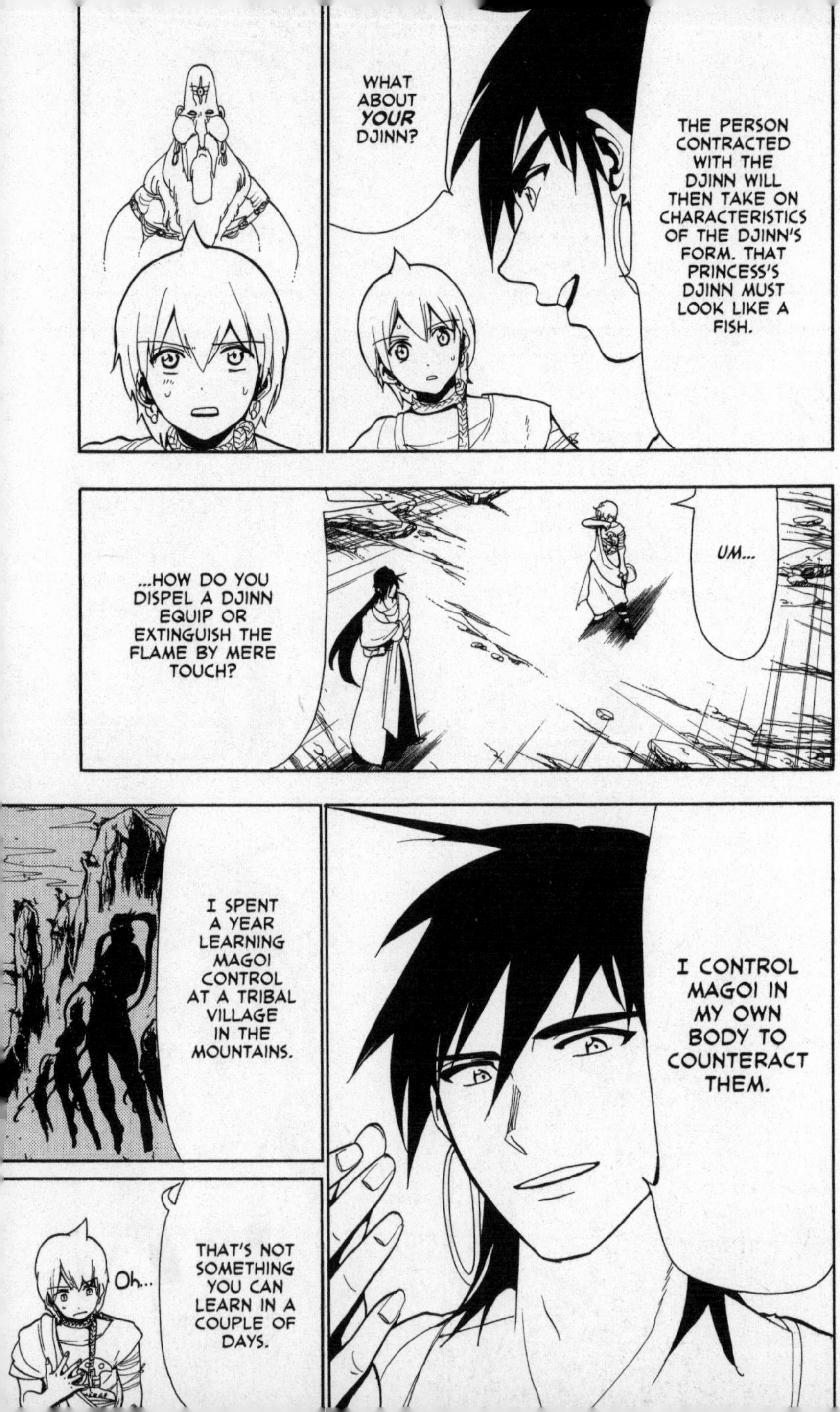
THE PERSON CONTRACTED WITH THE DJINN WILL THEN TAKE ON CHARACTERISTICS OF THE DJINN'S FORM. THAT PRINCESS'S DJINN MUST LOOK LIKE A FISH.
WHAT ABOUT *YOUR* DJINN?
UM...
...HOW DO YOU DISPEL A DJINN EQUIP OR EXTINGUISH THE FLAME BY MERE TOUCH?
I CONTROL MAGOI IN MY OWN BODY TO COUNTERACT THEM.
I SPENT A YEAR LEARNING MAGOI CONTROL AT A TRIBAL VILLAGE IN THE MOUNTAINS.
THAT'S NOT SOMETHING YOU CAN LEARN IN A COUPLE OF DAYS.
Oh...

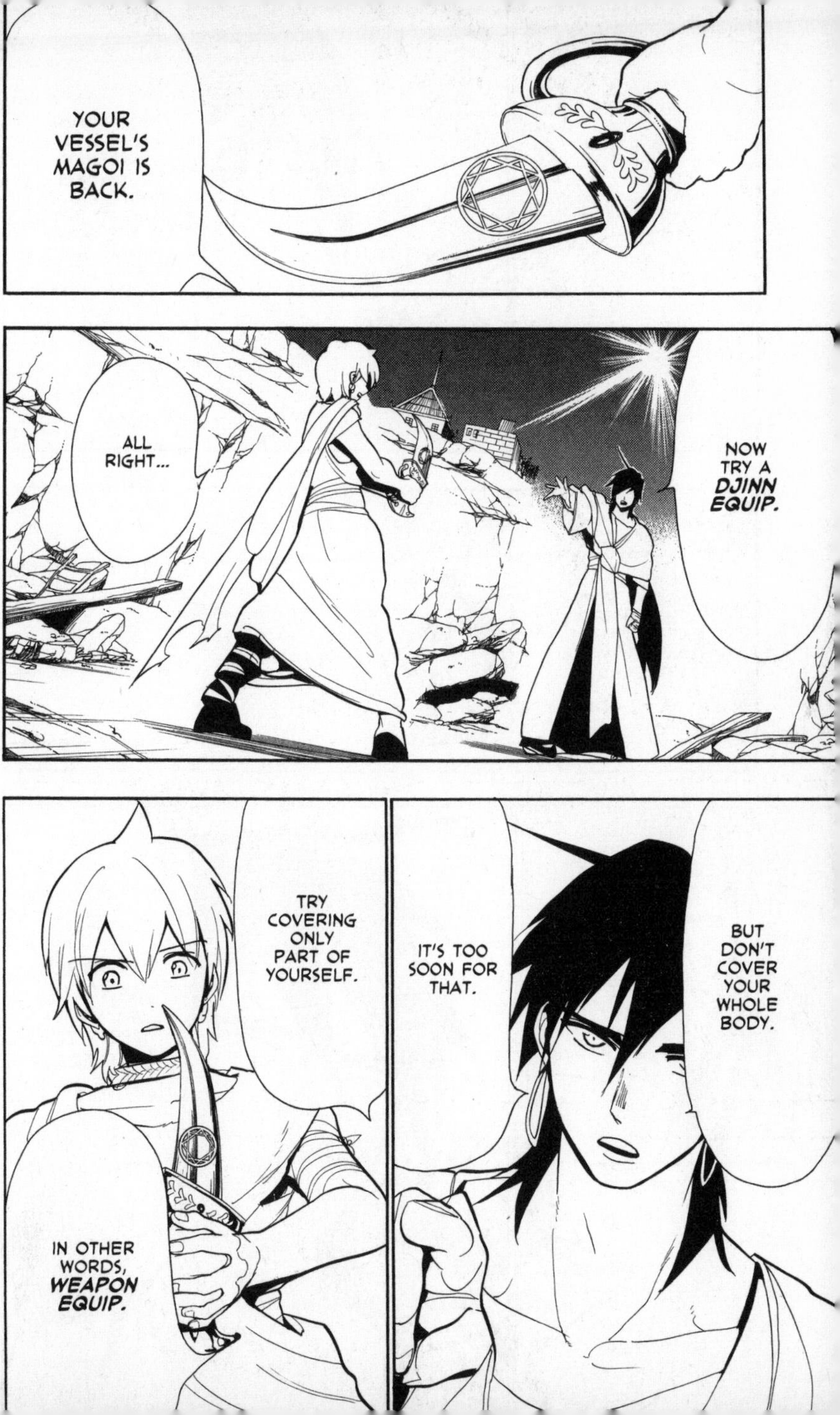
YOUR VESSEL'S MAGOI IS BACK.
NOW TRY A *DJINN EQUIP.*
ALL RIGHT...
BUT DON'T COVER YOUR WHOLE BODY.
IT'S TOO SOON FOR THAT.
TRY COVERING ONLY PART OF YOURSELF.
IN OTHER WORDS, *WEAPON EQUIP.*

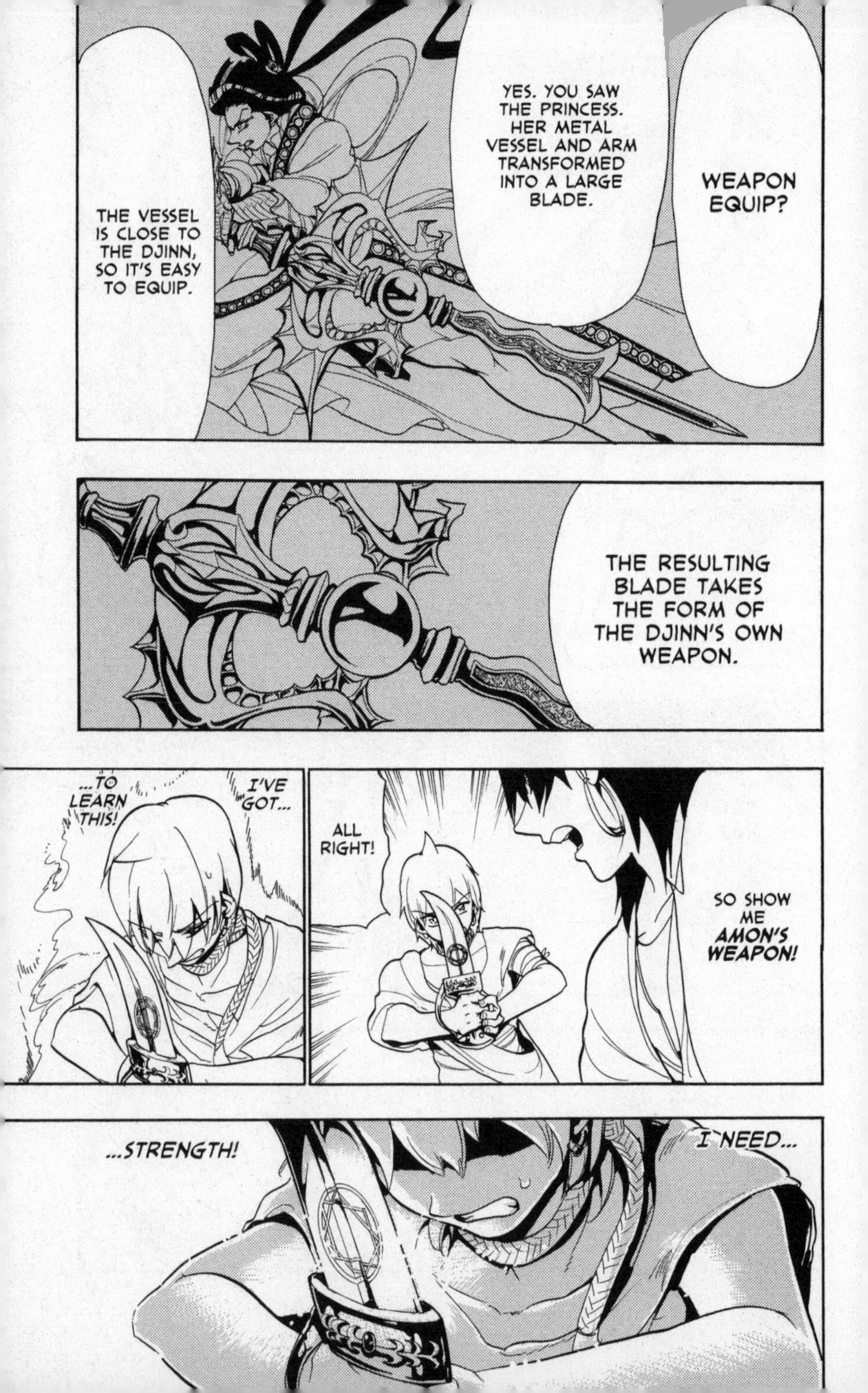
WEAPON EQUIP?
YES. YOU SAW THE PRINCESS. HER METAL VESSEL AND ARM TRANSFORMED INTO A LARGE BLADE.
THE VESSEL IS CLOSE TO THE DJINN, SO IT'S EASY TO EQUIP.
THE RESULTING BLADE TAKES THE FORM OF THE DJINN'S OWN WEAPON.
SO SHOW ME AMON'S WEAPON!
ALL RIGHT!
I'VE GOT...
...TO LEARN THIS!
I NEED...
...STRENGTH!

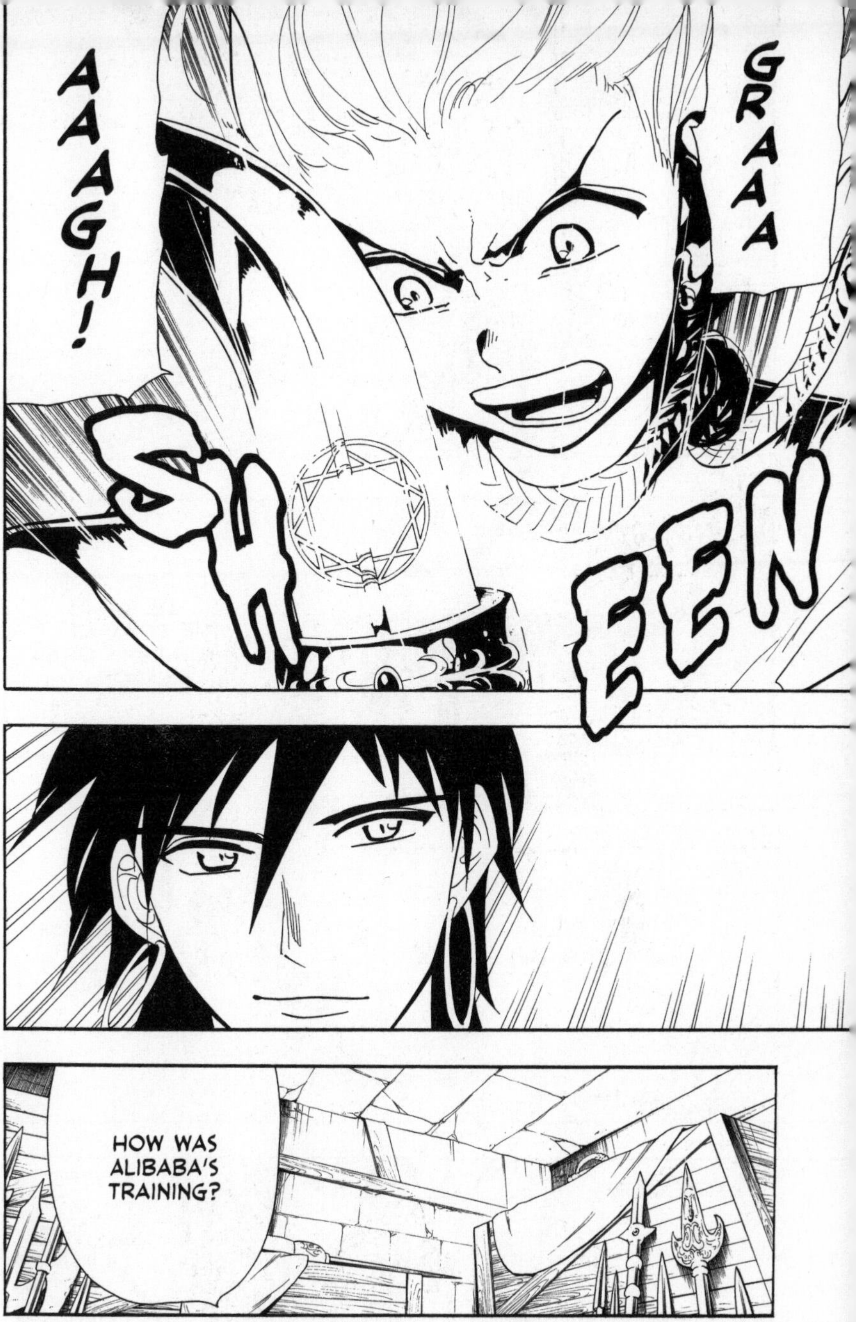
GRAAA
AAAGH!
SHEEN
HOW WAS ALIBABA'S TRAINING?

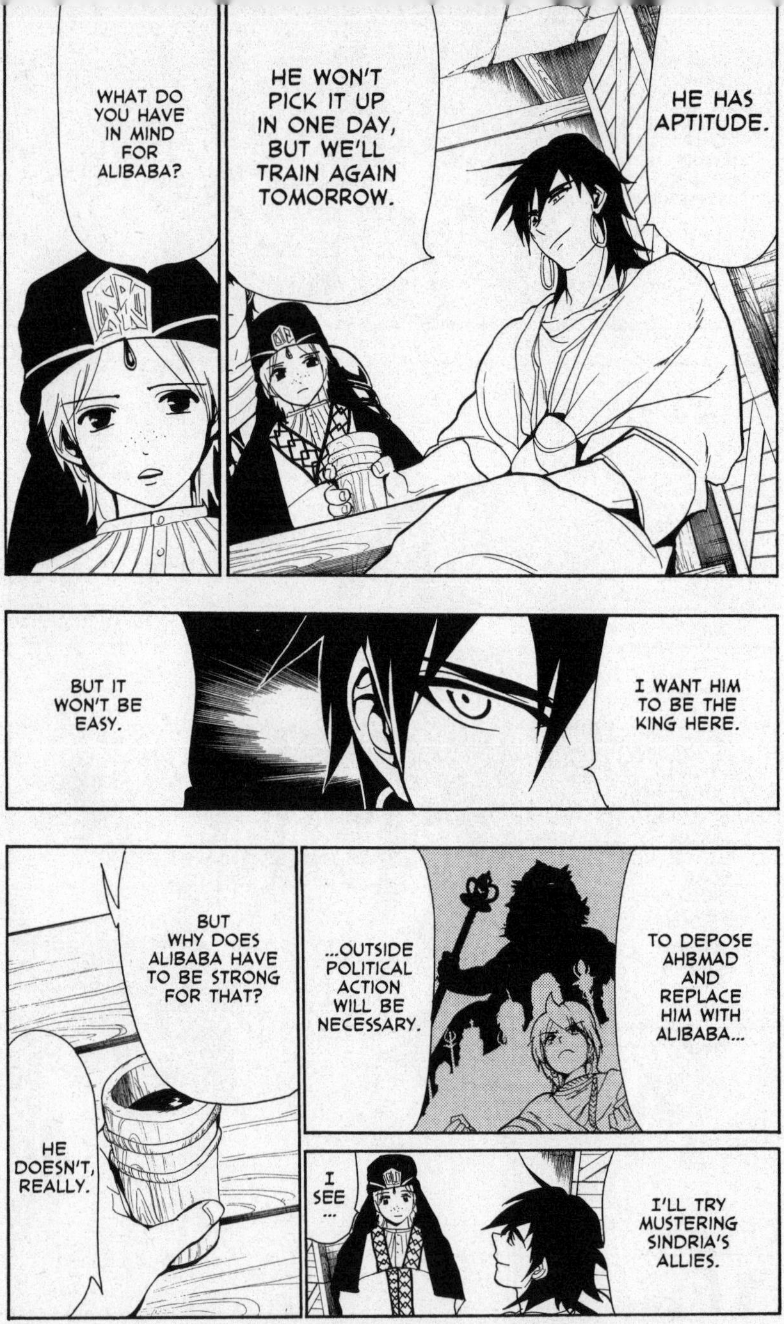
HE HAS APTITUDE.
HE WON'T PICK IT UP IN ONE DAY, BUT WE'LL TRAIN AGAIN TOMORROW.
WHAT DO YOU HAVE IN MIND FOR ALIBABA?
I WANT HIM TO BE THE KING HERE.
BUT IT WON'T BE EASY.
TO DEPOSE AHBMAD AND REPLACE HIM WITH ALIBABA...
...OUTSIDE POLITICAL ACTION WILL BE NECESSARY.
I'LL TRY MUSTERING SINDRIA'S ALLIES.
I SEE...
BUT WHY DOES ALIBABA HAVE TO BE STRONG FOR THAT?
HE DOESN'T, REALLY.

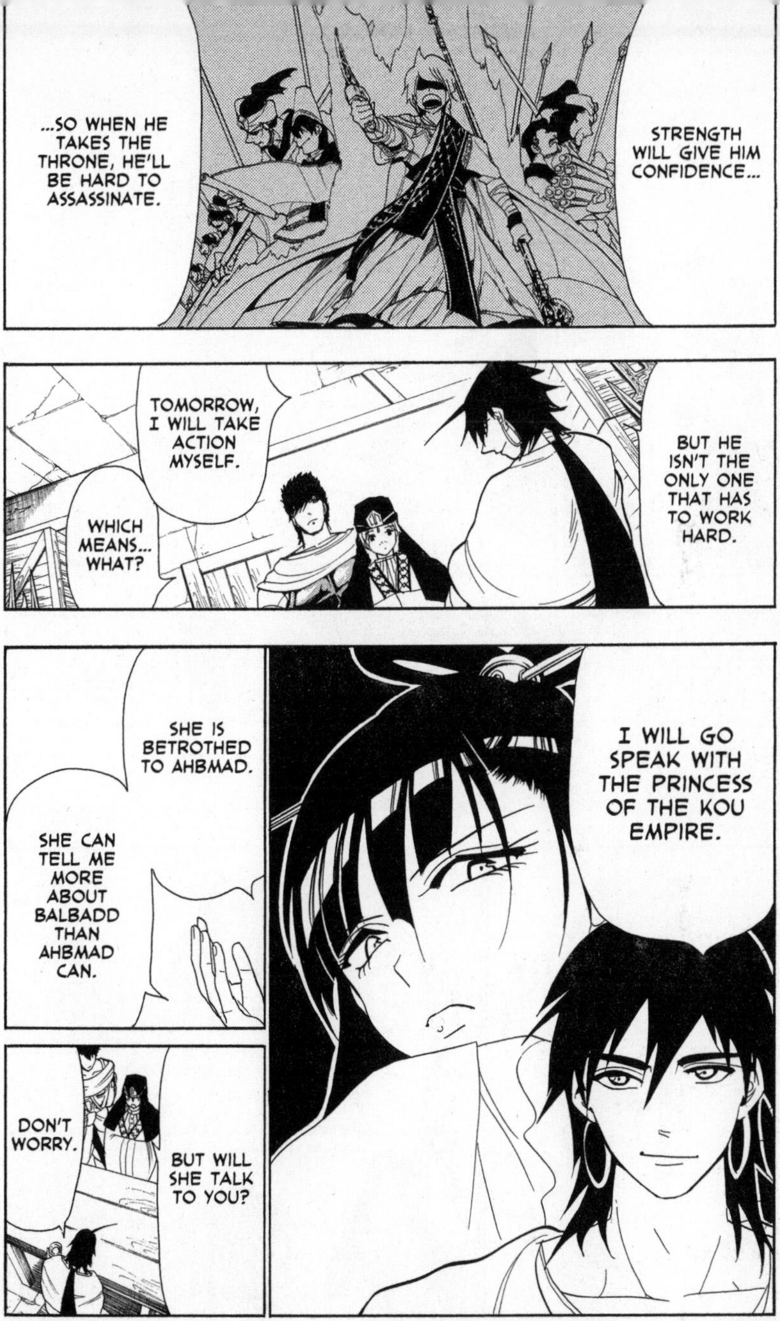
STRENGTH WILL GIVE HIM CONFIDENCE...
...SO WHEN HE TAKES THE THRONE, HE'LL BE HARD TO ASSASSINATE.
BUT HE ISN'T THE ONLY ONE THAT HAS TO WORK HARD.
TOMORROW, I WILL TAKE ACTION MYSELF.
WHICH MEANS... WHAT?
I WILL GO SPEAK WITH THE PRINCESS OF THE KOU EMPIRE.
SHE IS BETROTHED TO AHBMAD.
SHE CAN TELL ME MORE ABOUT BALBADD THAN AHBMAD CAN.
BUT WILL SHE TALK TO YOU?
DON'T WORRY.

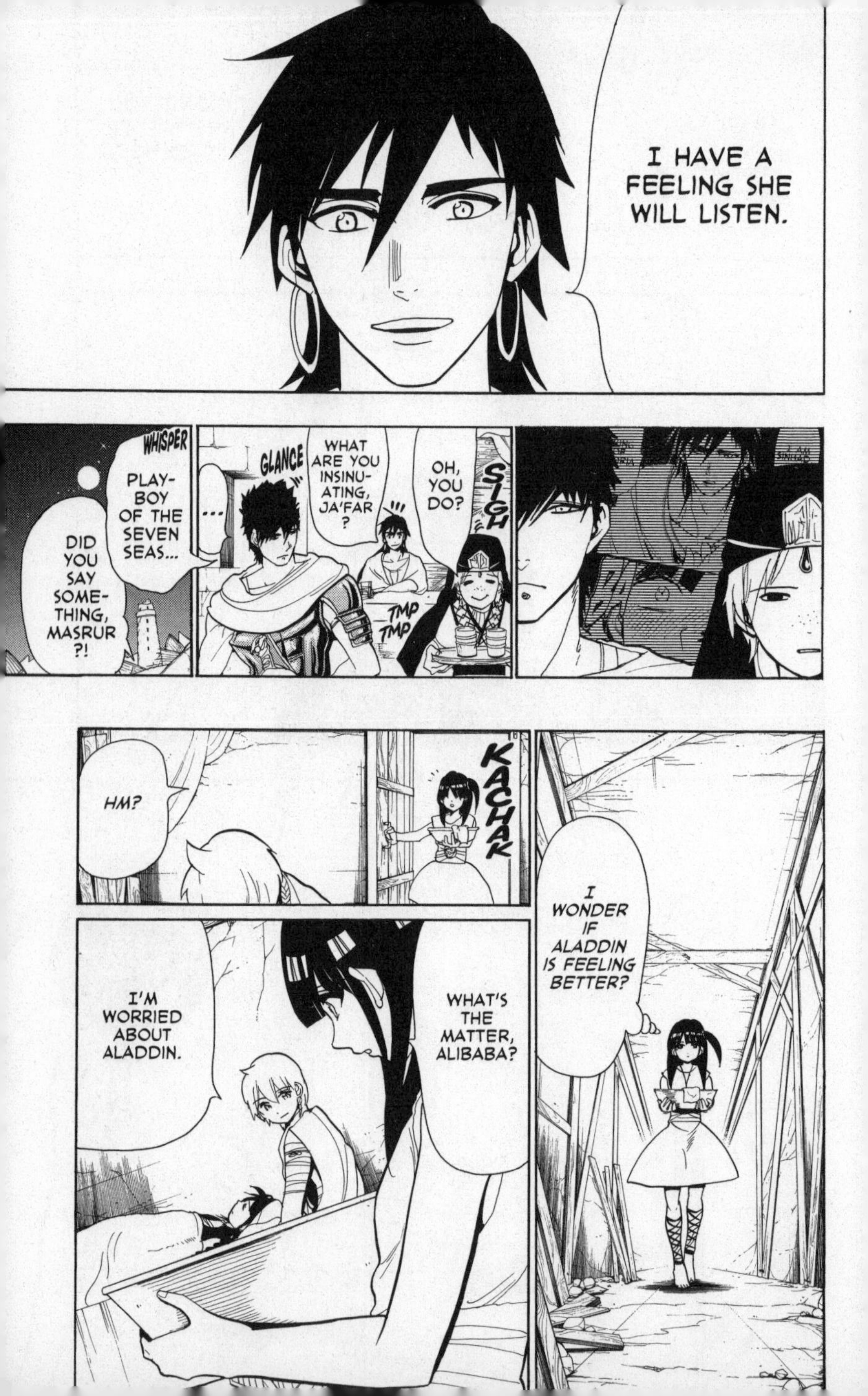
I HAVE A FEELING SHE WILL LISTEN.
SIGH
OH, YOU DO?
WHAT ARE YOU INSINUATING, JA'FAR?
GLANCE
...
TMP TMP
WHISPER
PLAYBOY OF THE SEVEN SEAS...
DID YOU SAY SOMETHING, MASRUR?!
I WONDER IF ALADDIN IS FEELING BETTER?
KACHAK
HM?
WHAT'S THE MATTER, ALIBABA?
I'M WORRIED ABOUT ALADDIN.

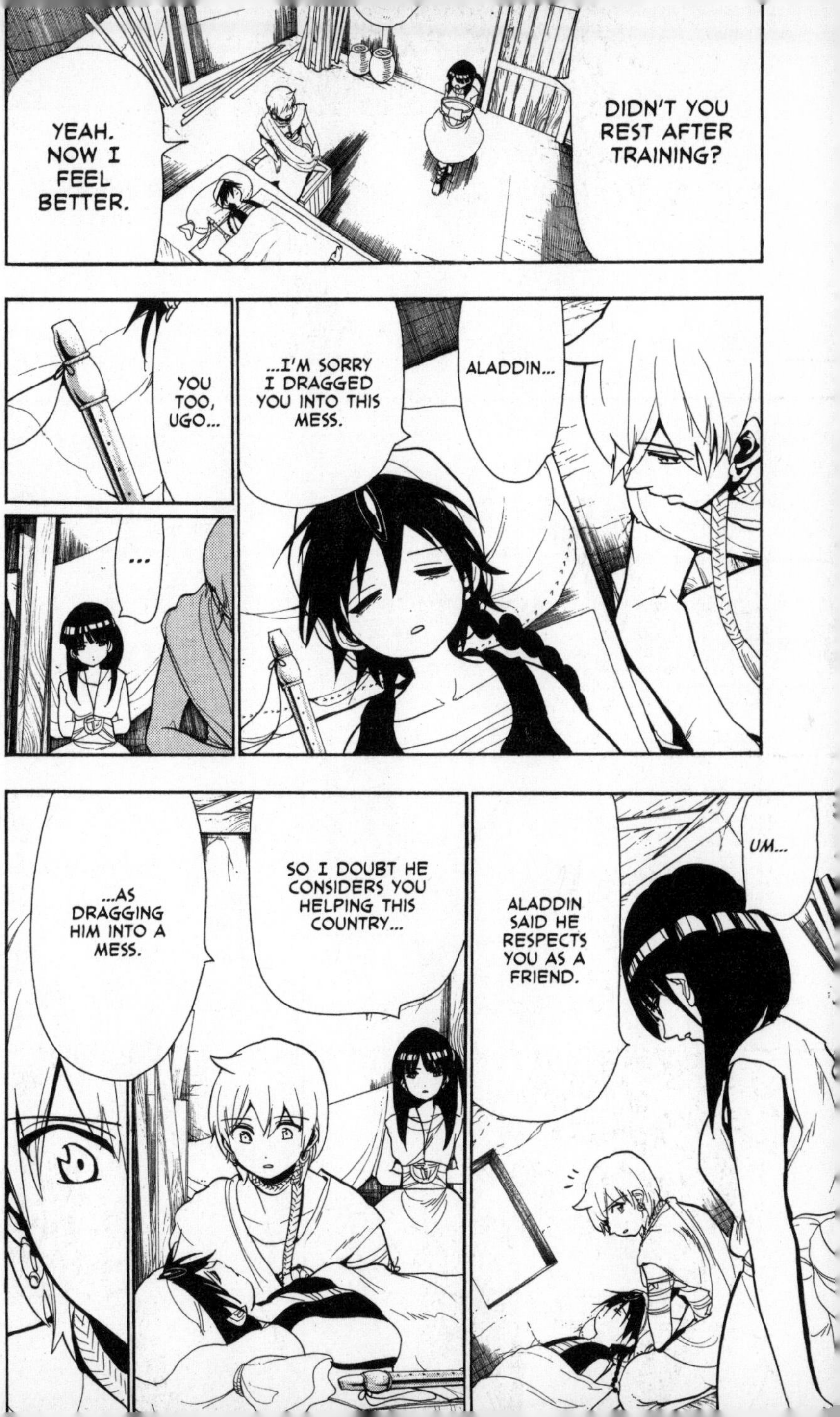
DIDN'T YOU REST AFTER TRAINING?
YEAH. NOW I FEEL BETTER.
ALADDIN...
...I'M SORRY I DRAGGED YOU INTO THIS MESS.
YOU TOO, UGO...
...
UM...
ALADDIN SAID HE RESPECTS YOU AS A FRIEND.
SO I DOUBT HE CONSIDERS YOU HELPING THIS COUNTRY...
...AS DRAGGING HIM INTO A MESS.

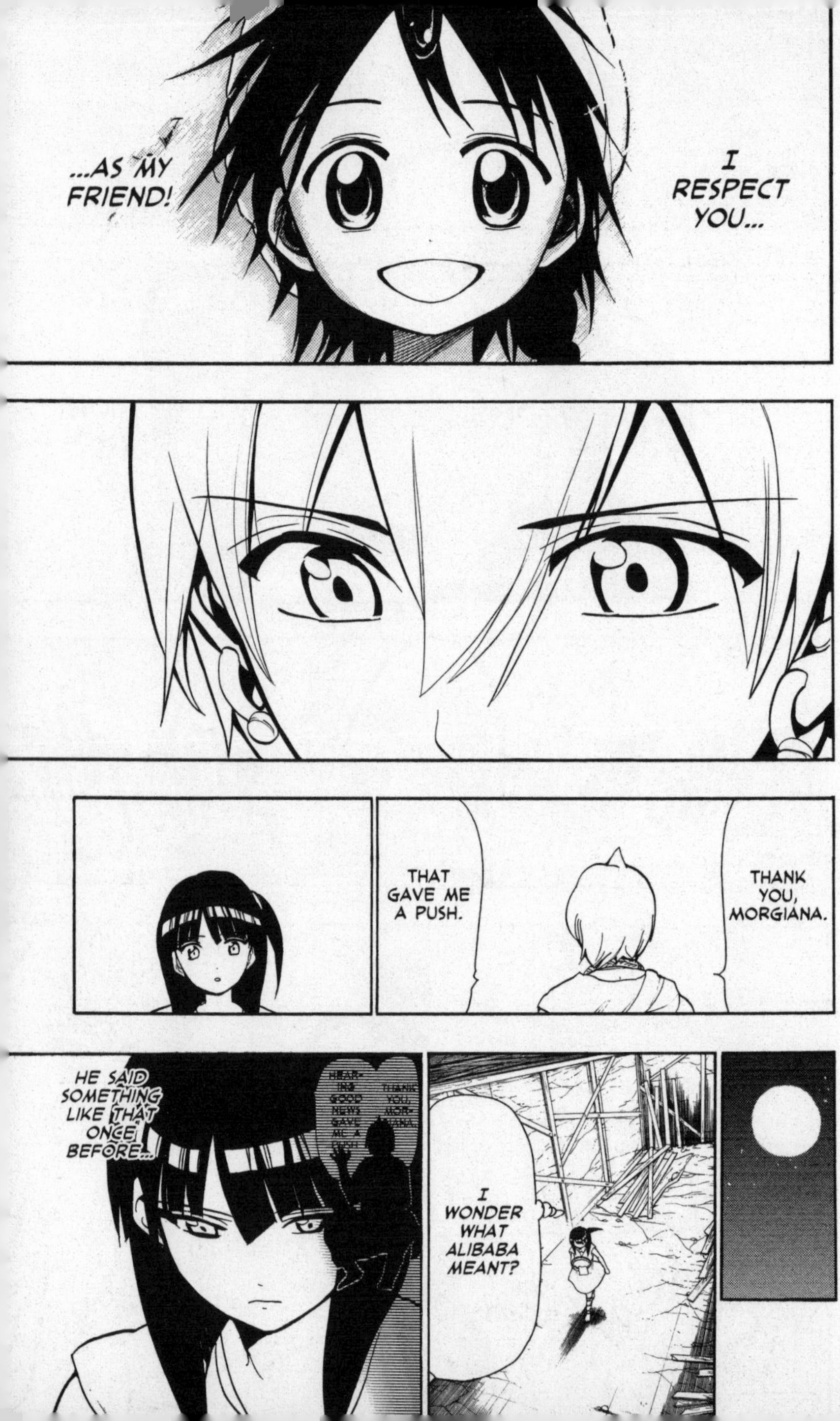
I RESPECT YOU...
...AS MY FRIEND!
THANK YOU, MORGIANA.
THAT GAVE ME A PUSH.
I WONDER WHAT ALIBABA MEANT?
THANK YOU, MOR-GIANA.
HEAR-ING GOOD NEWS GAVE ME A PUSH
HE SAID SOMETHING LIKE THAT ONCE BEFORE...

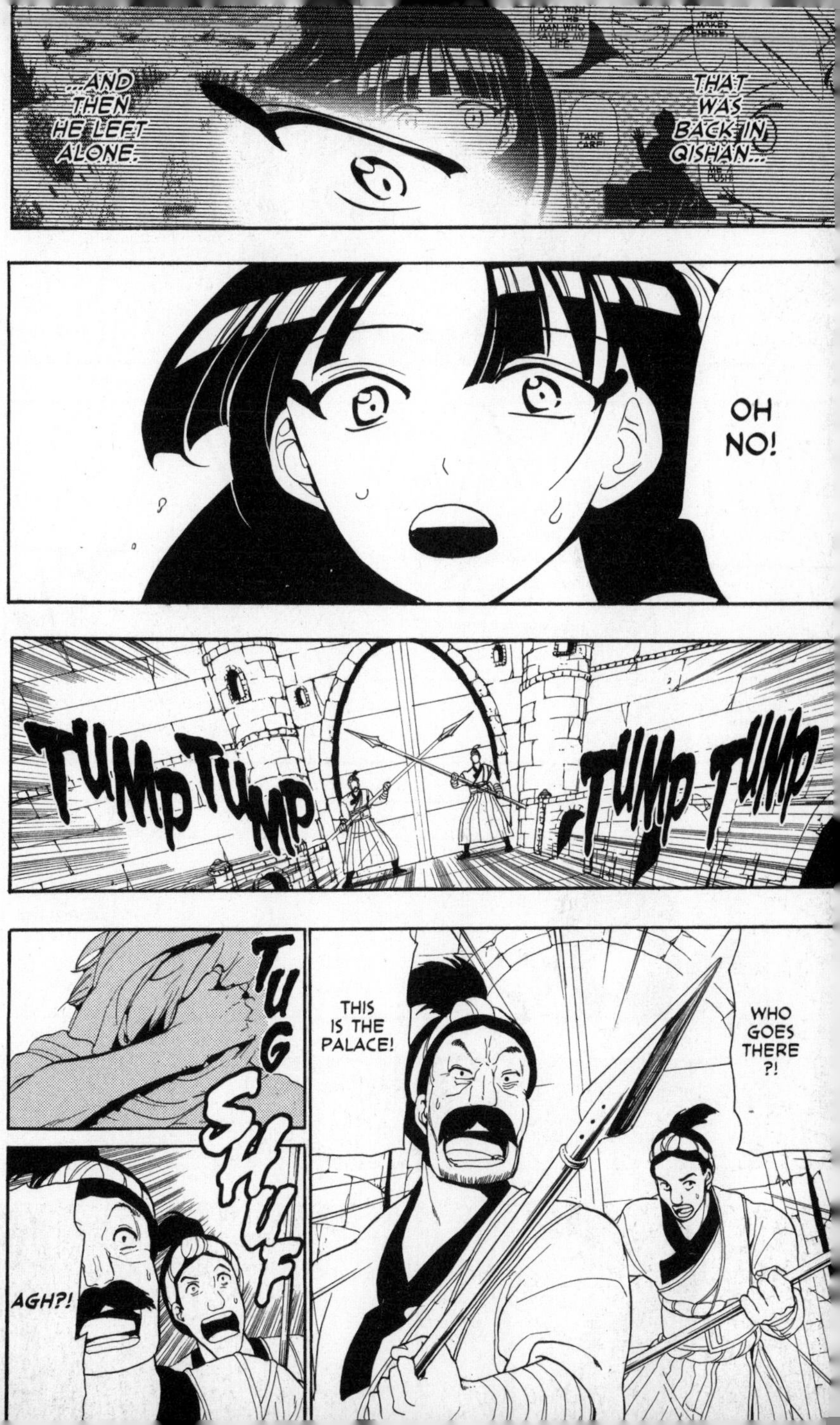
THAT WAS BACK IN QISHAN...
THAT MAKES SENSE
TAKE CARE!
...AND THEN HE LEFT ALONE.
OH NO!
TUMP TUMP
TUMP TUMP
WHO GOES THERE ?!
THIS IS THE PALACE!
TUG
SHUF
AGH?!

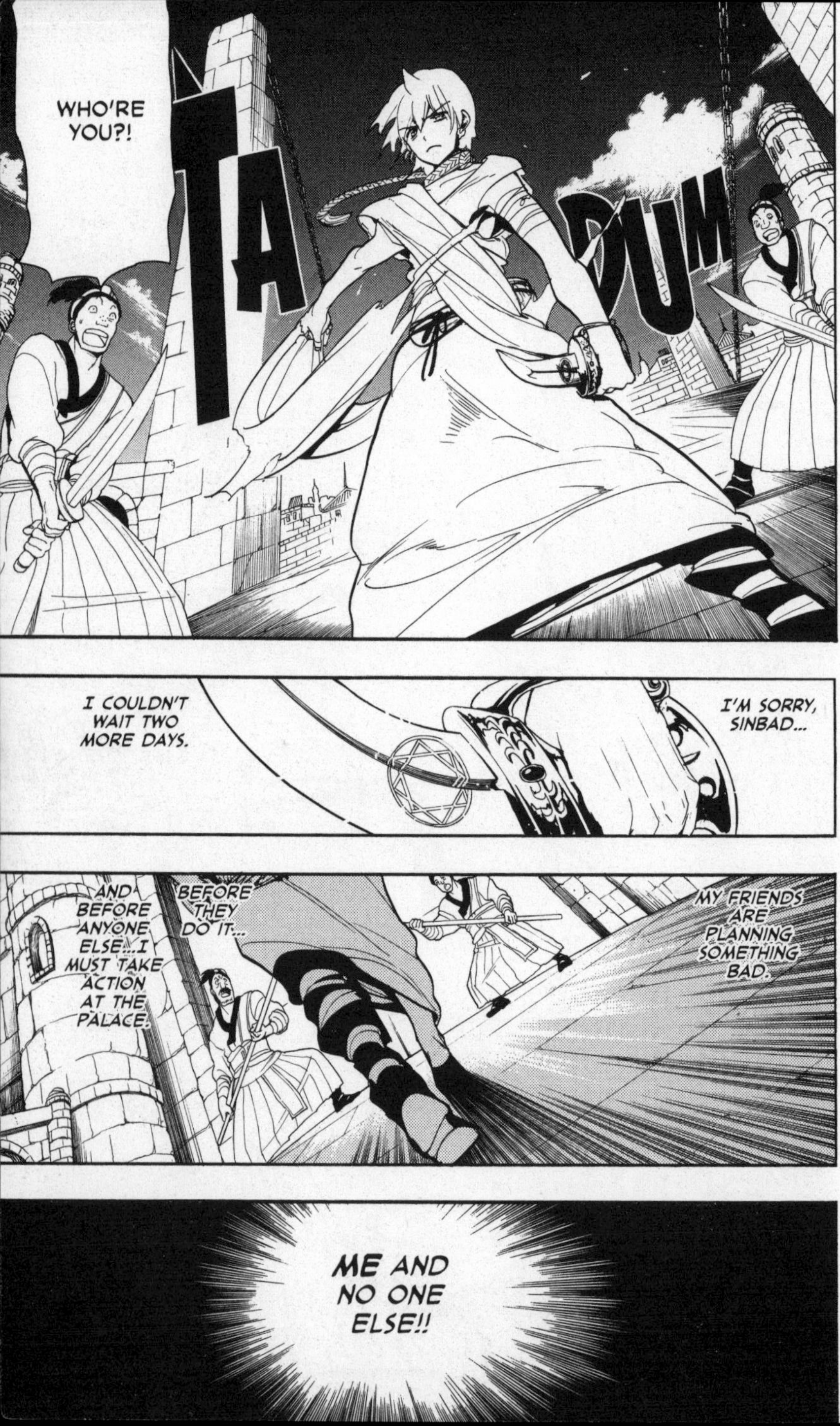
WHO'RE YOU?!
TA DUM
I'M SORRY, SINBAD...
I COULDN'T WAIT TWO MORE DAYS.
MY FRIENDS ARE PLANNING SOMETHING BAD.
BEFORE THEY DO IT...
AND BEFORE ANYONE ELSE...I MUST TAKE ACTION AT THE PALACE.
ME AND NO ONE ELSE!!

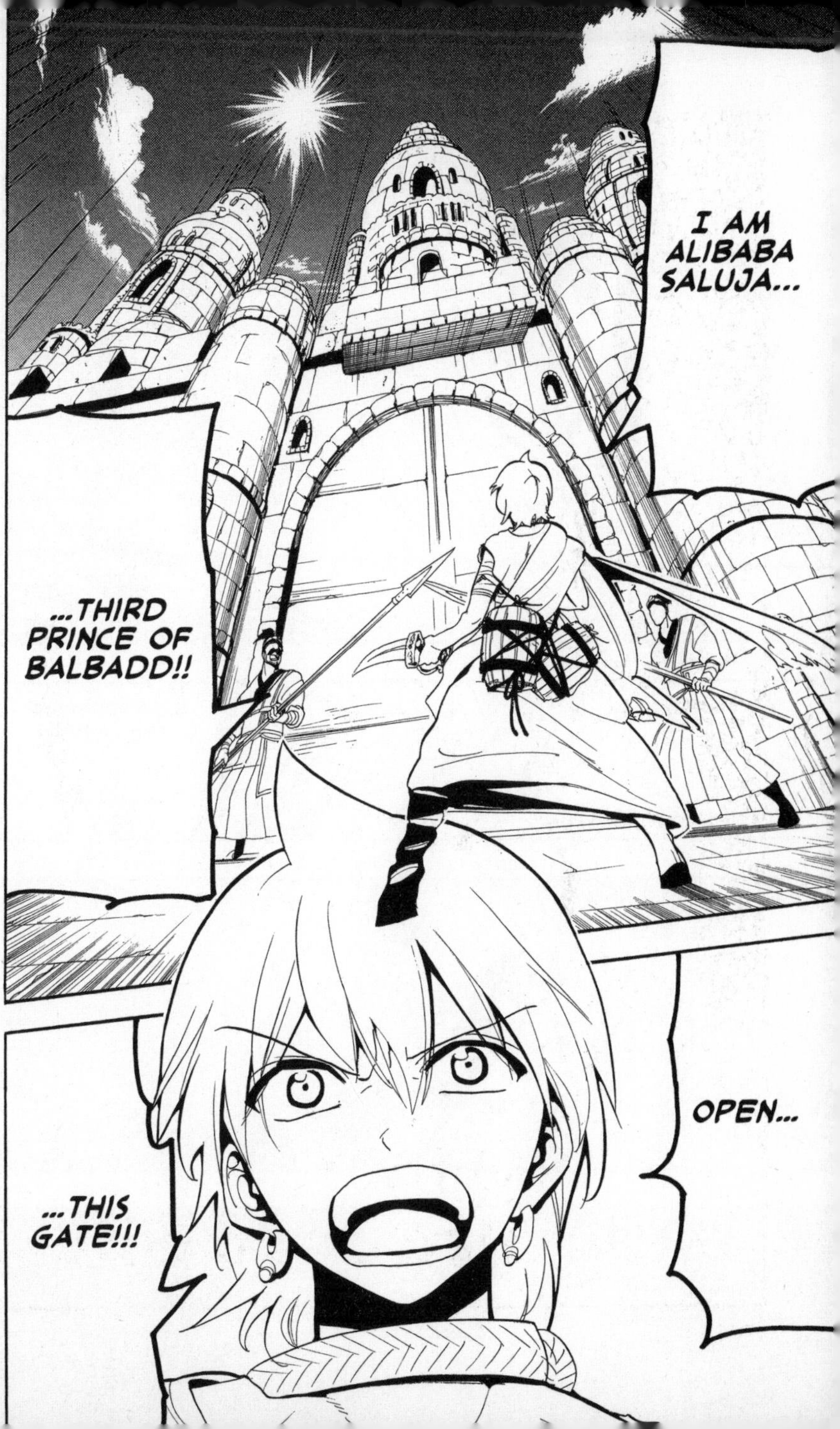
I AM ALIBABA SALUJA...
...THIRD PRINCE OF BALBADD!!
OPEN...
...THIS GATE!!!

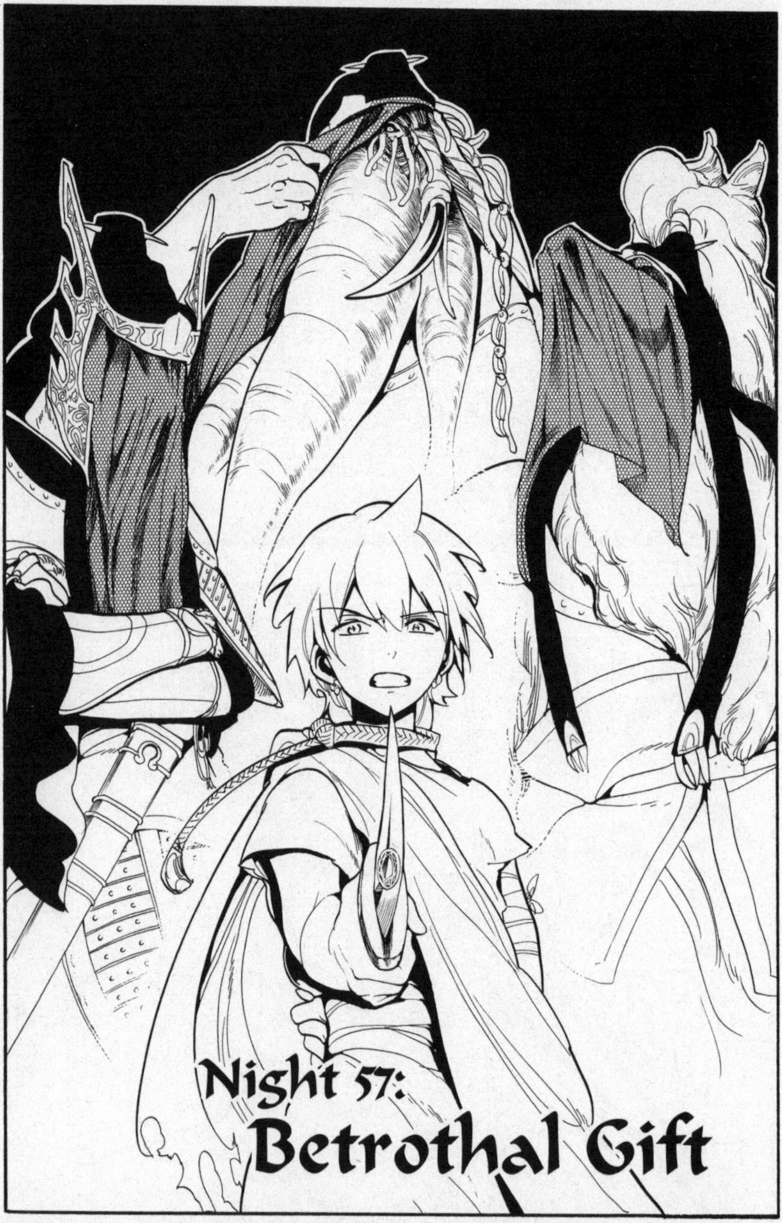
Night 57:
Betrothal Gift

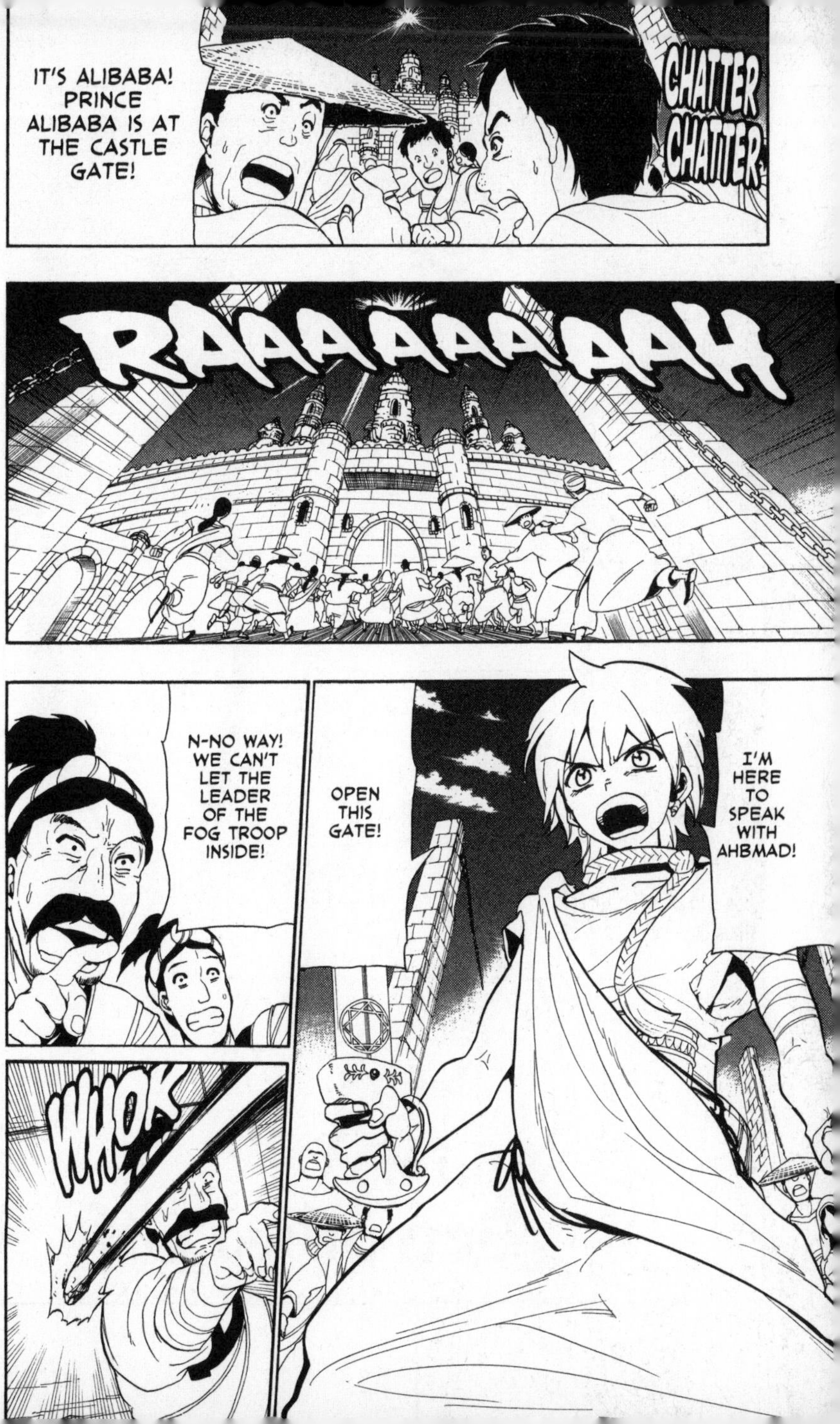
CHATTER CHATTER
IT'S ALIBABA! PRINCE ALIBABA IS AT THE CASTLE GATE!
RAAAAAAAH
I'M HERE TO SPEAK WITH AHBMAD!
OPEN THIS GATE!
N-NO WAY! WE CAN'T LET THE LEADER OF THE FOG TROOP INSIDE!
WHOK

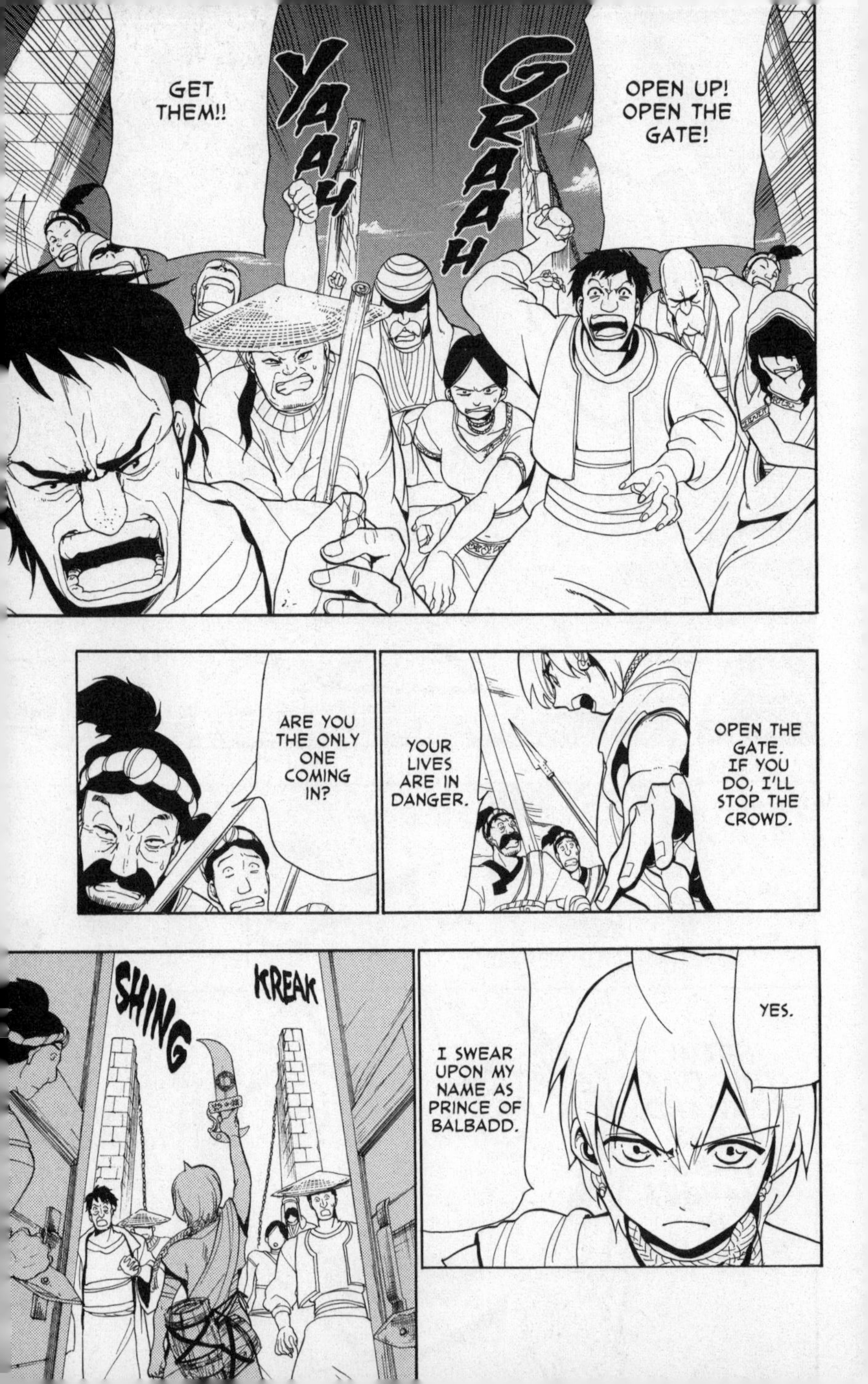
OPEN UP! OPEN THE GATE!
GRAAH
YAAH
GET THEM!!
OPEN THE GATE. IF YOU DO, I'LL STOP THE CROWD.
YOUR LIVES ARE IN DANGER.
ARE YOU THE ONLY ONE COMING IN?
YES.
I SWEAR UPON MY NAME AS PRINCE OF BALBADD.
KREAK
SHING

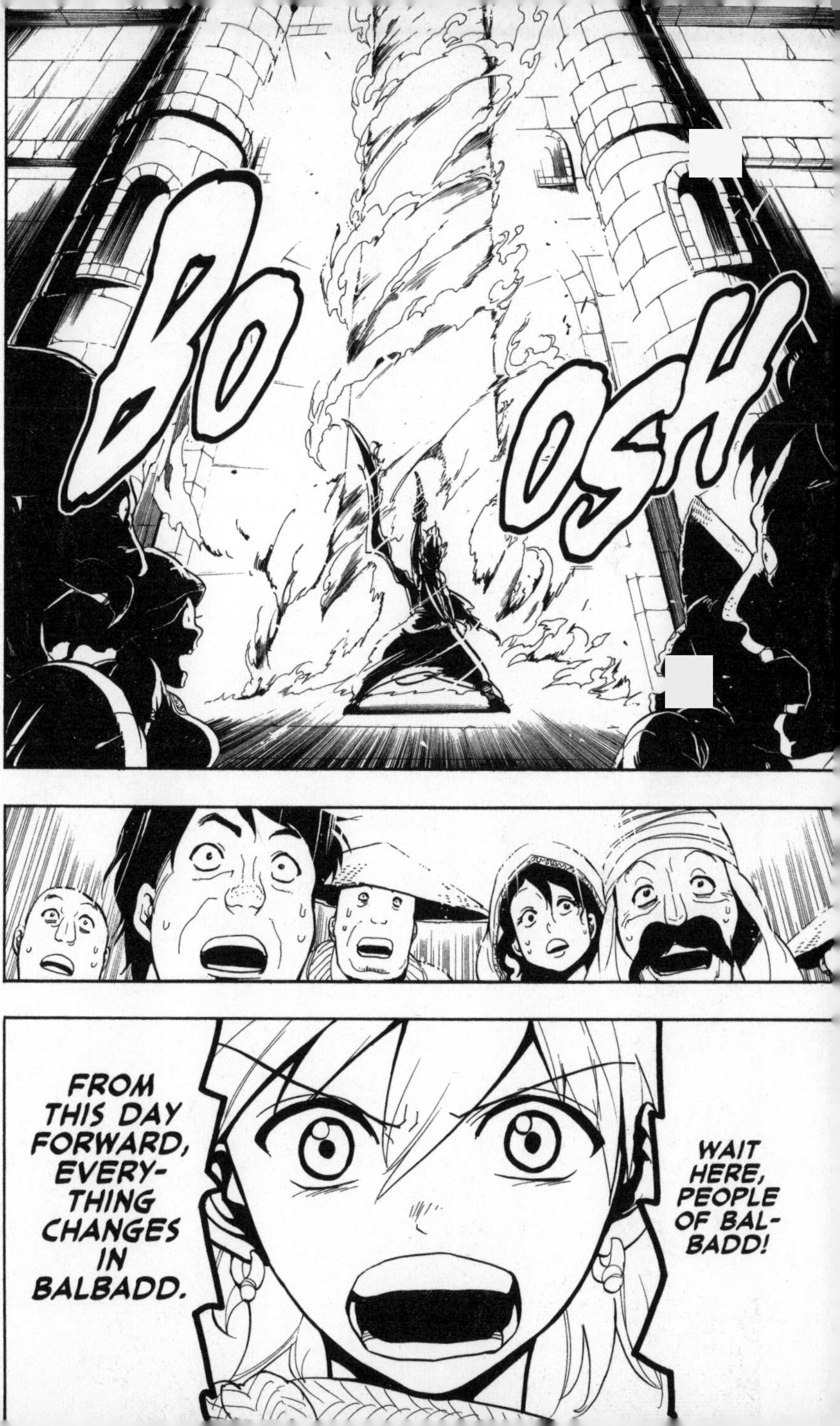
BOOSH
WAIT HERE, PEOPLE OF BAL-BADD!
FROM THIS DAY FORWARD, EVERY-THING CHANGES IN BALBADD.

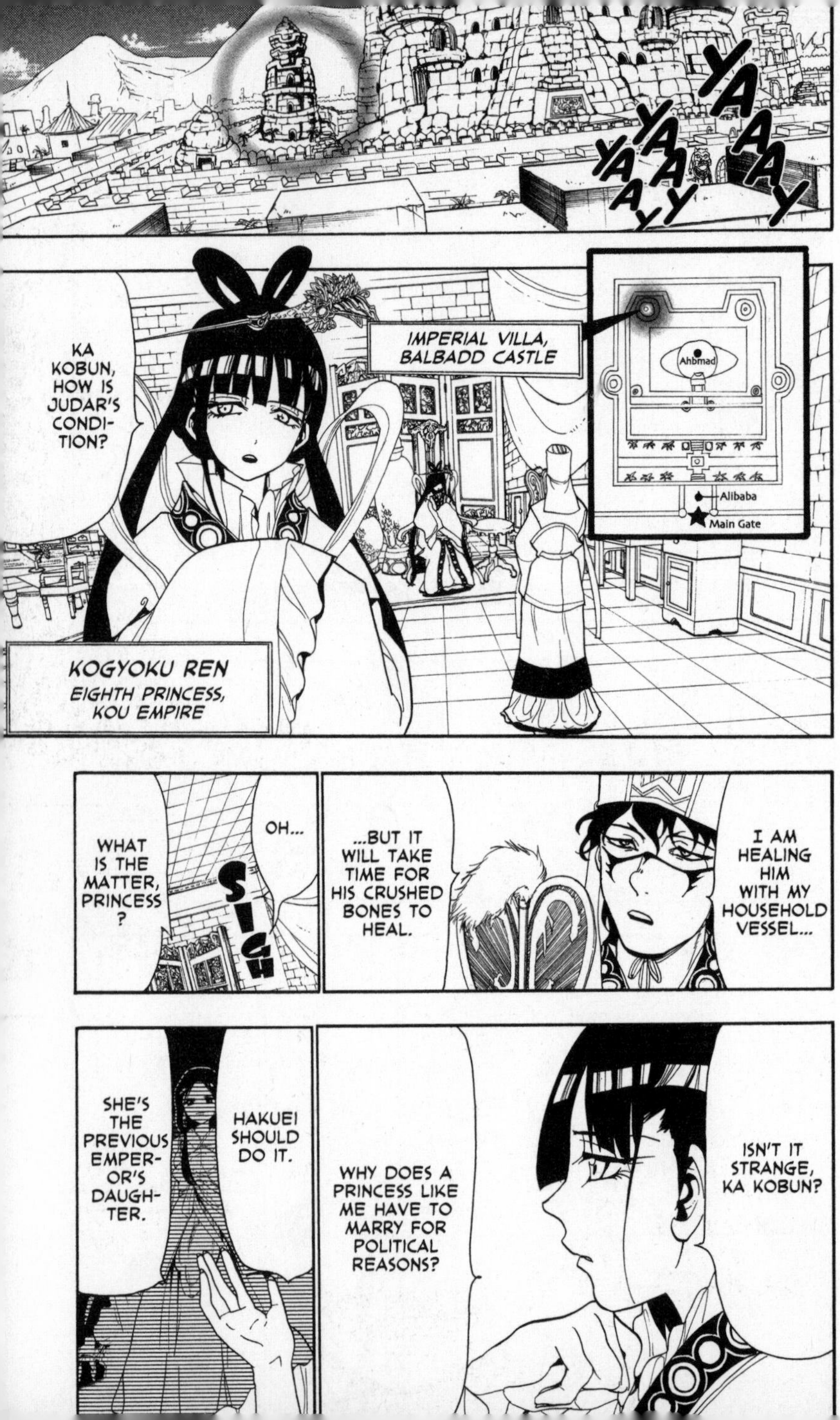
YAAAAY
YAAAY
YAAY
Ahbmad
Alibaba
Main Gate
IMPERIAL VILLA, BALBADD CASTLE
KA KOBUN, HOW IS JUDAR'S CONDITION?
KOGYOKU REN
EIGHTH PRINCESS, KOU EMPIRE
I AM HEALING HIM WITH MY HOUSEHOLD VESSEL...
...BUT IT WILL TAKE TIME FOR HIS CRUSHED BONES TO HEAL.
OH...
SIGH
WHAT IS THE MATTER, PRINCESS?
ISN'T IT STRANGE, KA KOBUN?
WHY DOES A PRINCESS LIKE ME HAVE TO MARRY FOR POLITICAL REASONS?
HAKUEI SHOULD DO IT.
SHE'S THE PREVIOUS EMPEROR'S DAUGHTER.

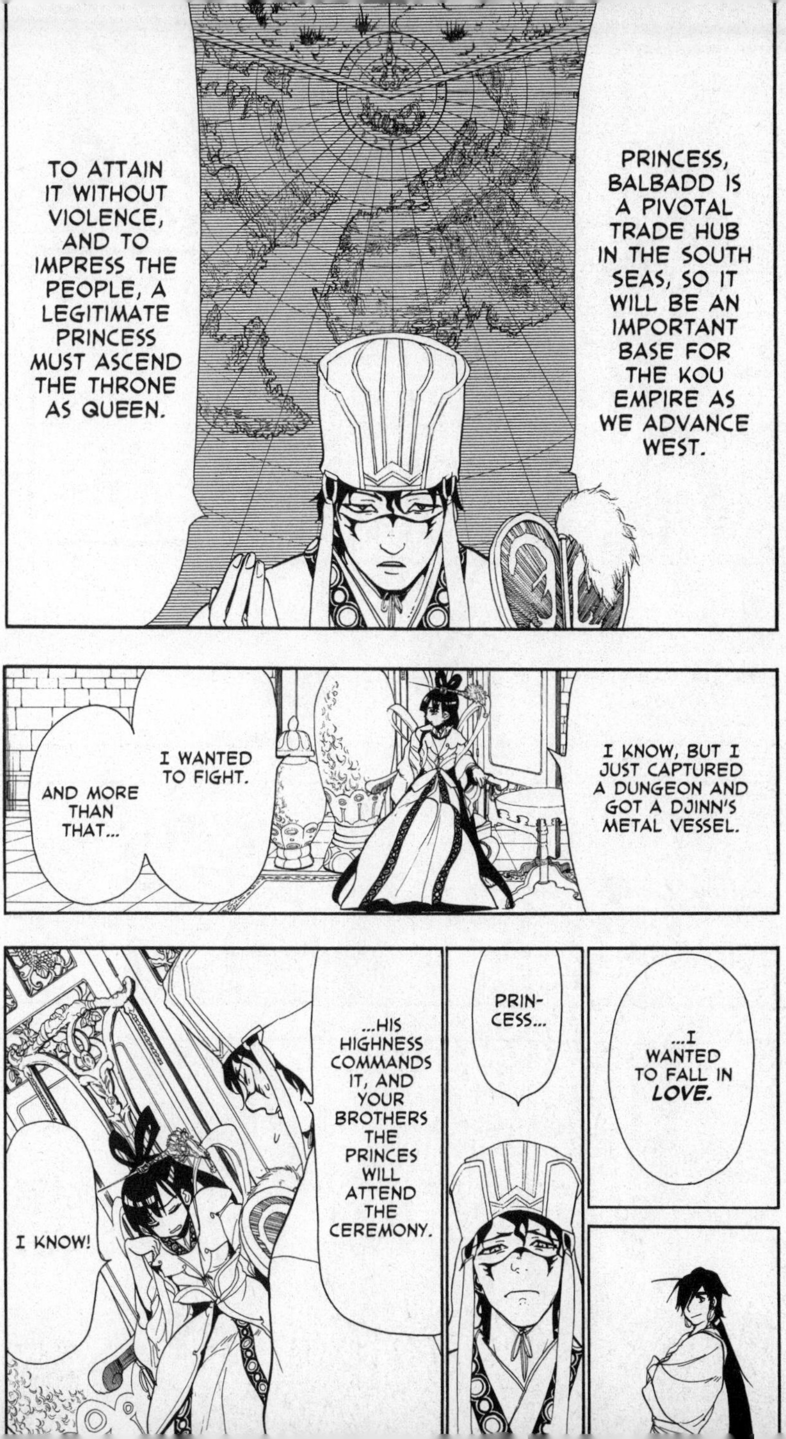
PRINCESS, BALBADD IS A PIVOTAL TRADE HUB IN THE SOUTH SEAS, SO IT WILL BE AN IMPORTANT BASE FOR THE KOU EMPIRE AS WE ADVANCE WEST.
TO ATTAIN IT WITHOUT VIOLENCE, AND TO IMPRESS THE PEOPLE, A LEGITIMATE PRINCESS MUST ASCEND THE THRONE AS QUEEN.
I KNOW, BUT I JUST CAPTURED A DUNGEON AND GOT A DJINN'S METAL VESSEL.
I WANTED TO FIGHT.
AND MORE THAN THAT...
...I WANTED TO FALL IN *LOVE.*
PRIN-CESS...
...HIS HIGHNESS COMMANDS IT, AND YOUR BROTHERS THE PRINCES WILL ATTEND THE CEREMONY.
I KNOW!

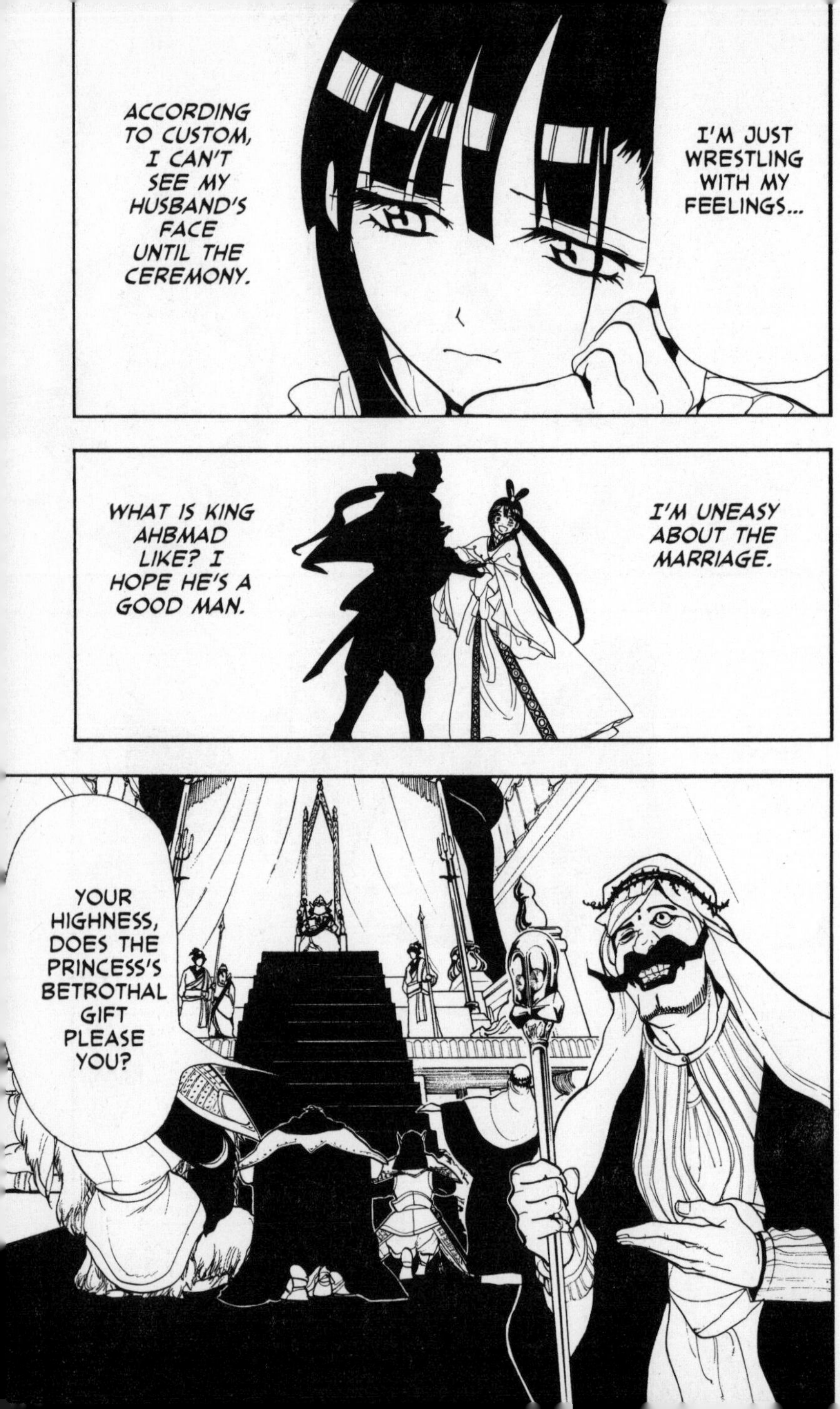
I'M JUST WRESTLING WITH MY FEELINGS...
ACCORDING TO CUSTOM, I CAN'T SEE MY HUSBAND'S FACE UNTIL THE CEREMONY.
I'M UNEASY ABOUT THE MARRIAGE.
WHAT IS KING AHBMAD LIKE? I HOPE HE'S A GOOD MAN.
YOUR HIGHNESS, DOES THE PRINCESS'S BETROTHAL GIFT PLEASE YOU?

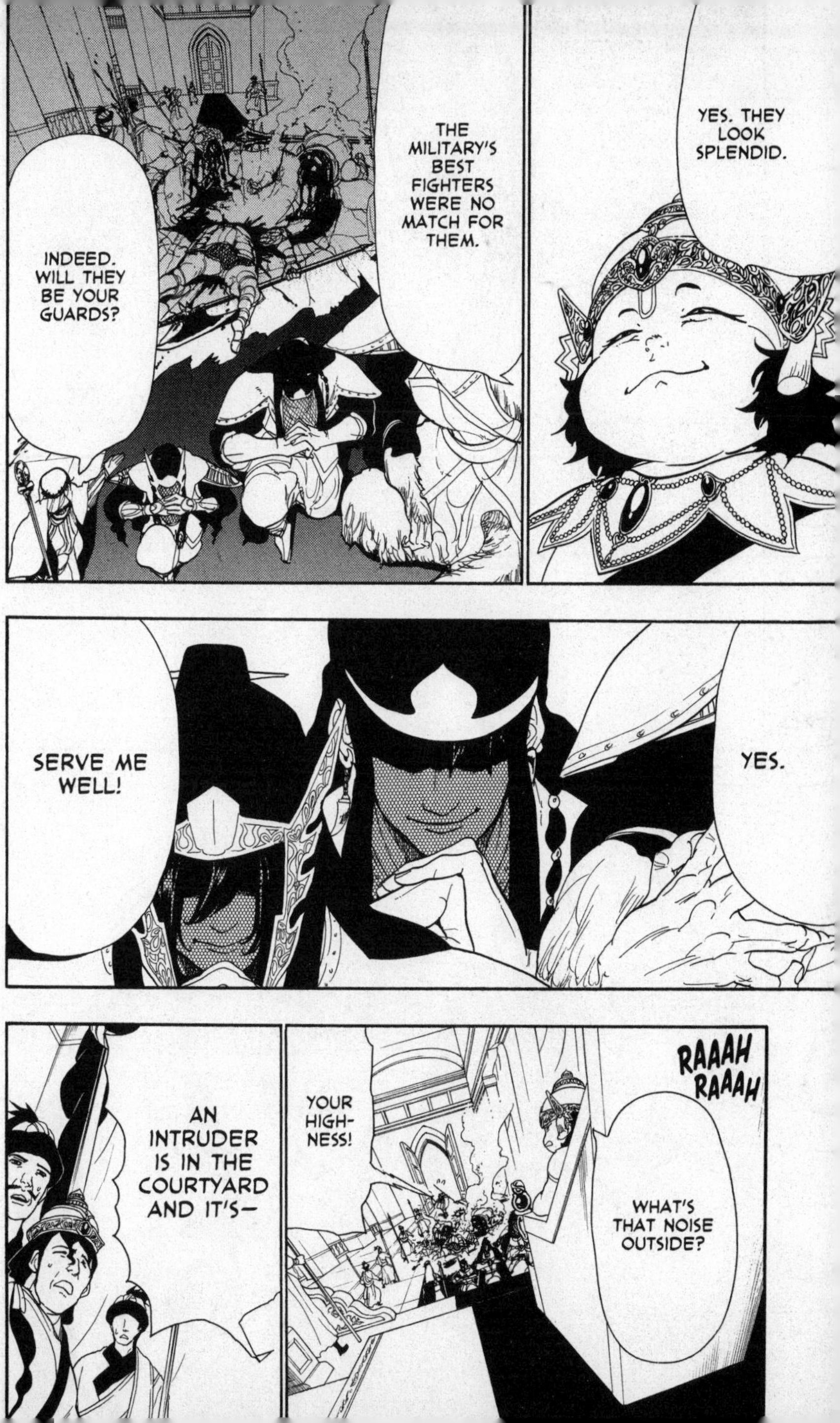
YES. THEY LOOK SPLENDID.
THE MILITARY'S BEST FIGHTERS WERE NO MATCH FOR THEM.
INDEED. WILL THEY BE YOUR GUARDS?
YES.
SERVE ME WELL!
RAAAH RAAAH
WHAT'S THAT NOISE OUTSIDE?
YOUR HIGH-NESS!
AN INTRUDER IS IN THE COURTYARD AND IT'S—

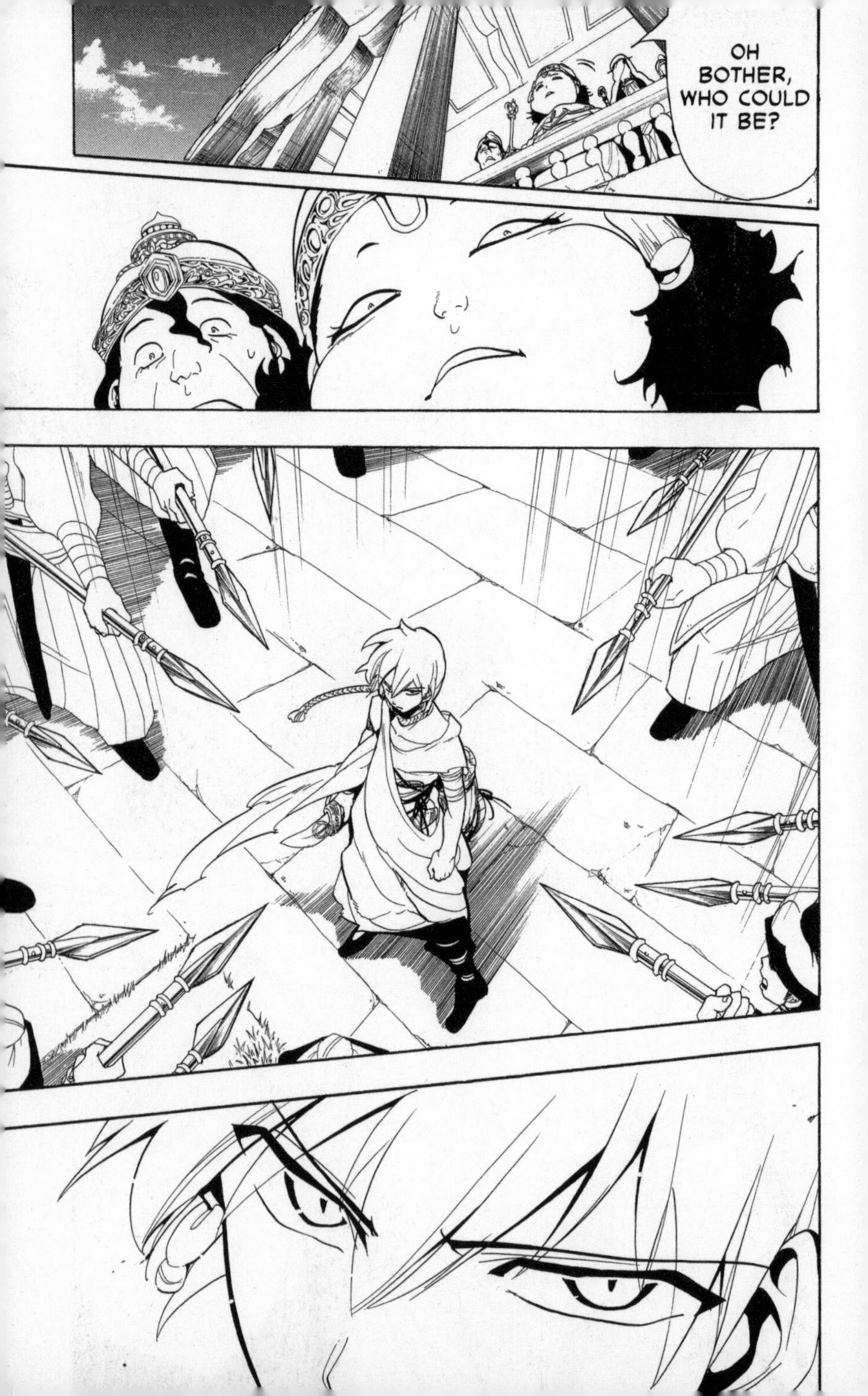
OH BOTHER, WHO COULD IT BE?

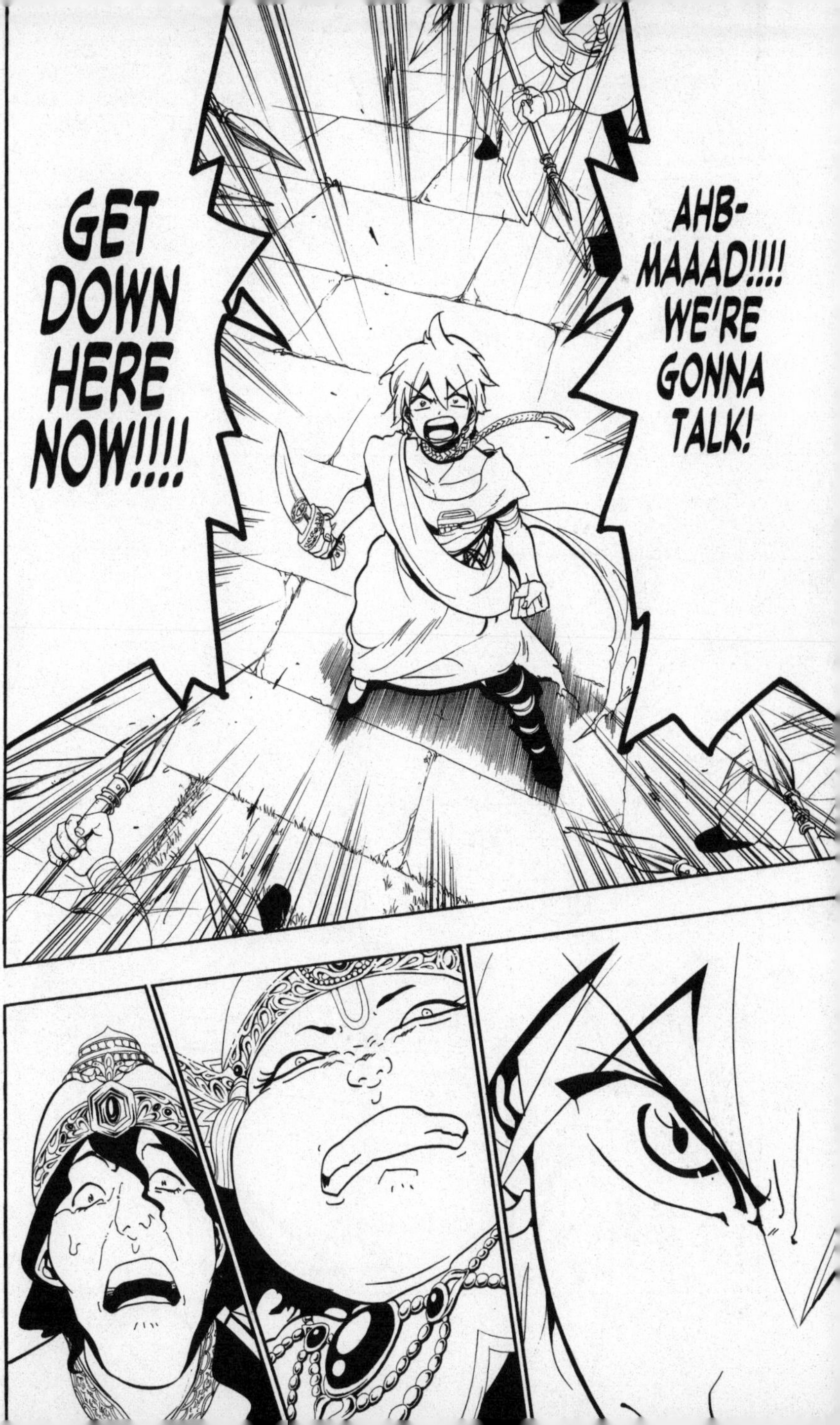
AHB-MAAAD!!!! WE'RE GONNA TALK!
GET DOWN HERE NOW!!!!

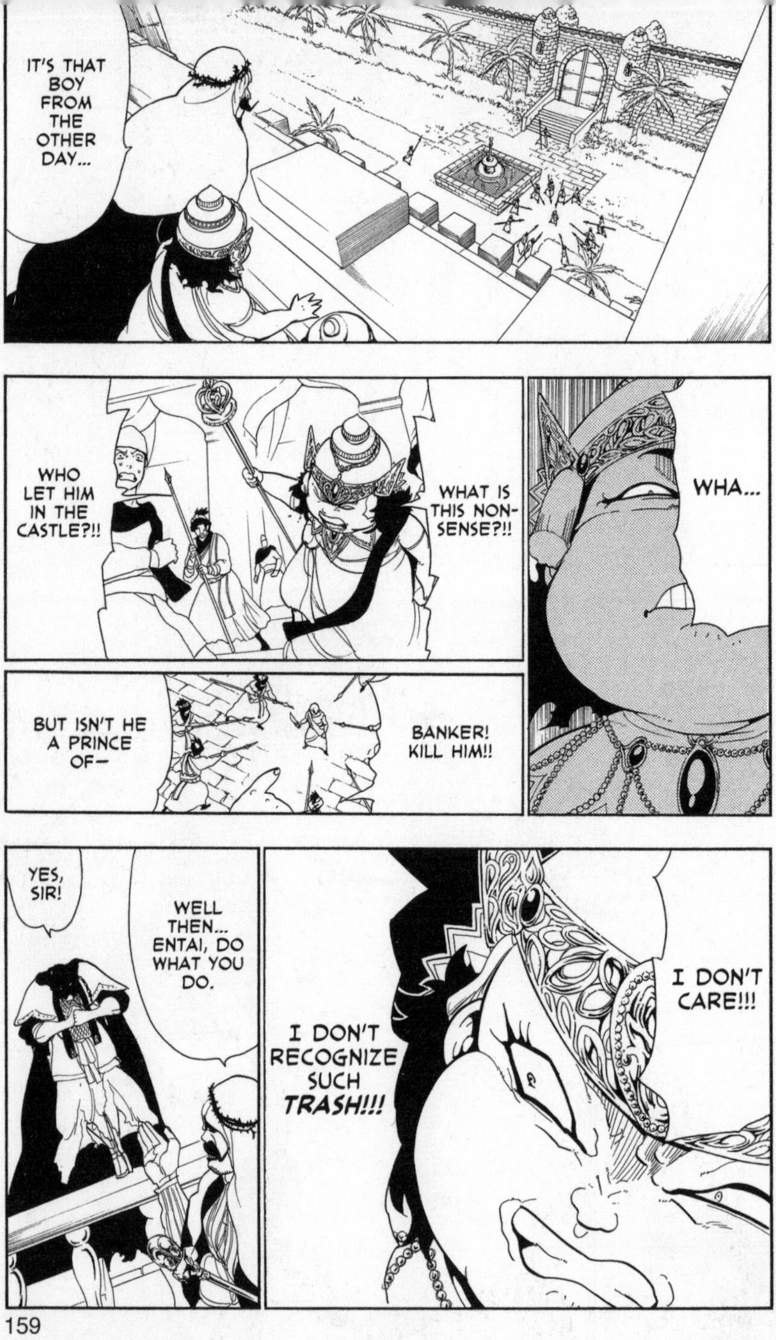
IT'S THAT BOY FROM THE OTHER DAY...
WHA...
WHAT IS THIS NON-SENSE?!!
WHO LET HIM IN THE CASTLE?!!
BANKER! KILL HIM!!
BUT ISN'T HE A PRINCE OF—
I DON'T CARE!!!
I DON'T RECOGNIZE SUCH *TRASH*!!!
WELL THEN... ENTAI, DO WHAT YOU DO.
YES, SIR!

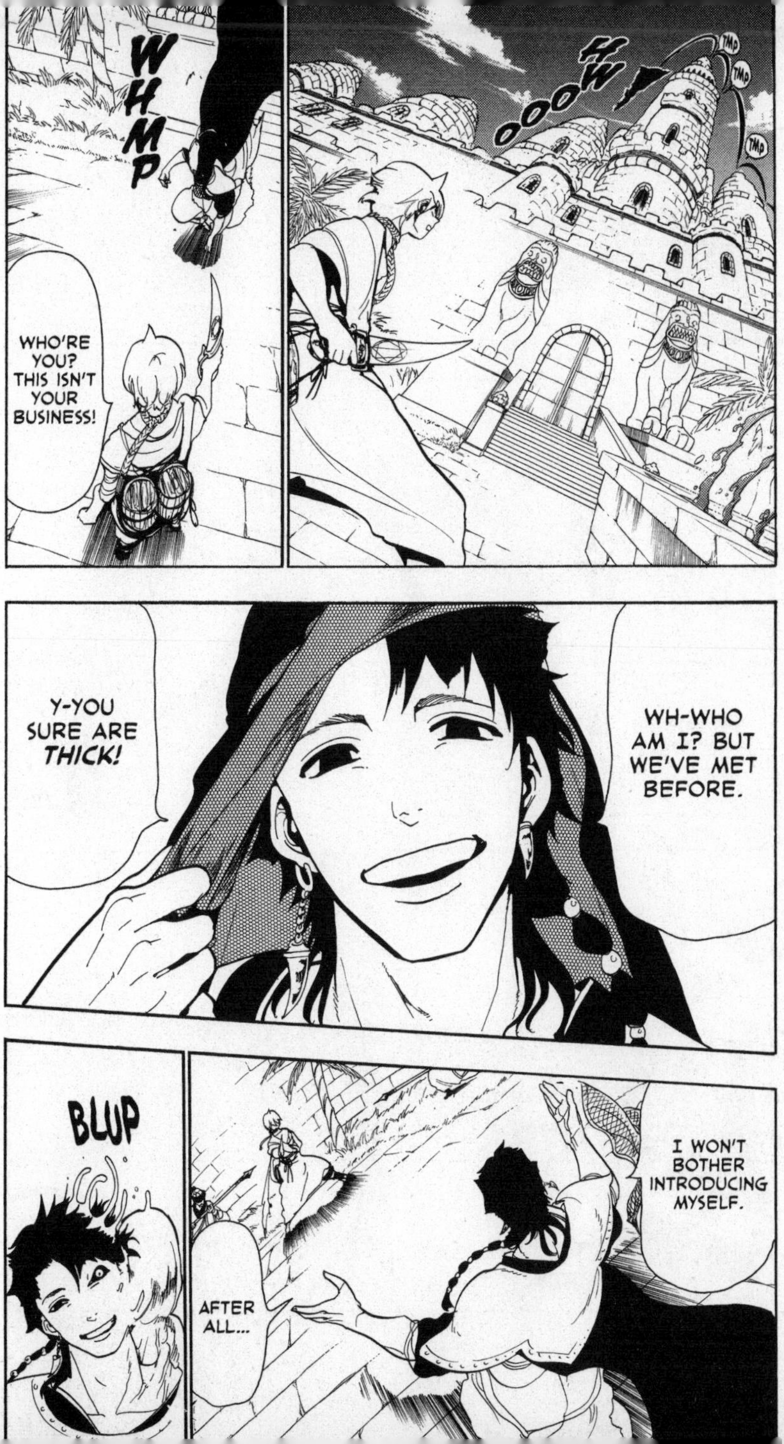
TMP
TMP
TMP
WHMP
WHO'RE YOU? THIS ISN'T YOUR BUSINESS!
WH-WHO AM I? BUT WE'VE MET BEFORE.
Y-YOU SURE ARE *THICK!*
I WON'T BOTHER INTRODUCING MYSELF.
AFTER ALL...
BLUP

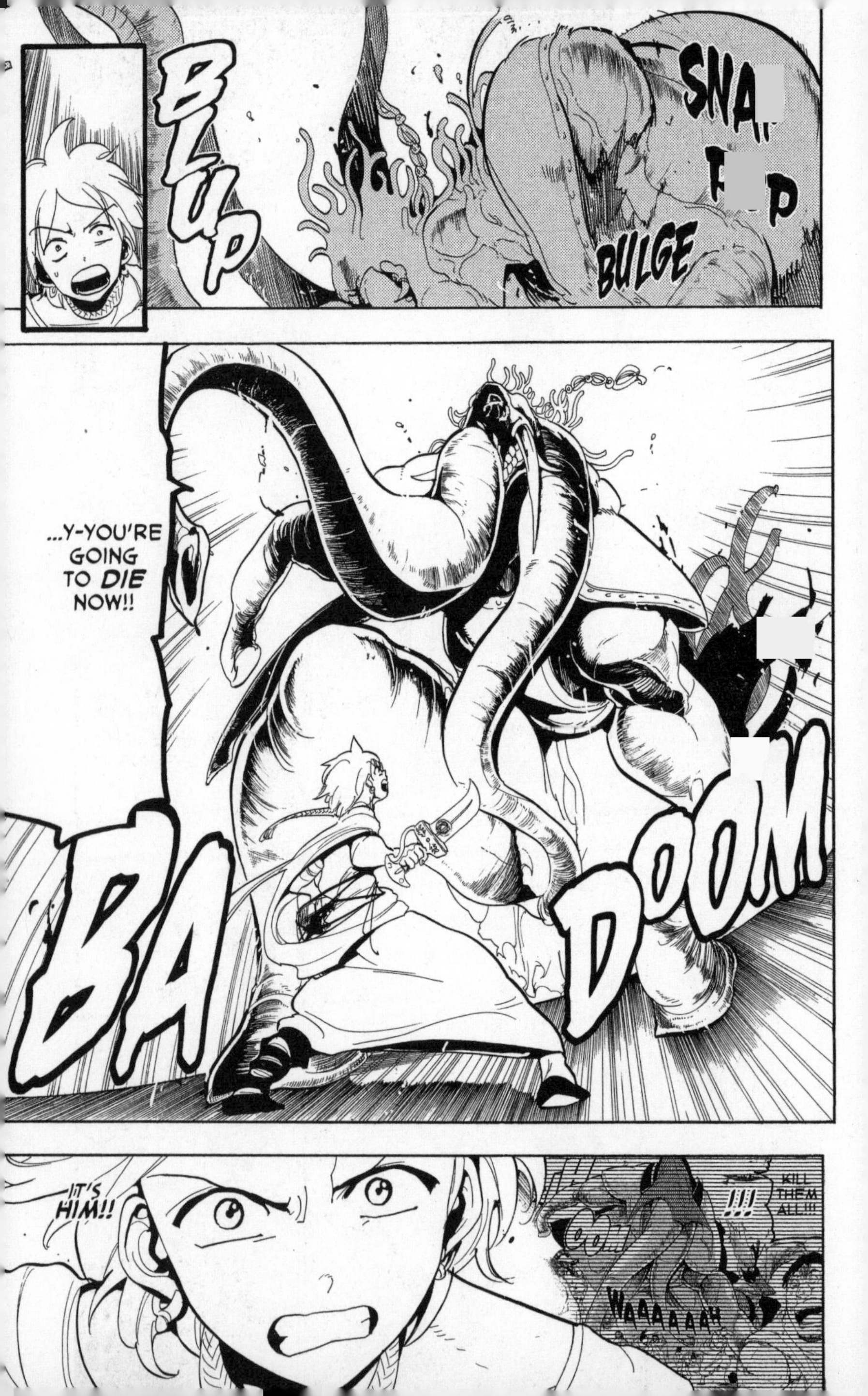

BULGE
BLUP
...Y-YOU'RE GOING TO *DIE* NOW!!
BADOOM
KILL THEM ALL!!!
!!!
WAAAAAAH
IT'S HIM!!

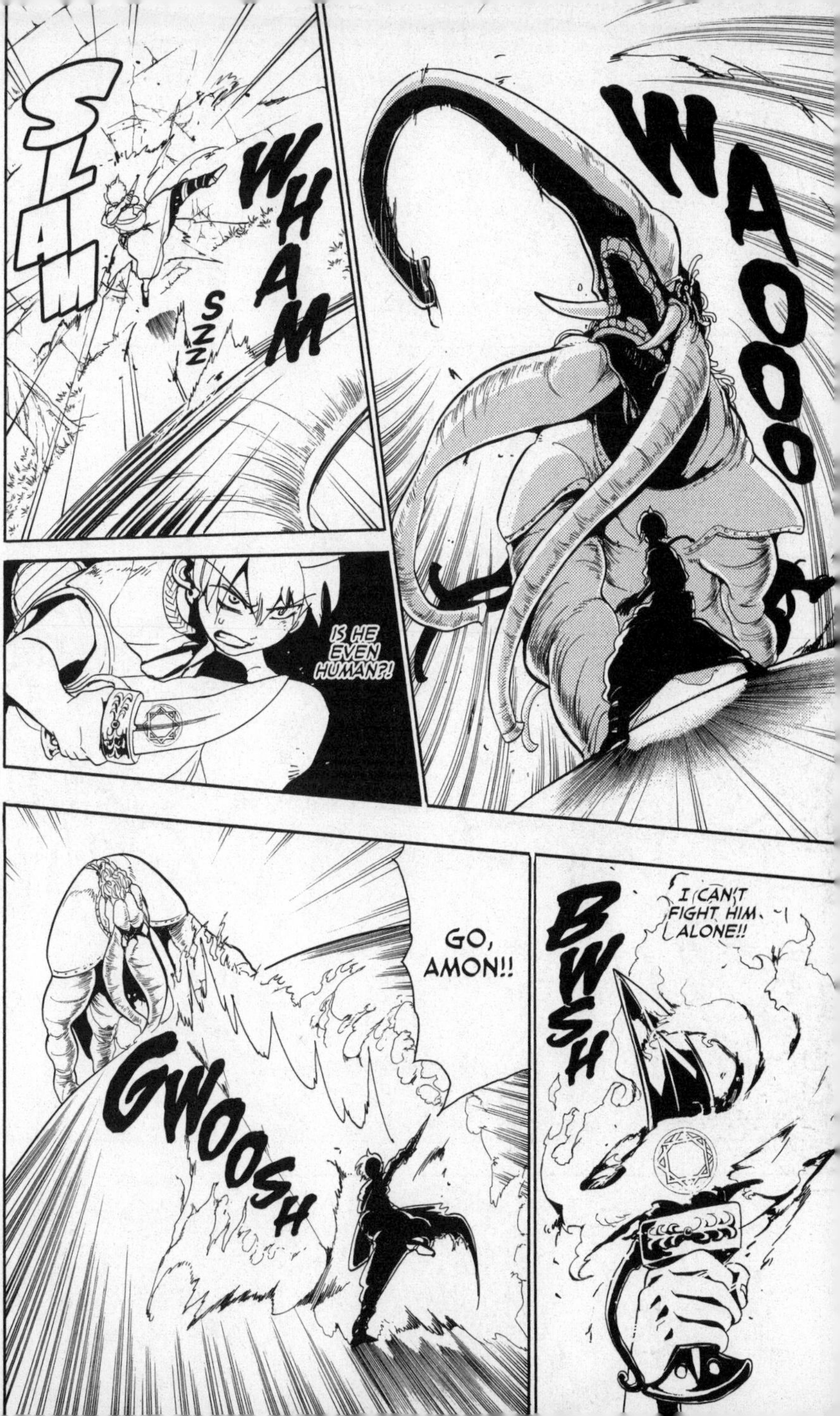
WAOOO
WHAM
SLAM
SZZ
IS HE EVEN HUMAN?!
I CAN'T FIGHT HIM ALONE!!
BWSH
GO, AMON!!
GWOOSH

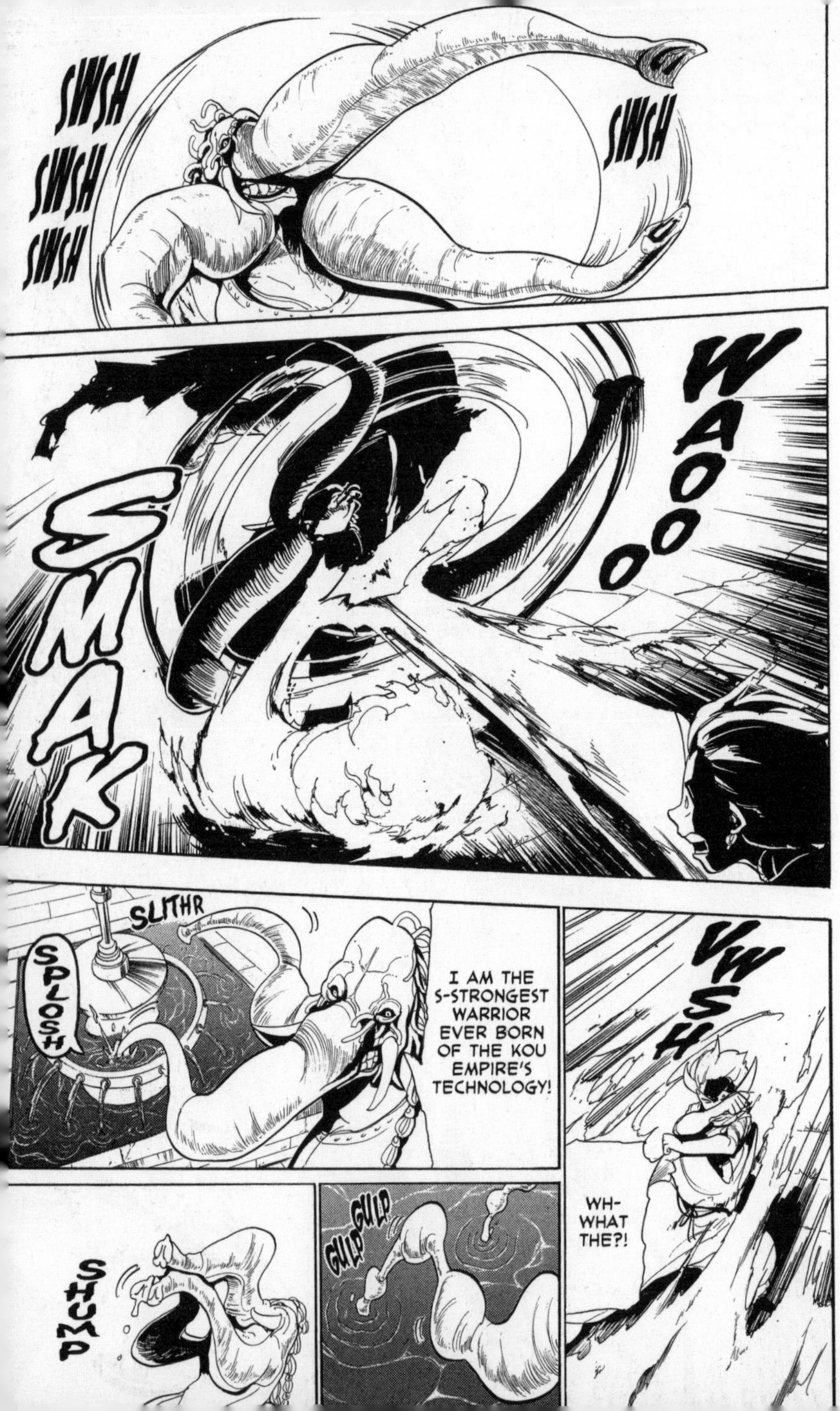
SWSH
SWSH SWSH SWSH
WAOOOO
SMAK
VWSH
WH- WHAT THE?!
I AM THE S-STRONGEST WARRIOR EVER BORN OF THE KOU EMPIRE'S TECHNOLOGY!
SLITHR
SPLOSH
GULP GULP
SHUMP

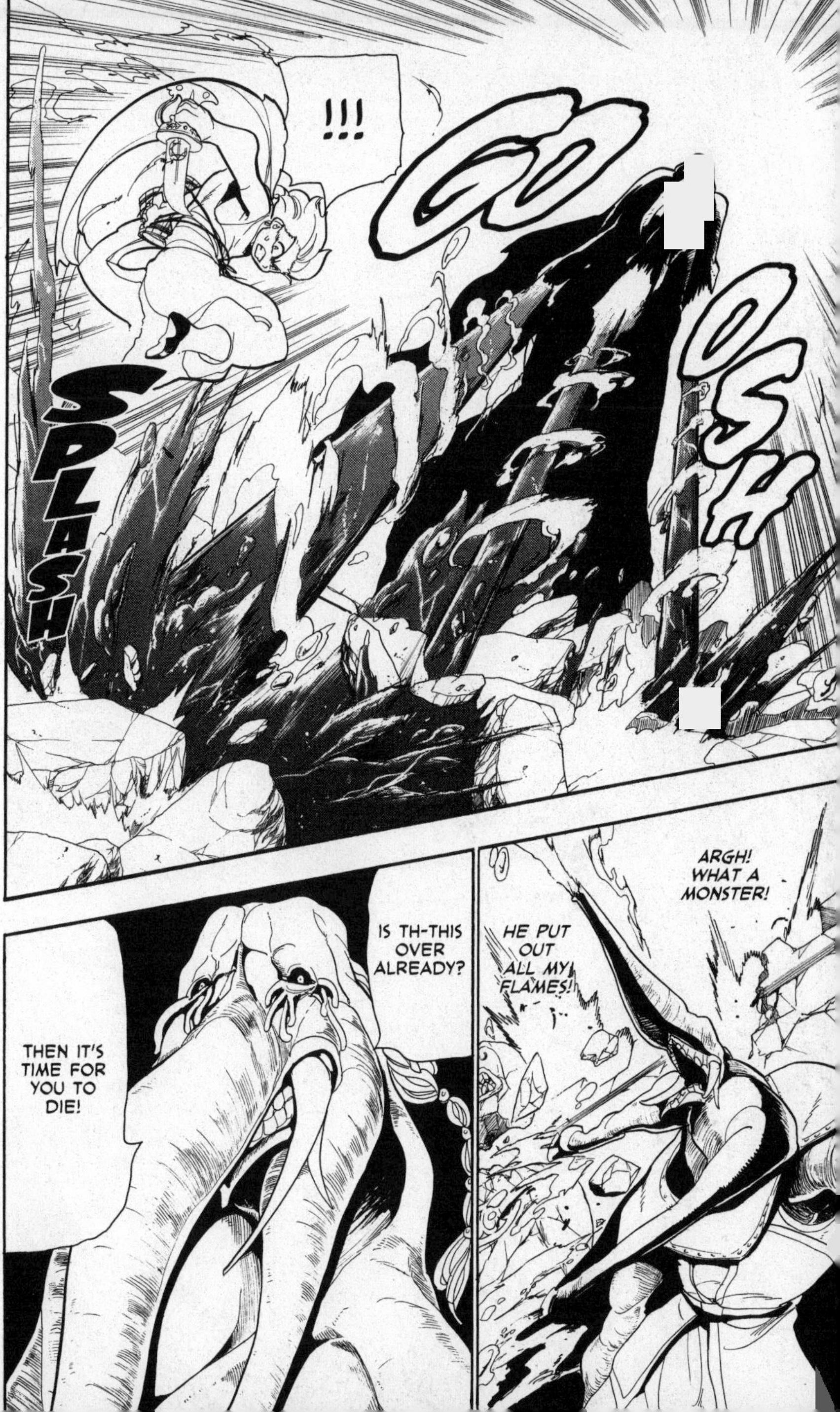
GOOSH
!!!
SPLASH
ARGH! WHAT A MONSTER!
HE PUT OUT ALL MY FLAMES!
IS TH-THIS OVER ALREADY?
THEN IT'S TIME FOR YOU TO DIE!

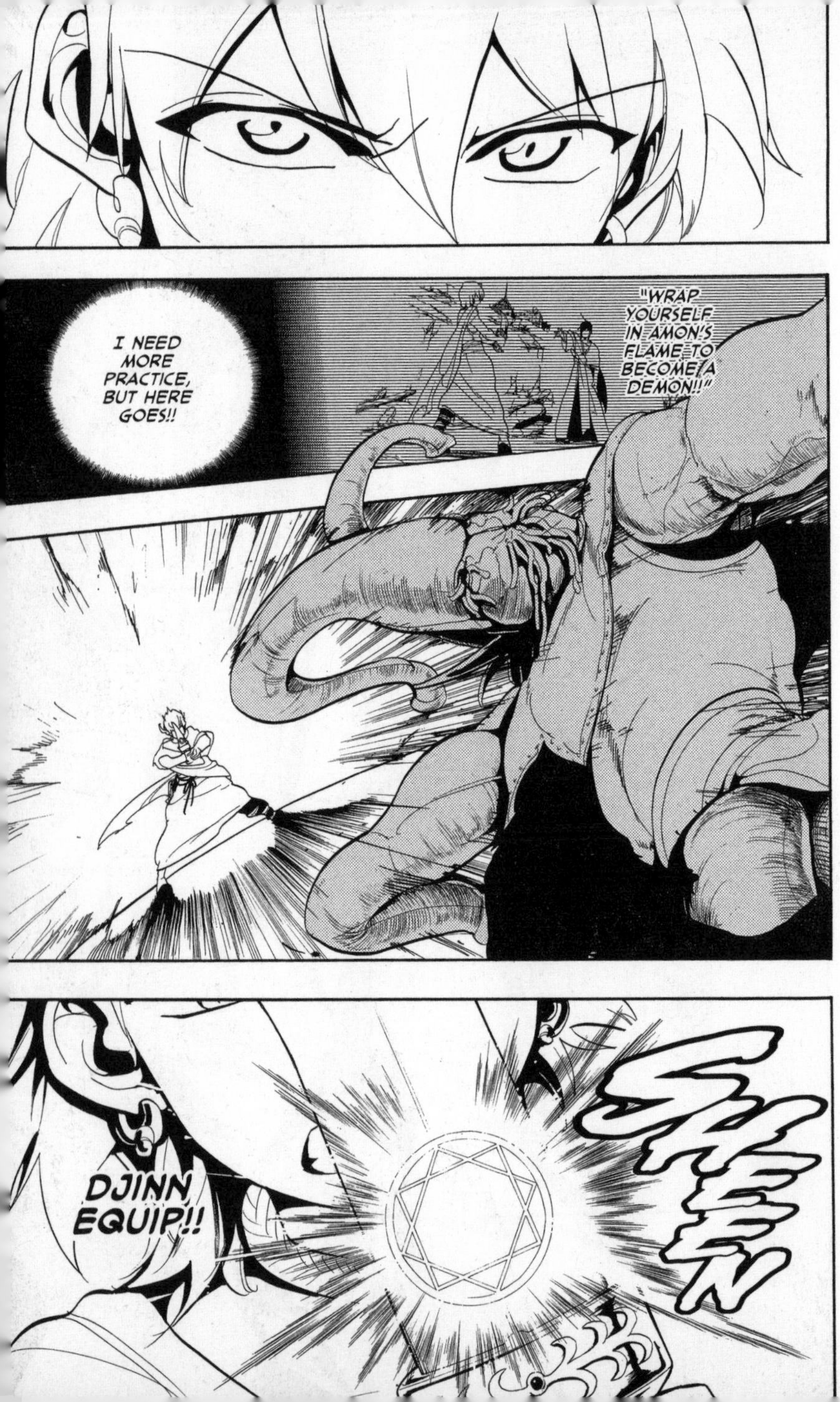
"WRAP YOURSELF IN AMON'S FLAME TO BECOME A DEMON!!"
I NEED MORE PRACTICE, BUT HERE GOES!!
SHEEN
DJINN EQUIP!!

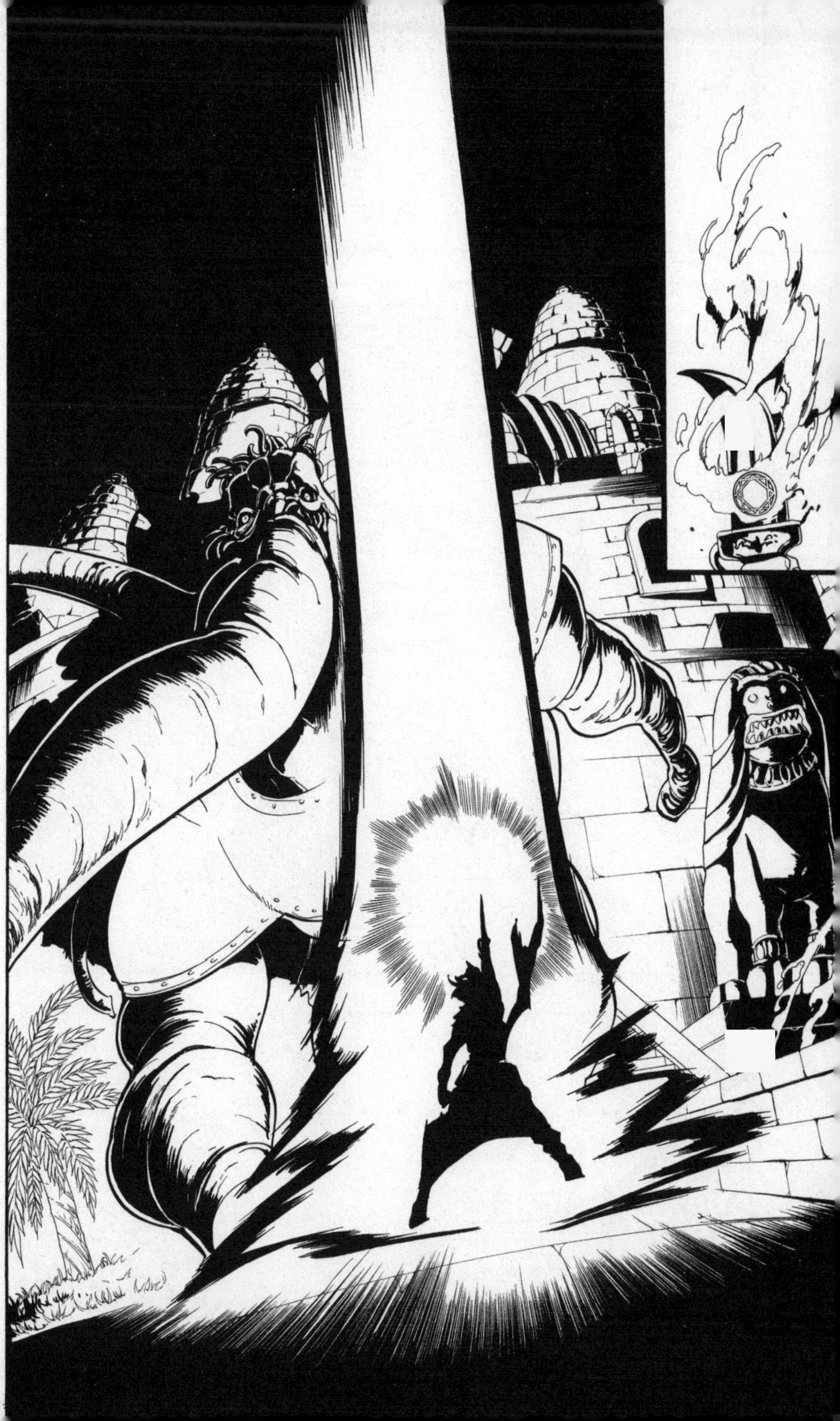

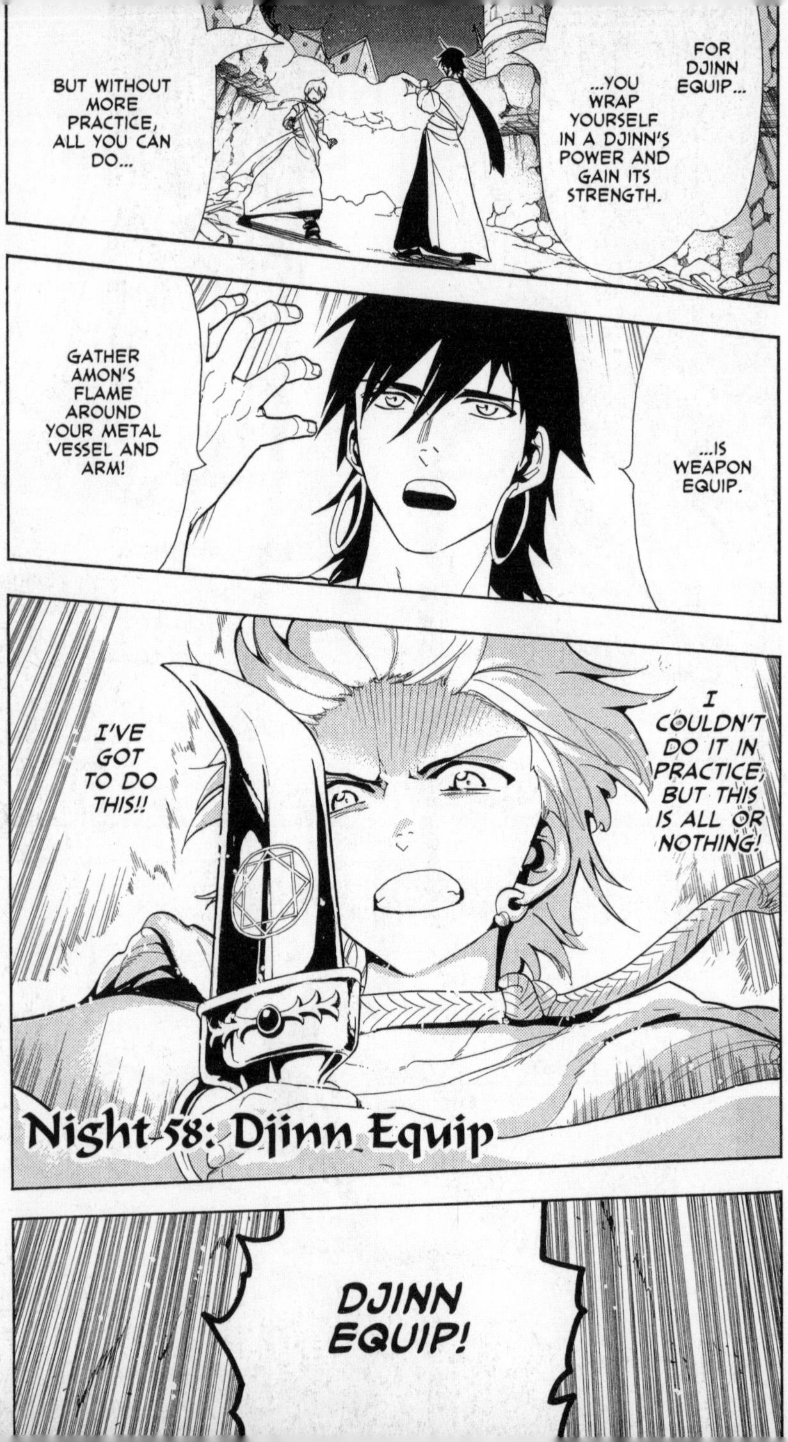
FOR DJINN EQUIP...
...YOU WRAP YOURSELF IN A DJINN'S POWER AND GAIN ITS STRENGTH.
BUT WITHOUT MORE PRACTICE, ALL YOU CAN DO...
...IS WEAPON EQUIP.
GATHER AMON'S FLAME AROUND YOUR METAL VESSEL AND ARM!
I COULDN'T DO IT IN PRACTICE, BUT THIS IS ALL OR NOTHING!
I'VE GOT TO DO THIS!!
Night 58: Djinn Equip
DJINN EQUIP!

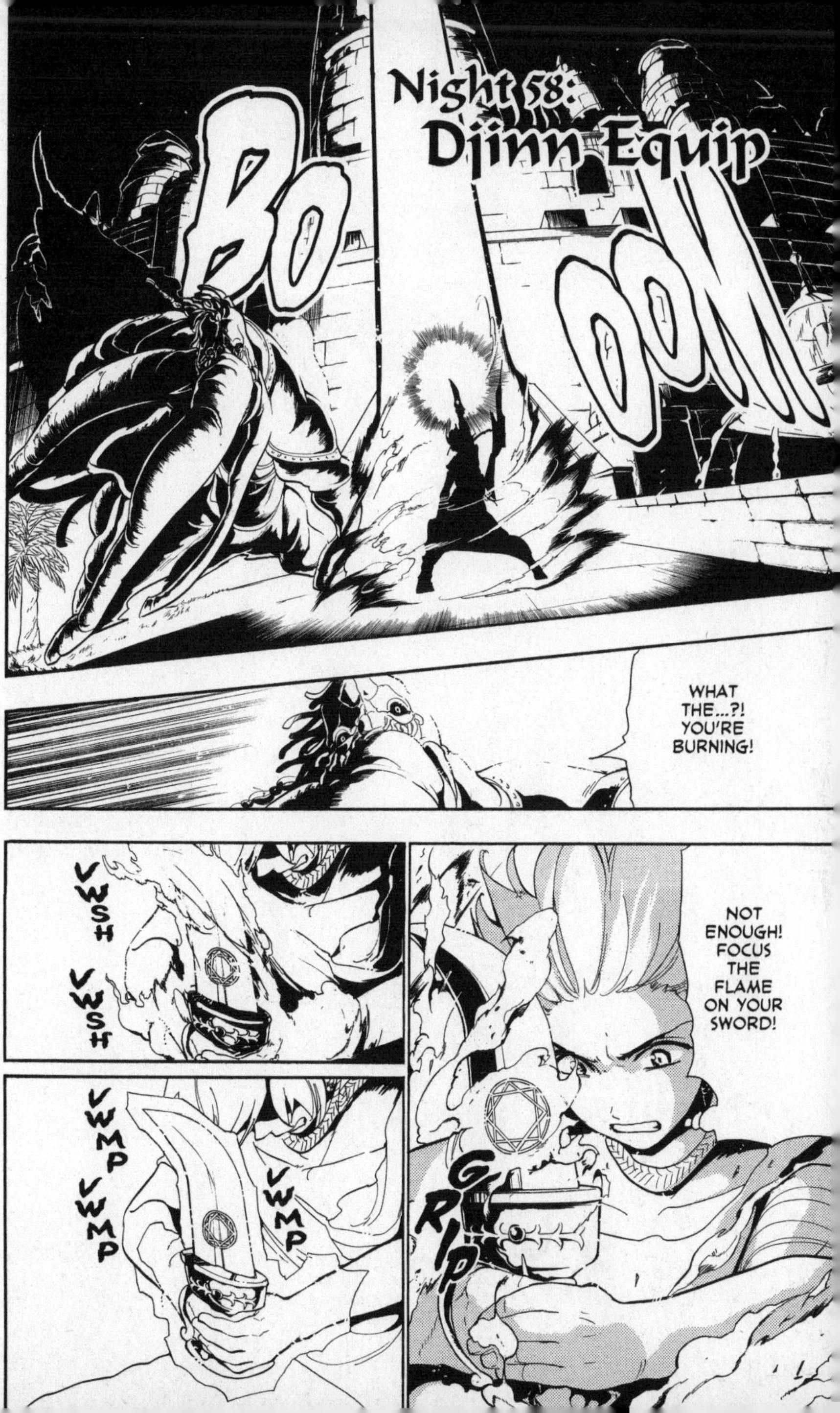
Night 58: Djinn Equip
BOOOM
WHAT THE...?! YOU'RE BURNING!
NOT ENOUGH! FOCUS THE FLAME ON YOUR SWORD!
GRIP
VWSH VWSH
VWMP VWMP VWMP

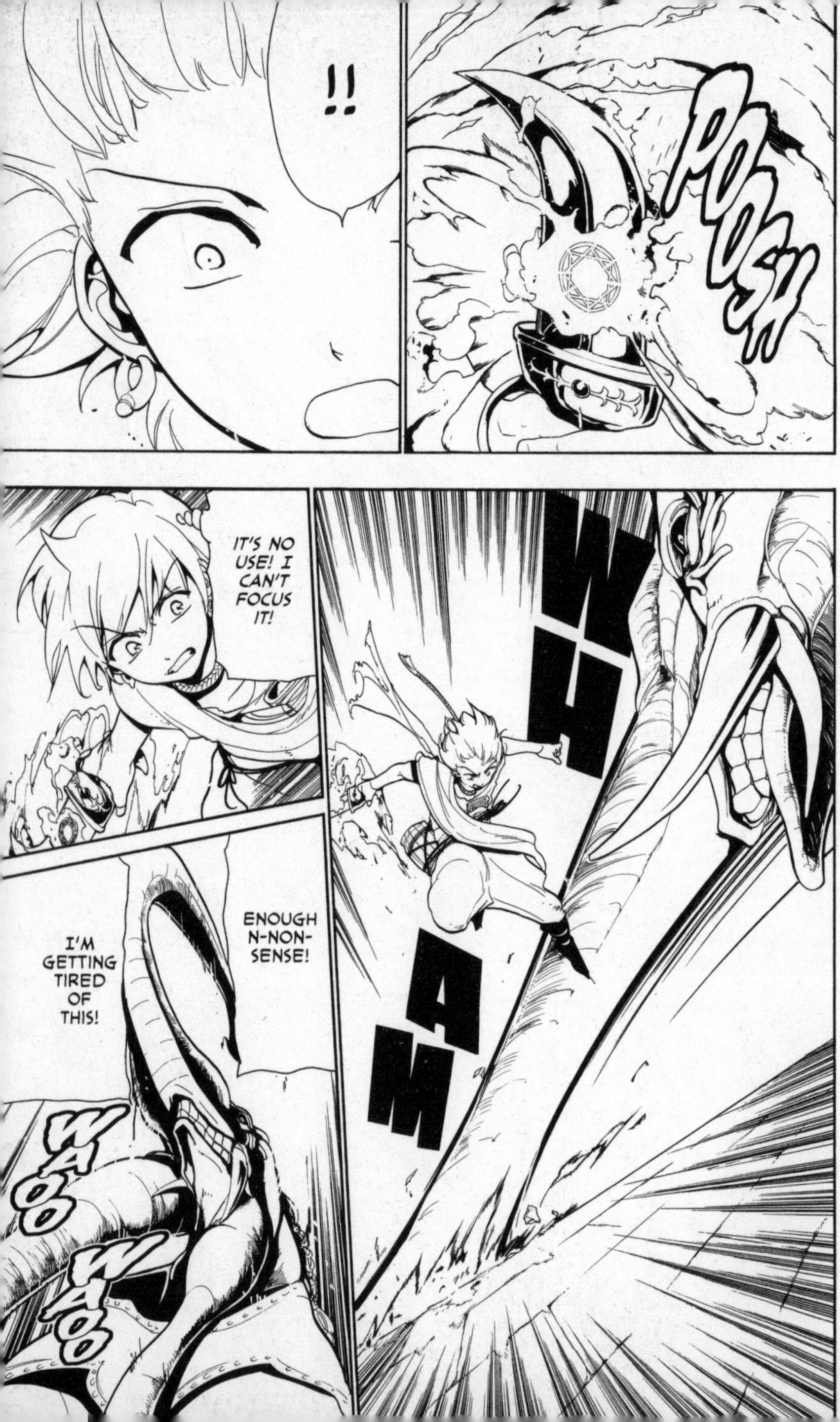
POOSH
!!
WHAM
IT'S NO USE! I CAN'T FOCUS IT!
ENOUGH N-NON-SENSE!
I'M GETTING TIRED OF THIS!
WAOO
WAOO

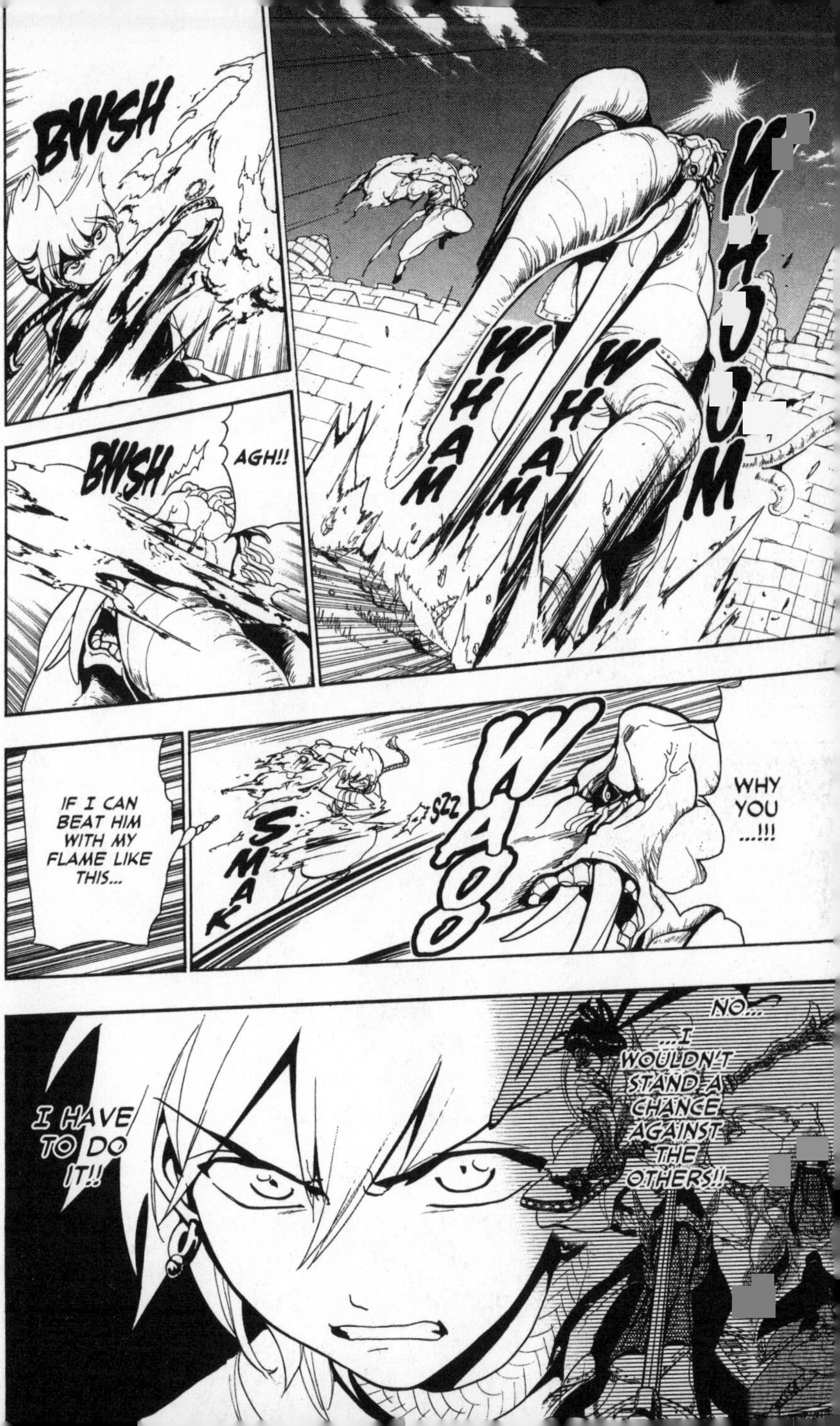
WHOOM
WHAM
WHAM
BWSH
BWSH
AGH!!
WHY YOU...!!!
WAOOO
SZZ
SMAK
IF I CAN BEAT HIM WITH MY FLAME LIKE THIS...
NO...
...I WOULDN'T STAND A CHANCE AGAINST THE OTHERS!!
I HAVE TO DO IT!!

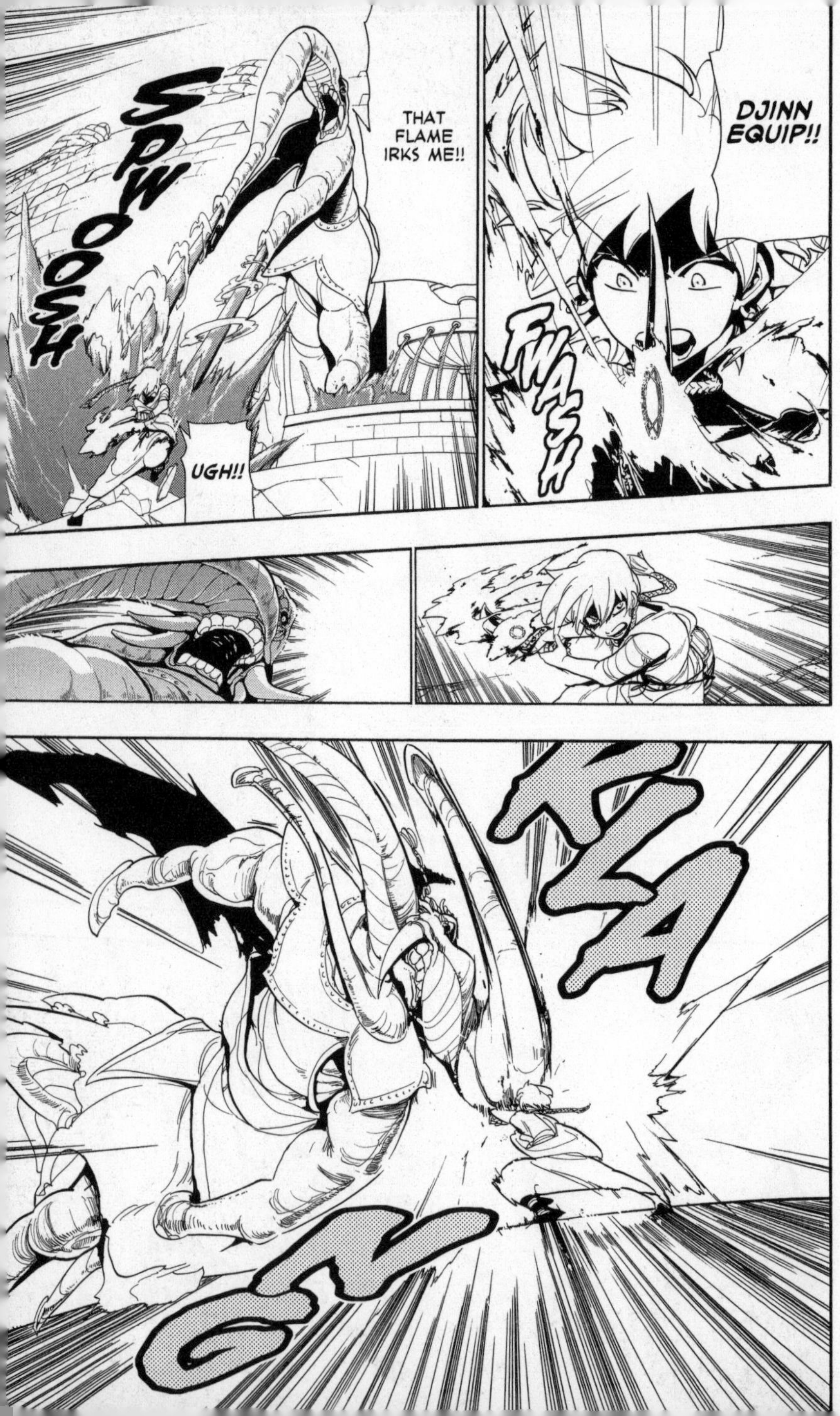
DJINN EQUIP!!
FWASH
THAT FLAME IRKS ME!!
SPWOOOSH
UGH!!
KLANG

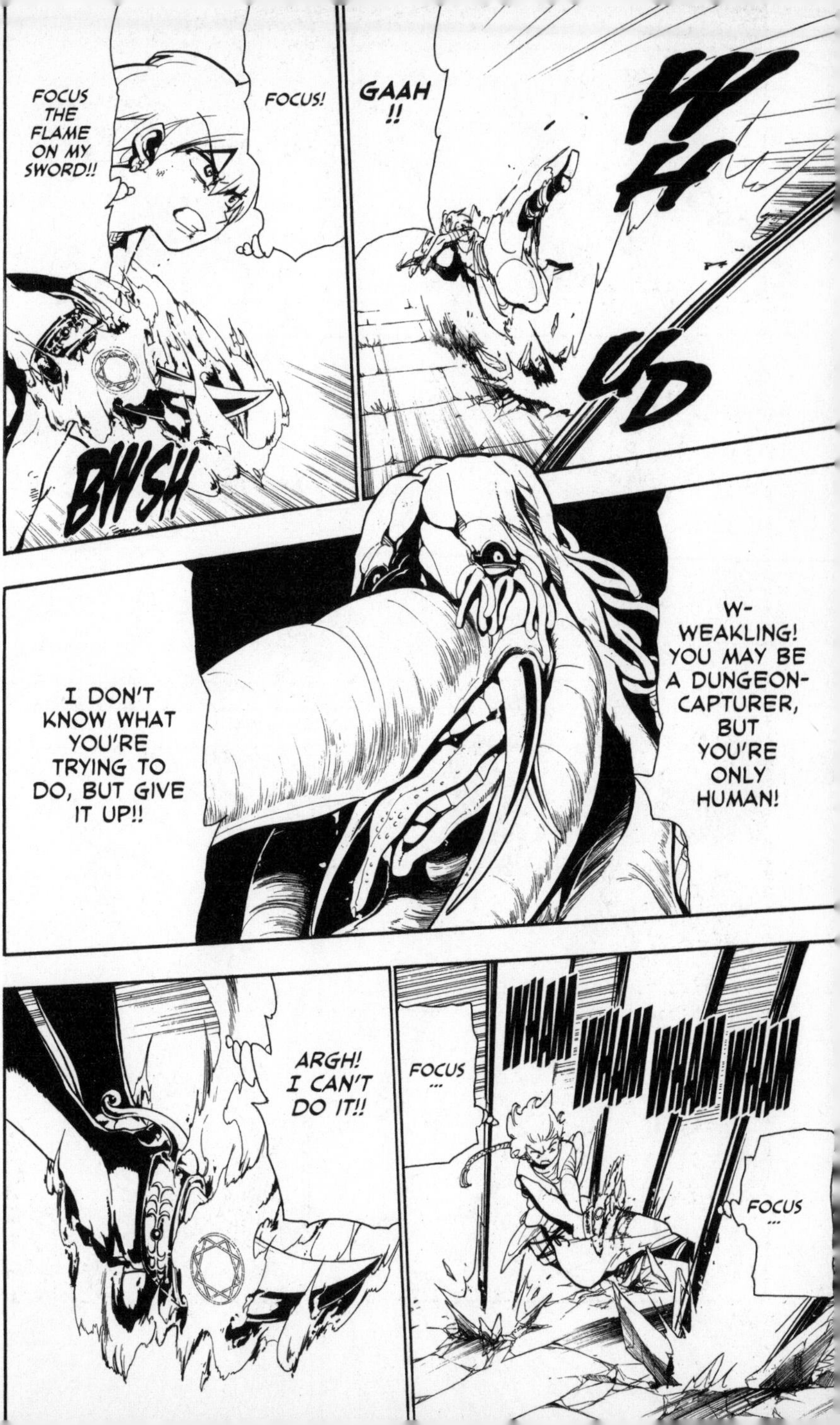
WHUD
GAAH!!
FOCUS!
FOCUS THE FLAME ON MY SWORD!!
BWSH
W-WEAKLING! YOU MAY BE A DUNGEON-CAPTURER, BUT YOU'RE ONLY HUMAN!
I DON'T KNOW WHAT YOU'RE TRYING TO DO, BUT GIVE IT UP!!
WHAM WHAM WHAM WHAM
FOCUS...
FOCUS...
ARGH! I CAN'T DO IT!!

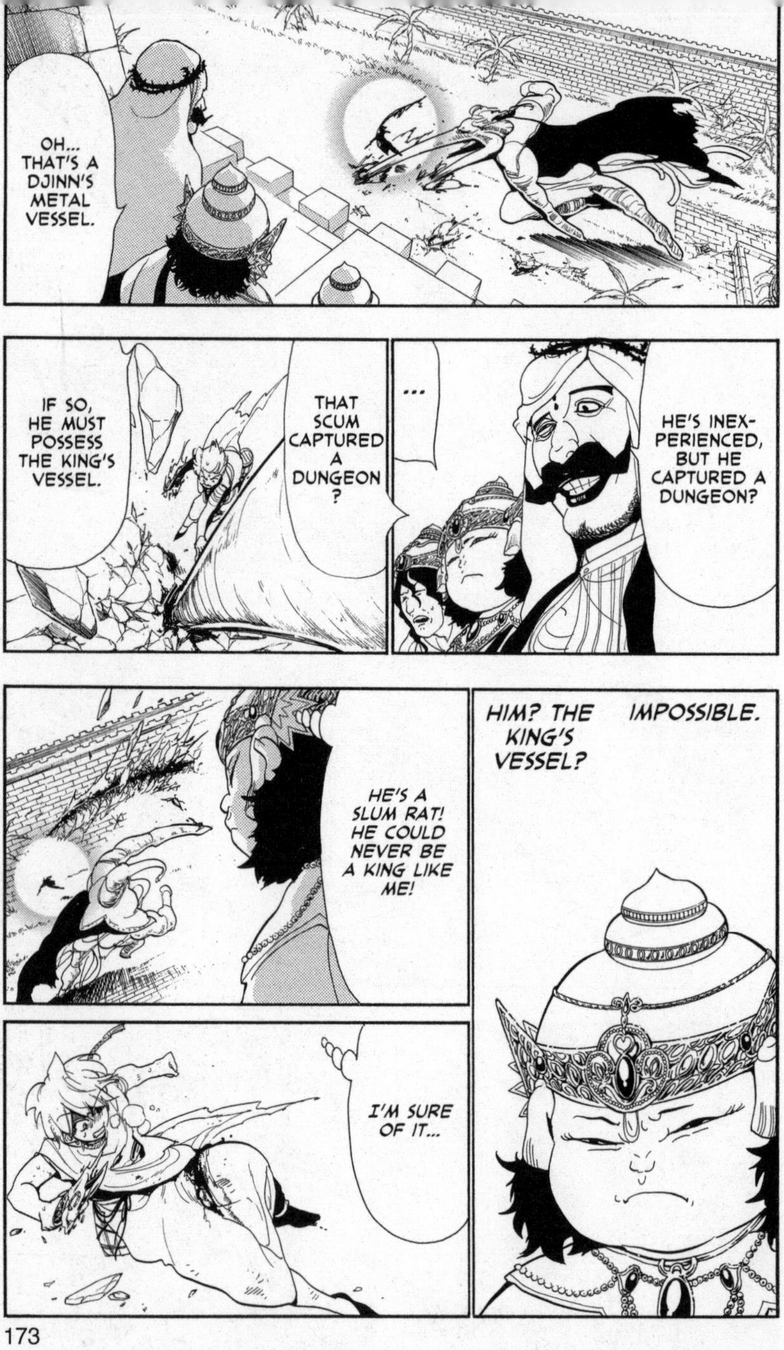
OH... THAT'S A DJINN'S METAL VESSEL.
HE'S INEXPERIENCED, BUT HE CAPTURED A DUNGEON?
...
THAT SCUM CAPTURED A DUNGEON?
IF SO, HE MUST POSSESS THE KING'S VESSEL.
IMPOSSIBLE.
HIM? THE KING'S VESSEL?
HE'S A SLUM RAT! HE COULD NEVER BE A KING LIKE ME!
I'M SURE OF IT...

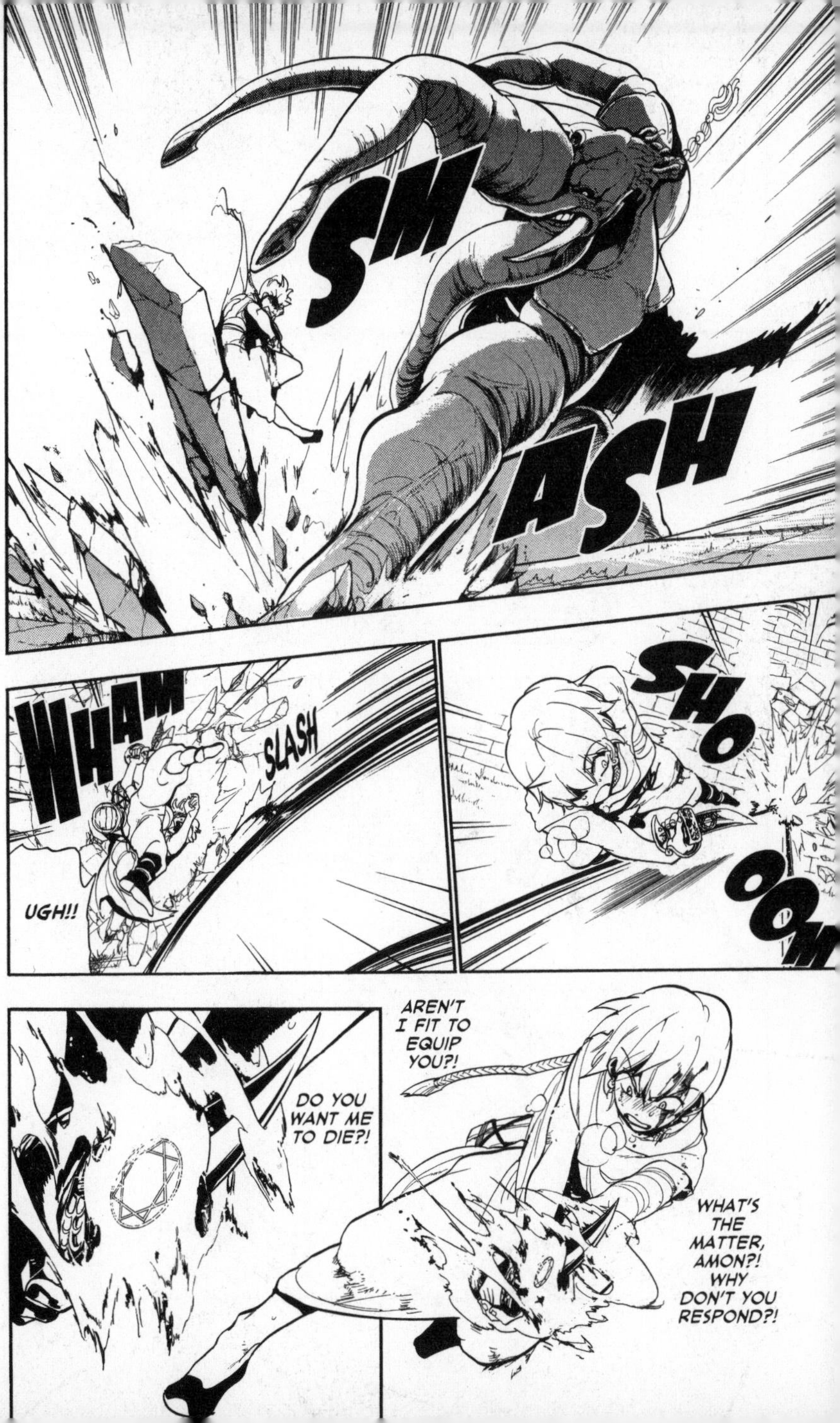
SMASH
SHOOOM
WHAM
SLASH
UGH!!
WHAT'S THE MATTER, AMON?! WHY DON'T YOU RESPOND?!
AREN'T I FIT TO EQUIP YOU?!
DO YOU WANT ME TO DIE?!

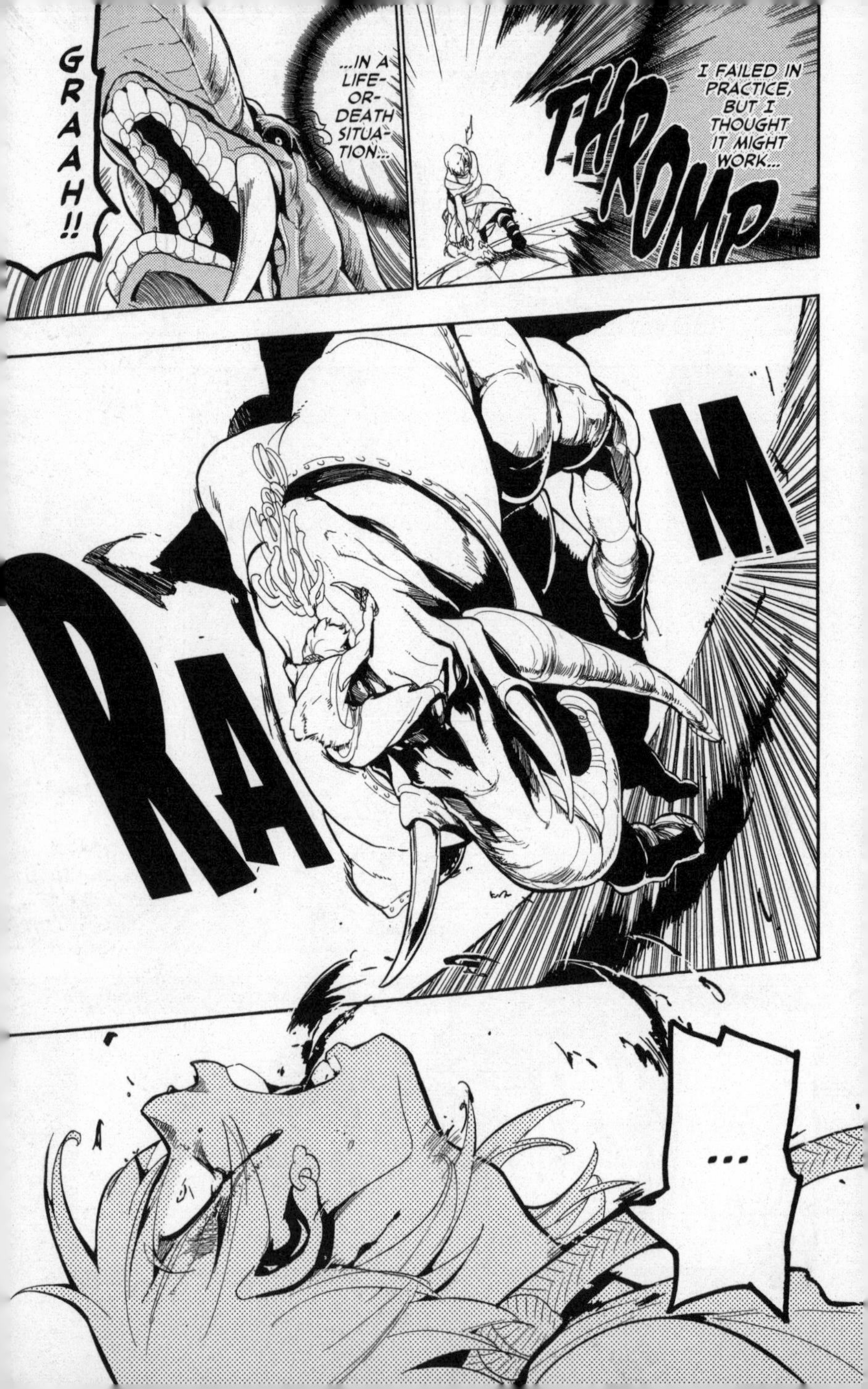
I FAILED IN PRACTICE, BUT I THOUGHT IT MIGHT WORK...
THROMP
...IN A LIFE-OR-DEATH SITUATION...
GRAAAH!!
RA
M
...

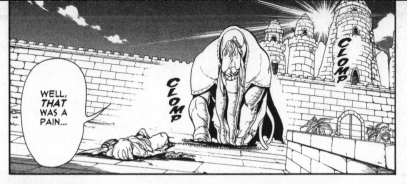

WELL,
THAT
WAS A
PAIN...

CLOMP

CLOMP

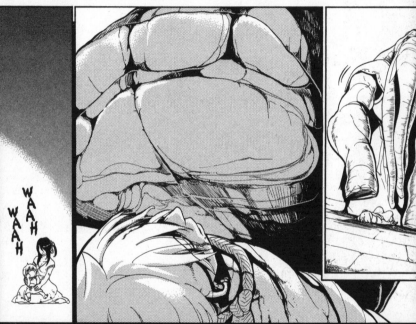

WAAH

WAAH

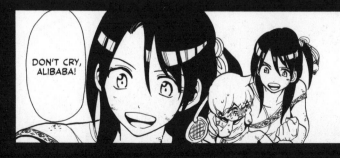

DON'T CRY,
ALIBABA!

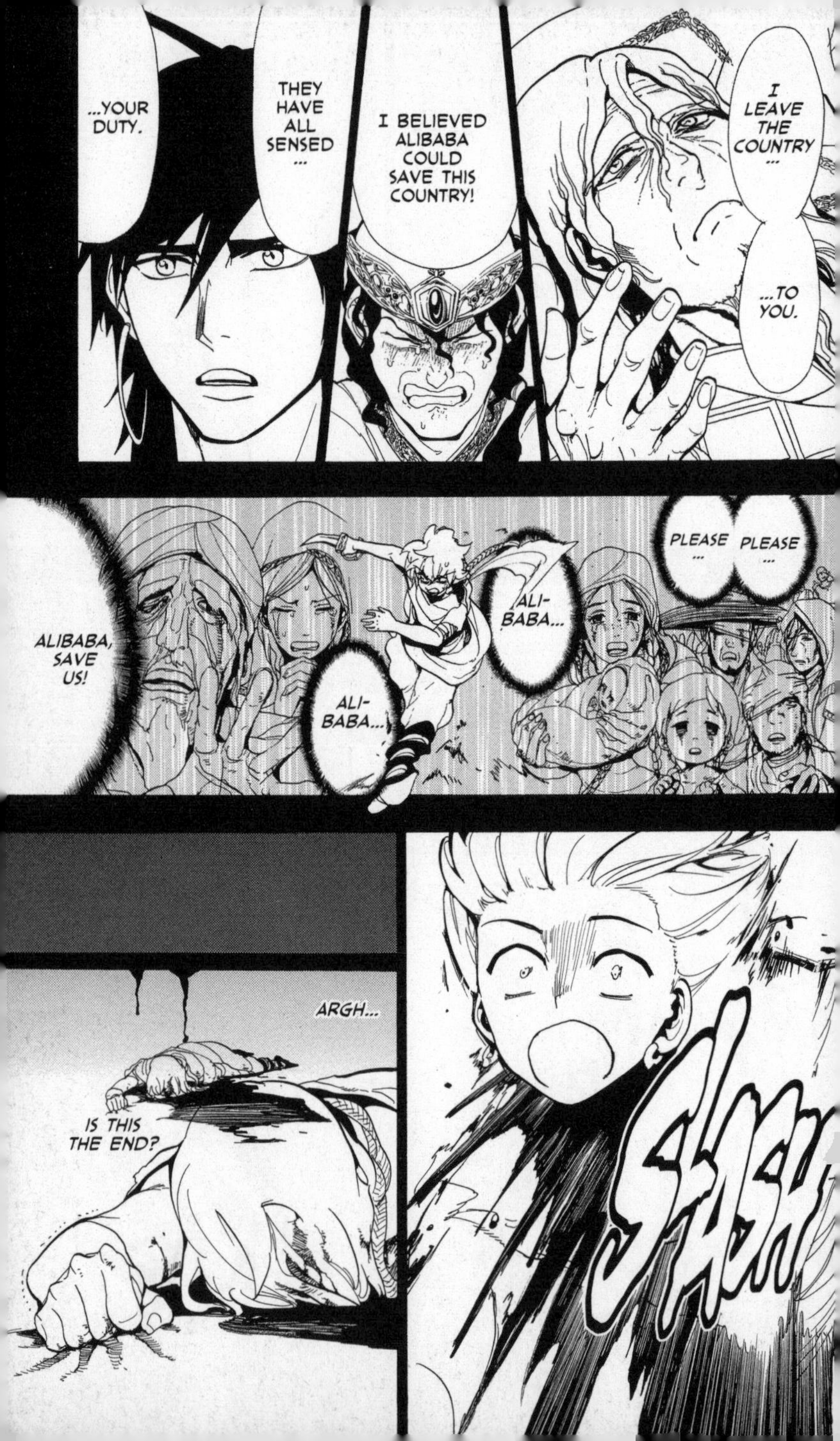
I LEAVE THE COUNTRY...
...TO YOU.
I BELIEVED ALIBABA COULD SAVE THIS COUNTRY!
THEY HAVE ALL SENSED...
...YOUR DUTY.
PLEASE...
PLEASE...
ALI-BABA...
ALI-BABA...
ALIBABA, SAVE US!
ARGH...
IS THIS THE END?

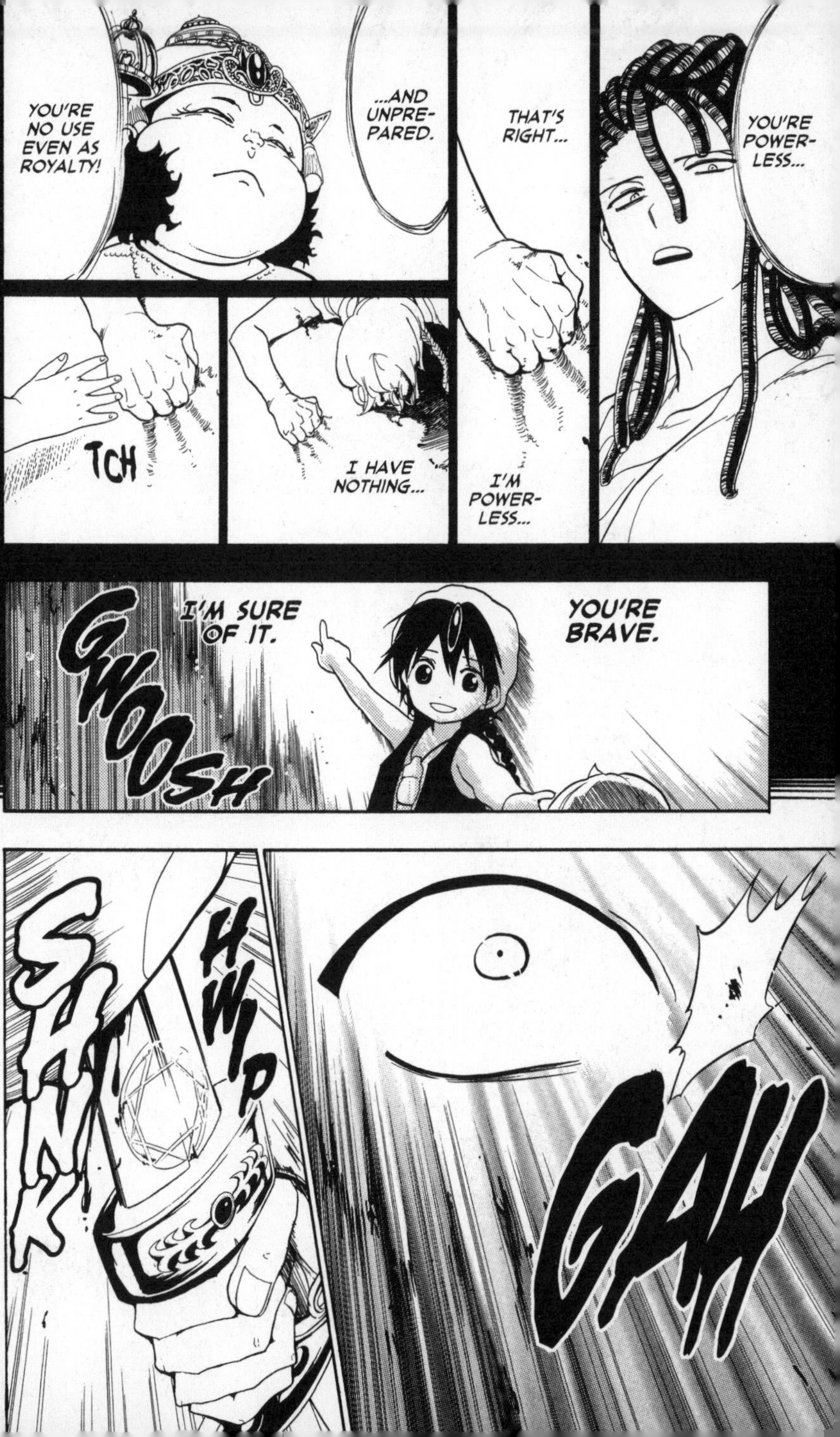
YOU'RE POWERLESS...
THAT'S RIGHT...
I'M POWERLESS...
...AND UNPREPARED.
YOU'RE NO USE EVEN AS ROYALTY!
I HAVE NOTHING...
TCH
YOU'RE BRAVE.
I'M SURE OF IT.
GWOOSH
GAH
WHIP
SHANK

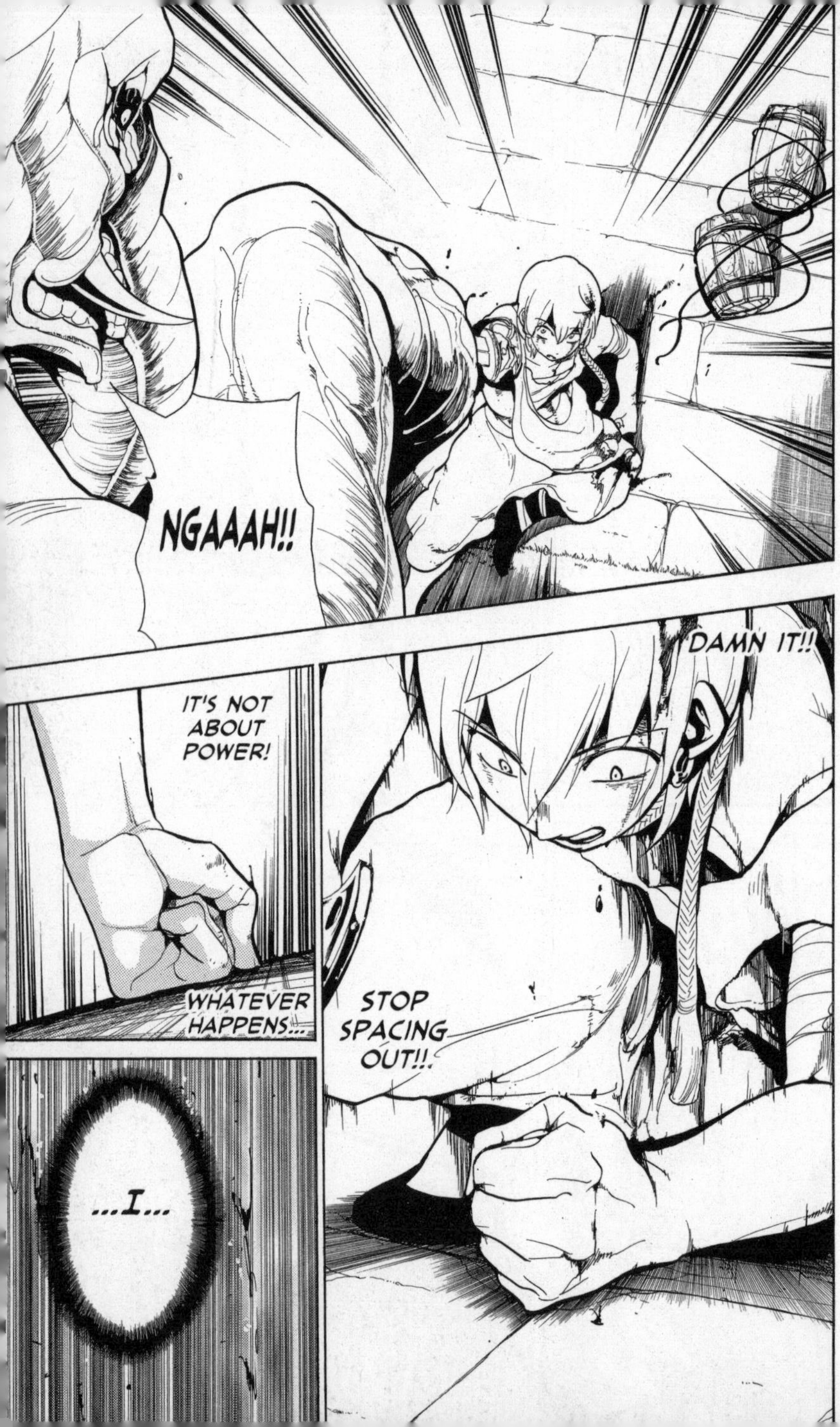
NGAAAH!!
DAMN IT!!
STOP SPACING OUT!!.
IT'S NOT ABOUT POWER!
WHATEVER HAPPENS...
...I...

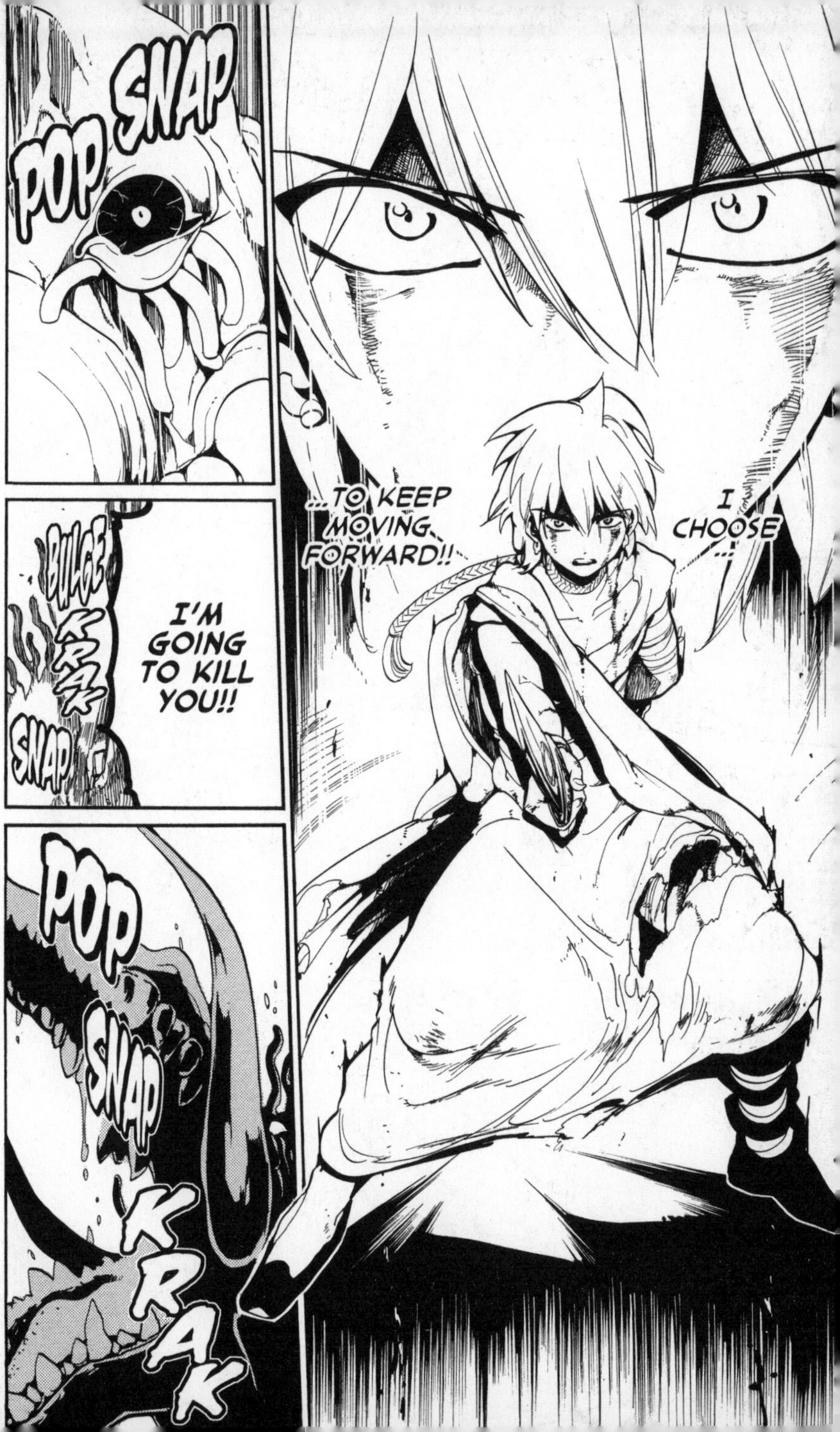
I CHOOSE...
...TO KEEP MOVING FORWARD!!
SNAP
POP
I'M GOING TO KILL YOU!!
BULGE
KRAK
SNAP
POP
SNAP
KRAK

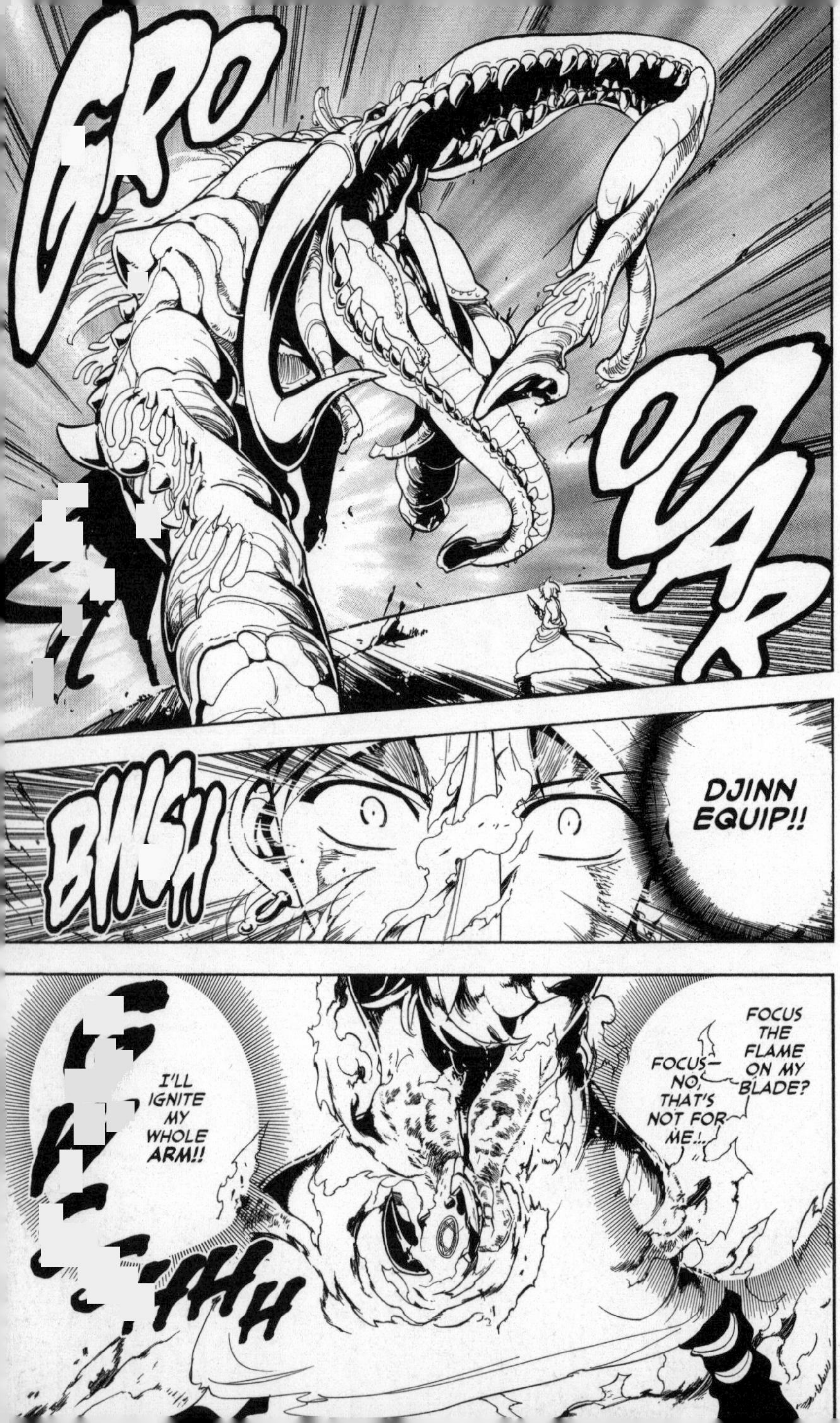
GRO
OOAR
DJINN EQUIP!!
BWSH
FOCUS THE FLAME ON MY BLADE?
FOCUS— NO, THAT'S NOT FOR ME...
I'LL IGNITE MY WHOLE ARM!!

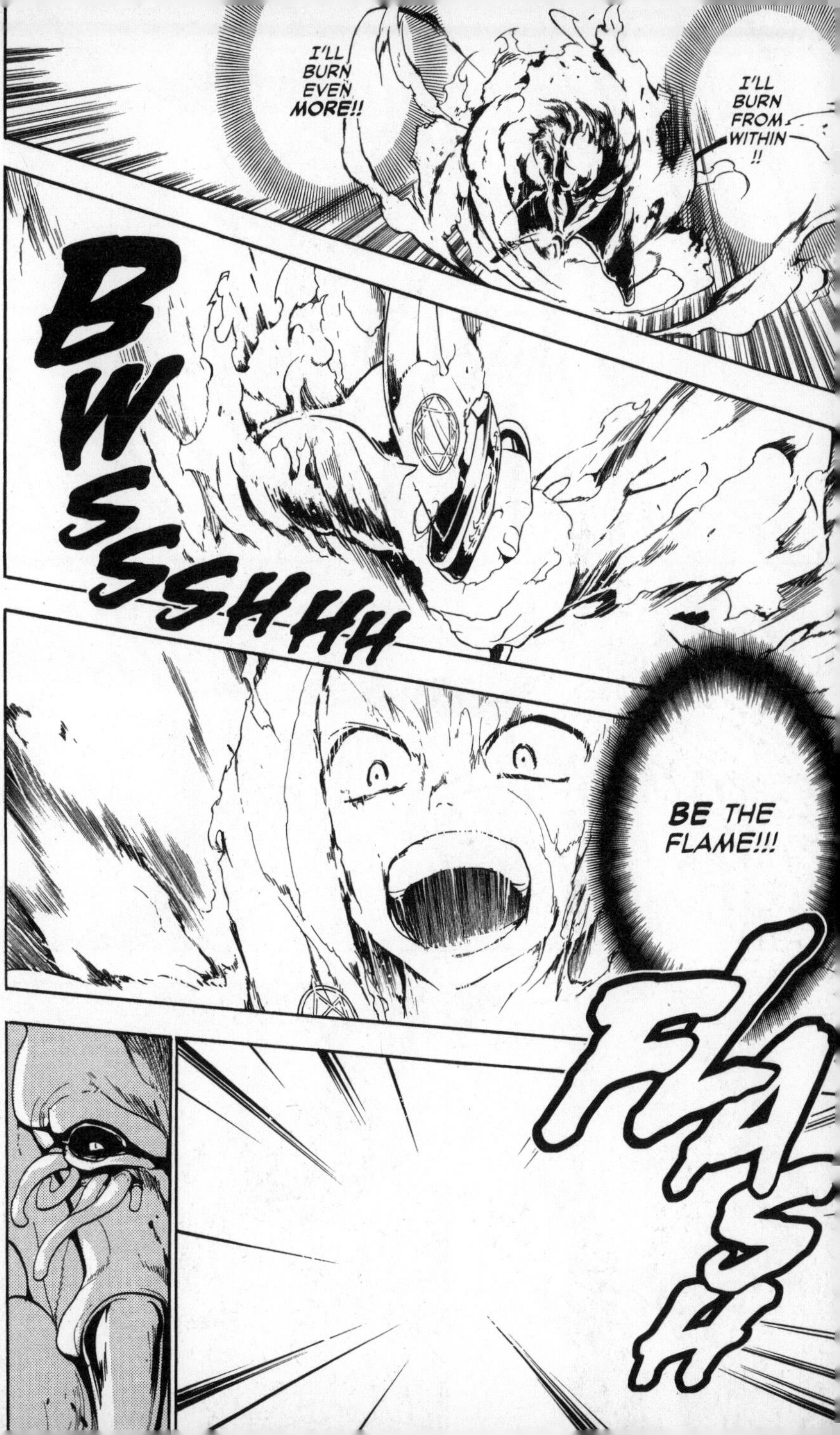
I'LL BURN FROM WITHIN !!
I'LL BURN EVEN MORE!!
BWSSSHHH
BE THE FLAME!!!
FLASH

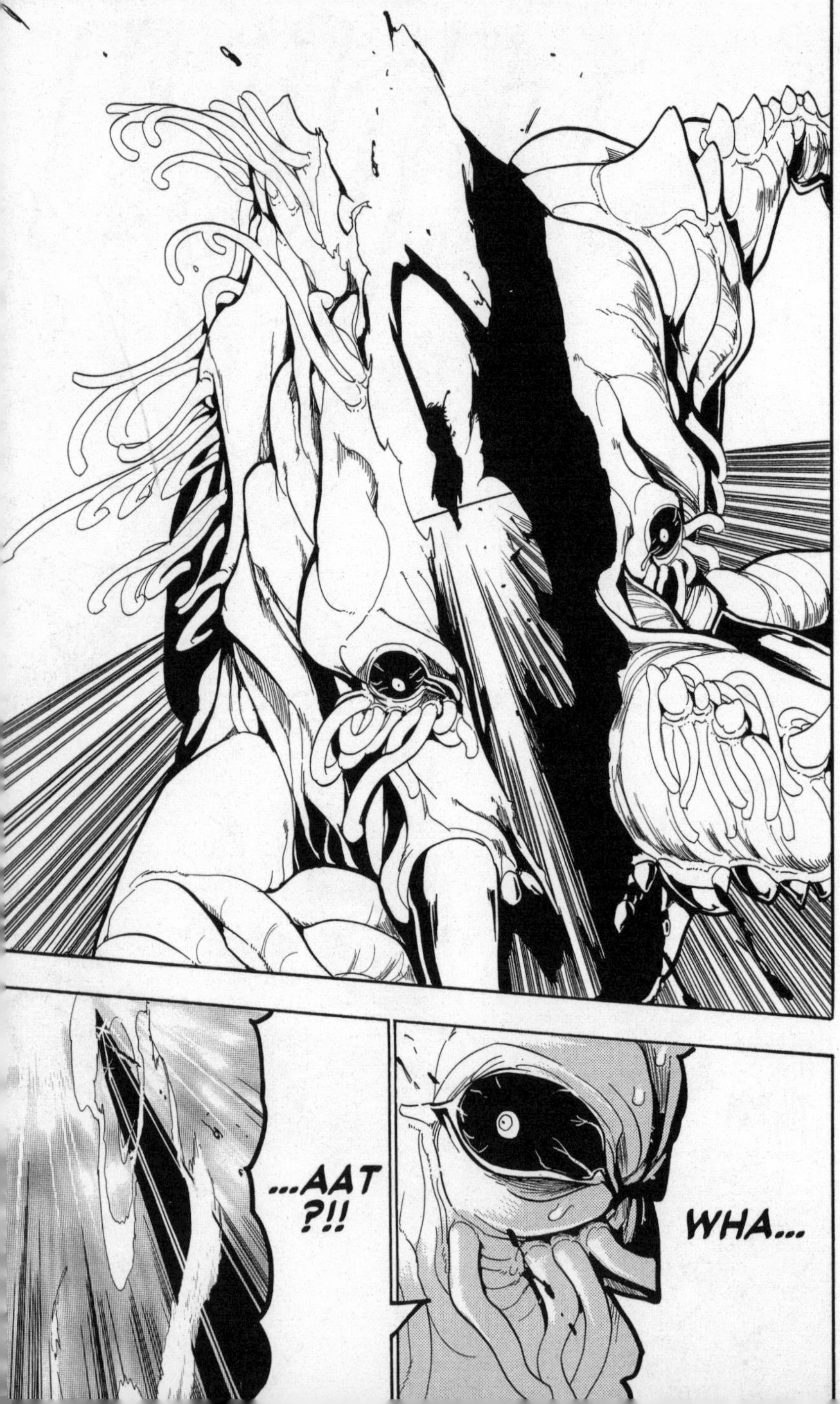
WHA...
...AAT ?!!

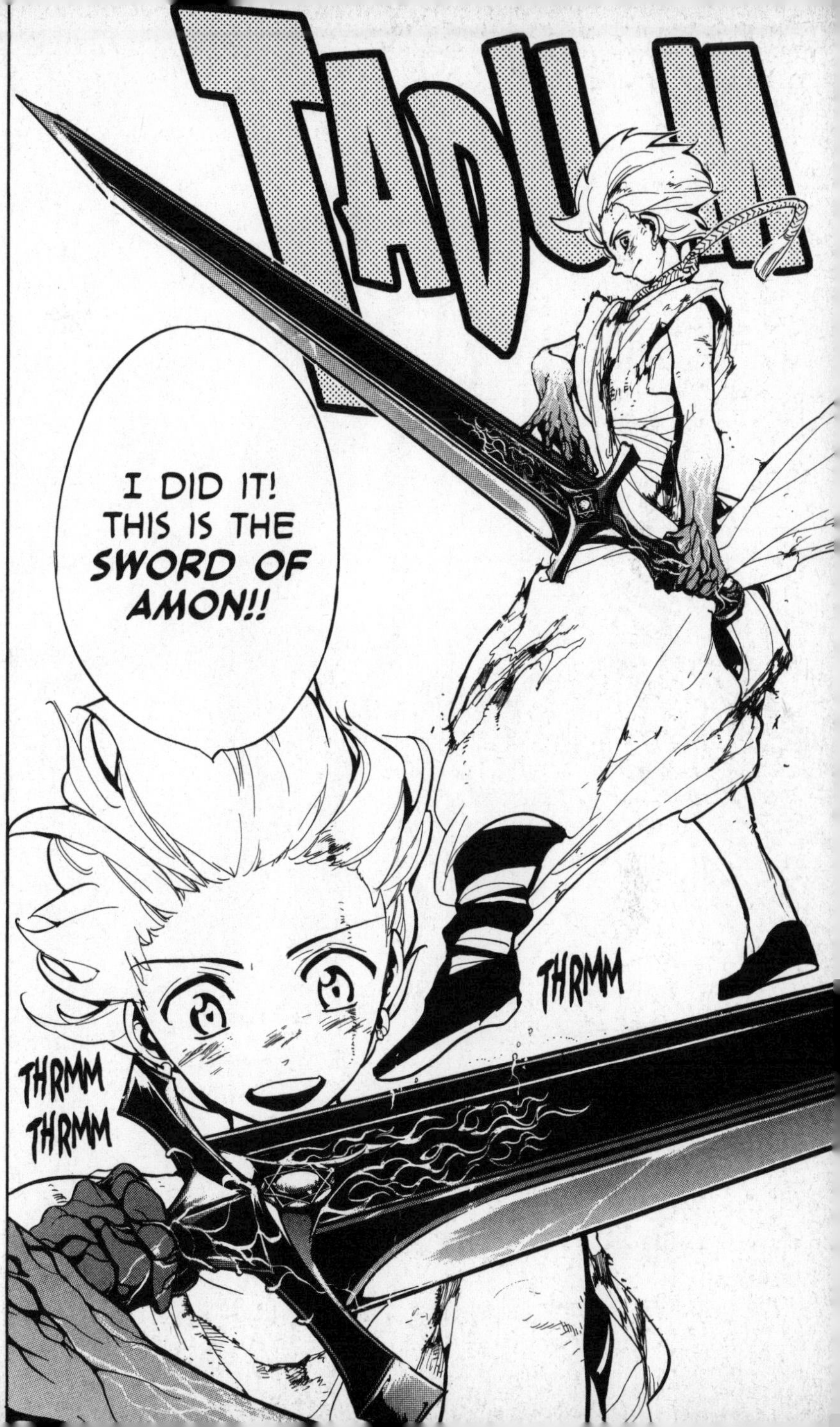
TADUM
I DID IT! THIS IS THE SWORD OF AMON!!
THRMM
THRMM THRMM

MAGI
The labyrinth of magic

6

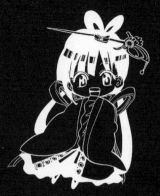

Staff

■ Story & Art

Shinobu Ohtaka
Shinobu Ohtaka

■ Regular Assistants

Matsubara
Matsubara

Miho Isshiki
Miho Isshiki

Akira Sugito
Akira Sugito

Tanimoto
Tanimoto

Yamada
Yamada

■ Editor

Kazuaki Ishibashi
Kazuaki Ishibashi

■ Sales & Promotion

Shinichirou Todaka
Shinichirou Todaka

Tsunato Imamoto
Tsunato Imamoto

■ Designer

Yasuo Shimura + Bay Bridge Studio
Yasuo Shimura + Bay Bridge Studio

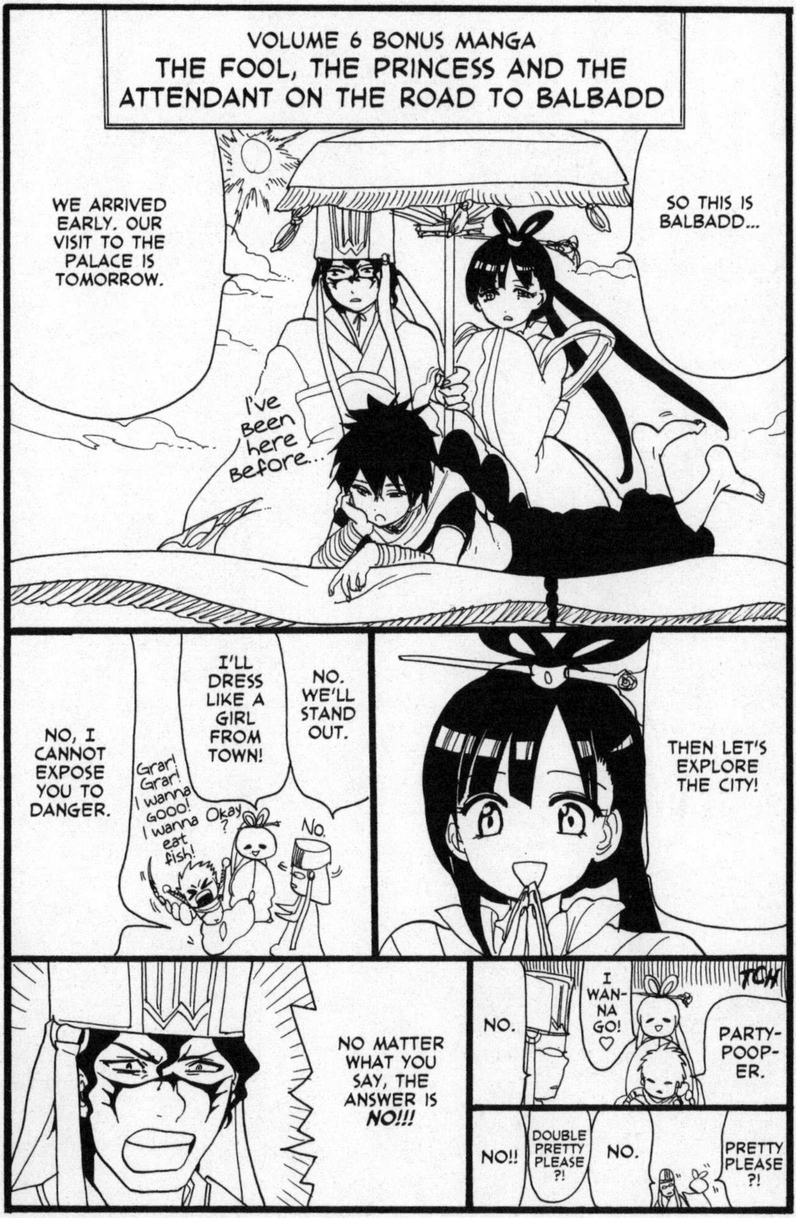
VOLUME 6 BONUS MANGA
THE FOOL, THE PRINCESS AND THE ATTENDANT ON THE ROAD TO BALBADD
SO THIS IS BALBADD...
WE ARRIVED EARLY. OUR VISIT TO THE PALACE IS TOMORROW.
I've Been here Before...
THEN LET'S EXPLORE THE CITY!
NO. WE'LL STAND OUT.
I'LL DRESS LIKE A GIRL FROM TOWN!
NO, I CANNOT EXPOSE YOU TO DANGER.
No.
Okay?
Grar! Grar! I wanna Gooo! I wanna eat fish!
TCH
PARTY-POOPER.
I WANNA GO! ♡
NO.
PRETTY PLEASE ?!
NO.
DOUBLE PRETTY PLEASE ?!
NO!!
NO MATTER WHAT YOU SAY, THE ANSWER IS ***NO!!!***

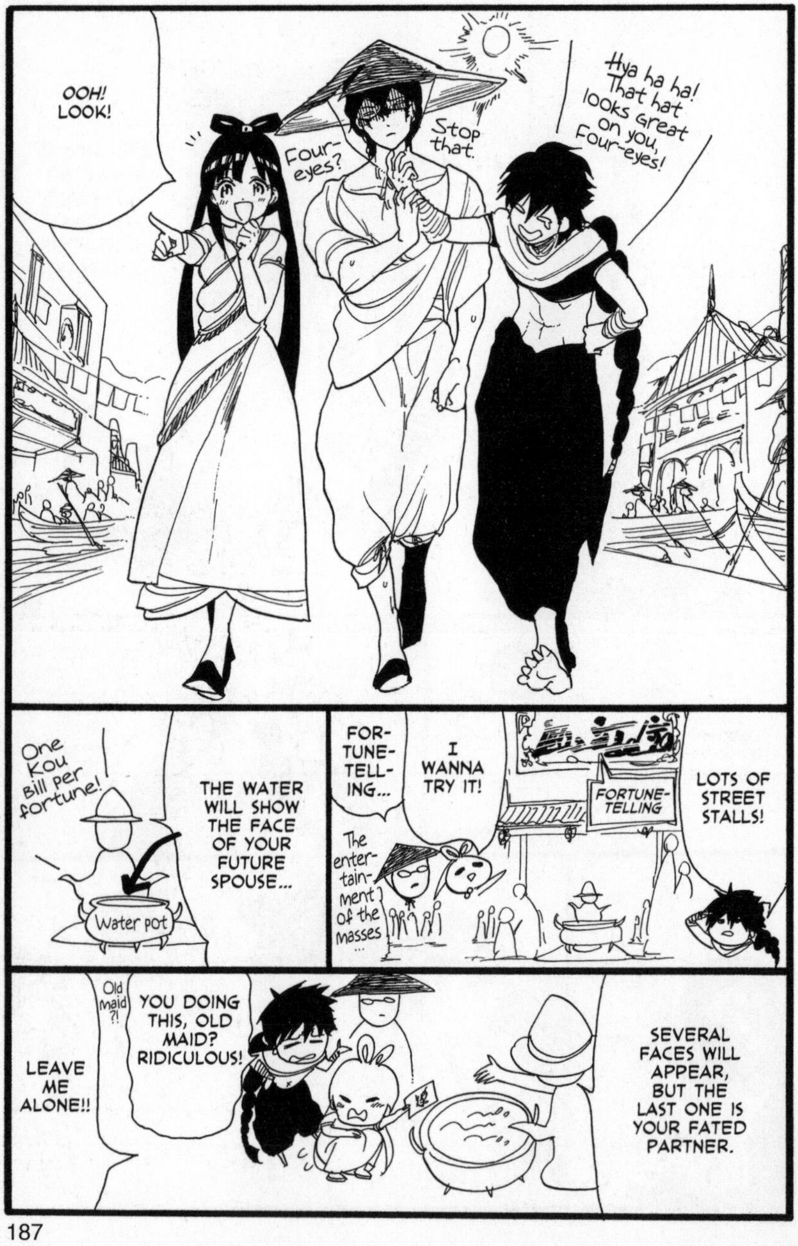
Hya ha ha! That hat looks great on you, Four-eyes!
Stop that.
Four-eyes?
OOH! LOOK!
LOTS OF STREET STALLS!
FORTUNE-TELLING
I WANNA TRY IT!
FOR-TUNE-TELL-ING...
The enter-tain-ment of the masses...
THE WATER WILL SHOW THE FACE OF YOUR FUTURE SPOUSE...
One Kou Bill per fortune!
Water pot
SEVERAL FACES WILL APPEAR, BUT THE LAST ONE IS YOUR FATED PARTNER.
YOU DOING THIS, OLD MAID? RIDICULOUS!
Old maid?!
LEAVE ME ALONE!!

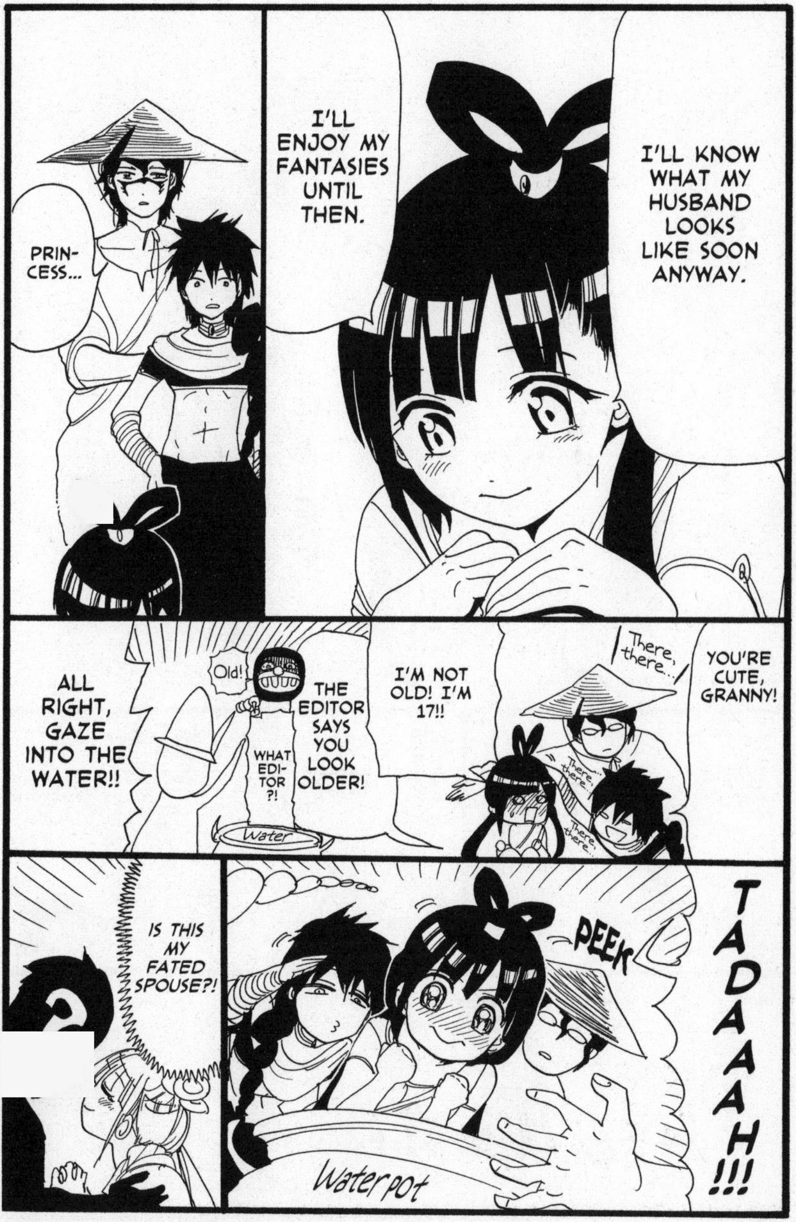
I'LL KNOW WHAT MY HUSBAND LOOKS LIKE SOON ANYWAY.
I'LL ENJOY MY FANTASIES UNTIL THEN.
PRIN-CESS...
YOU'RE CUTE, GRANNY!
There, there...
There, there...
There, there...
I'M NOT OLD! I'M 17!!
THE EDITOR SAYS YOU LOOK OLDER!
WHAT EDI-TOR ?!
Old!
Water
ALL RIGHT, GAZE INTO THE WATER!!
TADAAAAH!!!
PEEK
Waterpot
IS THIS MY FATED SPOUSE?!

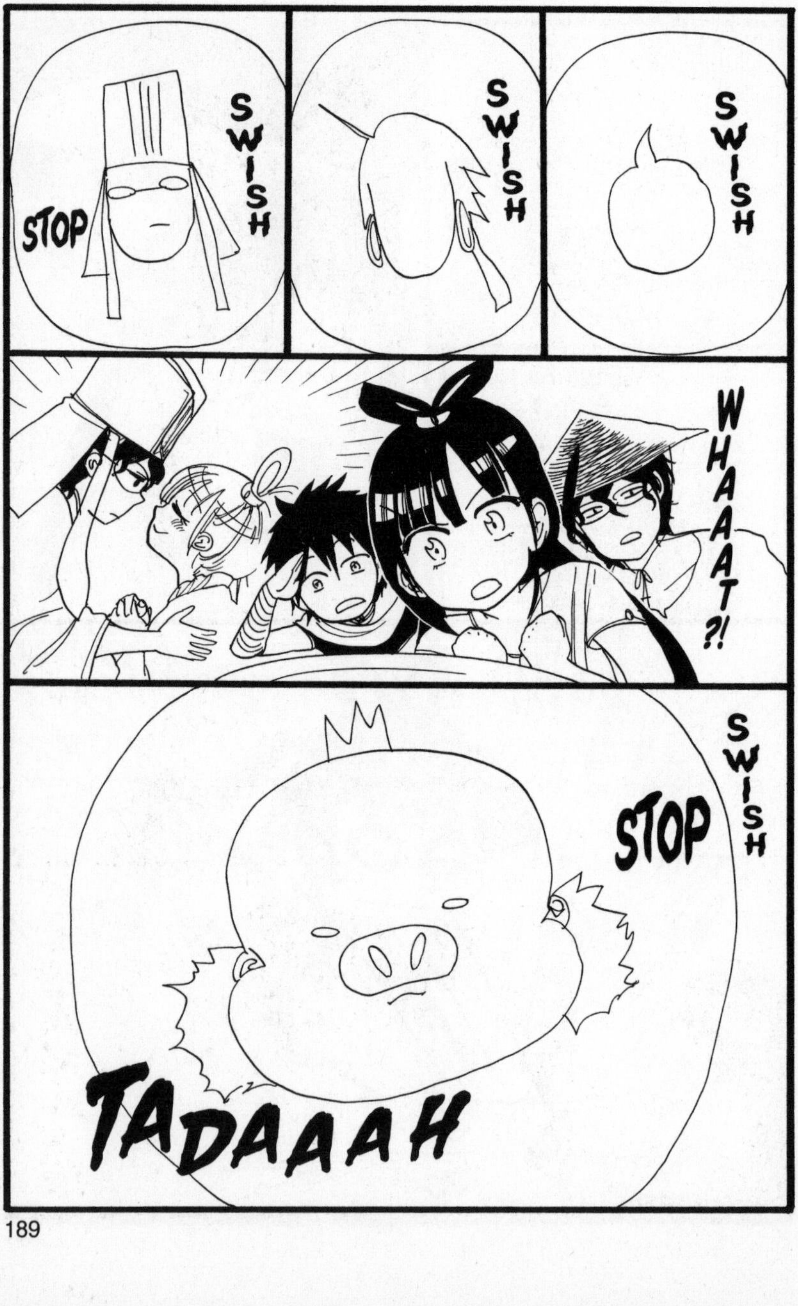
SWISH
SWISH
SWISH
STOP
WHAAAAT?!
SWISH
STOP
TADAAAH

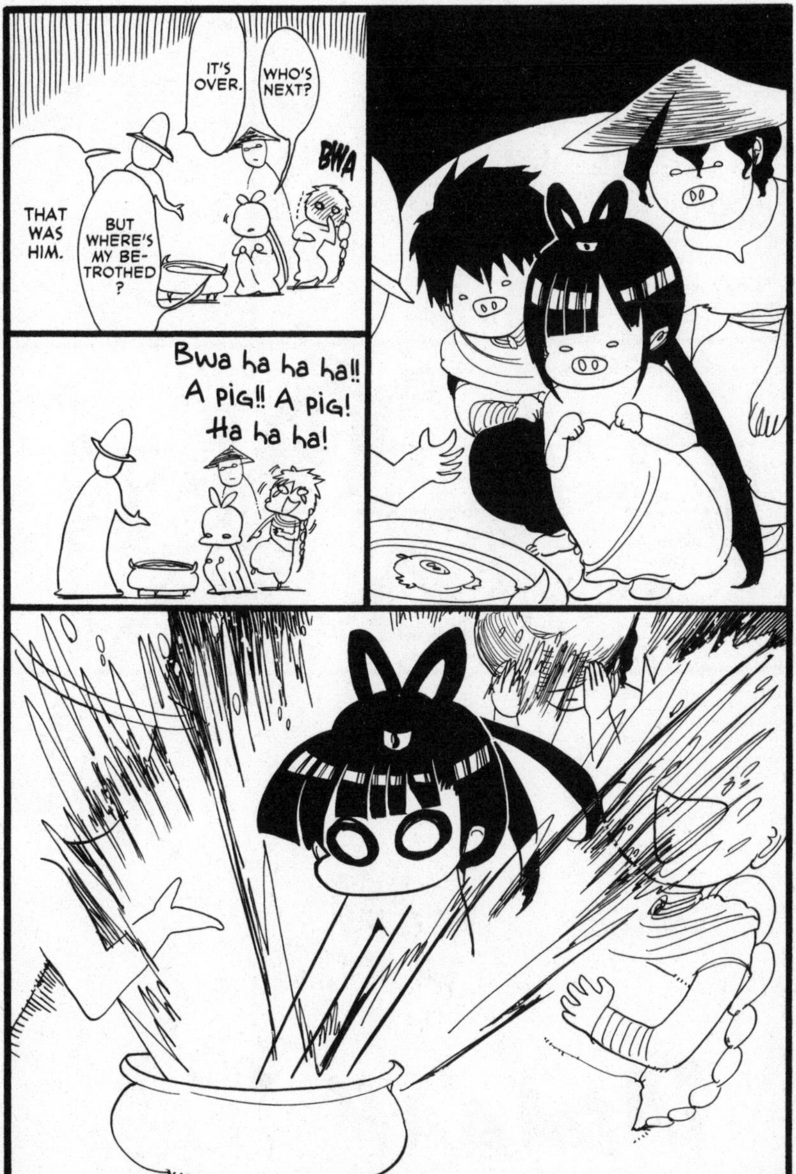
BWA
WHO'S NEXT?
IT'S OVER.
BUT WHERE'S MY BE-TROTHED?
THAT WAS HIM.
Bwa ha ha ha!! A PIG!! A PIG! Ha ha ha!

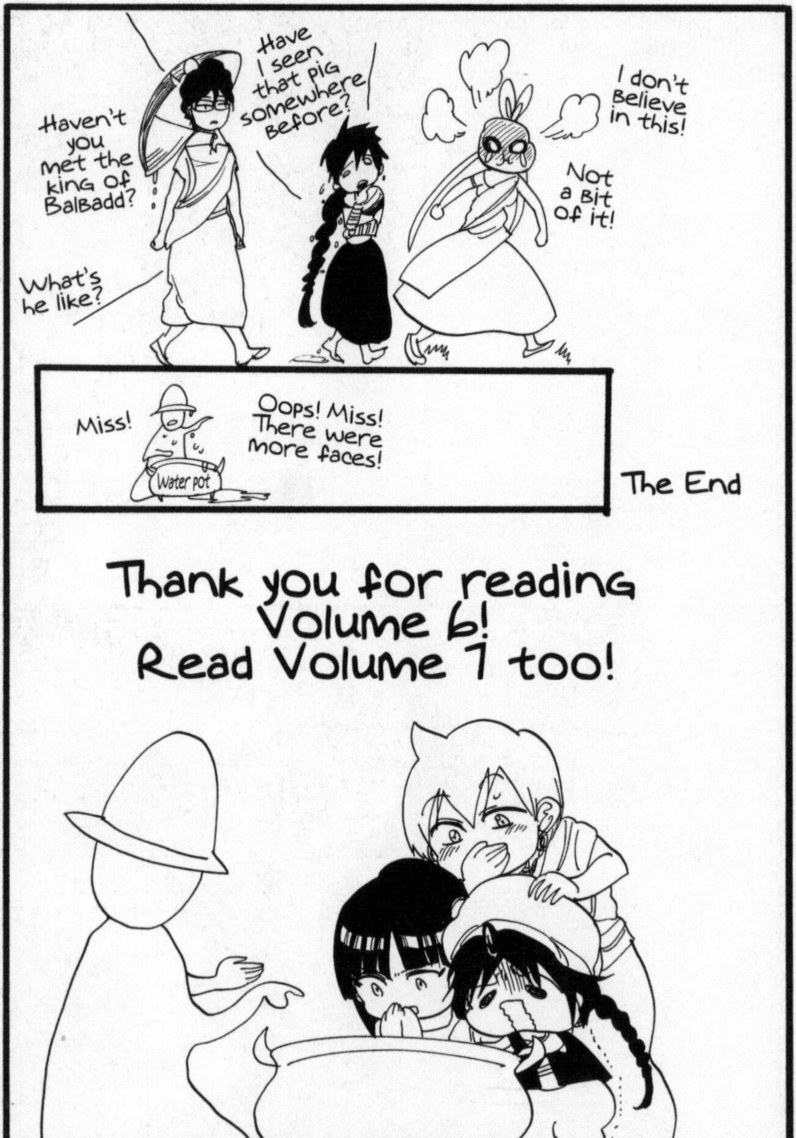
I don't Believe in this!
Not a Bit of it!
Have I seen that pig somewhere before?
Haven't you met the king of Balbadd?
What's he like?
Oops! Miss! There were more faces!
Miss!
Water pot
The End
Thank you for reading Volume 6! Read Volume 7 too!

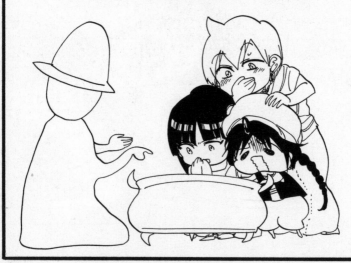

SHINOBU OHTAKA

MAGI6

Please read!

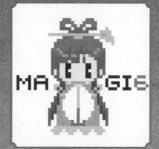

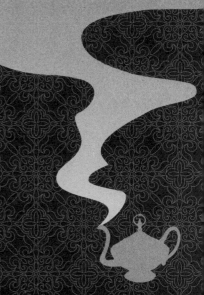

MAGI

Volume 6
Shonen Sunday Edition

Story and Art by
SHINOBU OHTAKA

MAGI Vol.6
by Shinobu OHTAKA
© 2009 Shinobu OHTAKA
All rights reserved.
Original Japanese edition published by SHOGAKUKAN.
English translation rights in the United States of America, Canada,
the United Kingdom and Ireland arranged with SHOGAKUKAN.

Translation & English Adaptation ◇ John Werry

Touch-up Art & Lettering ◇ Stephen Dutro

Editor ◇ Mike Montesa

Printed in the U.S.A.

Published by VIZ Media, LLC
P.O. Box 77010
San Francisco, CA 94107

10 9 8 7 6 5 4 3 2 1
First printing, June 2014

WWW.SHONENSUNDAY.COM

PARENTAL ADVISORY
MAGI is rated T for Teen.
This volume contains
suggestive themes.
ratings.viz.com

www.viz.com

At Your Indentured Service

Hayate's parents are bad with money, so they sell his organs to pay their debts. Hayate doesn't like this plan, so he comes up with a new one—kidnap and ransom a girl from a wealthy family. Solid plan... so how did he end up as her butler?

Find out in *Hayate the Combat Butler*— buy the manga at store.viz.com!

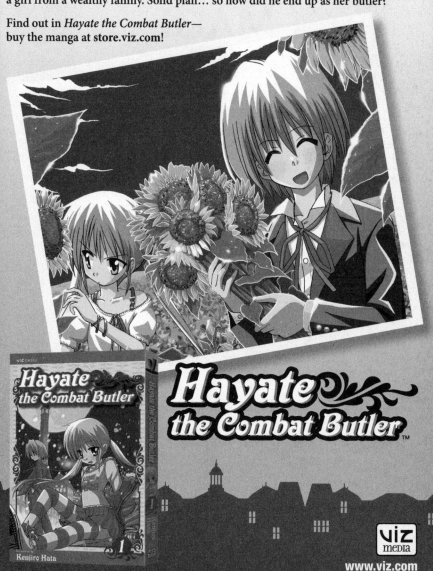

www.viz.com
store.viz.com

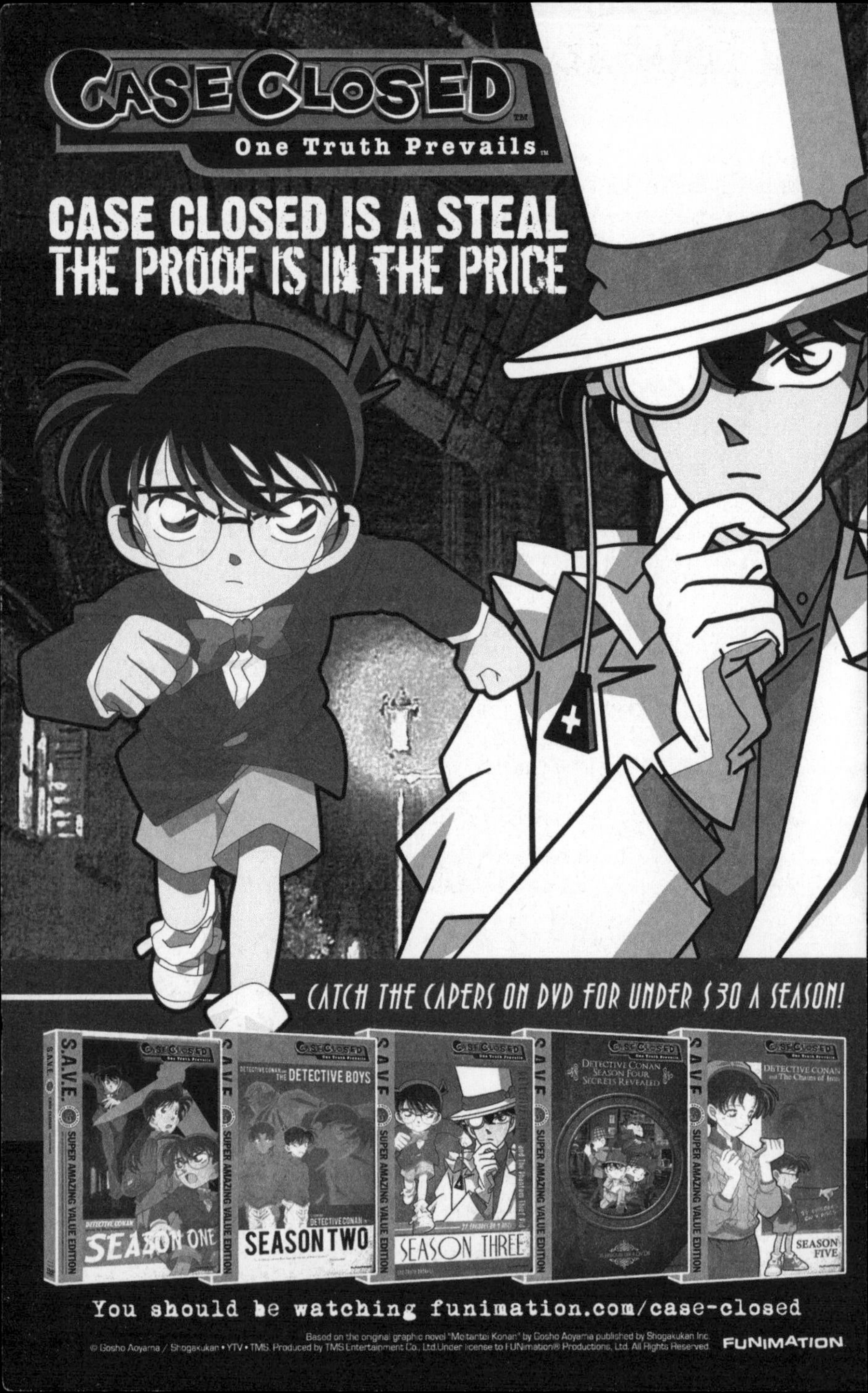

CASE CLOSED
One Truth Prevails
CASE CLOSED IS A STEAL
THE PROOF IS IN THE PRICE
CATCH THE CAPERS ON DVD FOR UNDER $30 A SEASON!
S.A.V.E. SUPER AMAZING VALUE EDITION
SEASON ONE
DETECTIVE CONAN THE DETECTIVE BOYS
SEASON TWO
SEASON THREE
DETECTIVE CONAN SEASON FOUR SECRETS REVEALED
DETECTIVE CONAN and The Chains of Iron
SEASON FIVE
You should be watching funimation.com/case-closed
Based on the original graphic novel "Meitantei Konan" by Gosho Aoyama published by Shogakukan Inc.
© Gosho Aoyama / Shogakukan • YTV • TMS. Produced by TMS Entertainment Co., Ltd.Under license to FUNimation® Productions, Ltd. All Rights Reserved.
FUNIMATION

Ranma½ Returns!

REMASTERED AND BETTER THAN EVER!

One day, teenaged martial artist Ranma Saotome went on a training mission with his father and ended up taking a dive into some cursed springs at a legendary training ground in China. Now, every time he's splashed with cold water, he changes into a girl. His father, Genma, changes into a panda! What's a half-guy, half-girl to do?

Find out what fueled the worldwide manga boom in beloved creator Rumiko Takahashi's (*Inuyasha, Urusei Yatsura, RIN-NE*) smash-hit of martial arts mayhem!

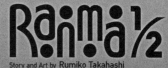

Story and Art by Rumiko Takahashi

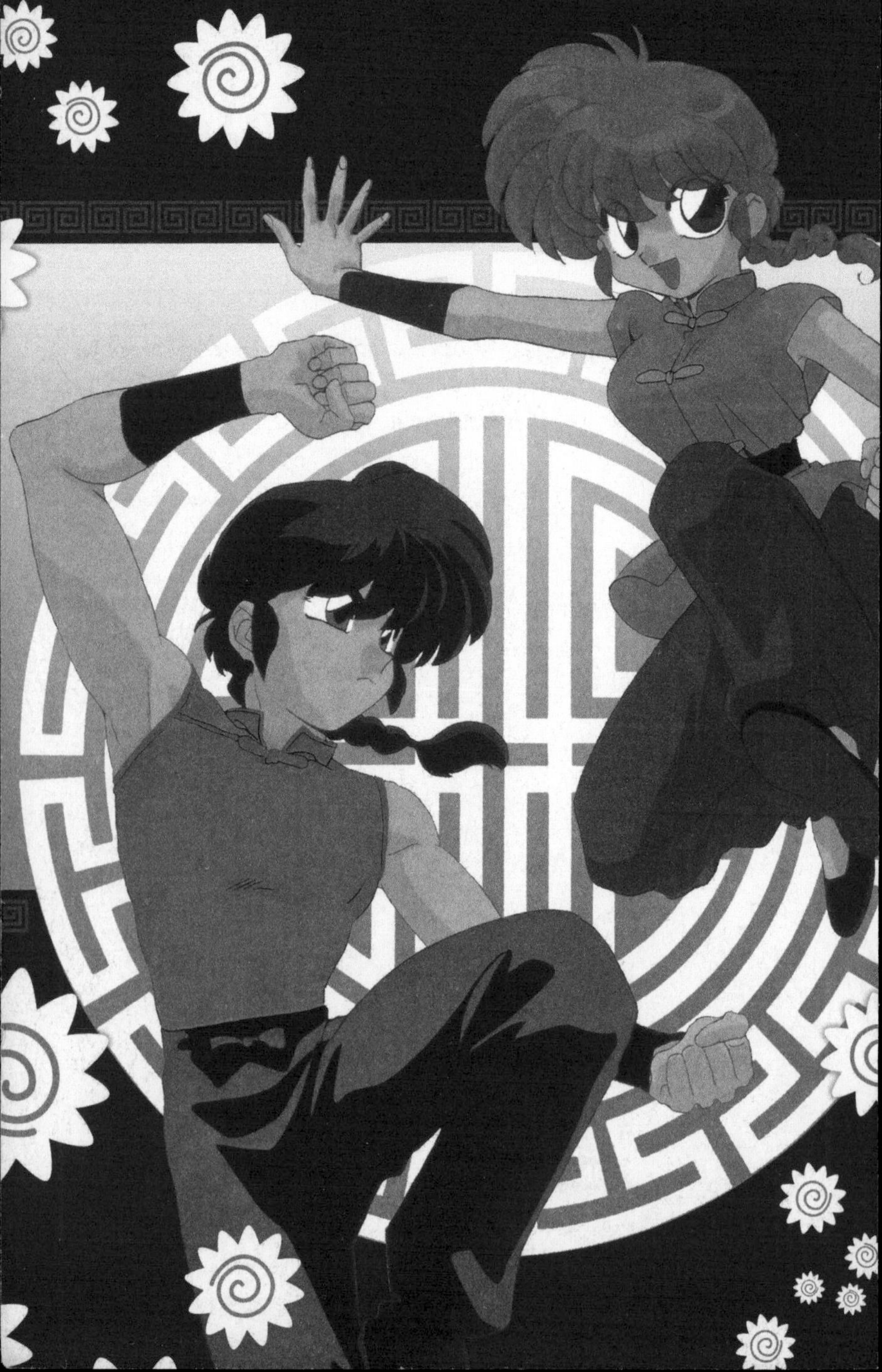

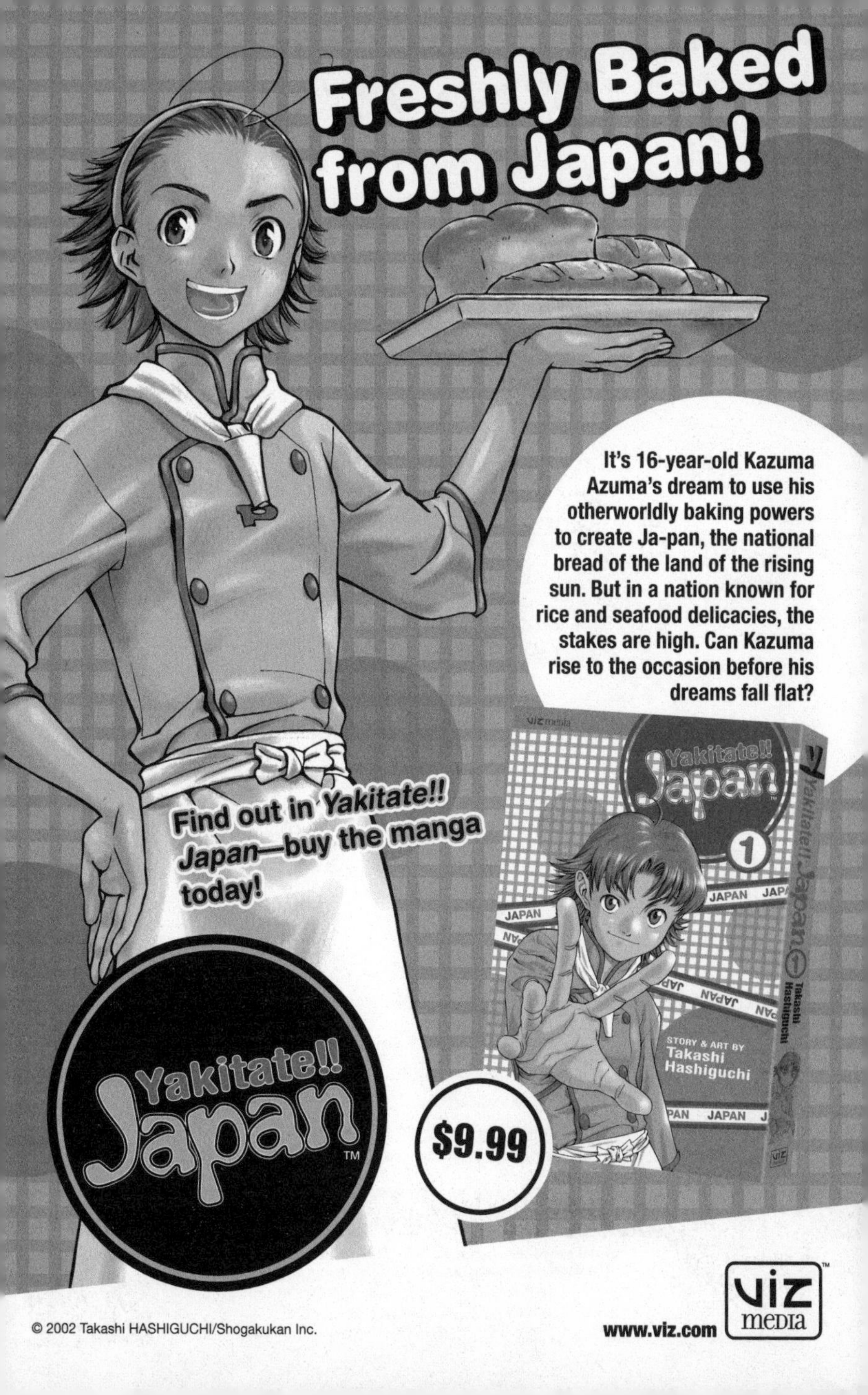
Freshly Baked from Japan!
It's 16-year-old Kazuma Azuma's dream to use his otherworldly baking powers to create Ja-pan, the national bread of the land of the rising sun. But in a nation known for rice and seafood delicacies, the stakes are high. Can Kazuma rise to the occasion before his dreams fall flat?
Find out in Yakitate!! Japan—buy the manga today!
Yakitate!! Japan™
$9.99
viz media
Yakitate!! Japan™
1
JAPAN
STORY & ART BY
Takashi Hashiguchi
© 2002 Takashi HASHIGUCHI/Shogakukan Inc.
www.viz.com
viz media™

ᗐIZMᗩNGᗩ
Read manga anytime, anywhere!

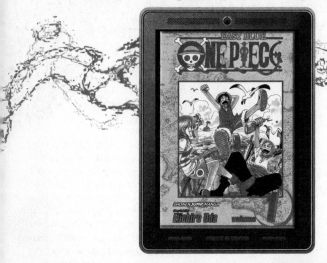

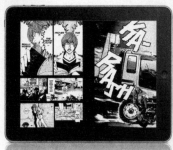

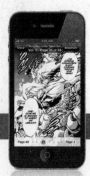

From our newest hit series to the classics you know and love, the best manga in the world is now available digitally. Buy a volume* of digital manga for your:

- iOS device (**iPad®**, **iPhone®**, **iPod® touch**) through the **VIZ Manga** app
- Android-powered device (**phone or tablet**) with a browser by visiting VIZManga.com
- **Mac or PC computer** by visiting VIZManga.com

VIZ Digital has loads to offer:

- 500+ ready-to-read volumes
- New volumes each week
- FREE previews
- Access on multiple devices! Create a log-in through the app so you buy a book once, and read it on your device of choice!*

To learn more, visit www.viz.com/apps

* Some series may not be available for multiple devices. Check the app on your device to find out what's available.

viz.com/apps

You're reading the
WRONG WAY

◇◇◇◇◇◇◇◇◇◇◇◇◇◇◇◇◇◇◇◇◇◇◇◇

MAGI reads from right to left, starting in the upper-right corner. Japanese is read from **right** to **left**, meaning that action, sound effects, and word-balloon order are completely reversed from English order.

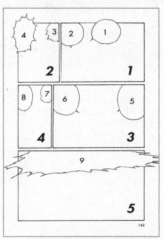